W9-CDH-255

Resources for Teaching

THE STORY AND ITS WRITER

An Introduction to Short Fiction

Sixth Edition

PREPARED BY

Ann Charters
University of Connecticut

Sam Charters

William E. Sheidley
University of Southern Colorado

BEDFORD/ST. MARTIN'S   Boston ◆ New York

Copyright © 2003 by Bedford/St. Martin's

All rights reserved.
Manufactured in the United States of America.

8 7 6 5 4 3
f e d c b a

For information, write: Bedford/St. Martin's, 75 Arlington Street, Boston, MA
02116 (617-399-4000)

ISBN: 0–312–39730–5

Cover Design: Donna Lee Dennison

Cover Art: Ken Howard, *Interior at Oriel,* 1982–4. Oil on canvas. Courtesy of
Richard Green, London.

Instructors who have adopted *The Story and Its Writer,* Sixth Edition, as a
textbook for a course are authorized to duplicate portions of this manual for
their students.

PREFACE

The entries in this manual include commentaries on each story in the anthology, along with questions for discussion, writing assignments, and suggested readings. The commentaries offer brief critical analyses of the stories and suggest ways to approach them in class. Like the questions that follow, the commentaries aim to promote a lively exchange of responses and perceptions without insisting on any particular interpretation or critical methodology.

Within many of the Topics for Writing are Connections questions, which ask students to link selections in the book. These questions promote critical thinking and are designed to provide both stimulating topics for writing assignments and material for fruitful class discussions. We have also added Responding Creatively questions, which enable you to incorporate creative writing assignments into your course. Instructors using these resources will readily see ways to rephrase, restructure, and reapply these assignments to suit their own purposes and the needs of their students. Some writing topics may serve equally well as discussion questions, and vice versa.

The suggested reading lists that conclude most entries are neither exhaustive nor highly selective; they simply cite interesting and, when possible, readily available criticism that proved useful in preparing the manual or that contains information and approaches to the stories that could not be incorporated in the commentaries. Thanks are due to the authors mentioned, to whose insights and scholarship these resources are generally indebted.

At the end of these resources are a thematic index of stories, a guide to commentaries, and a directory of short stories on film and video.

CONTENTS

STORIES

CHINUA ACHEBE

Civil Peace (p. 10)

Achebe narrates this story about the "civil peace" prevailing in war-torn Nigeria after the Biafran war with an ironic control that provides a strong contrast to the human suffering portrayed in the story. When the story opens, we learn that the protagonist, Jonathan Iwegbu, considers himself lucky to have survived the war with his wife and three of their four children. The terms of his survival, and the price he continues to pay for his own and his family's safekeeping despite the official end to the civil war, are dramatized in the events of the story.

Jonathan Iwegbu is an excellent example of what the critic Frank O'Connor called "the little Man" in short story literature, a figure projecting a distinctive aura of human dignity despite his all-too-apparent vulnerability and isolation. Like the clerk in Gogol's story "The Overcoat," Jonathan Iwegbu is tormented by the people around him (the soldiers who threaten to shoot up his house and force him to give up his money), yet his fundamental decency speaks so directly to us that we seem to hear him say, as in Gogol's story, "Why do you [bother] me? . . . I am your brother."

Questions for Discussion

1. Is "Civil Peace" a fully developed short story or an anecdote? What qualities in the narrative — characterization, setting, plot — lead you to your answer?
2. Explain the irony in the title of the story.
3. Jonathan Iwegbu acts as a self-reliant head of his family throughout the narrative. Why then does Achebe emphasize the "miracle" of his family's survival and the "monumental blessing" of his house's survival, and why does he repeat the phrase "nothing puzzles God" at the end of the story?

Topic for Writing

1. **RESPONDING CREATIVELY** Translate into conventional English the words of the leader of the group who knocks on the door of Jonathan's house and demands money from him in the middle of the night. Analyze the dramatic effect of this dialogue as the climax of the story.

Related Commentary

Chinua Achebe, An Image of Africa: Conrad's "Heart of Darkness," p. 1447.

Suggested Readings

Achebe, Chinua. *Girls at War and Other Stories.* New York: Ballantine, 1973.
Chargois, J. A. *Two Views of Black Alienation: A Comparative Study of Chinua Achebe and Ralph Ellison.* Bloomington: Indiana UP, 1973.
Wren, R. W. *Achebe's World.* Washington, D.C.: Three Continents, 1980.

SHERMAN ALEXIE

The Lone Ranger and Tonto Fistfight in Heaven (p. 14)

Although students will have little difficulty understanding the content of Alexie's story, they may be unfamiliar with the reference of the story's title, which seems to have no immediate connection to the story itself. In the story there is no specific mention of the Lone Ranger or Tonto, and nothing about a fistfight, in heaven or on earth. Some students will be familiar with the fictional characters in the title, but there may be students who are not, since it has been many years since they were a ubiquitous presence in American popular culture.

The Lone Ranger was a member of the Texas Rangers, a law enforcement group that was instituted in the nineteenth century to bring justice to the wild Texas frontier. In the fictional story, a group of rangers riding in a deserted area were ambushed by bandits, and all but one of them was killed. The survivor, severely wounded, was found by an "Indian," Tonto, who nursed him back to health. Together they set out to find the killers, and then rode on together through a long career, bringing justice to the West in Saturday matinee film serials, books, comic books, radio programs, and television. The Lone Ranger wore a mask to protect his identity and fought his enemies with silver bullets. When they had accomplished their mission, he and Tonto would move on, always leaving behind one of the silver bullets as a sign to the people he had helped.

The characters have obvious connections to other figures of myth and legend, such as Robin Hood, who also reinforced the belief in the power of the lone individual to effect change in society. The role of the "Indian," who was usually played by a white actor in dark make-up, was secondary, even though Tonto saved the Lone Ranger's life again in several episodes. There was also a suggestion of the fictional characters Don Quixote and Sancho Panza in the Lone Ranger's idealism and in Tonto's dependent role. Despite their years together, Tonto never learned English, expressing himself in a kind of pidgin English dialect. With the title of the story Alexie seems to be telling the reader that the myth is dead, and with the death of the myth the natural antagonism between the white man and the Indian can now be openly expressed. Native Americans had long complained about Tonto's role as a virtual servant to the white ranger, and in the years when the figures became fixtures of popular culture there were already cynical jokes questioning the relationship.

As students read the story more closely, they will realize that on another level Alexie is suggesting that the fistfight between the Lone Ranger, who represents white society, and Tonto, who represents Indian society, reflects a deep conflict within himself. There is almost no plot to the story. The only thing that happens — and we don't learn about it until close to the end — is that the narrator receives a phone call from the white woman whom he once lived with, abused emotionally, and finally left in the middle of the night. The story is a series of remembered incidents through which he is made conscious of the conflict he feels between his Indian background and the white culture he has chosen to enter. By presenting the story as memory, he is able to introduce other elements that his memory dredges up — from failed treaties between the Indians and the whites, to memories of old basketball games, to his self-conscious description of his attempt to frighten the clerk of an all-night store. The reader is aware that Alexie himself was a good basketball player, and that he consciously participated in white culture on many levels, so the story has a strong element of autobiography.

Questions for Discussion

1. Is the title of the story meant seriously or ironically?
2. Why does the protagonist purposefully frighten the clerk of the 7-Eleven?
3. When he describes the clerk swallowing hard "like a white man does," is he suggesting that someone else — an African American or an Asian American — would not be frightened in the same situation?
4. In the italicized sentence beginning "We'll take Washington and Oregon," to what is the author referring? Is it a specific or a general reference?
5. When he describes three white soldiers playing polo with a dead Indian woman's head and compares this to the U.S. policy in Central America, what is he saying about America's treatment of other races and peoples?
6. When he says that his failure to do anything with his life is normal "for almost any other Indian in the country," is he speaking cynically or out of genuine despair?

Topics for Writing

1. Some critics have suggested that Alexie is making a career by manipulating white Americans' guilt over the destruction of the Native American peoples. Discuss this idea in terms of the actions of the protagonist in the story.
2. In the story, there are two examples of police mistrust of minority peoples. Have students discuss whether these are, or are not, valid descriptions of police attitudes.

Suggested Reading

Alexie, Sherman. *The Lone Ranger and Tonto Fistfight in Heaven.* New York: HarperCollins, 1994.

Woody Allen

The Kugelmass Episode (p. 21)

Like most works of fiction based on impossible or unlikely suppositions, "The Kugelmass Episode" entertains us with the device on which it is grounded. Rather than developing the intellectual puzzles of science fiction, however, Allen mainly offers gently satiric jokes made possible by the incongruities arising from his donnée. When her class notices that on page 100 "a bald Jew is kissing Madame Bovary," the teacher in South Dakota, without consulting her desk copy, blames the problem on a mass-media stereotype, drug-crazed students; a professor at Stanford sees in the incredible instability of the text a confirmation of a mindless academic cliché: "Well, I guess the mark of a classic is that you can re-read it a thousand times and always find something new." Thus we transform what is unfamiliar into bricks for the wall of presupposition that barricades us from the truth. Meanwhile, Allen delights in collapsing the distance between "good literature" and everyday banality. Emma admires Kugelmass's leisure suit; he thrills her with black panties and designer slacks; and, like every other good-looking girl who goes to New York, she dreams of a career on the stage.

But the fantasy on which Allen bases his tale has deeper roots. Like Faust, Kugelmass dreams of transcending human limitations, of living for a while free from the constraints of time and ordinary causation. He abandons human science and philosophy, here represented by his shrink, and turns to magic. Although Persky resembles an auto mechanic more than Mephistopheles, he offers an equally dangerous and meaningful temptation to Kugelmass. If the professor lacks the poetry and grandeur of his Faustian predecessors, he is motivated by parallel desires. Bored with his life and unable to love the people he shares it with (who can blame him?), he bargains for something he expects will be better. Appropriately, given the diminished scale of modern heroism, he signs away not his soul but merely a "double sawbuck." As happens especially with Marlowe's Dr. Faustus, for his reward Kugelmass gets only what he is capable of imagining. Emma Bovary as he experiences her talks and acts like any woman he could have picked up at Elaine's — exactly what he wanted, and what he turns her into by bringing her out of the novel and into the Plaza Hotel.

After the near-disaster of his affair with Emma, Kugelmass swears off philandering, but of course he has not learned his lesson. When he asks Persky to use the wondrous machine to send him for a date with "The Monkey" of *Portnoy's Complaint*, Kugelmass reveals the utter emptiness of spirit that hides behind his glib pop-culture romanticism, and it is fitting that he ends up scrambling through a desert inhabited by predatory words without meaning.

The intellectual and moral universe that Kugelmass inhabits even before his final translation is no less devoid of meaning. Allen's fantasy shows how the sophistication of modern life can drain the spirit out of human language, desires, and relationships. Kugelmass claims to have "soul," but his needs are quoted from advertisements in *The New Yorker*. The language of commercial psychology debases even his dreams, whose imagery is third hand and probably phony: "I was skipping through a meadow holding a picnic basket and the basket was marked 'Options.'" Kugelmass picks his mistress as from a menu; he decides to plunge into the supernatural (but for exceedingly *natural* reasons) more easily than he chooses between red and white wine (as if those were the only possibilities); significantly, he is most comfortable minimizing the importance of what he is doing: "'Sex and romance,' Kugelmass said from inside the box. 'What we go through for a pretty face.'"

Through the fantastic device of Persky's box, Allen achieves the small dislocation necessary to reveal that remark of Kugelmass's as a pitifully inadequate cliché. The story is full of such instances, and the technique embodies its larger vision. We choose the things we say to describe our lives to ourselves because they have been purged of discomforting truths. Allen shows that these statements are illusions. Kugelmass regards his life as a novel that has turned out badly. Rather than seeking to understand why he has come to a second marital dead end burdened with financial obligations and bored with his family, he tries to escape from the present and reenact the past. He wants only to enter *Madame Bovary* before page 120, and he dreams of starting life over in Europe, selling the (long defunct) *International Herald Tribune* "like those young girls used to."

The story leaves us with an implicit question: What redemption is possible for Kugelmass and the culture — our culture — that he represents? Is there an alternative to the Hobson's choice between desperation and meaninglessness?

WILLIAM E. SHEIDLEY

Questions for Discussion

1. Comment on the situation of Kugelmass as described in the first two paragraphs. Do you think his circumstances are unusual? Where should we lay blame for his predicament?
2. Kugelmass "had soul." What does that term seem to mean in this context?
3. Interpret Kugelmass's dream. Is it profoundly symbolic?
4. How effective is Dr. Mandel? Why does Kugelmass need a magician?
5. Discuss Persky. What might be Allen's basis for this character? How important is Persky to the story?
6. What factors enter into Kugelmass's choice of a mistress? What does this event suggest about his attitude toward literature? toward women?
7. Explore the implications of this quip: "She spoke in the same fine English translation as the paperback."
8. Review the first conversation between Kugelmass and Emma. Has Kugelmass really been transported into *Madame Bovary*? Does it resemble the novel as you read it or as you imagine it to be?
9. What does Allen achieve by noting the effect of the sudden appearance of the Kugelmass episode in the novel on various readers?
10. "By showing up during the correct chapters, I've got the situation knocked," Kugelmass says. Consider the implications of that idea. Would you like to live only certain chapters of your life?
11. Why does Emma want to come to New York? Why does Kugelmass want to take her there? Are the ensuing problems entirely the result of her being a character in a novel?
12. As Persky struggles to repair his box and Emma consumes "Dom Pérignon and black eggs," Kugelmass becomes more and more agitated. Finally, he contemplates suicide ("Too bad this is a low floor") or running away to Europe to sell the *International Herald Tribune*. How serious is he? Explain why those ideas accord with his character.

13.   Why does it take Kugelmass only three weeks to break his resolution, "I'll never cheat again"?
14.   *Portnoy's Complaint* examines, among other things, masturbation and adolescent sexual fantasies. What does it imply about Kugelmass that he chooses that book for his next adventure?
15.   Do you think the ending of the story is appropriate? Why should Allen choose a remedial Spanish grammar for Kugelmass's hell rather than, say, a book in which adulterers are punished or in which none of the characters is a good-looking young woman?

Topics for Writing

1.   Analyze how Allen crosses the border between life and art in "The Kugelmass Episode" and in his film *The Purple Rose of Cairo*.
2.   Discuss the theme of meaningless language in "The Kugelmass Episode."
3.   Study the use of language in Allen's story. List familiar phrases. What are their sources? Examine the conversations between characters. How much communication is taking place?
4.   **RESPONDING CREATIVELY**   People often wish aloud for something they know to be impossible or speak of what they would do *if only*: "If only I had her looks and his money." "If only I were in charge." Imagine a character — yourself or someone you know, perhaps — whose impossible wish comes true. Then what? Follow Allen's lead by using the device to express the real truth in a surprising new way.
5.   **CONNECTIONS**   Compare and contrast the responses to marvels in Allen's "The Kugelmass Episode" and García Márquez's "A Very Old Man with Enormous Wings."

Suggested Readings

Gianetti, L. "Ciao, Woody." *Western Humanities Review* 35 (1981): 157–61.
Jacobs, Diane. *Magic of Woody Allen*. London: Robson, 1982.
Reisch, M. S. "Woody Allen: American Prose Humorist." *Journal of Popular Culture* 17 (1983): 68–74.
Rose, L. "Humor and Nothingness." *Atlantic* 255 (1985): 94–96.
Shechner, Mark. "Woody Allen: The Failure of the Therapeutic." *From Hester Street to Hollywood*. Ed. Sarah B. Cohen. Bloomington: Indiana UP, 1983. 231–44.
"Woody Allen on the American Character." *Commentary* 76 (1983): 61–65.

Isabel Allende

And of Clay Are We Created *(p. 30)*

"And of Clay Are We Created" is the last story in Allende's *The Stories of Eva Luna*, published after her third novel, *Eva Luna*, about a woman who "defeats the odds of her fate with generosity and candor." Rolf Carlé, the television journalist in the story who befriends Azucena, the thirteen-year-old girl caught in the mudpit after the volcano's eruption destroys her village, also writes the prologue to *The Stories of Eva Luna*. There Carlé comments on Allende the storyteller: "You think in words; for you, language is an inexhaustible thread you weave as if life were created as you tell it."

In Allende's hands, a story about the tragedy of a natural disaster is the occasion for a celebration of life. In an essay titled "Writing as an Act of Hope," Allende has said that writing *clearly* is the first duty of the storyteller: "Not simply — that only works with soap advertising; we don't have to sacrifice aesthetics for the sake of ethics. On the contrary, only if we are able to say it beautifully can we be convincing. Most readers are perfectly able to appreciate subtleties and poetic twists and symbols and metaphors." In "And of Clay Are We Created," the volcano's eruption elicits the young girl's heroism, which in turn frees the journalist who befriends her so that he is able to confront his own deeply repressed fears about his traumatic youth in Austria thirty years before.

One aspect of "And of Clay Are We Created" that could stimulate discussion in the classroom is how Allende suggests the difference between a television reporter's coverage of a story and a short story writer's handling of the same event. Rolf Carlé has at his disposal an expensive arsenal of technical equipment: helicopter, video camera and microphone, "spools of cable, tapes, film, videos, precision lenses, recorders, sound consoles, lights, reflecting screens, auxiliary motors, cartons of supplies, electricians, sound technicians, and camera men." Allende, on the other hand, has only her words and the blank page. Yet she is able to get beneath the surface of the natural disaster and tell the story in depth, so that we learn of the impact of the girl's heroism on Rolf Carlé. Allende's handling of the sequence of events communicates a moral lesson as well as a historical one.

Questions for Discussion

1. Analyze how the opening paragraph of the story foreshadows the events to come in the narrative.
2. What is the effect of Allende's description of the girl's "head budding like a black squash from the clay" after we are told that her name is *Azucena*, meaning "Lily"?
3. In the second paragraph of the story, Allende employs irony to describe the events leading up to the volcano's eruption. How does her tone establish her emotional control over her material?
4. What other examples of irony can you find in the story?
5. Discuss the significance of the title of the story.

Topics for Writing

1. **RESPONDING CREATIVELY** Write a book review of Allende's novel *Eva Luna*.
2. Allende has said that "it's hard for a book to stand against the message of the mass media; it's an unfair battle. Writers should therefore look for other forms of expressing their thoughts, avoiding the prejudice that only in books can they make literature. All means are legitimate, not only the cultivated language of academia but also the direct language of journalism, the mass language of radio, television and the movies, the poetic language of popu-

lar songs and the passionate language of talking face to face with an audience. These are all forms of literature." Agree or disagree with her statement.

3. **CONNECTIONS**   Compare and contrast Allende's description of a disaster
    in this story with the disaster described by Bharati Mukherjee in "The Man-
    agement of Grief."

Suggested Readings

Allende, Isabel. *The Stories of Eva Luna.* Trans. Margaret Sayers Peden. New York
     Atheneum, 1991.
Zinsser, William, ed. *Paths of Resistance: The Art and Craft of the Political Novel.*
     Boston: Houghton, 1989. Contains Isabel Allende's "Writing as an Act of
     Hope."

DOROTHY ALLISON

River of Names (p. 39)

Allison explains the title near the end of her story: "I've got a dust river in
my head, a river of names endlessly repeating. That dirty water rises in me, all
those children screaming out their lives in my memory, and I become someone
else, someone I have tried so hard not to be." The conflict in her story is both
physical and emotional: the protagonist's memories of the violence endured by
the members of her family, dramatized in a series of flashbacks, and the hatred
she feels for herself since she is still haunted by what she considers her "dirty"
poverty-stricken childhood in the American South. The story is open-ended, since
the narrator finds no possibility of resolution for either conflict, except in the act
of storytelling itself.

Perhaps students will enhance their reading of Allison's story by comparing and contrasting it with Susan Sontag's AIDS story "The Way We Live Now."
The subject of both stories is the often brutal nature of human experience. The
authors find no easy solutions, nor do they suggest that misery ennobles humankind. On the contrary. The voice of the narrator in each story is the only calm,
stable point in the storm of events conjured up by the act of storytelling. The
characters are dehumanized, presented by name only in a passing parade of sentences. Yet the reader senses relationships between the names and anticipates some
development or deeper revelation of character. Instead, the fictional relationships
merely continue until the end of the stories (as when Allison's narrator tells us
about her Aunt Raylene's disastrous attempt to leave her abusive husband after
she learns that her son Bo would never be "right"). However, there is no satisfy-
ing closure for any of the characters in the stories, including the narrators.

Allison's achievement in "River of Names" is her skillful creation of a form
and a voice to handle her difficult subject. Her tone is reminiscent of Tillie Olsen's
voice in "I Stand Here Ironing" — the lyrical, strong expression of a woman who
has survived emotionally devastating experiences. Here the fictional narrator has
found a companion in her lover, Jesse, but her sense of happiness seems fragile.

She is a survivor, but she has not been able to come to terms with the trauma of what she was forced to endure in her brutal childhood.

Questions for Discussion

1. Is this an autobiographical or a fictional story? Who is the narrator?
2. What has happened to the narrator's cousin, Tommy, in the first paragraph of the story? How has Allison underscored the horror of his death by describing "the rope around his neck pulled up into the sunlit heights of the barn, fascinating, horrible"? In this description is she exploiting the sensational aspect of the child's death, or is she presenting it with restraint?
3. Does "River of Names" have a plot? Where is it set? Who are the characters? Why is it considered a short story instead of an essay?
4. What is the effect of the narrator's telling her lover "But I lie" at the end of the story? Does this cast doubt on everything the narrator has said, or is it Allison's attempt to avoid sentimentality?

Topics for Writing

1. **CONNECTIONS** Compare and contrast the use of names (instead of fully developed characters) in Allison's and Sontag's stories.
2. **CONNECTIONS** Compare and contrast the first-person narration in Allison's and Olsen's stories about family life.

Suggested Reading

Allison, Dorothy. *Skin: Talking about Sex, Class, and Literature.* Ithaca, NY: Firebrand, 1994.

MARTIN AMIS

The Immortals (p. 47)

Martin Amis, the son of the well-known British comic novelist Kingsley Amis, is widely regarded in his native England as a darkly misanthropic writer who directs the sharp edge of his satire at a wide range of targets. In this story, he has squared off at life and human existence itself — and when we come to the end of his tragic tale we see that, like most great satirists, he is more intensely driven by his disappointment at the failings of his fellow beings than he is enraged by their corruptibility. It is perhaps with some difficulty that students will reach this conclusion themselves, since Amis has chosen to shape his narrative at a double level of imaginative projection. On the primary level, he has imagined himself as something or someone that he chooses to call the Immortal, which is never clearly defined, and on the secondary level he suggests that this persona is a delusion of his real self. As he describes himself in the story, "Sometimes I have this weird idea that I am just a second-rate New Zealand schoolmaster who never did anything or went anywhere. . . . " The story's syntax leaves us ultimately with the conviction that the Immortal is indeed the delusion of a New Zealand schoolmaster.

The concept of the Immortal, which Amis leaves deceptively vague while at the same time investing it with considerable comic invention, presents an opportunity for classroom discussion. From the opening descriptions it is clear that we are being presented with some indefinable life force, since the Immortal's consciousness precedes the appearance of any other life forms on the planet. Though we try to give a specific identity to this life force, Amis has presented us with a dilemma, since he tells us, in the opening sentence of the third paragraph, that "I was born, or I appeared or materialized or beamed down." There is nothing here that gives us any certain clues. In the persona of the Immortal, he has left us free to sort through the world's stock of creation myths and choose the most comfortable. He is more specific in his description of the later beginnings of other life on earth: "I used to croon over those little warm ponds where space-seeded life began." If what we have is truly the delusion of the failed New Zealander, then perhaps an earlier sentence represents a reasonable idealization of that person: "I think I must have been a dud god or something." As he says of himself, "conceivably I came from another planet which ticked to a different clock."

The ruses the Immortal has used to endure such long periods of time, ranging from the narrator's casual description of himself picking his nose for a year and a half to spending a summer in a prolonged act of masturbation, illustrate the writer's inventiveness and imaginative gusto. The comic tone of the story is achieved through the careful delineation of the myriad ways the Immortal has managed to pass the past four or five billion years, give or take a billion or so. The beginnings of the story are so cheerless — he describes the people around him as sick and dying, and they are the last beings on Earth — that it doesn't seem possible he could wring laughter out of his subject. But the experiences of the Immortal, as he slouches through evolution and human history, are told in such an offhand, unconcerned manner that it is difficult to carry the despairing mood of the opening paragraph through the heart of the story. It is only at the end, when we return to the final days of this dying group, that we feel the depth of Amis's despair at the human condition. For the student reader, the story will be a rollercoaster ride through their emotions.

As a technical point for class discussion, the language of the story itself will be of interest. Perhaps to strengthen the suggestion that the central figure in the story is a deluded schoolmaster from New Zealand, Amis has used a syntax that is different from his own native dialect of English. To many students it will seem as much American in syntax as English, and some of the idioms and the slang expressions have clearly been borrowed from everyday American usage. Certainly he has used this literary device as yet another way for him to emphasize the universality of his despairing narrative.

Questions for Discussion

1.   What is the significance of the Immortal's statement that he made his appearance on Earth near a present-day city in Africa?
2.   Although the Immortal describes his life in the early eons of earthly experience as healthy and pleasant, he longs for what he calls "reciprocation." What does he means by that?

3. What is he suggesting about the human condition in comparing the people he knows to his pets?
4. Why does he describe the scene of the atomic bomb attack as Tokyo?
5. In his description of the headaches he experiences after the atomic explosion, he refers to someone he calls Dionysus. Who was Dionysus, and why would this name be familiar to a New Zealand schoolmaster?
6. What is Amis telling his readers when he describes the Battle of Agincourt as a "little huddle of retching tramps" across the way from "another little huddle of retching tramps"?
7. What is there in the story that suggests to the reader that the narrator is actually a deluded New Zealand schoolmaster?

Topics for Writing

1. Discuss some of the idioms and expressions in the story that seem to be American, and those that are English, and compare their effects on the syntax.
2. Although in the character of the Immortal Amis has presented someone who seems to be nonjudgmental, he writes, "I *saw* what you were doing to the place. What was the matter? Was it too *nice* for you or something? Jesus Christ, you were here only for about ten minutes. And look what you did." Discuss the moral point he is presenting in this statement.
3. **CONNECTIONS**   Amis's glimpse of the apocalypse is a popular device with satirists or writers with a moral concern for the human experience. Compare this story with other stories that take as their theme the ending of life on Earth through nucleur holocaust or some other disaster.
4. In his description of the group of people who still survive he writes, "They suffer from a mass delusion. . . . They all believe that they are eternal, that they are immortal." Discuss the basic tenets of two or more religious faiths as they pertain to immortality.

Suggested Reading

Diedrick, James. *Understanding Martin Amis.* Columbia, SC: U of South Carolina, 1995.

SHERWOOD ANDERSON

Death in the Woods (p. 55)

"Death in the Woods" presents a religious image of the earth mother, the principle of connectedness by which life is fostered and sustained. Anderson's depiction of the woman whose job it is to feed animal life, "in cows, in chickens, in pigs, in horses, in dogs, in men," congeals in the visionary revelation of her death scene. To the men and boys who stand around her, the moonlit glimpse of her naked breast — effectively foreshadowed in the incident in which, as a girl,

she had her dress ripped open by the German farmer she was bound to —
conveys a sense of wonder: They look upon a marble statue of a beautiful young
woman in the snow. Near her, or perhaps around her, lies the oval track left by the
dogs, at once a prayer ring and a symbol of the interdependence and endless
continuity of the life she has served.

It is appropriate that the basis of Mrs. Grimes's scant economy is eggs, whose
various connotations are obvious enough. As the nurse of living things, Mrs.
Grimes establishes bonds and fosters community. The world with which she must
deal, however, corrodes those bonds. When we first see her she is struggling alone:
"People drive right down a road and never notice an old woman like that." The
men she feeds are rapacious and cruel — to her and, as in the fight between Jake
and the German farmer, to each other. The town treats them all with cold suspicion. Even the butcher who loads her grain bag out of pity would deny the food
to Mrs. Grimes's husband or son: "He'd see him starve first." Not Mrs. Grimes,
who tacitly reaffirms her theme: "Starve, eh? Well, things had to be fed. . . . Horses,
cows, pigs, dogs, men." When she dies the forces for harmony and union that she
embodies achieve a momentary victory, as the townspeople fall into a ragged
communal procession to witness her death — a ceremony as instinctive as the
ring running of the dogs, if somewhat less orderly and beautiful.

Anderson's story progresses from an apprehension of drab poverty and
ugliness to a discovery of wonder and beauty. The agency that distills religious
and aesthetic emotion out of the profane world of the story is the inquiring imagination of the narrator, who muses over his recollections, reconstructs his story
from fragments, and in doing so explains the process of synthesis that takes place
as he writes. In its progress from the ordinary to the mystical, from ugliness and
privation to a soul-nourishing beauty, the story records a triumph of the creative
imagination, which penetrates the surfaces of things to find within them their
inherent mythic truth.

What makes that triumph possible is the narrator's subtly expressed identification with Mrs. Grimes. The fascination that causes him to cling to his recollections and finally to work them through may arise, as William J. Scheick argues,
from the shock of his initiation into an awareness "of the relation between feed-
ing, sex, and death" that blocks his sexual development; or it may arise from a
sense of the hitherto unexpressed mythic implications of the scene in the woods.
In either case, the narrator recognizes that the death of Mrs. Grimes has meaning
for him — as one who has worked for a German farmer, who has himself watched
dogs run in a ring, and who has kept silent; as one who is fed by women; and as
one who must die. The story's circular structure, like the ring of dogs and the ring
of men around the corpse, transforms compulsion into worship, just as Anderson's
art transforms the report of a frightening death into a celebration of life and of the
power of the sympathetic imagination to render its beauty.

WILLIAM E. SHEIDLEY

Questions for Discussion

1. Discuss the style of the opening paragraph. What qualities of the old
    woman's life are reflected in the syntax and rhythms of the prose?

2. How does Anderson modulate from generalization through recollection to specific narration? What change in narrative mode takes place in section II with the paragraph that begins "One day in Winter"? Does the story ever return to its original mode? Where?
3. "Her name was Grimes" — appropriately?
4. What does the narrator mean when he calls the Grimes men "a tough lot"? Are they alone in this in the story?
5. Describe the woman's life with the German farmer. How important to the story is the farmer's having torn "her dress open clear down the front"?
6. How big a part does love play in the relations between people in this story? What other factors are prominent — exploitation? mistrust? violence?
7. Does the butcher's generosity seem a welcome change? How does the butcher compare with Mrs. Grimes as a nurturer of life?
8. How does Anderson prepare us to accept it as probable that Mrs. Grimes would sit down under a tree and freeze to death?
9. Describe the behavior of the dogs. How does Anderson explain it? How does the narrator know it took place?
10. Comment on the tonal effect of the passage "It had been a big haul for the old woman. It was a big haul for the dogs now."
11. What does the corpse look like in the moonlight? Why does Anderson give a concise description of the corpse near the beginning of section IV rather than saving the whole revelation until the men and boys arrive on the scene at the end of that section?
12. Comment on the implications of this line: "Either mother or our older sister would have to warm our supper."
13. Explain the possible meanings of the word "everything" in the first sentence of section V.
14. Discuss the narrator's remarks about why he has told the story. What is "the real story I am now trying to tell"? To what extent is it a story about the narrator himself? About stories and storytelling?

Topics for Writing

1. In an essay, describe Anderson's circular notion of image and structure in "Death in the Woods."
2. Discuss the narrator's struggle "to tell the simple story over again."
3. Write an essay analyzing the role of the community in "Death in the Woods."
4. Describe Mrs. Grimes and the mythic roles of woman in "Death in the Woods."
5. On a second reading, make notes about the narrator. Rearrange his activities, experiences, and concerns into chronological order. What is the narrator's story? What is his conflict? What does he achieve? What does he learn?
6. **RESPONDING CREATIVELY** Read several myths from Ovid's *Metamorphoses*. Rewrite the story of Mrs. Grimes as an Ovidian myth. What changes of tone are necessary? What important themes have you had to abandon? What have you had to invent?

Related Commentary

Sherwood Anderson, Form, Not Plot, in the Short Story, p. 1453.

Suggested Readings

See page 15.

Sherwood Anderson

Hands (p. 64)

Anderson's story "Hands" might be called a portrait. Like a formal painted portrait, it depicts Wing Biddlebaum not only as he exists at a given moment but also in conjunction with certain props in the background that reveal who he is by recalling his past and defining his circumstances. The focal image of the portrait is Wing's hands, around which the other elements of the picture are organized and to which they lend meaning. Further, the story depends for a portion of its effect upon a series of painterly tableaux, from the sunset landscape with berry pickers with which it begins to the silhouette of Wing as a holy hermit, saying over and over the rosary of his lonely years of penance for a sin he did not commit.

In keeping with this achronological narration (which William L. Phillips has shown may in part result from Anderson's thinking his way through the story as he wrote it), neither Wing nor George Willard experiences any clear revelation or makes any climactic decision. Wing never understands why he was driven out of Pennsylvania, and George is afraid to ask the questions that might lead them both to a liberating understanding of Wing's experience.

The reader, however, is not permitted to remain in the dark. With the clear understanding of how the crudity and narrow-minded suspicion of his neighbors have perverted Wing's selfless, "diffused" love for his students into a source of fear and shame comes a poignant sorrow for what is being wasted. Wing's hands may be the pride of Winesburg for their agility at picking strawberries, but the nurturing love that they betoken is feared by everyone, including George, including even Wing himself, whose loneliness is as great as his capacity to love — from which, by a cruel irony, it arises.

WILLIAM E. SHEIDLEY

Questions for Discussion

1. Define Wing Biddlebaum's relationship to his community as it is implied in the first paragraph. To what extent is the impression created here borne out?
2. Why does Wing hope George Willard will come to visit? Does George ever arrive?

3. Wing's name, which refers to his hands, was given to him by "some obscure poet of the town," and telling the full story of those hands "is a job for a poet." What connotations of "wings" are appropriate? Why is "Wing" a better name for Biddlebaum than, say, "Claw," or "Hook," or "Picker"?
4. Could Wing himself have been a poet? Why does he tell his dreams only to George?
5. Why did the people of the town in Pennsylvania nearly lynch Adolph Myers? Why was he unable to defend himself?
6. Are the people in Ohio any different from those in Pennsylvania? Explain. What about George Willard? Evaluate his decision not to ask Wing about his hands.
7. What other hands do we see in the story? Compare them with Wing's.
8. Explain the implications of our last view of Wing. What is the pun in the last line?

Topics for Writing

1. Write an essay analyzing the crucifixion of Wing Biddlebaum.
2. Consider Anderson's comments in "Form, Not Plot, in the Short Story" (included in Part Two, p. 1453) as a key to his art in "Hands."
3. After reading the story once, jot down your response, including your feelings about Wing, George, the townspeople, and the narrator. Also write, in one or two sentences, a summation of the story's theme as you understand it. Then reread the paragraphs in the order they would have followed had Anderson told the story in chronological order. Would your responses differ? Would the story have an identical theme? Explain.
4. **RESPONDING CREATIVELY** Anderson claimed to have written this story at a sitting and to have published it without rearrangements or major additions or deletions of material. Imitating his process, write a vignette about a person unknown to you whom you see in a photograph. Start with the scene in the photo and end with the same, interpolating previous incidents and background information as they occur to you.
5. **CONNECTIONS** Compare and contrast Anderson's Wing and Flaubert's Félicité.

Related Commentary

Sherwood Anderson, Form, Not Plot, in the Short Story, p. 1453.

Suggested Readings

Anderson, David, ed. *Critical Essays on Sherwood Anderson.* Boston: G. K. Hall, 1981.
Anderson, Sherwood. *A Story Teller's Story.* Cleveland: The UP of Case Western Reserve, 1968.
———. *The Portable Sherwood Anderson.* New York: Viking, 1972.
———. *The Teller's Tales.* Introduction by Frank Gado. Schenectady, NY: Union College P, 1983.

Burbank, Rex. *Sherwood Anderson*. Twayne's United States Authors Series 65. New York: Twayne, 1964. 64–66.
Crowley, John W., ed. *New Essays on* Winesburg, Ohio. New York: Cambridge UP, 1990.
Joselyn, Sister Mary. "Some Artistic Dimensions of Sherwood Anderson's 'Death in the Woods.'" *Studies in Short Fiction* 4 (1967): 252–59.
Phillips, William L. "How Sherwood Anderson Wrote *Winesburg, Ohio*." *The Achievement of Sherwood Anderson*. Ed. Ray Lewis White. Chapel Hill: U of North Carolina P, 1966. 62–84, esp. 74–78. Originally published in *American Literature* 23 (1951): 7–30.
Rideout, Walter B., ed. *Sherwood Anderson*. Englewood Cliffs, NJ: Prentice, 1974.
Scheick, William J. "Compulsion toward Repetition: Sherwood Anderson's 'Death in the Woods.'" *Studies in Short Fiction* 11 (1974): 141–46.
Townsend, Kim. *Sherwood Anderson*. Boston: Houghton, 1987.
White, Ray Lewis. Winesburg, Ohio: *An Explanation*. Boston: Twayne, 1990.

Margaret Atwood

Happy Endings (p. 69)

Atwood's story can be read profitably in conjunction with Grace Paley's "A Conversation with My Father." In both, the authors use humor to suggest a certain impatience with the traditional short-story form. Both stories can be read as "metafictions," fictions that comment on the art of telling stories. Atwood's piece is harsher than Paley's in its insistence that happy endings are impossible in stories; Atwood tells us clearly that death is "the only authentic ending" to everyone's story. Paley, in contrast, clearly values both her relationship with her dying father and her own imagination, allowing (even half-jokingly) her fictional heroine the possibility of rehabilitation after her drug addiction and a valued place in society as a counselor in a center for young addicts.

The first time students read "Happy Endings," they may miss the way Atwood connects the stories from "A" to "F." "B" is the first unhappy ending (as Atwood warns us in the third sentence), with the "worst possible scenario" worked out in John and Mary's love affair. Atwood's vocabulary here is deliberately harsh and unromantic, unlike the sentimental clichés of the "A" scenario.

As Atwood continues her permutations of the couples' possible relationships, her stories get shorter and more perfunctory. Her language becomes more elemental, preparing the reader for her summary dismissal of all plots, since they all end in death. In the final three paragraphs, Atwood drops all pretense that she is telling stories and directly addresses her readers, revealing that her true subject is not the emotional life she is creating for her characters but her awareness of the elements of fiction. She defines plot as "what" or "just one thing after another." Then, like the instructor's manual of a short-story anthology, she leaves the rest up to her reader: "Now try How [character] and Why [theme.]"

Questions for Discussion

1. Atwood's authorial presence is the strongest element in "Happy Endings" — does this make the text closer to an essay than a short story? Explain.
2. How does Atwood elicit your curiosity, so that you continue to read this short story? Would you say that she has proven that plot is the most essential element in a story? Is there also an underlying, coherent theme to "Happy Endings"?
3. Would the story still be effective if Atwood omitted her direct address to the reader ("If you want a happy ending, try A.")? Explain.

Topics for Writing

1. **RESPONDING CREATIVELY** Rewrite the story, inventing additional outcomes for John and Mary's relationship.
2. In "Reading Blind" (p. 1456), Atwood gives her criteria for judging whether a story is "good." Using these criteria, how would you rate "Happy Endings"?
3. Ray Bradbury, in his book *Zen in the Art of Writing: Essays on Creativity* (Capra, 1990), writes, "The writer must let his fingers run out the story of his characters, who, being only human and full of strange dreams and obsessions, are only too glad to run. . . . Remember: *Plot* is no more than footprints left in the snow after your characters have run by on their way to incredible destinations. *Plot* is observed after the fact rather than before. It cannot precede action. It is the chart that remains when an action is through." Apply Bradbury's analysis to "Happy Endings."

Related Commentary

Margaret Atwood, Reading Blind, p. 1456.

Suggested Readings

Atwood, Margaret. *Murder in the Dark.* Toronto: Coach House, 1983.
———. *Second Words.* Toronto: Anansi, 1982.
Grace, Sherrill E., and Lorraine Weir. *Margaret Atwood: Language, Text and System.* Vancouver: U of British Columbia P, 1983.
Rigney, Barbara Hill. *Margaret Atwood.* Totowa, NJ: Barnes & Noble, 1987.
Stouck, David. *Major Canadian Authors.* Lincoln: U of Nebraska P, 1988.

Margaret Atwood

Rape Fantasies (p. 71)

In this story, Atwood, a writer of considerable courage and political astuteness, seems to come close to trivializing a subject that is of particular concern to students. It is certainly a subject that is generally handled with considerable sensitivity and as an opportunity for students to present their own views. In this story the protagonist is presented with the subject, fantasies of rape, by one of the women at her lunch table, who tells her, "It says here all women have rape fantasies." Her dismissive reply is "For Chrissake, I'm eating an egg sandwich." It is in the development of this response that Atwood has created the story. It is one in which nothing could be said to "happen," but a careful reading will show how skillfully Atwood has presented us with a portrait of an individual woman's deepest response to the threat of physical violation.

The tone of the story's opening pages is flippant and casual, almost as though the woman were chatting idly for effect. In fact, as we reach the final paragraphs we realize that the woman *is* chatting, and she intends the tone of what she is saying to be casual, but at the same time she reveals much more about herself than she intends. A student who reads the story quickly may not be able to place the woman's long monologue in a physical setting, since Atwood doesn't reveal the situation until just before the end of the story. The woman is, in fact, sitting in a bar, it is Friday afternoon, and she is having a drink by herself to escape from the pressures of the week at her job. She explains carefully, "I'm not what you would call a drinker but I like to go out now and then for a drink or two in a nice place." She is talking to someone she has just met — probably someone who has just struck up a conversation with her. She explains herself to her listener: "I don't know why I'm telling you all this, except I think it helps you to get to know a person, especially at first."

The woman is comfortable and feels secure in the bar, since she has come there before and she knows the waiters, but she is still upset by the conversation she had two days before with her co-workers dealing with the subject of rape fantasies. In answer to another woman's questions, she related a comic fantasy of her own escape from a potential rapist by asking him to hold all the things in her purse so she could search for the plastic squeezer of lemon juice she always carried with her in case a rapist did approach her. When she eventually finds the squeezer at the bottom of her purse she asks the man to take the top off for her, and when he does, she squirts lemon juice in his eyes. It is difficult for the reader to decide at first whether the woman is being serious or if she is denying the threat of rape. In the series of fantasies that she relates to the man listening to her, she describes, in each instance, a comic response that prevents the rape from taking place. What becomes clear to the reader is that in these scenarios she is denying to herself the possibility of physical violence.

The author, however, takes the story further, and presents the reader with an unanticipated aspect of the woman's character, and it is this final revelation that leaves the reader with a consciousness of something more complex than the woman's flippant humor and her determined denials. In the same ostensibly casual tone, the woman has allowed the person sitting with her to understand that she is lonely, that she hopes to meet a man she could love, and that even an accidental meeting with someone who is intending to rape her could turn into a real relationship. As she describes her fantasy, "we're happy we've found the only other person in the world who can understand what we're going through, it's almost like fate, and after a while we just sort of look at each other and our hands touch, and he comes back with me and moves into my apartment."

In her final sentences the woman allows the reader to glimpse her real fears, but she also reveals her wistful defense. If she simply talks with the person, as she is talking to the man in the bar now, how could that person harm her? That is something she never would understand. As she insists, "I mean, I know it happens, but I just don't understand it, that's the part I really don't understand." With the ending of the story Atwood has taken us beyond the brittle humor of the woman's casual jokes. We have seen her longings and her hopes, and her final naive trust that her life will bring her what she dreams, even if her dreams reveal themselves only through the complex mirror of her fantasies.

Questions for Discussion

1. In her presentation of the woman the author has used small, trivial details to reveal aspects of her character, as well as to place the story in time. What is Atwood telling us when her protagonist says she would "prefer a June Allyson movie any time" or that she dreams of someone "like Mr. Clean"? The author also uses this technique to reveal more about the women of the story. What is she telling us about them with the paragraph that says of one of them, "she worked in Detroit for three years"?
2. What is the distinction the woman is making when she tells the other women that their fantasies are not about rape? Are her own fantasies any more real than theirs?
3. What is the woman telling us about her attitude toward herself in her references to her work in the Filing Department?
4. Do the fantasies the women describe relate to real men and to the fantasies the men themselves might have? Is there any reality in the woman's statement that for her, " . . . the rest of the time, [the rapists] must lead a normal life"?
5. What is the woman revealing about herself by saying, "At work they call me the office worry wart, but it isn't so much like worrying, it's more like figuring out what you should do in an emergency"?
6. The woman is presenting herself as rather simple and naive, but is she as unwary as she pretends to be?

Topics for Writing

1. The woman has revealed many things about herself in her fantasies. Discuss some of the aspects of her character that we understand through these fantasies, and extend the discussion to consider what we have learned about the other women through their fantasies.
2. Discuss the nature of denial, as it is presented in the woman's fantasies about physical violation.
3. The question of rape was a central theme in the early years of modern feminism. Discuss whether this question is relevant today or whether it is more closely associated with the older feminist agenda.

Isaac Babel

My First Goose (p. 80)

The narrator in this story is an outsider, a lonely and hungry intellectual who wins a meal and the acceptance of the Cossacks by killing the old peasant woman's goose. He does it roughly, demonstrating that he will "get on all right" at the front. The act is portrayed partly as a rape, partly as a crucifixion. The quartermaster tells him, "you go and mess up a lady, and a good lady too, and you'll have the boys patting you on the back," and that is what he does, trampling her goose under his boot and plunging his sword into it while she repeats, "I want to go and hang myself," and he says, "Christ!" But the narrator recoils from his self-debasement: The night that enfolds him resembles a prostitute; the moon decorates it "like a cheap earring." Lenin says there is a shortage of everything, and though Surovkov believes that Lenin strikes straight at the truth "like a hen pecking at a grain," the narrator uses the spectacles of his learning to discern "the secret curve of Lenin's straight line," the hidden purpose of the speech. The narrator, too, has taken an apparently bold and forthright step in killing the goose, but the secret curve of his straight line has been to gain acceptance by the Cossacks and a share of *their* dinner, which reminds him of his home. As he sleeps with his new friends he dreams of women, just as he saw female beauty in the long legs of Savitsky. But in taking his first goose he has messed up a good lady and stained his heart with bloodshed, and his conscience is not at peace.

Questions for Discussion

1. Describe Savitsky. What is the narrator's attitude toward him? Why does Babel begin the story with this character, who never reappears?
2. What advice does the quartermaster give? Does the narrator follow it?
3. Why are the narrator's "specs" an object of derision? Who else in the story wears glasses?
4. Why does the Cossack throw the narrator's trunk out at the gate?
5. When the narrator first tries to read Lenin's speech, he cannot concentrate. Why?
6. How does the narrator win the respect of the Cossacks?
7. Discuss the difference between Surovkov's understanding of Lenin's speech and the narrator's.
8. Explain the last sentence. What is the narrator's feeling about himself? about the situation he is in?
9. "Lenin writes that there's a shortage of everything." Of what is there a particular shortage in the story?

Topics for Writing

1. Write an essay analyzing the function of sexual imagery in "My First Goose."
2. Explain why the narrator stains himself in "My First Goose."
3. What is the effect of Babel's extreme brevity in "My First Goose"? Describe the way it is achieved.

4. **RESPONDING CREATIVELY** Before beginning to read "My First Goose,"
    write your prediction of what its subject might be on the basis of its title
    alone. Write a second guess as well. After reading the story, review your
    predictions. To what extent were the expectations aroused by the title —
    even if they were not confirmed — relevant to an understanding of Babel's
    narrative?

Related Commentary

Francine Prose, The Bones of Muzhiks: Isaac Babel Gets Lost in Translation, p.
1562.

Suggested Readings

Carden, Patricia. *The Art of Isaac Babel.* Ithaca: Cornell UP, 1972. 97, 100, 110, 130–
31.
Falen, James E. *Isaac Babel: Russian Master of the Short Story.* Knoxville: U of Tennessee P, 1974. 142–45.

JAMES BALDWIN

Sonny's Blues (p. 84)

The marvel of this story is the way the narrator — Sonny's older brother —
narrows the physical and emotional distance between himself and Sonny until
Sonny's plight is revealed and illuminated in a remarkable moment of empathy
and insight. This story of drug addiction in the inner city's black ghetto is as valid
today as it was when it was written. By juxtaposing the two brothers — a straight
high school math teacher and a heroin addict blues pianist — Baldwin makes it
possible for readers to enter the world of the story regardless of their racial background or their opinions about drugs. The author doesn't judge Sonny's plight.
Instead, through the brother, he helps us understand it, sympathize with it, and
transcend it in a brief shared experience of Sonny's inspired musical improvisation.

This is a long story, and its plot consists mostly of flashbacks, more "told"
than "shown" in the reminiscences of Sonny's older brother. Yet the power of
Baldwin's sympathy for his characters and his eloquent style move the reader
along. Baldwin captures the African American culture of strong family allegiances
in the face of American racism. Both Sonny and his brother are trying to survive,
and we respect them for their courage.

One of the ways to discuss the story is through an analysis of the narrator's
growing sympathy for Sonny. Baldwin tells us that the narrator thinks, after the
death of his little daughter Grace from polio, "My trouble made his real." This
realization motivates the first scene with the two brothers in which Baldwin begins to build the bridge between them. Separately they watch three sisters and a
brother hold a revival meeting on the sidewalk opposite the narrator's apartment,

and after they hear the gospel music, the silence between Sonny and his brother begins to give way to shared sound. The scene leads directly to the two brothers going to the bar where Sonny plays and creates an opportunity for the narrator (and the reader) to enter Sonny's world and satisfy his anguished need to share his music with someone who will listen to it and understand.

Questions for Discussion

1.   Analyze the following speech, in which Sonny explains to his brother how he has survived (however tenuously) the experience of racism in America:

> "It's terrible sometimes, inside," he said, "that's what's the trouble. You walk these streets, black and funky and cold, and there's not really a living ass to talk to, and there's nothing shaking, and there's no way of getting it out — that storm inside. You can't talk it and you can't make love with it, and when you finally try to get with it and play it, you realize *nobody's* listening. So *you've* got to listen. You got to find a way to listen."

How does this explanation make Sonny a sympathetic character?

2.   Discuss Baldwin's comment on the blues Sonny plays with Creole and the two other musicians at the end of the story:

> Creole began to tell us what the blues were all about. They were not about anything very new. He and his boys up there were keeping it new, at the risk of ruin, destruction, madness, and death, in order to find new ways to make us listen. For, while the tale of how we suffer, and how we are delighted, and how we may triumph is never new, it always must be heard. There isn't any other tale to tell, it's the only light we've got in all this darkness.

Baldwin's subject is the music, of course, but he is also talking about other forms of creation. What might they be?

Topics for Writing

1.   Chinua Achebe describes Baldwin as having brought "a new sharpness of vision, a new energy of passion, a new perfection of language to battle the incubus of race" in a eulogy titled "Postscript: James Baldwin (1924–1987)" (*Hopes and Impediments*, 1990). How does "Sonny's Blues" embody these qualities?

2.   **CONNECTIONS**   Baldwin's commentary "Autobiographical Notes" (p. 1459) states that he found it difficult to be a writer because he was forced to become a spokesman for his race: "I have not written about being a Negro at such length because I expect that to be my only subject, but only because it was the gate I had to unlock before I could hope to write about anything else." Yet Baldwin's depiction of the life lived by African Americans is unique and very different from Richard Wright's or Ralph Ellison's, Toni Cade Bambara's or Alice Walker's accounts. Compare and contrast "Sonny's Blues" with a story by one or more of these writers to describe how each finds his or her own way to dramatize what Baldwin calls "the ambiguity and irony of Negro life." Could "Sonny's Blues" be set in an Italian American or Jewish American family?

3. **CONNECTIONS** Compare and contrast "Sonny's Blues" with Willa Cather's "Paul's Case."

Related Commentary

James Baldwin, Autobiographical Notes, p. 1459.

Suggested Readings

Bloom, Harold. *James Baldwin.* New York: Chelsea House, 1986.
Burt, Nancy. *Critical Essays on James Baldwin.* Boston: G. K. Hall, 1986.
Campbell, James. *Talking at the Gates: A Life of James Baldwin.* New York: Viking, 1991.
Chametzky, Jules, ed. *A Tribute to James Baldwin: Black Writers Redefine the Struggle.* Amherst: U of Massachusetts P, 1989.
Kinnamon, Kenneth, ed. *James Baldwin.* Englewood Cliffs, NJ: Prentice, 1974.
Macebuh, Stanley. *James Baldwin: A Critical Study.* New York: Third, 1973.
Pratt, Louis H. *James Baldwin.* Twayne's United States Authors Series 290. Boston: G. K. Hall, 1978.
Standley, F. L., ed. *Conversations with James Baldwin.* Jackson: U of Mississippi P, 1989.

Toni Cade Bambara

The Lesson (p. 108)

Relationships are an organizational key to this story. "The Lesson" is narrated by Sylvia, one of a group of eight African American children living in an uptown slum in New York City who are "treated" by their neighborhood guide Miss Moore to an educational visit to the F.A.O. Schwarz toy store at Fifth Avenue and Fifty-seventh Street. The group consists of four girls (Sylvia and her best friend Sugar, the relatively affluent Mercedes and her friend Rosie Giraffe) and four boys (Big Butt [Ronald] and Junebug, and Little Q.T. and Flyboy).

The "lesson" of the story is learned first by Sugar and then by Sylvia. All along Sylvia has assumed Sugar to be her ally, sharing her hostility to all adults as authority figures and to the idea of education. There's a suggestion of foreshadowing when the girls pay the taxicab driver outside F.A.O. Schwarz and Sugar steps in when Sylvia can't figure out the 10 percent tip on the 85-cent fare — "Give him a dime." (This is a taxi fare from twenty-five years ago, when the story was written.) But Sugar plays dumb as usual in her next appearance in the story, when she asks Miss Moore outside the toy store, "Can we steal?"

After the children learn about the high prices of the luxury toys at F.A.O. Schwarz, they return to their homes uptown. Sugar's remark to Miss Moore before they disperse reveals that the afternoon's lesson in economics hasn't been wasted: "this is not much of a democracy if you ask me. Equal chance to pursue happiness means an equal crack at the dough, don't it?" Bambara doesn't tell us whether Sugar intends to begin studying hard in school or to begin dealing drugs (this is the early 1970s), but the blinders formed by her life in the inner-city ghetto have fallen away, and she's clearly dissatisfied with her customary smart-aleck role. In her first response Sylvia is dumbfounded by her friend's betrayal, but within a few minutes she awakens to a sense of rivalry: "But ain't nobody gonna beat me at nuthin." Again Bambara leaves the lesson unspecified, and the reader must imagine *how* Sylvia intends to win the new game she's playing.

Questions for Discussion

1. What is the effect of the inner-city ghetto language in the story?
2. Is Sylvia a reliable or an unreliable narrator?
3. How does Bambara evoke a sense of sympathy for the people enduring the poverty and filth in Sylvia's neighborhood through her descriptions of the relationship of the winos and the newly arrived families from the South?
4. Describe the eight children and their relationships within the neighborhood group. How dependent is Sylvia on her friend Sugar?
5. Who is Miss Moore? Why does she personify the hostile force of "education" to the ghetto children?
6. Why does Sylvia keep the four dollars' change from the taxi fare? What does she do with the money? Is this a convincing ending to the story?

Topics for Writing

1. **RESPONDING CREATIVELY**   Write a story using a special dialect that you have learned from your family or friends.
2. **CONNECTIONS**   Compare and contrast the authors' uses of African American speech in this story and in Richard Wright's "The Man Who Was Almost a Man." Analyze the different ways the two writers keep the dialect from distracting readers and causing them to lose interest in the stories.

Suggested Readings

Bambara, Toni Cade. *The Sea Birds Are Still Alive: Stories*. New York: Vintage, 1982.
Bell, Roseann P., Bettye J. Parker, and Beverly Guy-Sheftall, eds. *Sturdy Black Bridges: Visions of Black Women in Literature*. New York: Anchor, 1979.
Butler-Evans, Elliot. *Race, Gender, and Desire: Narrative Strategies in the Fiction of Toni Cade Bambara, Toni Morrison, and Alice Walker*. Philadelphia: Temple UP, 1989.
Cartwright, Jerome. "Bambara's 'The Lesson.'" *Explicator* 47.3 (Spring 1989): 61–63.
Evans, Mari, ed. *Black Women Writers (1950–1980): A Critical Evaluation*. New York: Anchor, 1984. 41–71.
Giddings, P. "Call to Wholeness from a Gifted Storyteller." *Encore* 9 (1980): 48–49.
Lyles, Lois F. "Time, Motion, Sound and Fury in *The Sea Birds Are Still Alive*." *College Language Association Journal* 36.2 (December 1992): 134–44.
Morrison, Toni. "City Limits, Village Values: Concepts of the Neighborhood in Black Fiction." *Literature and the Urban Experience: Essays on the City and Literature*. Ed. Ann Chalmers Watts and Michael C. Jaye. New Brunswick: Rutgers UP, 1981.

Tate, Claudia, ed. *Black Women Writers at Work*. New York: Continuum, 1983. 12–38.

Vertreace, Martha M. "A Bibliography of Writings about Toni Cade Bambara." *American Women Writing Fiction: Memory, Identity, Family, and Space*. Ed. Mickey Pearlman. Lexington: U of Kentucky P, 1989.

———. "Toni Cade Bambara: The Dance of Character and Community." *American Women Writing Fiction: Memory, Identity, Family, and Space*. Ed. Mickey Pearlman. Lexington: U of Kentucky P, 1989.

RUSSELL BANKS

Black Man and White Woman in Dark Green Rowboat (p. 115)

In an afterword to a recent collection of his short stories (*The Angel on the Roof*, 2000), Russell Banks justified his interest in the short story by explaining, "I've written a dozen or so novels, but the story form thrills me still. It invites me today, as it did back then, to behave on the page in a way that is more reckless, more steadily painful."

"Black Man and White Woman in Dark Green Rowboat" is a painful story, although on its quiet surface it could be said that the prevailing mood is a calm that matches the day Banks describes. He has left it to the reader to intuit the pain of each of the protagonists. We know the boundaries and the dimensions of the pain because the story at its deepest level is about something we live with daily; it is a story about race. The event that the author narrates, the young woman's decision to have an abortion, is just one incident in lives that have known many similar. To allow us to judge the effect of the woman's decision on the life of the man she is with in the green rowboat, as well as on her own life, the author has stripped the story of any secondary action. We see everything with the bright clarity of the sunlight on the hot summer day. A man swims, people leave for work, a woman sits and reads a book, a second woman walks to get her mail, a teenager sits on his trailer steps and smokes a joint, an old man scrapes paint from the bottom of a boat. The scene is set for the couple and their afternoon of fishing in the dark green rowboat.

Everything about the scene is completely ordinary, except that the man is black. His blackness, because of the reader's consciousness of the implications of this blackness, places him just outside the scene. As both the man and woman are aware, the decision she has made, despite her denials, will shut him outside of the scene forever. If the author had chosen to allow her any other explanation for her decision — she is young, they aren't married, she has recently been ill — we might have been presented with a plausible justification for her decision. She says that her mother is concerned because of her problems with depression, but she never offers a reason of her own, and so we are left with an awareness that to her race is in itself sufficient reason for what she is going to do.

One of the brilliant technical aspects of the story is its use of color as a series of symbols for the events of the afternoon. At no point in the story is the phrase *African American* or the word *Negro* used to describe the man. We are only told the color of his skin. The word *nigger* appears once, but it is used by the man himself in angry derision. Instead, the ordinary scene of the lake and the trailers is given a spare, stripped dimension that is clarified with moments of color. The title itself gives us colors — black, white, and dark green — and the other tonalities in the story are set against them. The morning haze is blue-gray, the swimmer is wearing a white bathing cap, the water is a dark green plain. The woman who comes out to read is wearing white shorts and halter, the skin of the swimmer is a chestnut color, the woman going for her mail is wearing a T-shirt that had turned pink in the wash. The boy smoking the joint is blond, the blonde girl who walks toward the rowboat is wearing a lime-green bikini, and her skin is tanned a light brown. The trailers, from the lake, are like "pastel-colored shoe boxes." The reader is given continual, almost subliminal hints throughout the story to be conscious of color.

Although students probably have no familiarity with other stories by Russell Banks, they would be interested to learn that he has written about this group of people many times. The trailer park is outside a small, imaginary New Hampshire mill town named Catamount, and the people who have jobs work in the town. The man taking the early swim is a retired captain in the American army, Dewey Knox; the woman reading the book, the girl's mother, is named Nancy Hubner; and the girl herself is Noni Hubner. She is home from college and recuperating from a nervous breakdown. Her father died two years earlier, and she and her mother are still struggling to go on with their lives. The boy smoking the joint is named Bruce Severance, and he will be shot to death in a few months as the result of a bad drug deal. The manager's name is Marcelle Chagnon, and the man scraping down the boat is named Merle Ring. He brought considerable confusion to the trailer park the winter before by winning $50,000 in the state lottery and showing a complete lack of interest in what might become of the money. This is the world of the little trailer park backed up against the boundary of the state forest at the edge of the lake. Did the author mean to emphasize the black man's inability to enter the white world at even this level by having his rejection come from someone who would be described as "trailer trash"?

Students will find it interesting to contrast this story with Ernest Hemingway's "Hills Like White Elephants (p. 647). This is also a story about a young woman who is about to have an abortion, but the circumstances and emotions of the two stories reflect entirely different social and personal conditions.

Questions for Discussion

1. The author has been careful to describe the setting of his story in considerable detail, but could the same story have been set in another part of the United States with the same effect?
2. How much of the emotional effect of the story depends on the events that are described, and how much depends on the reader's understanding of the implication of the woman's decision?
3. Does the young woman's lack of interest in fishing and the contents of the magazine she is reading suggest some of the emotional uncertainties that have gone into her decision?
4. Although no direct reference is made to the man's race, there is emphasis on the historical implications of his color, first when he ties his shirt over his head so that he looks, in her words, like an Arab sheik and in his words, like

a galley-slave, then when his face is described as "somber and ancient." What is the author suggesting with these allusions?

5. Is there any moment in the story when the man is given an opportunity to express his wishes regarding the situation? What is the implication of her statement, "Well. We've been through all this before. A hundred times"?

Topics for Writing

1. Discuss the way in which colors are used in the story.
2. **CONNECTIONS** Contrast this story with Hemingway's "Hills Like White Elephants" and discuss the similarities and the differences in the woman's role in the decision she has made.
3. Discuss how the reader's consciousness of race is crucial to his or her understanding of the story.

Related Story

Ernest Hemingway, Hills Like White Elephants, p. 647.

Related Commentary

Russell Banks, Author's Note, p. 1464.

Suggested Reading

Niemi, Robert. *Russell Banks.* New York: Twayne; London: Prentice-Hall International, 1997.

JOHN BARTH

Lost in the Funhouse (p. 122)

In a brief comment written for the collection *Writer's Choice*, edited by Rust Hills (New York: McKay, 1974), Barth describes this story as occupying a medial position in a development from conventional to less conventional techniques and from youthful and presumably more personal versions of Ambrose in the earlier stories in the volume *Lost in the Funhouse* to later "more mythic avatars of the narrator." He goes on to repudiate "merely cerebral inventions, merely formalistic tours de force," and to declare his hope that the story is "accessible, entertaining, perhaps moving." Just as Ambrose is portrayed "at that awkward age," so the narrator who portrays him (a being hard to distinguish from Ambrose on the one hand and Barth on the other) appears in a transitional stage, the adolescence of his art. Quoting to himself the supposedly infallible principles of composition that he seems to have learned in a creative writing course, he struggles forward self-consciously, complaining that what is supposed to be happening as he writes does not seem to be taking place. Just as for Ambrose in the toolshed or at his baptism, observation of the proper forms does not necessarily bring the expected results. Yet, just as Ambrose is capable of experiencing unusual transports at inopportune moments, so the story, in spite of or apart from the conventions, renders a poignant account of the time and place in which it is set, of its protagonist's initiation into the mysteries of life and art, and of the narrator's unexpected triumph over the difficulties he confronts.

Readers may compare their experience of the story to the difficult progress through a funhouse, with its sudden surprises, its maddening reflections, its obvious contrivances, and the heavy atmosphere of sexuality. We enter perhaps violently yawning in the nervous anticipation that shocks are in store, but surely few readers are prepared for the upending of expectation that takes place even in the first paragraph. We stagger forward with the narrator, bumping into the pasteboard screens of his contrivance, glimpsing the pulleys and levers by which the story is operated but nonetheless responding to the images thrust before us. When the narrator complains, "We haven't even reached Ocean City yet: we will never get out of the funhouse," the reader knows he is referring to the story itself as well as to the boardwalk attraction.

Fiction is traditionally supposed to be an imitation of life, made the more credible, as the narrator remarks, by the artifice of illusion. By extension, then, the funhouse can be called an imitation of life, and of that part of life called art (the commentator wanders in these mazes too). While the funhouse may be fun for lovers, for Ambrose and the narrator it begins as *"a place of fear and confusion,"* mastered only by the fantasy of control with which the story concludes. Life, too, which resembles the funhouse in having seduction, coupling, and propagation as its central purpose, appears to the sensitive adolescent a frightening labyrinth that he must enter. The realities of war, death, and suffering — masked by the diversions of the funhouse or glimpsed behind them — lie in wait, and perhaps the Operator of the whole show is dozing at the controls. Although Ambrose has theoretical access in Magda to the "fun" life has to offer, he recoils with nausea from his visions of the universal copulation, can bear only the lightest contact with her body, and recalls their precocious experience in the toolshed mainly by reference to the image of a muselike woman with a lyre printed on a cigar box, her lower parts peeled away. When he loses Magda in the funhouse, Ambrose feels relief, and although he finds his name, with its suggestions of enlightenment (or vision) and divinity, he loses *himself* in the multiple reflections of the mirrors.

The narrator knows that a conventionally structured story would reach its climax in Ambrose's escape from the funhouse, but what would this story become if its culminating image were the emergence of Ambrose from the funhouse in uneasy companionship with a blind, black Ariadne? Barth's self-regarding experimental narrative technique enables him to beg the question of his protagonists escape from the literal funhouse and to leave him lost in the figurative one, blocked from enjoying the "fun" but assured of his ability to create through his art even better "funhouses for others."

The discovery of this assurance constitutes a victory for Ambrose over his initial *"fear and confusion,"* and it proclaims the narrator's triumph over the problems of his art with which he has struggled throughout the story. It is a triumph gained in large measure by means of acknowledging the struggle. Like Joyce's *A Portrait of the Artist as a Young Man,* to which Barth alludes more than once, "Lost in the Funhouse" combines a nostalgic realization of the circumstances that determine the protagonist's vocation with the assertion of a provisional theory according to which he intends to carry it out. Just as Stephen Dedalus's resolution to take wing is subject to an ironic interpretation that sees it as an expression of his emotional immaturity, so Ambrose's decision to *substitute* the detached manipulation of the funhouse for living his life might be regarded as an expression of adolescent neuroses that he will outgrow. Barth makes clear, however, that the combined sensitivity to and detachment from his experience that make Ambrose an artist do not simply result from a trauma in the toolshed; rather, as existing qualities of his personality (perhaps inherited from his father, whom he resembles as Peter resembles Uncle Karl), they have conspired to render that occasion a tangible memory for Ambrose while for Magda it remains, if it lingers at all, an aspect of her vague but condescending warmth to Peter's little brother. Barth's handling of the double *pas de trois* that evolves its intricate parallels and contrasts in the front and back seats of the La Salle and along the boardwalk at Ocean City demonstrates that the artist's way of revealing the hidden realities of life does not have to follow the repellent naturalism of Ambrose's flashlight view below the boardwalk or the oversimplifications of his fantasies about the essential activities of his ancestors and the world at large. No less than *A Portrait*, Barth's story is a tour de force whose own principles of composition criticize the conclusions reached by its protagonist.

William E. Sheidley

Questions for Discussion

1. How are italics used most frequently in this story?
2. Examine the remarks about nineteenth-century realistic fiction in the second paragraph. If Barth's story seeks to convey an illusion of reality, what reality does it represent? A family's trip to Ocean City, or a writer's effort to narrate that trip? or to narrate his effort to narrate that trip?
3. Starting with the fourth sentence in the story, trace all references to American history, society, and current events, including World War II. How important are these concerns? What do you think Barth intends to accomplish by bringing them up?
4. Describe the seating arrangements in the car. What parallels do you notice between the two rows of people? Later, as they walk on the boardwalk similarly disposed, the narrator remarks, "Up front the situation was reversed." Explain. The name Peter means "rock." What objects and qualities are associated with Uncle Karl?
5. The narrator worries that "if one imagines a story called 'The Funhouse,' or 'Lost in the Funhouse,' the details of the drive . . . don't seem especially relevant." What does Barth accomplish on this drive with his characters, setting, and theme?
6. What does Barth succeed in communicating about Ambrose by tracing the chain of associations involving cigars, the banana, and Magda?
7. Immediately after chiding himself for having "nothing in the way of a *theme*," the narrator produces the account of Ambrose's visit to the toolshed with Magda. Explain the thematic implications of that passage. Do they account for Ambrose's moving away his hand as Magda sits down?
8. Why does Uncle Karl warn the young people to "stay out from under the boardwalk"? How are the various elements of this and the next few paragraphs related? Trace the associations in Ambrose's mind; in the narrator's.
9. Who asks, "How long is this going to take?"

10. Why does the narrator remark, "Nobody likes a pedant"? Is his attention to language part of what separates Ambrose from Magda?
11. If driving is a literary symbol, what does it symbolize? Judging from his choice of words, what is Ambrose thinking of as he talks to Magda about Peter's diving?
12. The next two paragraphs leap ahead to the funhouse and back to the toolshed, ending with another grammatical error. What does Barth achieve by thus manipulating chronology, here and elsewhere?
13. Analyze the paragraph that begins, "Let's ride the old flying horses!" Whose thoughts are transcribed there? What kinds of alternative plots are envisioned? In the next paragraph, the narrator contemplates still other ways of ending his story. What is the effect of our discovery that one of these endings may be more or less what "actually" happened?
14. Why do Ambrose's initiations — toolshed, baptism, Boy Scouts — all leave him cold?
15. Is Ambrose correct in his insight about the point of the funhouse?
16. One effect of Barth's manner of narration is to put off Ambrose's entry into the funhouse until the last possible moment. What does he gain by doing so?
17. Referring to the second diagram, a variant of "Freitag's Triangle," what event or events in the story of Ambrose should be represented by *C*? by *CD*? And what events in the story of the narrator's effort to tell the story?

Topics for Writing

1. Write an essay describing Barth's use of realistic narration in "Lost in the Funhouse."
2. Discuss the meaning of nausea in Barth's story
3. Analyze Barth's funhouse technique — obvious imagery, abrupt changes, and surprising drafts from below.
4. "Lost in the Funhouse" resembles an author's journal or an early draft of a traditional story coming into existence on the page. Outline that story as it finally emerges, and outline the story of the process by which it develops. Do you believe that this is an accurate account of how stories are written?

Suggested Readings

Beinstock, Beverly Gray. "Lingering on the Autognostic Verge: John Barth's *Lost in the Funhouse*." *Critical Essays on John Barth*. Ed. Joseph J. Waldmeir. Boston: G. K. Hall, 1980. 201–09. Esp. 206–09. (Originally published in *Modern Fiction Studies* 19 (1973): 69–78.)

Knapp, Edgar H. "Found in the Barthhouse: Novelist as Savior." *Critical Essays on John Barth*. Ed. Waldmeir, cited above. 183–89. (Originally published in *Modern Fiction Studies* 14 [1968–69]: 446–51.)

Morrell, David. *John Barth: An Introduction.* University Park: Pennsylvania State UP, 1976. 87–90.

Schulz, Max F. *Black Humor Fiction of the Sixties: A Pluralistic Definition of Man and His World.* Athens: Ohio UP, 1973. 34–36, 129–30.

Seymour, Thom. "One Small Joke and a Packed Paragraph in John Barth's 'Lost in the Funhouse.'" *Studies in Short Fiction* 16 (1979): 189–94.

Donald Barthelme

Me and Miss Mandible (p. 139)

Students will recognize that this story is one of a genre of narratives that have their roots in the earliest shared myths of human society. Every language and every culture has a tradition of narrative in which a figure with a human consciousness is placed in circumstances that permit the individual to observe human life from a perspective different from our common reality. The myth takes many forms, including myriad early examples in which a human being is changed into an animal, and in the form of an animal continues to observe the actions of the people close to him or to her. In the examples of the myth in which the human does not change form there are two main patterns. In the first, the individuals remain recognizably human, but their physical circumstances are abruptly changed. A current example of this form is the popular series of films beginning with *Honey, I Shrank the Kids*, in which first children, and later adults, face the everyday world as figures the size of a child's finger. A classic example of the second form of this myth is the famous section of Jonathan Swift's *Gulliver's Travels* in which Gulliver, who is a very ordinary person, wakes up in a land of tiny people to whom he seems a giant. Barthelme's playful story is a variant of the second form. The protagonist is not a giant, but he is a mature man playing the role of a pupil in a classroom of eleven-year-olds. The comic effect of the story depends on our acceptance of the fiction that not only has he been assigned to his cramped seat, but that no one else in the class, including the teacher, seems to notice his predicament.

The use of a mythical situation such as an adult in a children's classroom or a traveler who wakes up in a land of people the size of his thumb allows the writer or narrator to change our accustomed perspectives. Just as Swift used Gulliver to vent his contempt for his fellow human beings, and the makers of the *I Shrank* series introduced us to the marvels of our everyday life as seen from the fibers of the living room carpet, Barthelme's point of view allows us to intrude on the sixth grade in an ordinary American school. What the man, like all classic figures in this form of narrative, sees is what he sees within himself. To him the classroom seethes with "aborted sexuality." As he describes it, "The sixth grade at Horace Greeley Elementary is a furnace of love, love, love." But it is clear from the opening sentence that it is his consciousness of his own sexuality that sustains him in his adventure. As he writes in his first journal entry, "Miss Mandible wants to make love to me." Although Miss Mandible's feelings are not made entirely clear at the beginning of the story, he certainly would like to make love to *her*.

Unlike most of the mythic figures who share an experience like his, Barthelme's protagonist does not have large statements to make about the human condition, but he has become wise in small, personal things that justify, to him, the situation in which he finds himself. His generalizations represent small but satisfactory illuminations in the darkness that has characterized his life so far. He states in one entry in his journal, "The distinction between children and adults, while probably useful for some purposes, is at bottom a specious one, I feel. There are only individual egos, crazy for love." Later, as he considers the signs he gets from people around him and the symbolic righteousness of the American flag, he decides, "I say, looking about me in this incubator of future citizens, that signs are signs, and that some of them are lies. This is the great discovery of my time here."

Certainly for today's students the scandal of actor Eddie Fisher's affair with actress Liz Taylor and his divorce from his young wife, the actress Debbie Reynolds, has lost most of its immediacy, but the list of magazine articles that the author includes still has some of its satiric bite. The same series of articles is being written today, using virtually the same language, for any current romantic scandal involving a well-known figure who may be a politician, a movie personality, or a popular musician. Students can choose their own candidate and make up their own list of articles from today's scandal press.

Barthelme is conscious of each word in his stories, and he certainly used the word *mandible* as the name for the teacher for its suggestive meanings. It denotes the jaw, but its connotation is suggestive of eating or biting. Although the teacher he presents seems to be anything but fierce in her classroom demeanor, Barthelme clearly wants the reader to think of her as voracious, even though this perception of her seems to be a projection of the protagonist's own desires. The children's prepubescent consciousness of sexuality is presented through the responses of the young girls around him. He is smuggled magazines about Liz and Eddie and Debbie, and he is kicked sharply in the ankle. If Barthelme had chosen to place his protagonist in a high school classroom the man would have found himself the object of responses from the young women in the class that would be more familiar.

Questions for Discussion

1. Barthelme's hero speculates on reasons why he finds himself in his predicament. What are some reasons he suggests to himself?
2. What are some of the differences he finds between a sixth-grade classroom now and what he remembers of his first classroom experience?
3. Are these differences that anyone would expect to occur over a period of twenty years, or is the tempo of change in contemporary life presented as speeding up?
4. The protagonist has, for the moment, dropped out of his life as an insurance adjustor. What did he regard as the "clues" that he was succeeding in this life?
5. What was the significance of the love affair between Liz Taylor and Eddie Fisher, and his subsequent divorce from his wife Debbie Reynolds, for the protagonist's eleven-year-old classmates?
6. He describes the boy who sits behind him as turning to another object of interest as an emotional defense against the class's concern with sexuality. What is the boy's other interest? Is this kind of emotional substitution typical of eleven-year-olds? Is it something that ends in childhood?
7. Why does he ask that his experience be like everyone else's?

Topics for Writing

1. **CONNECTIONS** Compare this story to another myth in which a human changes form or consciousness and discuss the different kinds of knowledge that each protagonist discovers.
2. Discuss Barthelme's conclusion that "[t]he distinction between children and adults, while probably useful for some purposes, is at bottom a specious one, I feel. There are only individual egos, crazy for love."

3. Discuss his statement that "[t]he mysteries that perplexed me as an adult have their origins here."
4. Discuss the reasons why a writer would choose to tell a story in the form of a myth, and enumerate some of the observations the author could expect to find.

Suggested Readings

Barthelme, Donald. "Not-Knowing." *Voicelust.* Ed. Allen Wier and Dan Hendrie, Jr. Lincoln: U of Nebraska P, 1985.

Couturier, Maurice, and Regis Durand. *Donald Barthelme.* New York: Methuen, 1982.

Gitlin, Todd. *The Sixties: Years of Hope, Days of Rage.* New York: Bantam, 1987.

Gordon, Lois. *Donald Barthelme.* Twayne's United States Authors Series 416. Boston: G. K. Hall, 1981.

Johnson, Alexandra. *The Hidden Writer: Diaries and the Creative Life.* New York: Doubleday, 1997. 51–85.

Klinkowitz, Jerome. *Donald Barthelme: An Exhibition.* Durham, NC: Duke UP, 1991.

Leitch, Thomas M. "Donald Barthelme and the End of the End." *Modern Fiction Studies* 28.1 (1982): 129–43.

Molesworth, Charles. *Donald Barthelme's Fiction: The Ironist Saved from Drowning.* Columbia: U of Missouri P, 1982.

O'Hara, J. D. "Art of Fiction: Donald Barthelme." *Paris Review* 80 (1981): 181–210.

Stengel, Wayne B. *The Shape of Art in the Short Stories of Donald Barthelme.* Baton Rouge: Louisiana State UP, 1985.

Trachtenberg, Stanley. *Understanding Donald Barthelme.* Columbia: U of South Carolina P, 1990.

Wilde, Alan. *Middle Grounds: Studies in Contemporary American Fiction.* Philadelphia: U of Pennsylvania P, 1987. Contains "Barthelme, His Garden."

Ann Beattie

Find and Replace (p. 150)

This story by a contemporary American woman will immediately present a problem to the student. The author begins with the words "True story," and at moments in this unhappy narrative the student reader may be confused by the author's suggestion that this statement may not be simply another example of the time-honored literary device of pretending that what is obviously fiction is to be taken as fact. The story is so mundane, so ordinary, that the student certainly will suspect that it could be true — or at least as close to truth as a story on the page can come. The author identifies herself as Ann in the story, and there is enough suggestion of a knowledge of her earlier life that the reader continually encounters signs that stress the story's ambiguities. If it isn't a story — if it is "true" — then what is it? We would probably term it a memoir or a reminiscence. With her mother addressing her by the author's own name there is no way to be sure of what Beattie intends. We will have to see where the story finally is placed — in her autobiography or with her collected stories — to be certain, but it is presented now as a story, and that is how the student should read it.

However Beattie has chosen to classify her story, it is a corrosive self-portrait. The person who narrates the story reveals herself to be selfish, careless, dishonest, insecure, and spiteful. The reader is expected to excuse these traits because of an instinctive understanding that the woman is using them as a defense against her frightened vulnerability. Since, however, the reader is often not told enough to follow this line of intention, students may find that the story occasionally drifts from its emotional moorings. Also, in a mirroring of her own self-distaste, the woman manages to describe everyone else in the story as having some of her own shortcomings. Her mother is presented as near compulsive, the policeman attempts to pick her up, the boy at the car rental agency is helplessly vulnerable to her sophistication and experience, and even the man her mother intends to live with is glimpsed only as stiff, formal, and evasive. It is difficult to feel sorry for the narrator, since she spends so much of the story feeling sorry for herself. As she says, "I had left too many friends behind. I told myself it was because I travelled so much, because my life was so chaotic. But, really, maybe I should have sent a few more cards myself." At the story's end, however, we feel her desolation at her mother's decision to turn to someone else to give her life meaning and direction.

What students will respond to in the story is the complicated and ultimately sad relationship between the daughter and her mother. Like her Canadian contemporary Alice Munro, Beattie senses the drama in mundane domestic situations, and although the events she describes in the woman's visit to her mother are small in dimension, they have a deep emotional resonance within the woman herself. At the end of the story the reader understands that the woman's self-portrayal has shown us someone stripped of all emotional defenses. She is devastated by her mother's decision, and her response tells us that she still has not outgrown the dependencies and insecurities of her childhood. We are left with two contradictory portraits — a mother who is physically weak but strong and decisive in her social commitments, and a daughter who is physically strong but weak in almost every other aspect of her life. Somewhere in the two distinct portraits and in the uneasy areas where they blur together, many of Beattie's readers will find something to remind them of themselves.

Questions for Discussion

1.   What does the mother's compulsion about notes represent? Is the daughter's description of her mother's habit an attempt to focus her more clearly in the reader's mind, or is it a way of attacking her mother?
2.   Why does the woman tell us very quickly that she has a problem with speeding tickets? Is this a form of boasting?
3.   We are told that as she is driving to her mother's house she is listening to Mick Jagger on her car radio. Is she someone who is trapped in her identification with the '70s, or is this a story that might be set in the '70s? What details might tell us when it is set?
4.   In explaining her decision, her mother tells her, "You want to be compatible, but you can't let yourself get all involved in the dramas that have al-

ready played out." What does the daughter's refusal to accept this explanation tell us about her? Does she understand this herself?

5.   Does the author suggest that the woman had a closer relationship with her father than she had with her mother? Is this presented as a reason for her opposition to her mother's plans?

6.   Why is she so specific in her descriptions of her encounter with the boy at the car rental agency and with the policeman who stops her for speeding?

7.   When she returns to the house she sees her mother moving more slowly and needing help to climb the concrete steps. Were these things that she didn't see before, or did her mother conceal her weakness from her?

8.   Who are the people at the end of the story who are waiting to hear from the woman? From what we have learned about her, do we expect her to make any of the calls?

Topics for Writing

1.   It is a generally accepted writer's axiom that self-description is always self-serving. Discuss the character of the protagonist as she describes herself in the story and decide whether this statement applies to this instance.

2.   In this story the emotional strength is finely balanced between mother and daughter, but by the end of the story the reader senses that the balance has shifted. Discuss this change in the relationship and comment on its similarity to other mother-daughter relationships.

3.   **CONNECTIONS**   Compare this mother-daughter confrontation to other stories in the anthology, such as Gish Jen's "Who's Irish?" or Alice Munro's "Family Furnishings," with particular attention to disguised hostilities or misapprehensions and the contrast between this relationship and the daughter's relationship with her father.

4.   Although this story is clearly an archetype, the setting and the physical details of the daughter's trip and her car rental and encounter with the traffic officer have been presented with considerable detail. Discuss this description of the setting as a literary technique and comment on whether it heightens the effect of the narrative.

Suggested Readings

Beattie, Ann. *What Was Mine: Stories.* New York: Random, 1991.

———. *Where You'll Find Me and Other Stories.* New York: Simon, 1986.

Montresor, Jaye Berman. *The Critical Responses to Ann Beattie.* Westport, CT: Greenwood, 1993.

Murphy, Christina. *Ann Beattie.* Boston: Twayne, 1986.

GINA BERRIAULT

Who Is It Can Tell Me Who I Am? (p. 160)

Although Berriault's story was written in the mid-1990s, students will find its theme of fear and confusion in the face of a supposed terrorist threat even more valid in a world now facing the result of an actual terrorist act. For many Americans the threat of terrorism seemed distant, despite the destruction of the Alfred P. Murrah Federal Building in Oklahoma City by an American terrorist, but for someone like the librarian, who was only too aware of recent deadly attacks on individuals like him who worked in libraries, terrorism was an immediate fear. The sardonic twist of the story is that his fear is of an attack by someone from the political right, someone who during the attack would shout "a denunciation of all librarians for their heinous liberalism, a damnation for all the lies, the deceptions, the swindles, the sins preserved within the thousands of books they so zealously guarded." In the year 2001, the largest number of requests from action groups for books to be removed from American library shelves were directed against the popular *Harry Potter* series, so Alberto Perera's fears for himself were entirely justified.

Berriault's strong story is a character study of two very different men who seem to approach their lives and each other from opposite directions. One is Perera, a middle-aged bachelor librarian who is very set in his way of life and is looking forward to his retirement in a few more months. The other is a young San Francisco street person with a cough that suggests he is seriously ill and with pockets stuffed with scraps of paper. On the scraps of paper he has laboriously copied lines and verses from poems that he found on library shelves. The street person is never named, and except for Perera his death at the story's end will go unmourned. Although we might not have believed in a fictional character like the street person in another period, he seems at home on San Francisco's streets, where a ragged counterculture has managed to survive into this century. The 1960s and the spirit of Haight-Ashbury still live in San Francisco, and the man is recognizable as one of the holdovers from this half-forgotten era.

Although it is difficult for the librarian to understand the other man's respect for poetry, the belief in the power of poetry is the tenuous thread that they share — however each of them came to his own belief. After the man questions him closely about the poem by Rubén Darío he realizes that he will see him again. "Anybody who inquires so relentlessly into the meaning of a poem, and presses the words of the poets into the ephemerae of the streets, would surely return." Students may also be conscious that the man's questions about whether the bear would dance would be part of any classroom discussion of the poem.

As the story develops, the author lets us see that the librarian has also experienced life at its raw edges. He is a child of refugees who fled Franco's dictatorship in Spain, and he lives in a fourth-floor apartment in a crime-ridden section of San Francisco that is also home to many people whose lives are as threatened as the street person's. It is clear that Perera clings to his work and to his modest life with such determination because he is conscious that it was only his own decisions that kept him from a life like the one lived by the other man. It is because of his empathy for the man that he begins to gather clothing and bedding that the man can eventually take out onto the streets, even though he understands that the man is seriously ill. Despite the obvious differences in their lives, with poetry they meet on common ground.

Berriault has given us a satisfactory story, with a confidently realized story line, but we also sense an underlying theme. The author believes as passionately in poetry — and poetry here comes to symbolize everything that is worth saving in our society — as does each of these two very different men. In telling their story, Berriault affirms the strength of her own belief.

Questions for Discussion

1. Is there a reason the author chose a poem by Darío for the street person to question?
2. Is there a contradiction between Perera's fear of the man and his sympathies for the disadvantaged people in society?
3. How do you interpret his love of the objects he has collected from writers whose work he has loved?
4. Although we learn from the text that the woman Perera loved died of an illness three years earlier, would you say that his life is lonely?
5. The story suggests that there are many things to be taken from great literature. Does the author make it clear what some of them are? What are your own ideas about this theme of the story?
6. Why does the street person refer to the poets and the librarian as having beds to retire to? Does this basic need affect some of his other opinions about poetry?

Topics for Writing

1. Comment on Perera's expectation of suffering violence for his "heinous liberalism" and discuss what we have learned of his political views. As a conclusion decide whether or not his fears are justified.
2. Discuss Perera's perception that writers "down through the centuries" often looked more like criminals than writers.
3. Part of Perera's work is to order books for the library, and he has left three books on the floor by his bed, books that he wouldn't conceive of ordering. His experience was that "[o]ne had seduced and deceived him, the second was unbearably vain, and he was put to sleep by the third." Discuss what these opinions tell us about a man like Perera.
4. Discuss the view of life that would lead someone to write the following line, one that the street person has copied down: "Anything in books represents the godlike and anything in myself represents the vile."
5. Comment on Perera's awareness that the young man, by hiding in the library, was "breaking into a home of his own."

Suggested Readings

Berriault, Gina. *The Infinite Passion of Expectation: Twenty-five Stories.* San Francisco: North Point, 1982.
———. *Women in Their Beds: New and Selected Stories.* Washington, DC: Counterpoint, 1996.

Ambrose Bierce

An Occurrence at Owl Creek Bridge (p. 173)

What is the reason for the enduring interest of this contrived and improbable tale? Surprise endings frequently draw groans similar to those that greet bad puns, but Bierce's final twist is more likely to elicit shock and recoil. Perhaps the story's success results more from its realization of an intimate and familiar fear than from its sharp, vivid style or its tense pacing. The idea of continued life is all that the human mind, unable to imagine mere "darkness and silence," can propose in view of impending death. By narrating a fantasy of escape so persuasively that we succumb to it, and then by revealing it with the snap of a neck to have been only a fantasy, Bierce forces us to recognize once again the reality of our mortal situation.

If, out of the desire to evade that recognition, the reader seeks to repudiate the story as a piece of literary chicanery, he or she will not succeed. A clearheaded review of section III reveals that the exciting tale of escape could not have been real. Even before Farquhar enters the nightmare forest with its strange constellations and peculiar, untraveled roadway, he has experienced a preternatural heightening of sensory awareness that happens only when one sees with the eyes of the mind, and he has undergone sensations better explained by reference to a slow-motion expansion of a hanging than to his imagined plunge into Owl Creek. The images of his dream emerge from Farquhar's instinctual desire to live, and Bierce renders them with such clarity that the reader can cherish them as well. The same intensity of sensory awareness marks Bierce's conjecture about what it must be like when the noose jerks tight. We feel the constriction, see the flash of nervous discharge, and hear the cracking vertebrae.

Our close participation in the imaginary and real sensations of dying countervails the doomed man's symbolic isolation, which is the burden of section I. While the executioners enact the formal rituals that establish distance from the victim, who is being expelled from the human community (even the sentinels are turning their backs on him), Bierce leads the reader into an empathic communion with him. The agency of this imaginative projection is the coolly exact observational style, which carries us across the plank — Farquhar's first thought to which we are privy is his approval of this device — and into the psyche of the condemned.

Before launching into Farquhar's dying fantasy, however, Bierce goes back, in section II, to narrate the events leading up to the execution. Besides establishing for Farquhar an identity with which we can sympathize, this passage presents him as active rather than acted upon, and so generates a momentum that continues into the story of his escape. The section ends with one of several stark, one-line revelations that conclude passages of uncertainty, illusion, or false conjecture in the story: "He was a Federal scout"; "What he heard was the ticking of his watch"; "Peyton Farquhar was dead." This device of style expresses Bierce's major theme: Whatever we dream of, life is entrapment by death, and time is running out.

William E. Sheidley

Questions for Discussion

1. In what ways does section I suggest a psychological time much slower than actual time?
2. Why is it appropriate that the execution take place on a bridge over a river?
3. What is the function of Farquhar's conjectures about escape at the end of section I?
4. In what ways does Bierce try to gain the reader's sympathy for Farquhar? Why does he need to do this?
5. Which events in section III might be read as dislocations of sensations experienced by a man in the process of being hanged?
6. Contrast the descriptive style of a passage from section III with that of a passage from section I.
7. What would be the result if Farquhar's imagined reunion with his wife took place *after* the snapping of his neck?

Topics for Writing

1. Analyze Bierce's handling of time and chronology in "An Occurrence at Owl Creek Bridge."
2. **CONNECTIONS**   Discuss the fiction of effect as a fiction of despair in the works of Bierce, Gogol, and Poe.

Suggested Readings

Bierce, Ambrose. *The Complete Short Stories of Ambrose Bierce*. Lincoln: U of Nebraska P, 1984.

Davidson, Cathy N. *The Experimental Fictions of Ambrose Bierce*. Lincoln: U of Nebraska P, 1984.

Grenander, Mary E. *Ambrose Bierce*. New York: Twayne, 1971.

Stoicheff, Peter. "'Something Uncanny': The Dream Structure in Ambrose Bierce's 'An Occurrence at Owl Creek Bridge.'" *Studies in Short Fiction* 30.3 (Summer 1993): 349–58.

Wolotkiewicz, Diana. "Ambrose Bierce's Use of the Grotesque Mode: The Pathology of Society." *Journal of the Short Story in English* 16 (Spring 1991): 81–92.

JORGE LUIS BORGES

The End of the Duel (p. 181)

The particularly disquieting quality of this story derives from the value-neutral framework in which it is presented. Neither the narrative tone nor the structure of the plot allows the reader the escape of outrage or even the release of laughter. Although the narrator admits that the ending of the tale is "grim," that judgment is counterbalanced by his pleasant memory of the circumstances under which he heard it. And should the reader nonetheless be steeling himself for an instance of that gothic horror that is made tolerable, even delightful, by the very fact of its being extraordinary, Borges hastens to introduce Juan Patricio Nolan, whose name and reputation as a friendly rogue and prankster promise something to evoke a smile of sentimental indulgence.

Silveira and Cardoso, too, tempt the reader's stock responses. These colorful gauchos, caught up in the passion of their romantic hatred, will surely, we suppose, demonstrate in meeting their fate an innocent purity of motive or the dignity of the human heart; or they may learn a profound lesson at the satiric hands of Nolan. Such expectations are defeated. Not only does the feud, like most feuds, lack adequate motive, it elicits no elevated behavior. Their mutual hatred lends the only meaning there is to the lives of Silveira and Cardoso, and nothing else in the story has any meaning at all. Love does not conquer hatred here. Relations with La Serviliana are casual and sordid compared with the gauchos' enduring bond of animosity. Honor offers little more than love. The war between the Reds and the Whites, explained in a foreign language, is meaningless to Silveira and Cardoso. Killing a man is like killing a cow, and they are capable of feeling only whispers of fear. So limited are both men in imagination that as they line up for their final competition they are "eager." Cardoso, however, has previously expressed curiosity about "what it was like" to cut a man's throat, and for this, perhaps, he is rewarded with victory — though he is dead before he can savor it.

To summarize the gauchos' limitations, however, is to impose an unjustifiable scale of values on the story, for no one in it is any more sensitive. The executions are "expected"; the "understanding" Nolan gives in to the prisoners' desire to watch the race; and although as they await execution some of the condemned seem to be expressing emotions that call for a sympathetic response, when we hear their conversation it turns out that they simply envy the gauchos and resent one another.

The most appalling insinuation of the story is that Borges's vision may be true. The executioner's remark about birth pangs invites us to liken the race to life itself, which we stagger through already irrevocably doomed, no less than if our throats were slit, struggling for no permanent reward, in a world where, as Borges says of the feud, it is impossible to be sure "whether the events . . . are effects or causes." "This is what always happens," the author remarked of his story's ending in the interview quoted in Part Two (p. 1465). "We never know whether we are victors or whether we are defeated." The only hope Borges holds out for the reader who wishes to reject the universe portrayed in the story is that the narrative may be inaccurate, "since both forgetfulness and memory are apt to be inventive." To clutch at this straw, however, is to exchange absurdity for total indeterminacy, a bargain of questionable merit.

Questions for Discussion

1.   How appropriate are the memories the narrator associates with this anecdote?
2.   What kind of man do we expect Juan Patricio Nolan to be on the basis of the description given in the second paragraph? Are our expectations confirmed?
3.   Do the narrator's remarks on the provenance and uncertainty of the tale make the reader more or less receptive?
4.   Why are Silveira and Cardoso such loyal enemies?
5.   What impels the gauchos to join the Blancos' army?

6. Discuss Cardoso's request to his superior. Does he "handle himself like a man"?
7. The "proceedings" for the "expected" executions have been "arranged . . . down to the last detail." Comment on Borges's diction.
8. Why do the other prisoners want to watch the race?
9. Why does Borges have the executioner mention birth pangs?

Topics for Writing

1. Analyze the tone of "The End of the Duel."
2. Discuss the race of Cardoso and Silveira as a symbol of human existence.
3. Discuss whether or not there is a political theme in "The End of the Duel." (See the related commentary, p. 1465.)
4. **RESPONDING CREATIVELY**   Revise the story so that it becomes comic. Then revise it again so that it become inspiring. Change it only as much as is necessary to achieve the desired effect. What changes do you find essential for each purpose?

Related Commentary

Jorges Luis Borges, On the Meaning and Form of "The End of the Duel," p. 1465.

Suggested Readings

Agheana, Ion Tudro. *The Meaning of Experience in the Prose of Jorge Luis Borges.* New York: P. Lang, 1988.
Alazraki, Jaime. *Critical Essays on Jorge Luis Borges.* Boston: Twayne, 1987.
Borges, Jorge Luis. *The Book of Fantasy.* New York: Carroll and Graf, 1990.
———. *The Book of Sand.* New York: NAL-Dutton, 1979.
———. *Dream Tigers.* Austin: U of Texas P, 1984.
———. *A Personal Anthology.* New York: Grove Weidenfeld, 1961.
Christ, Ronald J. *The Narrow Act: Borges's Art of Allusion.* New York: New York UP, 1969.
Lindstrom, Naomi. *Jorge Luis Borges: A Study of Short Fiction.* Boston: Twayne, 1990.
McMurray, George R. *Jorge Luis Borges.* Modern Literature Monographs. New York: Ungar, 1980.
Stabb, Martin S. *Borges Revisited.* Boston: Twayne, 1991.

TADEUSZ BOROWSKI

This Way for the Gas, Ladies and Gentlemen (p. 186)

Borowski's story can be taught with another Holocaust story in this anthology, Cynthia Ozick's "The Shawl." "The Shawl" is told by an omniscient narrator describing the ordeal of a woman victim of the concentration camps. "This Way for the Gas, Ladies and Gentlemen" has a more complex point of view, since the narrator is a Polish political prisoner (indeed, he is the writer), and he voluntarily helps the Nazis unload and brutalize the newly arrived Polish Jews.

The thoughtful comments of the Italian concentration camp survivor Primo Levi are helpful here. In *The Drowned and the Saved* (Summit, 1988), Levi explores the situation of the prisoners of war who, like Borowski, survived to tell their tales. According to Levi, the survivors who wrote about their experiences were often political prisoners like Borowski. The camps held three categories of prisoners — political, criminal, and Jewish — and the political prisoners had "a cultural background which allowed them to interpret the events they saw; and because precisely inasmuch as they were ex-combatants or antifascist combatants even now, they realized that testimony was an act of war against fascism."

Furthermore, according to Levi, "the network of human relationships inside the Lagers [camps] was not simple: it could not be reduced to the two blocs of victims and persecutors." The context of the "prisoner-functionary" (like Borowski) is poorly defined, "where the two camps of masters and servants both diverge and converge. This gray zone possesses an incredibly complicated internal structure and contains within itself enough to confuse our need to judge."

Levi continues,

> The arrival in the Lager was indeed a shock because of the surprise it entailed. The world into which one was precipitated was terrible, yes, but also indecipherable: it did not conform to any model; the enemy was all around but also inside. . . . One entered hoping at least for the solidarity of one's companions in misfortune, but the hoped for allies, except in special cases, were not there; there were instead a thousand sealed off monads, and between them a desperate covert and continuous struggle. This brusque revelation, which became manifest from the very first hours of imprisonment, often in the instant form of a concentric aggression on the part of those in whom one hoped to find future allies, was so harsh as to cause the immediate collapse of one's capacity to resist. For many it was lethal, indirectly or even directly; it is difficult to defend oneself against a blow for which one is not prepared.

"This Way for the Gas, Ladies and Gentlemen" is one of many stories in this anthology that are based on personal experience, meticulously observed, remembered, and re-created as a "story" or work of autobiographical fiction, or "autofiction." Borowski, the narrator, was interned at Birkenau with Communists and Jews from France, Russia, Poland, and Greece. He survived the camp because he cooperated with his jailers in the persecution of victims less fortunate than himself. How does he present his story so that the reader is forced to sympathize with him, even while realizing that this sympathy is itself a faint mirror image of the prisoner's moral dilemma?

A highly rational structure holds together this totally irrational nightmare. The unities of place, time, and point of view are strictly observed. The passage of time is orderly, paralleling the organization of the transport of human beings from train to trucks to crematoria. The narrator is new to his job, and we learn it as he does. As train follows train through the stifling August afternoon and into the evening, we grow exhausted with him. The only variety is the ever-changing stream of prisoners who leave the train, take their brief walk on the platform, and disappear onto the trucks or are sorted out for the work camps. Occasionally an individual achieves humanity, like the young blonde who is so beautiful that she appears to descend "lightly" from the packed train, or the calm, tall, gray-haired woman who takes the bloated infants' corpses from the narrator, whispering to him, "My poor boy." For the narrator, such moments of grace are withheld: He hangs on to his self-control by concentrating on sheer physical endurance.

Questions for Discussion

1. How did the narrator become a storyteller? (The headnote might be helpful here, but students should be encouraged to talk about the cathartic process in the creation of fiction.)
2. What elements of narrative — plot, character, setting, language, theme — are most striking in this story?
3. Is it necessary to know the historic context of the Nazi atrocities in World War II to understand the story? Explain.

Topics for Writing

1. Report on a documentary film or a book about the Holocaust, such as Primo Levi's *The Drowned and the Saved*.
2. **CONNECTIONS** Compare Borowski's story with another example of Holocaust or prison literature you have read — Cynthia Ozick's "The Shawl," or Anne Frank's diary, or Alexander Solzhenitzyn's *One Day in the Life of Ivan Denisovich*.
3. **CONNECTIONS** Compare the psychology of prisoners in Borowski's story and in Frank O'Connor's "Guests of the Nation."

Suggested Readings

Borowski, Tadeusz. *This Way for the Gas, Ladies and Gentlemen*. Trans. Barbara Vedder. New York: Penguin, 1976.
Kuhiwczak, Piotr. "Beyond Self: A Lesson from the Concentration Camps." *Canadian Review of Comparative Literature* 19.3 (September 1992): 395–405.
Walc, Jan. "When the Earth Is No Longer a Dream and Cannot Be Dreamed Through to the End." *The Polish Review* 32.2 (1987): 181–94.

T. CORAGHESSAN BOYLE

Friendly Skies (p. 199)

At the time Boyle wrote this story he couldn't have foreseen the tragedy that awaited us in September 2001, but he has brilliantly captured the frightened reactions of people who find themselves first in a damaged plane, then in a plane threatened by a man who is drunk and angry. The title of the story is certainly intended to be ironic, and it echoes the advertising campaign of an American airline company that invited us to fly its "friendly skies." We realize after a few paragraphs, however, that the story is intended to be more than an ironic comic sketch. The author has clearly suffered on many cramped, delayed flights, and despite his best efforts it isn't something that he can consider with amused detachment.

It is against the background of the plane journeys that the central figure of the story tries to consider the life decision she has just made, but the events of her journey seem to outweigh anything else she tries to think about. The woman has set her life in a new and not entirely satisfactory direction, and Boyle makes us aware that often our decisions are made without the time or the tranquility to consider what we have done. The difficulties the woman experiences with the burning motor, the crowded airport passages, and the drunken passenger who becomes violent in the second plane could be considered aspects of her difficult emotional journey, but Boyle lets us see that her decisions have already been made and that the events of the journey are somehow less personally destructive than what she has recently experienced in her life. We might expect that the story's violent conclusion, her attack on the drunken, dangerous passenger with only a dinner fork, would provide her with some catharsis, but it is only another incident, and the pattern into which she has set her life is left unchanged.

Boyle is highly regarded for his vivid, risk-taking writing, and the story is filled with figurative language — a rich gathering of image, simile, metaphor — that brings the setting to life. The motor of the plane begins to "unravel a thin skein of greasy, dark smoke." The plane's window is "abraded," and outside she sees "tufted clouds." The plane lurches "like a balsawood toy struck by a rock." Many of the images describe the plane's cabin, and they help us to visualize the cramped seats and the narrow aisle. Many students who travel will find much that he describes very familiar. The woman's head is "filled with the sucking dull hiss of the air jets and the static of the speakers." Her fellow passengers slump "under the weight of their bags like penitents." She wakes in the middle of the night and finds that "[t]here was a sour taste in her mouth, her head was throbbing, and the armrest gouged at her ribs as if it had come alive." Boyle has won many awards in his literary career, but it is difficult to imagine that he will be presented with any kind of respectful recognition by the airline industry.

Questions for Discusson

1. We are told about the woman and the recent changes in her life in scattered sentences throughout the story. Who is she and what is happening to her?
2. The man who later becomes violent seems, when she first notices hiim, to be passive and calm. How does he change? What is it that changes him?
3. Many of the images in the story are easily identified, but others present more difficulties. What does the author mean by the phrase "a boviform line"? And how would we describe someone who has "[t]he bulb of his head in the grip of his hair"?
4. What are some of the images the author employs to describe the cramped conditions of the cabin?
5. We are ultimately told what it is that the woman is fleeing from. What has happened to her, and how does this affect the way she perceives the men she encounters on the flight?
6. What is the significance of the spider she remembers from her classroom?

Topics for Writing

1. List some of the uses of figurative language in the story and discuss their effect on the reader.
2. Describe some of your own unpleasant experiences on plane journeys.
3. When the woman thinks of her classroom she is remembering a fifth-grade class. Compare her description of her students with the description of the sixth-grade class in the story "Me and Miss Mandible" by Donald Barthelme. (p. 139) Consider whether it is only one year that accounts for the differences in the two classrooms.

Suggested Readings

Boyle, T. C. *After the Plague: Stories.* New York: Viking, 2001.
———. *Descent of Man: Stories.* New York: Penguin, 1987.
———. *Greasy Lake and Other Stories.* New York: Penguin, 1986.
———. *If the River Was Whiskey: Stories.* New York: Viking, 1989.
———. *The Collected Stories of T. Coraghessan Boyle.* New York: Viking, 1998.
———. *Without a Hero: Stories.* New York: Viking, 1994.

ALBERT CAMUS

The Guest (p. 211)

One of the key questions raised by Camus's narrative is, Who is the true guest in the story — the Algerian Arab prisoner or the Algerian French schoolteacher? Daru, the schoolteacher, thinks of the prisoner as his guest, but at the end of the story, after watching the freed Arab choose the path to prison, the schoolteacher returns to his classroom to find he has been judged an enemy by the Arabs — on the blackboard is the message, "You handed over our brother. You will pay for this." Daru, who feels at home in the landscape, learns that he is only a temporary guest there. Its Arab inhabitants have found him lacking.

Daru's fairness and impartiality are never in question; the Arab prisoner doesn't want to leave him and doesn't kill him when he falls deeply asleep. But Daru's sense of isolation and solitude is a false one. Camus tells the story in such a way that there is never a time when the schoolteacher is unaware of the presence of both Arabs and French in his environment, beginning with the opening sentence and continuing to the last sentence, when ironically Daru feels himself truly alone, caught between opposing hostile forces.

Given the history of political strife in Algeria, the reader may well ask if Daru hasn't recognized before the story opens that he cannot remain neutral after war is declared as a result of Algeria's struggle to break free of French rule. The story takes place shortly before the French-Algerian war (1954–1962). The schoolmaster's friend Balducci, the old gendarme, warns, "Things are brewing, it appears. There is talk of a forthcoming revolt. We are mobilized, in a way." Then he goes even further, telling Daru, "If there's an uprising, no one is safe, we're all in the same boat." Daru denies the truth of his friend's words, but they nevertheless foreshadow the hostile message on the schoolmaster's blackboard the next day. Daru is unable to continue what Balducci refers to as the soothing routine of the "comfortable life" he has enjoyed, caring for the poverty-stricken Islamic schoolchildren and tacitly endorsing the status quo.

To be sure, Daru seems to have earned the right to his peaceful life after his service in World War II. After what he has been through he feels anger toward "all men with their rotten spite, their tireless hates, their blood lust." His love for his Arab charges and for the barren, arid landscape of the country of his birth is what sustains him. Denying the political reality of his situation, carefully drawing maps of the distant rivers of France on the blackboard of his one-room schoolhouse, he has retreated to a dream world, until the advent of his uninvited guest brings him back to the world of bloodshed and civil war.

Questions for Discussion

1. Why does Balducci have a different attitude than Daru toward the Arab prisoner?
2. How does the Arab show that he shares Daru's respect for the ancient rule of hospitality — that a guest is never to be harmed?
3. Why has Daru drawn the four rivers of France on the blackboard of his Algerian schoolroom? Why does his action turn out to have ironic implications at the end of the story?
4. How does the scorched landscape of the story contribute to its theme? What is the story's theme?
5. What crime did the Arab commit? Why doesn't he tell Daru he is sorry for what he has done?
6. Why does Daru let the Arab go free?
7. Why do the Arabs watching Daru leave their message on his blackboard?

Topics for Writing

1. Camus once wrote in an essay titled "The Wager of Our Generation" (1957), "No great work has ever been based on hatred or contempt. On the contrary, there is not a single true work of art that has not in the end added to the inner freedom of each person who has known and loved it." Write an essay in which you evaluate "The Guest" in light of Camus's statement.
2. Analyze the story to account for the presence of both a limited omniscient narrator and an omniscient narrator in the narrative.

Suggested Readings

Eberhard, Greim. "Albert Camus's 'The Guest': A New Look at the Prisoner." *Studies in Short Fiction* 30.1 (Winter 1993): 95–98.
Knapp, Bettina L., ed. *Critical Essays on Albert Camus.* Boston: G. K. Hall, 1988.
McBride, Joseph. *Albert Camus: Philosopher and Litterateur.* New York: St. Martin's, 1992.
McDermott, John V. "Albert Camus's Flawed Guest." *Notes on Contemporary Literature* 14.3 (May 1984): 5–7.

Meagher, Robert E., ed. *Albert Camus: The Essential Writings.* New York: Harper
   Colophon, 1979.

ANGELA CARTER

The Company of Wolves (p. 221)

In her collection *The Bloody Chamber,* Carter included two stories based on
the Little Red Ridinghood tale. She placed "The Company of Wolves" after "The
Werewolf," a shorter narrative in which the grandmother is a witch who can take
the form of a wolf. In this version, the girl meets the wolf in the forest on the way
to her grandmother's house and fearlessly slashes off its right forepaw. She puts
it in her basket and continues her walk to her grandmother's cottage. There the
paw falls out of the basket and is transformed into a human hand that the girl
recognizes as her grandmother's by the wart on the index finger. Little Red
Ridinghood calls in the neighbors, who drive the old woman out into the snowy
forest and stone her to death. This version empowers Little Red Ridinghood to
vanquish the wolf with the support of her community, united in their effort to
replace pagan superstition with Christian belief.

"The Company of Wolves" is a longer story imagining Little Red Ridinghood
as a feminist hero. Christianity is absent, paganism rules with its complex superstitions, and the girl is on her own. But she is a hero in her society because reason,
not superstition or faith in the supernatural, is her support, and it does not let her
down. When "this strong-minded child" enters her grandmother's house, after
flirting with the attractive hunter in the forest with whom she has entered into a
bet about which of them will come first to the cottage, the girl finds "[n]o trace at
all of the old woman [whom the hunter has eaten] except for a tuft of white hair
that had caught in the bark of an unburned log." For the first time in her life, the
girl shivers with fear, recognizing that the young man/wolf is a murderer. But
then Carter tells the reader that "since her fear did her no good, she ceased to be
afraid." Many readers will experience this sentence as the climax of the story.
Little Red Ridinghood takes off her clothes and goes to bed with the wolf, and the
tale ends with her "sweet and sound" in her grandmother's bed, safe "between
the paws of the tender wolf."

Carter's version is true to the original in that it remains a fantasy tale with a
happy ending, but she has created it as a story for grownups instead of children.
The celebration of female sexuality is the theme here, not the fear of death or
strangers.

Questions for Discussion

1. What does Carter accomplish in the first five paragraphs of her tale, before
   introducing the voice of Little Red Ridinghood's mother?
2. How does Carter gradually make the girl older in the story, from "the good
   child" at the beginning of the narrative to the satisfied young woman sleeping with the wolf at the end? Is she a round or a flat character?

3. How important is the setting of the story? Why does the hunter take out a compass and explain how it works to Little Red Ridinghood?
4. What does Carter's description of the way the grandmother has furnished her cottage suggest about the old woman?
5. Why did Little Red Ridinghood owe the hunter a kiss?

Topics for Writing

1. Analyze "The Company of Wolves" from a feminist critical perspective.
2. **CONNECTIONS**   Compare and contrast Carter's tale with Hawthorne's "Young Goodman Brown" or with Irving's "Rip Van Winkle."

Related Commentary

Salman Rushdie, On Angela Carter's *The Bloody Chamber*, p. 1570.

Suggested Readings

Carter, Angela. *Burning Your Boats: The Collected Short Stories.* New York: Holt, 1996.
———. *Come Unto These Yellow Sands.* Newcastle upon Tyne: Bloodaxe, 1985.
———. *Fireworks: Nine Profane Pieces.* New York: Penguin, 1987.
———. *Nothing Sacred: Selected Writings.* London: Virago, 1982.
Fowl, Melinda G. "Angela Carter's 'The Bloody Chamber' Revisited." *Critical Survey* 3.1 (1991): 71–79.
Michael, Magali Cornier. "Feminism and the Postmodernist Impulse: Doris Lessing, Marge Piercy, Margaret Atwood, and Angela Carter." *Dissertation Abstracts International* 51.5 (Nov. 1990): 1609A.
Rushdie, Salman. "Angela Carter, 1940–92: A Very Good Wizard, A Very Dear Friend." *New York Times Book Review* Mar. 8, 1992, p. 5.
Wilson, Robert Rawdon. "SLIP PAGE: Angela Carter, in/out/in the Postmodern Nexus." *Ariel: A Review of International English Literature* 20.4 (Oct. 1989): 96–114.

RAYMOND CARVER

The Bath (p. 230)

"The Bath," one of Raymond Carver's early stories, reflects his initial commitment to bare, minimalist prose. It is interesting to compare this story to his later, more expansive rewrite, "A Small, Good Thing," to see how Carver's concerns as a writer have changed. "The Bath" concentrates our attention on the *event* of the story: A young boy is hit by a car and goes into a coma, and we witness the repercussions of this accident on his parents. The account, however, is shorn of sentimentality and most of its emotion by the hard-edged way in which the characters are drawn. We observe an evidently wearing drama without being asked to become involved in any way. Carver's choice of title reflects this flat aspect of the story; bathing, after all, is a fairly mundane, everyday aspect of life. It is as if all the emotions have been cleansed from the prose. Carver enjoys forcing his readers to witness events from an original perspective by drawing their attention to an aspect of an event that might seem peripheral — here the bath of the title. For each parent, taking a bath is meant to be a moment of respite from the horror of their son's ordeal in the hospital. In each case the bath is interrupted by the baker's phone call, causing the parents to panic about the cold truth of their son's condition, from which there is no escape. Cold truths, like cold baths, tend to wake one up, and these parents must face the fact that all life is tenuous, everyone is prone to loss, but we must continue to live nonetheless.

Most of the characters in this story seem to lack compassion: the stricken boy's school friend who, on seeing Scotty hit by a car, wonders if he should finish his chips; the noncommittal, uncommunicative doctors and nurses; the baker who badgers the poor parents because they never picked up their cake; even the parents themselves. The family members are referred to dispassionately as "the mother," "the father," and "the child" rather than being personalized for the reader with names (except for the occasional indirect reference). But they do not lack compassion so much as they lack the means of expressing it; it all comes down to poor communication skills.

The baker would not seem to be a very important player in the story, yet his role is uncomfortably memorable. He is a man of few words, socially awkward or possibly a recluse. His character remains undeveloped and unexplained, as it matters little who he is; it is more important what he *does* — make those phone calls. The reader realizes that the baker is only attempting to claim recompense for his work on the birthday cake, but for the parents he becomes a cruel reminder of their inability to protect their son from harm. The baker's attempt to get the husband to pay for the cake fails because the husband does not know that the cake has been ordered. However, the husband's instant rebuttal exasperates the baker who feels that he is being cheated. While the baker thinks the parents are playing games with him, the parents feel the same about the baker; none of them is capable of understanding the situation from the other's perspective. Both parties are obsessed by their own concerns, which deafen them to those of others. Carver depicts an innate human selfishness that is hard to avoid. The conflict between the parents and the baker is unnecessary; if they spoke and communicated with each other more efficiently there would be better understanding, eradicating much of the conflict. However, the reality is that people are poor communicators. The fact that the futile attempt at communication between the parents and the baker takes place over the phone, a symbol and agent of modern communication, is particularly ironic.

When words fail them, the parents attempt to communicate through body language: The husband holds his wife's head and later places her hand in his lap. But such gestures are open to interpretation and are not as clear as open speech. The wife withdraws her hand and seems to purposefully distance herself from her husband by this gesture, yet she is all the time trying to make sense of a world which has been turned inside out by her son's accident.

At first it seems as though the mother is trying to distance herself from reality by her speculative observation of others: the doctor, the lady in the car, or the other family in the hospital. This allows her to displace her own concerns, even to see that elsewhere life continues, although her personal world has been placed on hold. One reason that she explains all the details of her son's case to total strangers may be to make it more real for herself and to understand what has happened. She even tells them her name, as if to assert her identity in an effort to make sure that she exists, as everything has become so unreal to her.

The ending of the story is deliberately ambiguous. Carver leaves matters hanging with someone on that instrument of miscommunication, the phone. It is most likely the baker, but it could also be the hospital calling with bad news. We never discover whether or not the boy comes out of his coma, and it is interesting to consider how much the reader cares. The characters in the tale are so incapable of showing emotion that it is hard for them to elicit any emotional response from those observing their lives. We are left with a cold, unpleasant picture of the world; one profoundly different from that of the revised version of the story.

Susan C. W. Abbotson

Questions for Discussion

1. To which bath does the title refer — that of the husband or the wife — and why should this detail be given such prominence?
2. How does irony operate in this story?
3. What is the effect of referring to the characters primarily by type rather than by name?
4. How does each parent respond to the son's coma?
5. Why do the parents respond so violently to the baker's phone calls? Why does the baker keep calling?
6. What do we know about the baker? Why does Carver tell us so little?
7. Where in the story does miscommunication take place, and why?
8. Which characters in the story seem to respond with the least compassion for the son's situation? Why are they so lacking in compassion?
9. To what extent does this story emotionally involve its readers?
10. How would you interpret the ending of the story? What happens to Scotty?

Topics for Writing

1. Discuss how "The Bath" is a story about people's poor communication, and how this affects their lives.
2. **RESPONDING CREATIVELY**   Before reading "A Small, Good Thing," continue the story of "The Bath" from where Carver leaves off.
3. **CONNECTIONS**   Compare and contrast Raymond Carver's "The Bath" and "A Small, Good Thing."

Related Commentaries

Raymond Carver, "Creative Writing 101," p. 1610.
Raymond Carver, "On Writing," p. 1605.
Jim Naughton, "As Raymond Carver Muses, His Stature Grows," p. 1614.
A. O. Scott, "Looking for Raymond Carver," p. 1624.
Kathleen Westfall Shute, "On 'The Bath' and "A Small, Good Thing,'" p. 1617.

Suggested Readings

See page 56.

Raymond Carver

A Small, Good Thing (p. 235)

Two years after publishing "The Bath," Carver returned to this story of a family disaster and rewrote it as "A Small, Good Thing." This version of the story is far more expansive, and the central characters are presented in much more detail. By switching the emphasis from action to emotion, Carver creates a very different story, even though the situation remains the same. His more personal terms of reference for the characters — pronouns and actual names rather than "the mother," "the father," "the child" — underline a more sympathetic concern with their personal and emotional lives.

Carver has also depicted new characters as exhibiting compassion for each other, which helps the reader to empathize with them. Now the son's friend, instead of wondering if he should finish his chips after Scotty is hit by a car, drops his chips and cries. The various nurses and doctors we meet are similarly more human and sympathetic. The greater detail throughout the story engages the reader more closely than did "The Bath." We learn more of the specifics of Scotty's injuries, and there is now communication between the parents, from their discussing the phone calls to sharing their mutual feelings and fears about their son's condition.

From the start of the story, the baker is more fully developed than in "The Bath," where he remains much of a mystery. Carver allows the reader to better understand the reasons for the baker's behavior by offering more personal information. The mother, Ann, assumes the baker has a family, but the reader learns that the baker is utterly alone, and has been for years, which accounts for his poor social skills. All he has for companionship is his radio, and his isolation from other people is further emphasized by the sound of machinery, which is present in the background of his phone calls. This does not, however, excuse his malicious behavior as he continuously calls the couple in revenge for their failure to pick up the cake. The fact that on a number of his phone calls he remains silent reveals his calls to be motivated by malice rather than an honest attempt to seek payment for his work.

Communication remains a concern for Carver, and here he explores both its possibilities and failures. Dr. Francis's initial refusal to use the word *coma* in order not to alarm the parents indicates the importance of the words we choose. It is, after all, just semantics as to whether Scotty is in a coma or a deep sleep, as it amounts to the same thing — he is neither awake nor receptive. The doctor's excessive chatter reveals that he does not know what is causing Scotty's coma, although his kindly concern for the parents allows the reader to forgive him for this human fallibility. With the doctor's repeated reassurance that there is nothing to worry about, the boy's eventual death comes as a bigger shock to everyone. By making Scotty's death so unpleasant, Carver ensures that the reader continues to sympathize with the parents, even as they attack the baker.

The parents appear very close; they kiss and touch each other on numerous occasions, acknowledging each other's needs and pain. Carver frequently describes them as being "together." Both are equally upset by their son's accident and struggle not to panic. They are also both obsessed with blame. They initially blame fate, then later turn inward to self-blame; finally they become focused on the baker as a handy scapegoat on whom they can take out their frustrations. In "The Bath," Ann was a fairly complacent, passive figure who was struggling to assert her own identity, but here she is depicted as prone to anger — demanding answers from the hospital staff and later declaring a desire to kill the baker. When she wishes to become the woman she sees in the car, it is not to run away from her situation but to exert some force to reunite her with her son. The husband, Howard, also becomes more sympathetic as the reader learns details of his suffering.

The episode in which Ann meets the other family who is waiting for news of their son's condition is presented differently than in "The Bath." The family is described in detail, and they interact more closely with Ann; the husband even offers Ann sympathy and an explanation of what happened to *his* son. Grief is shared, and the reader sees a greater camaraderie and connection between the two families. When Ann later learns that Franklin has died, it is a foreshadowing of her own son's fate.

"The Bath" ends with Ann's getting out of her bath to answer the phone; Carver continue the story in "A Small, Good Thing." The reader learns not only Scotty's fate but also his parents' subsequent response. On a number of occasions, the parents' lack of desire and inability to eat is emphasized. They are so obsessed with Scotty they can think of little else, including their own well-being and comfort. The accident threatens to consume them. Scotty's death offers no relief — especially because Scotty dies in great pain, without recognizing his parents. The apologies of the doctors and assurances that Scotty's condition was a "one-in-a-million" circumstance also offer no comfort, despite the good intentions and sympathies of the medical staff.

Ann and Howard switch off their emotions in order to cope with their grief. Dr. Francis embraces Ann, but she responds stiffly, without feeling. Both parents are in a state of shock and act for some time as if in a dream, unable to pick up toys or even take off their coats. Suspecting it is better to feel nothing than the pain of loss, they try to numb themselves through intense self-control. However, there are reminders of their son everywhere, and the baker's continued calls provoke them once more toward feeling. Although the feeling is anger, it is better than no feeling at all, and foreshadows their eventual return to life.

As Ann and Howard approach the bakery, its deserted appearance offers little hope. But inside the bakery is light. The baker is suspicious, but allows them entrance, only to be strongly criticized by the couple, who unleash their frustration and anger over their son's death on this stranger. In a way, by telling the baker their son is dead, the event finally becomes real to them, and they feel an immediate sense of relief.

The baker initially tries to defend himself, but then the true miracle occurs — he responds compassionately and accepts their blame. Their grief draws out his buried humanity, and he not only apologizes but offers them comfort in the form with which he is most familiar — food. "Eating," he tells them, "is a small, good thing in a time like this." They eat and are immediately comforted. The warm sanctuary of the bakery allows them to relax. Their resulting hunger reminds the parents and the reader that despite tragedy, life goes on.

The baker tries to explain his actions to the couple, and their responding sympathy helps to draw him out, and so he is rewarded for his kindness. They break the heavy bread and share it between them; it is like a kind of communion, a ritual in which they bond and offer each other comfort. They share their grief with this stranger (whose life also contains disappointment and loss) as he shares his bread with them, and this allows the couple to cope with their own loss. Unlike the bleak, discomforting end of "The Bath," "A Small, Good Thing" ends with a more hopeful image of human camaraderie and connection.

SUSAN C. W. ABBOTSON

Questions for Discussion

1. How does Carver elicit the reader's sympathy for the characters in this story?
2. How would you describe the baker? Why does he keep calling? How does your impression of him alter by the end of the story?
3. How would you describe the doctor? Why does he talk so much?
4. What was your reaction to learning of the boy's death, and why?
5. What is the state of the relationship between the parents, and how is this shown? Who do they blame for their son's condition?
6. What is the function of Franklin's family in the story?
7. Why do the parents go to see the baker?
8. What is the "small, good thing" referred to in the title?
9. How does Scotty's death initially affect the parents? How do they manage to transcend their grief and find comfort?
10. How does Carver use the idea of eating in the story? What does the sharing of bread near the close of the story represent?

Topics for Writing

1. Discuss whether or not you see "A Small, Good Thing" as a pessimistic or optimistic story.
2. Carver is concerned with the ways in which human beings communicate or fail to communicate with each other and how that affects people's lives. Discuss how this concern is depicted in "A Small, Good Thing."
3. **CONNECTIONS** Compare and contrast Raymond Carver's "The Bath" and "A Small, Good Thing."

Related Commentaries

Raymond Carver, "Creative Writing 101," p. 1610.
Raymond Carver, "On Writing," p. 1605.
Jim Naughton, "As Raymond Carver Muses, His Stature Grows," p. 1614.
A. O. Scott, "Looking for Raymond Carver," p. 1624.
Kathleen Westfall Shute, "On 'The Bath' and 'A Small, Good Thing,'" p. 1617.

Raymond Carver

What We Talk About When We Talk About Love (p. 252)

The scarcely veiled animosity between Dr. Mel McGinnis and his wife, Terri, gives tension to this story of three married couples. Through Mel's thoughts and experiences, Carver is investigating the nature of married love. Like the naive boy in Sherwood Anderson's classic short story "I Want to Know Why," Mel insists on asking an impossible question: What is the nature of love? What is the meaning of sharing?

The three pairs of lovers represent different stages of marriage. At one end of a spectrum are Laura and Nick (the narrator), married only a year and a half, still infatuated, glowing with the power of their attraction for each other.

At the other end of the spectrum are the old married pair in the hospital whom Mel and the other doctors have patched up after a catastrophic highway accident. Glad to learn his wife has survived, the old man — as Mel tells the story — is depressed, not because of their physical suffering but because he can't see his wife through the eye holes in his bandages. As Mel says, "Can you imagine? I'm telling you, the man's heart was breaking because he couldn't turn his goddamn head and *see* his goddamn wife."

Between the two extremes of perfect love, Mel and Terri are veterans (four years married to each other), who are past the bliss of their first attraction and not yet two halves of a whole because they've survived the long haul together. Each has been married before, and each is obsessed with the earlier partner. First Terri talks too much about her sadistic ex-husband Ed; then Mel reveals that he hates his first wife because she kept their kids. Terri says, "she's bankrupting us." The talk appears to ramble, but Carver keeps it under control by sticking to his subject — specific examples of the different varieties of love — and organizing the four friends' conversation by chronicling the stages of their drunkenness as they go through two bottles of gin in the afternoon.

The passing of time is brilliantly described, paralleling the waxing and waning of the stages of love. When the story opens, sunlight fills the New Mexico kitchen where the four friends with their gin and tonics are talking around the table. Midway, when the narrator is beginning to feel the drinks, he describes the sun like the warmth and lift of the gin in his body. "The afternoon sun was like a presence in this room, the spacious light of ease and generosity." As the conversation wears on and Mel tells Terri to shut up after she's interrupted one too many times, the light shifts again, the sunshine getting thinner. The narrator is a shade drunker, and his gaze fixes on the pattern of leaves on the windowpanes and on the Formica kitchen counter, as if he's staying alert by focusing deliberately on the edges of the objects around him. "They weren't the same patterns, of course." Finally, mysteriously, the light drains out of the room, "going back through the window where it had come from." The alcoholic elation has evaporated. At the end of the story, the couples sit in darkness on their kitchen chairs, not moving. The only sound the narrator hears is everyone's heart beating, separately.

The person we know least about is the narrator, Nick. Perhaps Carver deliberately echoes the name of Nick Adams, Hemingway's autobiographical narrator in his stories of initiation; or Nick Carraway, the narrator of Fitzgerald's *The*

Great Gatsby. The role of Carver's Nick in the story is also like that of Marlow in Conrad's "Heart of Darkness," as Nick voyages through the conversation of Mel and Terri into uncharted, deep waters of the heart. But this Nick is also a participant, through the gin and the sunlight, in the feelings of his troubled, overworked doctor friend.

Questions for Discussion

1. As the story opens, what is the setting in time, place, and situation?
2. How would you describe Terri? What type of person is Mel?
3. What was Terri's experience with her first husband, Ed? In what way was Mel involved in this experience? How does Terri's view of Ed contrast with Mel's view of him? What does this contrast reveal about the character of Mel and Terri's relationship?
4. In the discussion about Ed, what do we discover about the couple with whom Mel and Terri are socializing? What is their relationship both to each other and to Mel and Terri? Compare and contrast their marriage with Terri and Mel's.
5. What is the point of view in this story? Who is the narrator? How reliable is he?
6. Does Mel view his first wife in the same way he does Terri? What are we told about his first wife?
7. What are some of the questions about love that Carver raises through his characters? Does he offer any answers to these questions?
8. A third couple is introduced in the story. What astonishes Mel about their relationship?
9. What changes in the setting, if any, can you identify over the course of the story? In what way does the setting mirror Carver's message about the stages of love?
10. What does each of the couples represent? What is the significance of the last paragraph?

Topics for Writing

1. Write an essay discussing theme and characterization in "What We Talk About When We Talk About Love."
2. Explore the question posed by the title of this story: What does Carver (and the reader) talk about when he (and we) talks about love?
3. Think about married couples you know and discuss what their views on love might be as well as the quality of their relationships.
4. **CONNECTIONS** Compare and contrast the types of love in Carver's story and Joyce's "The Dead."

Related Commentaries

Raymond Carver, The Ashtray, p. 1613.
Raymond Carver, Creative Writing 101, p. 1610.
Raymond Carver, On Writing, p. 1605.
Jim Naughton, As Raymond Carver Muses, His Stature Grows, p. 1614.

Arthur M. Saltzman, A Reading of "What We Talk About When We Talk About Love," p. 1622.
A. O. Scott, Looking for Raymond Carver, p. 1624.

Suggested Readings

Adelman, Bob. *Carver Country — The World of Raymond Carver.* New York: Scribner's, 1991. A photographic essay with quotations from Carver's writing.
Carver, Raymond. "The Art of Fiction LXXVI." Interview in the *Paris Review,* No. 88 (Summer, 1983).
———. *Fires: Essays, Poems, Stories.* Santa Barbara, CA: Capra, 1983.
———. *Where I'm Calling From: New and Selected Stories.* New York: Atlantic Monthly, 1988.
Gentry, Marshall B., and William A. Stuff, eds. *Conversations with Raymond Carver.* Jackson, UP of Mississippi, 1990.
Halpert, Sam, ed. *When We Talk About Raymond Carver.* Layton, UT: Gibbs Smith, 1991.
Stull, W. L. "Beyond Hopelessville: Another Side of Raymond Carver." *Philological Quarterly* 64 (1985): 1–15.

WILLA CATHER

Paul's Case (p. 263)

Students may feel repelled by this story and reject its ending as heavy-handed. The structure of the plot, which pits a sensitive adolescent against an ugly and confining bourgeois society, invites us to admire Paul's rebellion and to glamorize his suicide, but Cather takes great pains to make Paul as unattractive in his way as the family, school, and neighborhood he hates. Quite apart from his supercilious mannerisms, which his teachers feel some inclination to forgive, Paul's quest for brightness and beauty in the world of art and imagination is subjected to Cather's devastating criticism, so readers who were ready to make a stock tragic response to his demise may find it difficult to care.

Try meeting this objection directly by examining the implications of the story's concluding passage. The vision presented here comes close to formulaic naturalism. Paul is not only caught in a universal machine, he is himself a machine. The imagination that has sustained him against the ugliness of his surroundings is dismissed as a "picture making mechanism," now crushed. The world against which Paul rebels is plain, gray, narrow, and monotonous. Its combination of saints (Calvin, Washington) and customary homilies precludes all that is in itself beautiful, pleasant, and fulfilling in the present moment. Paul's reaction, however, is merely the obverse. His habitual lies reflect his general resort to the artificial. He may be "artistic," but not in the sense of being creative, and his romantic fantasies involve no more satisfactory relations with others than does his ordinary life. Paul's world is so intolerable to his sensitivity that he is driven to escape from it, even at the cost of sitting in the cellar with the rats watching him from the corners. His escape inevitably becomes a form of self-destruction, as manifested in his criminal act — which to him feels like confronting "the thing in the corner" — and finally in his suicide. Paul passes through the "portal of Romance" for good, into a dream from which "there would be no awakening."

If it could be termed a choice, it would clearly be a bad choice, but Cather presents it rather as a symptom of Paul's "case," a disease of life from which he suffers, has suffered perhaps since his mother died when he was an infant, and for which, at first glance, there seems to be no cure. No wonder readers may be inclined to dismiss the story as unduly negative because unduly narrow. But Cather, at the same time that she meticulously documents the inexorable progress of Paul's illness, defines by implication a condition of health whose possible existence gives meaning to Paul's demise. As Philip L. Gerber explains: "Although [Cather] extolled the imaginative, her definition of imagination is all-important; for rather than meaning an ability 'to weave pretty stories out of nothing,' imagination conveyed to her 'a response to what is going on — a sensitiveness to which outside things appeal' and was an amalgam of sympathy and observation."

Paul's refuge is the product of the first, false kind of imagination, but the reality and the power of an imagination of the second sort is evident throughout the story, in the masterful evocations of Cordelia Street, of the school and its all-too-human teachers, and not least of Paul himself. When Paul's case finally becomes extreme enough to break through the insensitivity of bourgeois Pittsburgh, the world of the street that bears the name of King Lear's faithful daughter at last begins to live up to its name, sympathizing with Paul's plight and offering to embrace him with its love. To Paul, however, whose own unregenerate imagination is still confined to making pretty pictures rather than sympathetic observations, the advances of Cordelia Street seem like tepid waters of boredom in which he is called upon to submerge himself. The potential for growth and change that is reflected in his father's abandoning his usual frugality to pay back the money Paul has stolen and in his coming down from the top of the stairs into Paul's world to reach out to him, escape Paul's notice — but not that of the reader.

WILLIAM E. SHEIDLEY

Questions for Discussion

1. Describe Paul's personality as Cather sets it forth in the opening paragraph of the story. Is this someone we like and admire?
2. Why do Paul's teachers have so much difficulty dealing with him? What does the knowledge that Cather was a teacher in Pittsburgh at the time she wrote this story suggest about her perspective on Paul's case?
3. What techniques does Cather use to establish the reader's sympathy for Paul? What limits that sympathy?
4. Contrast the three worlds — school, Carnegie Hall, and Cordelia Street — in which Paul moves. Why does Cather introduce them in that order?
5. What is the effect of Cather's capitalizing the word *Romance*?
6. Discuss the three decorations that hang above Paul's bed. What aspects of American culture do they refer to? What do they leave out?
7. Explore the allusion embodied in the name "Cordelia Street." Why does Paul feel he is drowning there?

8.   Discuss Paul's fear of rats. Why does he feel that he has "thrown down the gauntlet to the thing in the corner" when he steals the money and leaves for New York?
9.   Explicate the paragraph that begins "Perhaps it was because, in Paul's world, the natural nearly always wore the guise of ugliness." To what extent does this paragraph offer a key to the story's structure and theme?
10. Describe the effect of the leap forward in time that occurs in the white space before we find Paul on the train to New York. Why does Cather withhold for so long her account of what has taken place?
11. What is admirable about Paul's entry into and sojourn in New York? What is missing from his new life?
12. Why does Paul wink at himself in the mirror after reading the newspaper account of his deeds?
13. On the morning of his suicide, Paul recognizes that "money was everything." Why does he think so? Does the story bear him out?
14. What is the effect of Paul's burying his carnation in the snow? of his last thoughts?

Topics for Writing

1.   Analyze "Paul's Case" as an attack on American society.
2.   In an essay argue that Cather's commentary on Mansfield (printed in Part Two, p. 1467) is a basis for criticism of "Paul's Case."
3.   Cather's story is punctuated by several recurrent images and turns of phrase. Locate as many as you can and take note of their contexts. What does this network of internal connections reveal?
4.   **CONNECTIONS**   Compare Cather's account of Paul's death with accounts of dying in other stories, such as Tolstoy's "The Death of Ivan Ilych" and Bierce's "An Occurrence at Owl Creek Bridge."

Related Commentary

Willa Cather, The Stories of Katherine Mansfield, p. 1467.

Suggested Readings

Arnold, Marilyn. *Willa Cather: A Reference Guide.* Boston: G. K. Hall, 1986.
———. *Willa Cather's Short Fiction.* Athens: Ohio UP, 1984.
Brown, E. K., and Leon Edel. *Willa Cather: A Critical Biography.* Lincoln: U of Nebraska P, 1987.
Callander, Marilyn B. *Willa Cather and the Fairy Tale.* Ann Arbor: UMI Research P, 1989.
Cather, Willa. *Collected Short Fiction 1892–1912.* Introduction by Mildred R. Bennett. Lincoln: U of Nebraska P, 1965.
———. *Early Novels and Stories.* The Library of America. New York: Viking, 1986.
Daiches, David. *Willa Cather: A Critical Introduction.* Ithaca: Cornell UP, 1951. 144–47.
Gerber, Philip L. *Willa Cather.* Twayne's United States Authors Series 258. Boston: Hall, 1975. 72–73, 101, 141, 163.

Murphy, John J. *Critical Essays on Willa Cather.* Boston: G. K. Hall, 1984.
Thomas, Susie. *Willa Cather.* Savage, MD: Barnes and Noble, 1990.
Wasserman, Loretta. *Willa Cather: A Study of Short Fiction.* Boston: Twayne, 1991.

JOHN CHEEVER

The Swimmer (p. 279)

One way to reconstruct a naturalistic time scheme for the story, so Neddy's "misfortunes," the awareness of which he seems to have repressed, can be dated with regard to the other events in the narrative, is to imagine a gap in time covered by the line "He stayed in the Levys' gazebo until the storm had passed." The authoritative point of view in the opening paragraphs seems to preclude placing the misfortunes before Neddy begins his swim, while the gathering clouds and circling de Haviland trainer assert the continuity of the first phase of his journey. After the storm, however, signs of change appear, and it is possible to reconcile Neddy's subsequent encounters with the proposition that he is continuing his swim on another day or days under quite different circumstances. Before the storm, he visits the Grahams and the Bunkers, who greet him as the prosperous and popular Neddy Merrill described at the beginning of the story, but after the storm Neddy visits only the empty houses of the Lindleys and the Welchers; the public pool where any derelict may swim; the peculiar Hallorans, who mention his troubles; the Sachses, who have problems of their own and refuse him a drink; the socially inferior Biswangers, who snub him; and his old mistress Shirley, who implies that this call is not the first he has paid in this condition.

But Cheever is not interested in a realistic time scheme. If he were, he would not have burned the 250-page novelistic version of the story (mentioned in the headnote) that presumably filled in the blanks. Instead, he has constructed the story so Neddy's recognition of his loss strikes the reader with the same impact it has on Neddy. By telescoping time, Cheever thrusts us forward into a state of affairs that exists only as a dim cloud on the horizon on the day the story begins and at first seems to be entirely taking place.

What accounts for the reversal in Neddy's life? Surely it is possible to tax Neddy for irresponsibility and childishness in turning his back on his friends and family and so casually setting off on an odyssey from which he returns far too late. Neddy's own view of his adventure is considerably more attractive. The only member of his society who seems free from a hangover on this midsummer Sunday, Neddy simply wishes to savor the pleasures of his fortunate life: "The day was beautiful and it seemed to him that a long swim might enlarge and celebrate its beauty." Although he has been (or will be) unfaithful to his wife with Shirley Adams, and although he kisses close to a dozen other women on his journey, Neddy does not construe his departure as infidelity to Lucinda. Rather, to swim the string of pools across the suburban county is to travel along "the Lucinda River." As "a pilgrim, an explorer, a man with a destiny," Neddy plunges into this river of life aware of the gathering storm on the horizon but regarding it with pleasurable anticipation. When it finally breaks over the Levys' gazebo, he savors the exciting release of tension that accompanies the arrival of a thunder shower, but with the explosion of thunder and the smell of gunpowder that ensues, Neddy finds his happy illusions, his world of "youth, sport, and clement weather," lashed by a more unpleasant reality, just as the "rain lashed the Japanese lanterns that Mrs. Levy had bought in Kyoto the year before last, or was it the year before that?"

What Neddy now confronts, though he tries gamely to ignore it, are the twin recognitions that his youth is not eternal and that the pleasant society of the "bonny and lush . . . banks of the Lucinda River" is unstable, exclusive, and cruel. Grass grows in the Lindleys' riding ring, the Welchers have moved away, and the sky is now overcast. Crossing Route 424 in his swimming suit, Neddy is subjected to the ridicule of the public, and at the Recreation Center he finds that swimming does not convey the same sense of elegance, pleasure, and freedom that it does in the pools of his affluent friends. The validity of the society Neddy has previously enjoyed is called further into question by the very existence of the self-contradictory Hallorans, whose personal eccentricity is matched by their political hypocrisy. Neddy's visits to the Biswangers and to Shirley Adams complete the destruction of his illusions, but it is Eric Sachs, disfigured by surgery and (with the loss of his navel) symbolically cut off from the human community, who embodies the most troubling reflection of Neddy's condition. "I'm not alone," Shirley proclaims, but Neddy is, and as this man who "might have been compared to a summer's day" recognizes that his summer is over, it is not surprising that for "the first time in his adult life" he begins to cry. While the reader may relish Cheever's indictment of a society whose values have so betrayed Neddy, it is hard not to feel some admiration for a man who, by executing his plan to swim the county through the now icy autumn waters, has indeed become a legendary figure, an epic hero of a sort.

William E. Sheidley

Questions for Discussion

1. Who is referred to by the word "everyone" in the opening sentence? Who is not?
2. How does Neddy Merrill relate to the world in which he moves? Why does he decide to swim home?
3. Why does Neddy name his route "the Lucinda River"? The Levys live on "Alewives Lane." Alewives are a kind of fish that swim up rivers to spawn. Is there a sexual component to Neddy's journey?
4. Is the storm that breaks a surprise? How does Neddy feel about the beginning of the rain?
5. What differences can be noticed between what Neddy experiences before and after the storm? How might they be explained?
6. What new elements enter the story when Neddy crosses Route 424? Why do the drivers jeer at him?
7. Before he dives into the unappealing public swimming pool, Neddy tells himself "that this was merely a stagnant bend in the Lucinda River." How characteristic is this effort to assuage his own doubts and discontents?
8. Based on what the Hallorans, the Sachses, the Biswangers, and Shirley Adams say to Neddy, what is the truth about himself and his life of which he is unaware?
9. Cheever has his hero discover the season by observing the stars. What effect does that choice among various possibilities have on our attitude toward Neddy?
10. It is not difficult to say what Neddy has lost. What has he gained?

Topics for Writing

1. Explain why Neddy Merrill talks only with women.
2. Analyze the characters Rusty Towers, Eric Sachs, and Neddy Merrill.
3. Write an essay discussing Neddy Merrill's voyage of exploration and discovery.
4. Evaluate Cheever's attitude toward the swimmer.

Related Commentary

John Cheever, Why I Write Short Stories, p. 1472.

Suggested Readings

Cheever, John. *The Journals of John Cheever*. New York: Knopf, 1991.
Cheever, Susan. *Home before Dark*. Boston: Houghton, 1984.
Coale, Samuel. *John Cheever*. New York: Ungar, 1977. 43–47.
Collins, R. G., ed. *Critical Essays on John Cheever*. Boston: G. K. Hall, 1982.
O'Hara, James E. *John Cheever: A Study of the Short Fiction*. Boston: Twayne, 1989.
Waldeland, Lynne. *John Cheever*. Boston: Twayne, 1979.
Writers at Work, Fifth Series. New York: Penguin, 1981. Interview with John Cheever by Annette Grant, Fall 1976.

ANTON CHEKHOV

Angel [The Darling] (p. 289)

One of the liveliest discussions about a short story in this anthology could be started by a class debate based on the contradictory interpretations of "Angel" ["The Darling"] by Leo Tolstoy and Eudora Welty included in Part Two (pp. 1642 and 1645). Tolstoy was convinced that Chekhov was misguided in satirizing women's tendency to depend on men for meaning and direction in their lives. In Tolstoy's view, Chekhov had allowed himself to become a women's rights advocate under the pernicious influence of his "liberated" wife, the actress Olga Knipper. Welty, in contrast, reveals the subtle emotional tyranny of the protagonist, Olga. In Welty's interpretation, the schoolboy shows us at the end of the story that men want their "space" too. Students could be assigned Tolstoy's or Welty's interpretation and asked to support or refute it. Certainly neither interpretation is unassailable.

Other critical perspectives can also be applied to this provocative story. A feminist reader could argue that Olga has been handicapped by the environment around her: Uneducated for a profession, she can have no ideas or life of her own. A psychological interpretation could concentrate on the darling's early, possibly traumatic fixation on her father and his long mortal illness just as she reaches manageable age. A formalist approach might look closely at the words the schoolboy uses as he cries out in his sleep: "You watch out! You go away! Don't you pick quarrels with me!," or in another translation, "I'll give it you! Get away! Shut up!" Basing her analysis on the latter translation, Welty assumes that the boy is dreaming of Olga. He could just as well be dreaming of his teacher at school, other students fighting with him in the schoolyard, or his own mother, who appears to have abandoned him. He could even be repeating the cruel words his mother might have said to drive him away from her before she left him with Olga.

The English short story writer H. E. Bates interpreted the story yet another way. Comparing Chekhov's technique with Maupassant's, Bates writes, "Both like to portray a certain type of weak, stupid, thoughtless woman, a sort of yes-woman who can unwittingly impose tragedy or happiness on others. Maupassant had no patience with the type; but in Olenka [Olga], in the 'The Darling ["Angel"],' it is precisely a quality of tender patience, the judgment of the heart and not the head, that gives Chekhov's story its effect of uncommon understanding and radiance."

Bates saw Chekhov as subtle: His

> receptivity, his capacity for compassion, are both enormous. Of his characters he seems to say, "I know what they are doing is their own responsibility. But how did they come to this, how did it happen? There may be some trivial thing that will explain." That triviality, discovered, held for a moment in the light, is the key to Chekhov's emotional solution. In Maupassant's case the importance of that key would have been inexorably driven home; but as we turn to ask of Chekhov if we have caught his meaning aright, it is to discover that we must answer that question for ourselves — for Chekhov has gone. . . . Both [Maupassant and Chekhov] knew to perfection when they had said enough; an acute instinct continually reminded them of the fatal tedium of explanation, of going on a second too long. In Chekhov this sense of impatience, almost a fear, caused him frequently to stop speaking, as it were, in mid-air. It was this which gave his stories an air of remaining unfinished, of leaving the reader to his own explanations, of imposing on each story's end a note of suspense so abrupt and yet refined that it produced on the reader an effect of delayed shock.

Questions for Discussion

1. How does Chekhov characterize Olga at the beginning of the story?
2. Why does he have the "lady visitors" be the first ones to call her a "darling"?
3. Olga "mothers" each of her husbands. Could she have been both a good wife and a good mother if she had had children of her own? Why or why not?

Topics for Writing

1. Interpret Sasha's words at the end of "Angel." Identify the person he is talking to, and find details in the story that justify your interpretation.
2. **RESPONDING CREATIVELY** Continue "Angel," supposing that the "loud knock at the gate" is a message from Sasha's mother, who wants him to join her in Harkov.

Related Commentaries

Anton Chekhov, Technique in Writing the Short Story, p. 1631.
Richard Ford, Why We Like Chekov, p. 1632.
Leo Tolstoy, Chekhov's Intent in "The Darling," p. 1642.
Eudora Welty, Plot and Character in Chekhov's "The Darling," p. 1645.

Suggested Readings

See page 67.

ANTON CHEKHOV

A Blunder (p. 297)

Although this short fiction is little more than a sketch or an anecdote, Chekhov is still able to suggest to the reader, with only a handful of details, the complex attitudes toward love and marriage in the world of the village where the story is set. The reader understands, from the opening scene of the two parents eavesdropping outside the drawing-room door, the crucial importance of finding a husband for a daughter. From the mention of the man's status — schoolteacher — and the young woman's breathless response to the name of the author Nekrassov, the reader is aware of the family's modest social rank and their desire to find someone of importance for their daughter to marry. With the same quick strokes the author also presents the venality of the teacher. The man doesn't mind striking his students and he has intentions toward the daughter that her mother and father wouldn't approve. The young woman is such a vague simpleton that the reader has a desire to sit her down and explain life to her. The ending of the story is a comedy of errors that was the stock in trade of the writer of comic sketches, the young Chekhov's source of income in his family's struggling years.

As we read the story we find ourselves responding to the situation with annoyed interest. The mother and father are so clearly reprehensible that we are upset with their plan to trap the man in the next room into marriage. At the same time we sense their anxiety for their daughter. Somehow they have to get her married. For someone of Chekhov's time the situation would be as ridiculous, but the emotions would be uncomfortably familiar. The teacher is obviously feeling some physical attraction, enough that he has ventured into the little drawing-room alone with the young woman, and although the reader also is ambivalent about the teacher's impatience with his students, his pomposities, and his desires, the man himself is also a familiar figure. Only the young woman is described without emotional contradictions. She is just what the reader would expect, complete to the detail that her "fat little hand" smells of egg soap. Her sigh at the mention of the name of an author and her habit of "continually peeping at herself in the glass" confirm the reader's impression of her simple vanity.

What all of these conflicting characterizations present is a situation in which the reader is at first irritated with the parents for their plan to trick the teacher, then irritated with the teacher for his fatuous attitudes, and at the same time impatient with the young woman for her shallowness. The writer achieves all of this in the space of a page and a half, and he simultaneously builds the tension in the story around the folk custom of blessing a betrothed couple with a religious painting, a custom completely unknown to our own society! It is as though the young but supremely talented Chekhov were giving us a demonstration of his skills. He crowds the characters with their conflict of emotions into a small space, presents them with such skill that the reader can't help but become interested in the outcome of the situation, and then resolves the tension with a broad burlesque gesture that manages to humiliate everyone except the young woman, whose vanity is left unshaken. Whatever emotions the reader has been feeling during the story's delineation of its characters, there will be at least an amused smile at the story's tumultuous resolution.

Questions for Discussion

1. What do we understand about the importance of marriage in this society from the parents' effort to trick the schoolteacher?
2. What does the use of the religious painting imply about the power of religion in the lives of these people?
3. From the little we learn about the two young characters from their conversation, we understand that there has been a misunderstanding about some letters. Is it ever decided whether or not the teacher sent them?
4. How would you describe the teacher's interest in the young woman, and what does she expect from him? What in their situation has conditioned them to respond to each other in this way?
5. How would a woman today describe the role that the young woman is expected to play in her own life?
6. Would a reader of Chekhov's time have seen allusions in the story that a modern reader fails to perceive, or has the author based his story so solidly on shared human attitudes and ambitions that the reader today follows the sketch with the same appreciation of the situation?

Topics for Writing

1. The talent of the young Chekhov is evident in the presentations of the characters in this sketch. Compare the writer's characters in a later story, such as "The Woman with the Little Dog," and discuss Chekhov's writing as it matured.
2. The sketch describes a situation for women and their parents that is almost incomprehensible to us today. Discuss the expectations and ambitions of the young woman in the sketch and compare them to modern attitudes.
3. The importance of the name of one writer and the fact that the family has a portrait on the wall of another writer tell us something about the place of literacy and literature in the life of the village. Discuss the differences between this response to literature and our own response in the modern world.

Related Commentaries

Anton Chekhov, Technique in Writing the Short Story, p. 1631.
Richard Ford, Why We Like Chekhov, p. 1632.
Richard Ford, Editor's Note on "The Blunder," p. 1636.

Suggested Readings

See page 67.

ANTON CHEKHOV

The Lady with the Little Dog (p. 299)

Anna Sergeevna comes to Yalta because she wants "to live, to live!" Gurov begins his affair with her because he is bored and enjoys the freedom and ease of a casual liaison. At the outset both are undistinguished, almost clichés — a philandering bank employee escaping from a wife he cannot measure up to, a lady with a dog and a "flunkey" for a husband. By the end of the story, however, after having been captured and tormented by a love that refuses to be filed away in memory, the two gain dignity and stature by recognizing that life is neither exciting nor easy; and, by taking up the burden of the life they have discovered in their mutual compassion, they validate their love.

Chekhov develops the nature of this true love, so ennobling and so tragic, by testing it against a series of stereotypes that it transcends and by showing a series of stock expectations that it violates. Anna Sergeevna reacts differently from any of the several types of women Gurov has previously made love to, and Gurov finds himself unable to handle his own feelings in the way he is accustomed to. Anna Sergeevna proves neither a slice of watermelon nor a pleasant focus of nostalgia. Most important, as the conclusion implies, she will not remain the secret core of his life, bought at the price of falsehood and suspicion of others.

In observing the evolution of the lovers, the reader is led through a series of potential misconceptions. We may want to despise Gurov as a careless breaker of hearts, but it is clear that he has one of his own when he sees Anna Sergeevna as a Magdalene. Later, when Gurov is tormented by his longings for Anna Sergeevna, we are tempted to laugh the superior realist's laugh at a romantic fool: Surely when Gurov arrives at S——, disillusionment will await him. And in a sense it does. Just as there was dust in the streets at Yalta, the best room in the hotel at S—— is coated with dust; reality is an ugly fence; and even the theater (where *The Geisha* is playing) is full of reminders of how unromantic life really is. But Anna Sergeevna has not, as Gurov supposes at one point, taken another lover, nor has she been able to forget Gurov.

The antiromantic tone is but another oversimplification, and the story comes to rest, somewhat like Milton's *Paradise Lost,* at a moment of beginning. The lovers' disillusionment about the nature of the struggle they face creates in them a deep compassion for each other, which finds its echo in readers' final attitude toward them as fellow human beings whose lives are like our own and who deserve a full measure of our sympathy. Or perhaps they draw our pity; surely their fate, which Chekhov so skillfully depicts as probable and true, inspires tragic fear. Gurov and Anna Sergeevna have met the god of love, and Chekhov awes us by making him seem real.

WILLIAM E. SHEIDLEY

Questions for Discussion

1. Why does Gurov call women "an inferior race"?
2. At the end of section I, Gurov thinks that there is "something pathetic" about Anna Sergeevna. Is there? What is it?
3. Why is Anna Sergeevna so distracted as she watches the steamer putting in?
4. How does Anna Sergeevna differ from other women Gurov has known, as they are described in the paragraph that ends "the lace of their underwear seemed to him like scales"? Compare this passage with the paragraph that begins "His head was beginning to turn gray."
5. In view of what follows, is it appropriate that Gurov should see Anna Sergeevna as a Magdalene?
6. What is the function of the paragraph that begins "In Oreanda they sat on a bench not far from the church"?
7. What "complete change" does Gurov undergo during his affair with Anna Sergeevna at Yalta? Is it permanent?
8. Explain Gurov's remark at the end of section II: "High time!"
9. Why is Gurov enraged at his companion's remark about the sturgeon?
10. Discuss the possible meanings of the objects Gurov encounters in S——: the broken figurine, the long gray fence, the cheap blanket, and so on.
11. Seeing Anna Sergeevna enter the theater, Gurov "realized clearly that there was no person closer, dearer, or more important for him in the whole world." What is Chekhov's tone in this statement?
12. Explain Anna Sergeevna's reaction to Gurov's arrival. Why does she volunteer to come to Moscow?
13. Discuss the implications of Gurov's "two lives" as Chekhov explains them in section IV. Do you agree with the generalizations about the desire for privacy with which the paragraph ends? Relate these ideas to the story's ending.
14. What will life be like for Gurov and Anna Sergeevna? Anna has previously said, "I have never been happy; I am unhappy now, and I never, never shall be happy, never!" Is she right?

Topics for Writing

1. Write an essay describing Chekhov's characterization of the wronged spouse in "The Lady with the Little Dog."
2. Discuss the meaning of the three geographical locales in "The Lady with the Little Dog."
3. On your first reading of the story, stop at the end of each section and write down your judgment of Gurov and Anna Sergeevna and your prediction of what will happen next. When you have finished reading, compare what you wrote with what turned out to be the case and with your final estimate of the protagonists. To the extent that your initial impressions were borne out, what points in the text helped to guide you? To the extent that you were surprised, explain what led you astray. What might Chekhov have wanted to accomplish by making such misconceptions possible?

Related Commentaries

Anton Chekhov, Technique in Writing the Short Story, p. 1631.
Richard Ford, Why We Like Chekhov, p. 1632.
Vladimir Nabokov, A Reading of Chekhov's "The Lady with the Little Dog," p. 1637.

Suggested Readings

Bates, H. E. *The Modern Short Story.* Boston: The Writer, 1972.
Eekman, Thomas. *Critical Essays on Anton Chekhov.* Boston: G. K. Hall, 1989.
Friedland, Louis S., ed. *Anton Tchekhov's Letters on the Short Story, the Drama, and Other Topics.* Salem, NH: Ayer, 1965.
Kramer, Karl D. *The Chameleon and the Dream: The Image of Reality in Chekhov's Stories.* The Hague: Mouton, 1970. 171.
Matlaw, Ralph E., ed. *Anton Chekhov's Short Stories.* New York: Norton, 1979.
Meister, Charles W. *Chekhov Criticism, 1880 through 1986.* New York: St. Martin's, 1990.
Pritchett, V. S. *Chekhov: A Spirit Set Free.* New York: Random, 1988.
Rayfield, Donald. *Chekhov: The Evolution of His Art.* New York: Barnes, 1975. 197–200.
Smith, Virginia Llewellyn. "The Lady with the Dog." Anton Chekhov's Short Stories: Texts of the Stories, Backgrounds, Criticism. Ed. Ralph E. Matlaw. New York: Norton, 1979. Excerpted from Smith, *Anton Chekhov and the Lady with the Dog* (New York: Oxford UP, 1973). 96–97, 212–18.
Troyat, Henri. *Chekhov.* Trans. Michael Henry Heim. New York: Dutton, 1986.

CHARLES CHESNUTT

The Wife of His Youth (p. 312)

Like any great story, this masterful narrative can be read on many different levels. It can and will be read as a story about the experience of a single individual, but it is even more meaningful to consider its metaphoric implications and its relevance to the continuing debate within the African American community on the questions of assimilation and identity. Historically, these questions have been framed around the perceived necessity to assimilate within the mainstream white society to achieve any level of economic security and personal safety. At the same time there has been a perception that with assimilation comes a loss of the unique identity that has resulted from the long struggle by Africans who were brought as slaves to the new continent.

Students might at first decide that the opening paragraph, describing the social group known as the Blue Veins, is meant to be a satirical portrayal of people often called "strivers." At the time Chesnutt was writing, however, the questions of blood and lineage were considered of crucial importance to Americans, and the white society had its familiar term *bluebloods* to characterize its own "aristocracy." Skin that is light and clear allows the veins to show through the surface with a bluish tone. What Chesnutt is presenting here is the concept of blue veins as a symbol of assimilation, a sign that the members of the social club like the one he describes have become almost white. The subtle racism that is an uncomfortable aspect of the group's requirements for membership is predicated by the necessity to assimilate.

In a larger sense, however, the story is not about Mr. Ryder and his fancy dress ball and his love for Mrs. Dixon. The plot of the story, with the sudden appearance of the woman he had "married" many years before, should be seen as a symbol of Chesnutt's theme: the troubling dream of assimilation and its subsequent loss of a deeper identity. As Mr. Ryder sits on his pleasant front porch, he is considering the poetry he wants to quote in his talk at the ball, and he is reading his favorite poet, Tennyson. No writer could be further from the African American experience than the English poet laureate, but Mr. Ryder feels no incongruity in his choice. Mr. Ryder has educated himself, and it is English poetry that has stirred him. Tennyson represents assimilation — the desire of the man to immerse himself in a new sense of self.

The figure that comes to his gate a few moments later, a small, toothless, dark-skinned woman much older than he, is clearly a symbol of the other identity that he has rejected. As Chesnutt writes, "She looked like a bit of the old plantation life, summoned up from the past by the wave of a magician's wand." As she speaks — and her dialect is carefully imitated on the page so the reader understands that she is entirely a person of the slave past — the reader quickly suspects that she is the woman in the title of the story, the wife of Ryder's youth in the South. At the same time there is the poignancy of her earnest conviction that she would recognize her husband, even though she is unknowingly standing in front of him. She insists, "I'd know 'im 'mongs' a hund'ed men." She has even made the reader smile with her considered opinion that he wouldn't have made much of himself after he ran away. "I 'spec's ter haf ter suppo't 'im w'en I fin' 'im."

What is remarkable in Chesnutt's portrayal of the old woman is that he presents her without condescension. She is uneducated and she is poor, but her small figure is proud and dignified, and when she leaves Ryder and walks down the street, ". . . he [sees] several persons whom she passed turn and look back at her with a smile of kindly amusement." In Ryder's description of the woman at the ball later in the evening the words he uses are "devotion and confidence." On a symbolic level Chesnutt is saying that in the struggle toward assimilation it must not be forgotten that there was much good in the older self that assimilation denies. His story is an American masterpiece.

Questions for Discussion

1. Are there groups like the Blue Veins in African American society today?
2. What does Chesnutt mean when he describes the society as "a lifeboat, an anchor, a bulwark and a shield"?
3. For those members of the society who have become completely assimilated, what does this status imply?
4. Is the community that Chesnutt describes a specific town, or is it symbolic of the new life many African Americans achieved in northern cities?
5. What level of achievement does the list of professions of the group's members represent?

6. Although the dialect of the old woman seems at first to be difficult to understand, after a moment it is clearly comprehensible. Does it have the flavor of true vernacular speech? Why or why not?
7. Is a search like the old woman's something that could have happened in the turbulent conditions following the Civil War?

Topics for Writing

1. Discuss the place of a group like the Blue Veins in America's "classless" society.
2. Discuss the implications of Mr. Ryder's statement that "[o]ur fate lies between absorption by the white race and extinction in the black."
3. Discuss the speech of Mr. Ryder and his slave wife, considering whether the differences represent more than a difference in the level of education of the two people.
4. **CONNECTIONS** Compare this portrayal of African American life with the view that Zora Neale Hurston presents in her stories (p. 652–673).
5. Mr. Ryder has a deep love for the poetry of Tennyson. Discuss the importance of literature in the assimilation process.
6. Recently attention has been given to vernacular black speech as a unique form of English that is described by the term Ebonics. Consider the social implications of the use of Ebonics in everyday life, including education.

Suggested Readings

Chesnutt, Charles Waddell. *The Conjure Woman and Other Conjure Tales.* Ed. R. Broadhead. Durham, NC: Duke UP, 1993.
——. *The Wife of His Youth, and Other Stories of the Color Line.* Ridgewood, NJ: Gregg, 1967.
Render, Sylvia Lyons. *Charles W. Chesnutt.* Boston: Twayne, 1980.
——, ed. *The Short Fiction of Charles W. Chesnutt.* Washington, D.C.: Howard UP, 1974.

KATE CHOPIN

Désirée's Baby (p. 322)

It is difficult to imagine a reader who would not be horrified and disgusted by the tragic results of the racism and sexism that permeate this story. No one could believe that Armand Aubigny's inhuman cruelty to his wife Désirée and his child is warranted. The only real uncertainty the reader confronts regards Armand's foreknowledge of his own parentage: Did he know that his mother had "negro blood" before he married Désirée, or did he discover her revealing letter later on? If he *did* know beforehand (and it is difficult to believe that he did not) his courtship of and marriage to Désirée were highly calculated actions, with Désirée chosen because she was the perfect woman to be used in an "experimental" reproduction. If their child(ren) "passed" as white, everything would be fine. If not, Désirée, the foundling, would be the perfect victim to take the blame.

This may seem to be judging Armand too harshly, because the narrator does describe his great passion for Désirée, so suddenly and furiously ignited. Certainly Armand behaves like a man in love. But Chopin inserts a few subtle remarks that allow us to question this, at least in hindsight: "The wonder was that he had not loved her before; for he had known her since his father brought him home from Paris, a boy of eight, after his mother died there." It does seem unlikely that a man of Armand's temperament would conceive this sudden intense desire for "the girl next door," a sweet, naive young woman whom he has known for most of his life. Right from the beginning, Chopin also reveals details about his character that are unsettling, even to the innocent and loving Désirée. The basic cruelty of Armand's nature is hinted at throughout the story, particularly regarding his severe treatment of "his negroes," which is notably in sharp contrast to his father's example.

Armand's reputation as a harsh slavemaster supports the presumption that he has known about his own part-negro ancestry all along. He did not learn this behavior from his father, who was "easy-going and indulgent" in his dealings with the slaves. The knowledge that some of his own ancestors spring from the same "race of slavery" would surely be unbearable to the proud, "imperious" Armand, and the rage and shame that his knowledge brings would easily be turned against the blacks around him. In much the same way, when Armand realizes that his baby is visibly racially mixed, he vents his fury viciously on his slaves, the "very spirit of Satan [taking] hold of him."

Modern readers will find many disturbing aspects to this story. The seemingly casual racism is horrifying. And feminists will be likely to take exception (as they sometimes do to Chopin's *The Awakening*) to Désirée's passive acceptance of Armand's rejection of her and his child, and her apparently deliberate walk into the bayou. Suicide is not the strong woman's answer to the situation, but Désirée is definitely not a strong woman. What she does have is wealthy parents who love her and are willing to take care of her and the baby. So why would she feel that she has to end her life? Discussion of this issue will have to focus on the historical period and social setting of the story. Gender and class roles and structures were so rigid that it was impossible for a woman to cross those lines very far. If she tried, what would the cost be to her children? And of course, the most rigid barrier of all was racial. No mixing of black and white blood would ever be condoned in that society (thus, Armand's mother remained in France, keeping her family secrets), so Désirée's baby would never have acceptance anywhere. Désirée isn't able to see any viable way out of her terrifying situation, and her view is not entirely unrealistic, considering her time and place. Once again, Kate Chopin realistically depicts the cruelty and horror of a social structure that totally denies power to women, children, the poor, and most of all, to blacks.

Questions for Discussion

1. Describe your feelings toward Armand at the end of the story. What aspect of this last scene do you find the most shocking? Are you completely surprised by his behavior here? See if you can trace Chopin's gradual building of Armand's character, noting the things she chooses to reveal to us throughout the story.
2. What kind of person is Désirée? Does she seem to be a good match for Armand? Does your opinion of her change as the story progresses? How consistent is she as a character?

3. How do you feel about Désirée's final choice? Is suicide an understandable choice, or is she simply a weak character? What other options do you think she may have?

4. Should Madame Valmondé have told Désirée of her realization about the baby? When she sees the baby at four weeks of age, she obviously is startled by something in its appearance, but doesn't mention it. Then, she returns home and seems to wait for disaster to strike, never returning to visit Désirée. How do you explain this behavior, coming from an obviously protective, loving mother?

5. Armand is shown to be a very cruel master to his slaves, a direct contrast to the way in which his father ran the plantation. Does learning his family secret in the last scene suggest any explanation for this?

6. Do you think Armand knew about his own mother's negro ancestry before he courted and married Désirée? Look for evidence from the story to support your opinion.

Topics for Writing

1. Discuss the way the setting affects the action in this story.

2. Should Désirée have returned to her family home with her baby? Consider the pros and cons of her future there.

3. According to the critic Wai-chee Dimock, the racial injustice in "Désirée's Baby" is "only a necessary background against which Chopin stages her deadly dramatic irony. . . . The injustice here is not the injustice of racial oppression but the injustice of a wrongly attributed racial identity." Agree or disagree with this interpretation of the story.

Related Commentary

Kate Chopin, How I Stumbled upon Maupassant, p. 1474.

Suggested Readings

See page 73.

KATE CHOPIN

The Story of an Hour (p. 326)

Does the O. Henryesque trick ending of this story merely surprise us, or does Chopin arrange to have Louise Mallard expire at the sight of her unexpectedly still living husband in order to make a thematic point? Students inclined to groan when Brently Mallard returns "composedly carrying his gripsack and umbrella" may come to think better of the ending if you ask them to evaluate the doctors' conclusions about the cause of Mrs. Mallard's death. Although Richards and Josephine take "great care . . . to break to her as gently as possible the news of her husband's death," what actually kills Mrs. Mallard is the news that he is still alive. The experience of regeneration and freedom that she undergoes in the arm-chair looking out upon a springtime vista involves an almost sexual surrender of conventional repressions and restraints. As she *abandons herself* to the realization of her freedom that *approaches to possess her*, Mrs. Mallard enjoys a hitherto forbidden physical and spiritual excitement. The presumption that she would be devastated by the death of her husband, like the presumption that she needs to be protected by watchful, "tender" friends, reduces Mrs. Mallard to a dependency from which she is joyful at last to escape. Chopin best images this oppressive, debilitating concern in what Mrs. Mallard thinks she will weep again to see: "the kind, tender hands folded in death; the face that had never looked save with love upon her, fixed and gray and dead." Although had she lived Mrs. Mallard might have felt guilty for, as it were, taking her selfhood like a lover and pridefully stepping forth "like a goddess of Victory," Chopin effectively suggests that the guilt belongs instead to the caretakers, the "travel-stained" Brently, the discomfited Josephine, and Richards, whose "quick motion" to conceal his error comes "too late."

WILLIAM E. SHEIDLEY

Questions for Discussion

1. In view of Mrs. Mallard's eventual reactions, evaluate the efforts of Josephine and Richards to break the news of her husband's death gently.
2. What purpose might Chopin have in stressing that Mrs. Mallard does not block out the realization that her husband has died?
3. What might be the cause or causes of the "physical exhaustion that haunted her body and seemed to reach into her soul" that Mrs. Mallard feels as she sinks into the armchair?
4. Describe your reaction to the view out the window the first time you read the story. Did it change on a second reading?
5. Mrs. Mallard's face bespeaks repression. What has she been repressing?
6. Discuss the imagery Chopin uses to describe Mrs. Mallard's recognition of her new freedom.
7. What kind of man is Brently Mallard, as Mrs. Mallard remembers him? In what ways does he resemble Josephine and Richards?
8. Describe your feelings about Mrs. Mallard as she emerges from her room. Is the saying "Pride goeth before a fall" relevant here?
9. In what way is the doctors' pronouncement on the cause of Mrs. Mallard's death ironic? In what sense is it nonetheless correct?

Topics for Writing

1. Discuss the imagery of life and the imagery of death in "The Story of an Hour."
2. Write a paper analyzing "The Story of an Hour" as a thwarted awakening.
3. Describe the tragic irony in "The Story of an Hour."
4. On a second reading of "The Story of an Hour," try to recall how you responded to each paragraph or significant passage when you read it the first time. Write short explanations of any significant changes in your reactions.

To what extent are those changes the result of knowing the story's ending? What other factors are at work?

5. **RESPONDING CREATIVELY** Can falsehood be the key to truth? Narrate a personal experience in which your own or someone else's reaction to misinformation revealed something meaningful and true.

6. **RESPONDING CREATIVELY** How long is a turning point? Tell a story covering a brief span of time — a few minutes or an hour — in which the central character's life is permanently changed. Study Chopin's techniques for summarizing and condensing information.

Related Commentary

Kate Chopin, How I Stumbled upon Maupassant, p. 1474.

Suggested Readings

Bender, B. "Kate Chopin's Lyrical Short Stories." *Studies in Short Fiction* 11 (1974): 257–66.

Chopin, Kate. *The Complete Works of Kate Chopin.* Baton Rouge: Louisiana State UP, 1970.

Dimock, Wai-chee. "Kate Chopin." *Modern American Women Writers.* Ed. Elaine Showalter et al. New York: Collier, 1993.

Fluck, Winifred. "Tentative Transgressions: Kate Chopin's Fiction as a Mode of Symbolic Action." *Studies in American Fiction* 10 (1982): 151–71.

Miner, Madonne M. "Veiled Hints: An Affected Stylist's Reading of Kate Chopin's 'Story of an Hour.' " *Markham Review* 11 (1982): 29–32.

Seyersted, Per. *Kate Chopin: A Critical Biography.* Baton Rouge: Louisiana State UP, 1969. 57–59.

Skaggs, Peggy. *Kate Chopin.* Boston: Twayne, 1985.

Toth, Emily. *Kate Chopin.* New York: Morrow, 1990.

SANDRA CISNEROS

The House on Mango Street (p. 330)

Cisneros credits Jorge Luis Borges's *Dreamtigers* as an important influence on her choice of form in *The House on Mango Street.* Like Borges in "Everything and Nothing," a short piece from *Dreamtigers,* Cisneros works within short narrative forms, writing sketches rather than stories. Where Borges develops an idea about Shakespeare as his theme, Cisneros dramatizes emotions in her sketches. These emotions belong to the young narrator as she tells about her experiences of economic hardship and social marginalization within a Mexican American family. The economic and social realities of her life are difficult, but the emotional security she finds within her tightly knit family appears to have given her the strength to survive the difficulties she faces and enables her to speak in the positive tone of her stories.

"The House on Mango Street" starts in a voice that suggests muted protest, foreshadowing our awareness of the narrator's developing strength of character. In the opening paragraph, the narrator names the various streets her family has lived on as they moved from apartment to apartment during her early childhood. Her memories center on the difficult living conditions in the different rental apartments — for example, broken water pipes and a hostile landlord "banging on the ceiling with a broom" if the six members of her family made too much noise. Her parents have told their four children that they would eventually own their own home, and this promise gives them hope. Cisneros's book begins when the family has achieved its dream of home ownership. Then the author takes the difference between the American dream and its economic and social reality as the subject of her book.

Students should be aware that Cisneros and her young narrator are not identical. Cisneros has chosen the persona of a young girl to tell her stories, and this choice of first-person point of view adds considerable poignancy to her narratives. Reading "The House on Mango Street," we are aware that the (imaginary) narrator's naiveté is part of the emotional effect of what she tells us. We become emotionally involved in the story through her shy pride at moving into her "own" house on Mango Street, and through her confusion after she realizes that the dream house her parents have promised her isn't at all what she dreamed it would be.

We understand how important the house is to the narrator when she tells us about the apartment on Loomis where the family lived before moving to Mango Street. There a nun from her school made her "feel like nothing" by tactlessly wondering how her young pupil could live in a building that had been so brazenly burglarized. Yet among the descriptive details of the way the Loomis building looked, the narrator discloses that her father had nailed wooden bars on the windows of the family's third-floor apartment so that she and her brother Carlos and sister Nenny and the baby Kiki wouldn't fall out. The significance of this detail doesn't weigh as heavily on the narrator as her memory of her shame before the nun, but we register the father's concern for his young children's safety. There is little character description in Cisneros's stories, but the essential details giving coherence to the narrative are there.

Questions for Discussion

1. How does your awareness of the author's background help you to understand "The House on Mango Street"?
2. What clues does Cisneros give you to help you understand that she has created a fictional narrator in this story?
3. How does Cisneros's choice of a first-person narrator shape the way she tells her story?

Topics for Writing

2. **RESPONDING CREATIVELY** Write a sketch of your earliest memories of the home(s) you lived in as a young child.

Related Commentary

Marc Zimmerman, *U.S. Latino Literature: History and Development,* p. 1598.

Suggested Reading

Cisneros, Sandra. *Woman Hollering Creek.* New York: Random, 1991.

SAMUEL CLEMENS (MARK TWAIN)

The Celebrated Jumping Frog of Calaveras County (p. 333)

In this tall tale, Twain gently mocks the American literary genre of frontier humor. Alert readers encountering the story suspect that they are being mocked too, as Twain takes us by our noses and leads us into what R. V. Cassill calls "the maze of the entertainment."

This is a frame story, told to the narrator by "good-natured, garrulous old Simon Wheeler." Good-natured garrulousness permeates the tale, from its start in Wheeler's impartial admiration for the two con men and his deliberately block-ading the narrator in a corner so he'd be a captive audience for the "monotonous" and "interminable" tall tale, to its conclusion when the narrator politely but firmly refuses to listen to Wheeler's story about the one-eyed yellow cow with a tail "like a bannanner."

The story about the notorious jumping frog is neither "monotonous" nor "interminable," of course. Twain is playing with the oral tradition of storytelling here. We have all been bored by poor storytellers, but Simon Wheeler is a genius at spinning his yarns. His language abounds in figurative expressions, as well as a sense of his physical presence in his tone of voice and compulsion to buttonhole his listeners. In this short tale, Twain has caught the flavor of time and place in early California.

Questions for Discussion

1. During the course of Twain's classic short story, four different and distinct characters are described. Give a brief summary of each. How do their indi-vidual personalities contribute to the overall effectiveness of the story?
2. What is the general tone of this story, as revealed in the first paragraph?
3. What is ironic about describing Wheeler's account as "monotonous" and "interminable"? What is Twain's purpose in using such a description?
4. Note the animal imagery in the story. What contribution does it make to the total narrative?
5. What is ironic about the incident with Smiley's frog, Daniel Webster?
6. Twain appears to be mocking various factions of society here. How many can you identify? What was Twain's purpose in doing this? Would you say he was successful?

7. Carefully reread this story and discuss the elements that enable you to classify it as a tall tale, the variety of folktale that usually describes the deeds of a superhero.

Topics for Writing

1. Discuss the human tendency to be easily cheated or tricked as revealed in "The Celebrated Jumping Frog of Calaveras County."
2. Analyze levels of language as a representation of one's background and social class in this story.
3. What's the significance of the point of view in "The Celebrated Jumping Frog of Calaveras County"?
4. Discuss humor and irony in this tall tale.

Suggested Readings

Arnold, S. T., Jr. "Twain Bestiary: Mark Twain's Critters and the Tradition of Animal Portraiture in Humor of the Old Southwest." *Southern Folklore Quarterly* 41 (1977): 195–211.

Branch, E. M. "My Voice Is Still for Setchell: A Background Study of Jim Smiley and His Jumping Frog." *PMLA* 82 (1967): 591–601.

Cuff, Roger P. "Mark Twain's Use of California Folklore in His Jumping Frog Story." *Journal of American Folklore* 65 (1952): 155–58.

Rodgers, P. C., Jr. "Artemus Ward and Mark Twain's Jumping Frog." *Nineteenth Century Fiction* 28 (1973): 273–86.

JOSEPH CONRAD

Heart of Darkness (p. 339)

At the center of the concentric layers out of which Conrad constructs this story lies a case of atavism and the collapse of civilized morality. Kurtz casts aside all restraint and becomes as wild as his surroundings; or rather, the darkness around him calls out the darkness within his innermost being. Kurtz is a man of heroic abilities and exemplary ideals, yet at the end of the story, he explodes, unable to control his own strength.

Conrad does not provide an intimate inside view of Kurtz. To do so would destroy the aura of mystery and special significance that marks the story's theme as a profound revelation, the "culminating point of [Marlow's] experience," gained at "the farthest point of navigation." Instead, Conrad positions Kurtz in the midst of an impenetrable jungle, at "the very heart of darkness," as far from home and as remote from familiar frames of reference as possible. Then he causes the reader to approach Kurtz through a series of identifications that make the revelation of his debasement a statement not just about Kurtz, but about us all.

Conrad creates this effect mainly through his use of Marlow as narrator, and no discussion of the story can avoid exploring his function. He is on one hand a kind of prophet — his pose resembles that of an idol or Buddha — whose wisdom arises from his having looked beyond the veil that screens the truth from common view ("the inner truth is hidden — luckily, luckily"), and on the other hand an adventurer like the heroes of epic poems, descending into Hades and emerging shaken with his dark illumination. But Marlow's vision is neither of heaven nor of hell. His journey up the Congo River is in fact a descent into the inner reaches of the human soul. Forced by a combination of circumstances and preconceptions into a special association with Kurtz, Marlow recognizes in that "shadow" the intrinsic darkness of human nature, in which he shares. When he plunges into the jungle to redeem Kurtz, who has crawled away on all fours to rejoin the "unspeakable rites" of his worshipers, Marlow embraces what Kurtz has become no less than what he once was or might have been, acknowledging his own kinship with the deepest depravity. Kurtz dies crying, "The horror! The horror!" — apparently having regained from his rescuer enough of his moral bearings to recoil from his own behavior. Marlow, who judges the truth "too dark — too dark altogether," preserves the innocence of Kurtz's "Intended," leaving her "great and saving illusion" intact.

Conrad may be suggesting that only by a conscious lie or by willful blindness can we avoid sinking into the savagery that surrounds us, that dwells under externally maintained restraint within us, and that animates our civilization in various guises, such as the "flabby, pretending, weak-eyed devil of a rapacious and pitiless folly." The conquest of the earth, which is what the civilized society portrayed in the story is engaged in, "is not a pretty thing when you look into it too much," Marlow says. "What redeems it is the idea only . . . an unselfish belief in the idea — something you can set up, and bow down before, and offer sacrifice to." But such idolatry of our own idea is not far from its horrible perversion into the worship of himself that the would-be civilizer Kurtz sets up. It leads to a civilization aptly portrayed in Kurtz's symbolic painting of a blindfolded woman carrying a torch through darkness. If Conrad offers a glimmer of light in the dark world he envisions, it is in the sympathetic understanding that enables Marlow to befriend Kurtz and to lie for Kurtz and his Intended, even at the cost of having to taste the "flavor of mortality" he finds in lies, which he detests like the death it suggests to him.

WILLIAM E. SHEIDLEY

Questions for Discussion

1. What does Conrad gain by having his story told by Marlow to a group of important Londoners on a yacht in the Thames estuary? What is implied by the association of the Thames with the Congo? by Marlow's assertion, "And this also . . . has been one of the dark places on the earth"?

2. Marlow enters on his adventure through a city he associates with "a whited sepulcher"; he passes old women knitting who remind him of the Fates; the Company office is "as still as a house in a city of the dead." Locate other indications that Marlow's journey is like a trip into the underworld. What do they suggest about the story's meaning?

3. In what ways is the French warship "shelling the bush" an apt image of the European conquest of Africa? What does this historical theme contribute to our understanding of Marlow and Kurtz?

4. Discuss the Company's chief accountant. Why is it appropriate that Marlow first hears of Kurtz from him?
5. Marlow calls the men waiting for a post in the interior "pilgrims." Explain the irony in his use of the term.
6. Marlow is associated with Kurtz as a member of "the gang of virtue." Explain the resonance of that phrase.
7. Describe the journey up the Congo as Marlow reports it in the pages that follow his remark, "Going up that river was like traveling back to the earliest beginnings of the world." In what ways does Conrad make it a symbolic journey as well as an actual one?
8. Discuss Marlow's attitudes toward the natives. What do they mean to him?
9. As the boat draws near Kurtz's station, people cry out "with unrestrained grief" from the jungle. Why?
10. After the attack of the natives is repulsed and the narrative seems at the point of reaching the climax toward which so much suspense has been built — the meeting with Kurtz — Conrad throws it away by having Marlow stop to light his pipe and speak offhandedly and abstractly about what he learned. Why? Does this passage actually destroy the suspense? Is the story rendered anticlimactic? Or is the climax changed? What is the true climax of the story?
11. Why do you think the heads on stakes are facing Kurtz's house?
12. Discuss the Russian and his attitude toward Kurtz. Why does Conrad trouble to add this European to Kurtz's train of cultists?
13. Marlow is astonished that the Manager calls Kurtz's methods "unsound." Why? What does this passage reveal about each of them?
14. Explain what happens to Marlow when he goes into the bush after Kurtz. Explain what happens to Kurtz. Why does Marlow call Kurtz "that shadow"?
15. Marlow claims to have "struggled with a soul"; he tells Kurtz that if he does not come back he will be "utterly lost." Is Marlow a savior for Kurtz? Is Kurtz saved?
16. Why does Marlow lie to Kurtz's "Intended"?
17. Contrast the last paragraph of the story with the opening.
18. Comment on the title of Kurtz's pamphlet, about the "Suppression of Savage Customs," and on the significance of its scrawled postscript, "Exterminate all the brutes."

Topics for Writing

1. In an essay, explore Conrad's use of foreshadowing.
2. Discuss traditional symbolism and literary allusion as a way of universalizing the theme of "Heart of Darkness."
3. Analyze the function of the frame in this novella.
4. Marlow frequently concludes a segment of his narrative with a generalization that sums it up and takes on a quality of special significance, such as, "I felt as though, instead of going to the center of a continent, I were about to set off for the center of the earth"; or, "It was like a weary pilgrimage among hints for nightmares." Locate as many such passages as you can. What do they reveal about the mind of the narrator?
5. Conrad frequently uses an impressionist technique that Ian Watt has called "delayed decoding." When the steamboat is attacked, for example, Marlow first sees "little sticks" flying about, and only later recognizes them as ar-

rows. Find other instances of delayed decoding in the story, and then write a narrative of your own using a similar method.
6.   **CONNECTIONS**   Analyze the journey into madness in Conrad's "Heart of Darkness" and Gilman's "The Yellow Wallpaper."

Related Commentaries

Chinua Achebe, An Image of Africa: Conrad's "Heart of Darkness," p. 1447.
Edward Said, The Past and the Present: Joseph Conrad and the Fiction of Autobiography, p. 1572.
Lionel Trilling, The Greatness of Conrad's "Heart of Darkness," p. 1587.

Suggested Readings

Bender, Todd K. *Concordances to Conrad's "The Shadow Line" and "Youth": A Narrative.* New York: Garland, 1980.
Bennett, Carl D. *Joseph Conrad.* New York: Continuum, 1991.
Berthoud, Jacques. *Joseph Conrad: The Major Phase.* New York: Cambridge UP, 1978. 41–63.
Billy, Ted. *Critical Essays on Joseph Conrad.* Boston: G. K. Hall, 1987.
Cohen, Michael. "Sailing through *The Secret Sharer:* The End of Conrad's Story." *Studies in English* 10.2 (Fall 1988): 102–09.
Conrad, Joseph. *Heart of Darkness: An Authoritative Text, Backgrounds and Sources, Criticism.* Ed. Robert Kimbrough. Rev. ed. New York: Norton, 1971.
———. *Portable Conrad.* New York: Penguin, 1991.
Gekoski, R. A. *Conrad: The Moral World of the Novelist.* New York: Barnes, 1978. 72–90.
Gillon, Adam. *Joseph Conrad.* Boston: Twayne, 1982.
Graver, Lawrence. *Conrad's Short Fiction.* Berkeley: U of California P, 1969.
Hynes, Samuel, ed. *The Complete Short Fiction of Joseph Conrad. The Stories, Volume I.* New York: Ecco, 1991.
Page, Norman. *A Conrad Companion.* New York: St. Martin's, 1986.

JULIO CORTÁZAR

A Continuity of Parks (p. 402)

Students may be familiar with the kind of geometric drawings that present a pattern of lines that seem to create a perfectly logical form, except that the lines overlap and appropriate each other's space, resulting in a seemingly normal drawing of a physical impossibility. Cortázar's story has the same quality of a logical and reasonable appearance that turns itself inside out in the final lines of the story. A character from a book that a man has been reading suddenly turns up behind him in the room, poised to stab him to death. Since it seems to be a human instinct to try to "understand" any story we read, we make an effort to understand Cortázar's conundrum.

In the beginning of the story it is clear that the man is reading a novel. We are given the details about his reading, and we are told that "word by word" he has been "caught up in the sordid dilemma of the hero and heroine." Then the characters begin to take on a life of their own, and we are presented with a love scene with imprecise implications. As the love scene ends, the man who has been presented to us as a character in a novel leaves on a mission that has been described for him by the woman. Then, in a twist of reality, we are told in the final sentence of the story that his mission is to kill the man who sits reading. The opening of the story cannot be reasonable if that is its ending. Cortázar has presented us with the verbal equivalent of the geometric drawing that seems reasonable, but leaves us with an object that has no rational equivalent.

The student may ask why Cortázar has chosen to present us with this puzzle. On a direct and immediate level he could be showing us how powerfully we react to stories — so powerfully the characters can seem to come alive for us. Since the beginning of his career, however, Cortázar has again and again confronted his readers with the ambiguity of writing itself, teasing us for our insistence on trying to "understand" a story, even when there is nothing on the page but words and scenes that the writer can manipulate at will. In his first novel, the modernist classic *Hopscotch*, the chapters are deliberately left in no rational order, only listed in possible combinations at the end of the book, so the reader is forced to hop from one chapter to another. "A Continuity of Parks" could be read as a literary exercise that the author has deliberately created to emphasize his point. The story also could serve as a demonstration of "modernist" literary theory. If the student is interested in contemporary modernist stories, there are further examples in the text by Allen, Barth, Borges, and Calvino.

Questions for Discussion

1. Is there any way this story might be explained on a logical basis?
2. Is it true that readers can lose themselves so deeply in a book that they begin to believe that the characters have a life of their own?
3. What is the last reference the author makes to the fact that the man is reading a book?
4. What kind of story does the author suggest that the novel describes?
5. Why does he say "and underneath liberty pounded"?
6. Why does the killer expect the dogs to be silent and the estate manager to be away? How does he know how to find his way through the house?
7. Have both fictional characters now begun to direct the story themselves?

Topics for Writing

1. **CONNECTIONS**   Compare this story with another of the modernist stories in the anthology and discuss their similarities and their differences.
2. Examine the aesthetic and historical basis of modernist writing through a study of source material from your college library.

Suggested Readings

Alazraki, Jaime, and Ivar Ivask, eds. *The Final Island: The Fiction of Julio Cortázar.* Norman: U of Oklahoma P, 1978.

Cortázar, Julio. *Around the Day in Eighty Worlds.* Trans. Thomas Christensen. San Francisco: North Point, 1986. Esp. 17–23, 158–67.

———. *Blow Up and Other Stories.* London: Panther, 1967.

———. *Unreasonable Hours.* Trans. Alberto Manguel. Toronto: Coach House, 1995.

Stephen Crane

The Open Boat (p. 405)

Crane's story fictionalizes an actual experience. A correspondent himself, Crane happened to be aboard the *Commodore* when it went down, and he included in his newspaper report of the event this passage (as quoted by E. R. Hagemann):

> The history of life in an open boat for thirty hours would no doubt be instructive for the young, but none is to be told here now. For my part I would prefer to tell the story at once, because from it would shine the splendid manhood of Captain Edward Murphy and of William Higgins, the oiler, but let it suffice at this time to say that when we were swamped in the surf and making the best of our way toward the shore the captain gave orders amid the wildness of the breakers as clearly as if he had been on the quarter deck of a battleship.

It is good that Crane did not write "at once" but let his experience take shape as a work of art which, instead of celebrating the "splendid manhood" of two or four individuals, recognizes a profound truth about human life in general — about the puniness of humankind in the face of an indifferent nature and about the consequent value of the solidarity and compassion that arise from an awareness of our common fate. Crane's meditation on his experience "after the fact" enables him to become not simply a reporter but, as he puts it in the last line of the story, an *interpreter* of the message spoken to us by the world we confront.

Crane portrays the exertions of the four men in the boat without glamorizing them. His extended and intimate account of their hard work and weariness wrings out any false emotion from the reader's view of the situation. By varying the narrative point of view from a coolly detached objective observer to a plural account of all four men's shared feelings and perceptions to the correspondent's rueful, self-mocking cogitations, Crane defeats our impulse to choose a hero for adulation, at the same time driving home the point that the condition of the men in the dinghy — their longing, their fear, and their powerlessness before nature and destiny — reflects our own. By the end, what has been revealed is so horrible that there can be no triumph in survival. The good fortune of a rescue brings only a reprieve, not an escape from what awaits us. Billie the oiler drowns, but there is no reason it should have been he, or only he. His death could be anybody's death.

Crane's narration builds suspense through rhythmic repetition, foreshadowing, and irony. We hear the surf periodically: Our hopes for rescue are repeatedly raised and dashed; night follows day, wave follows wave, and the endless struggle goes on. The correspondent's complaint against the cruelty of fate recurs in diminuendo, with less whimsy and self-consciousness each time.

These recurrences mark the men's changes in attitude — from the egocentric viewpoint they start with, imagining that the whole world is watching them and working for their survival, to the perception of the utter indifference of nature with which the story ends. Some stages in this progression include their false sense of security when they light up the cigars; their isolation from the people on shore, epitomized by their inability to interpret the signal of the man waving his coat (whose apparent advice to try another stretch of beach they nonetheless inadvertently follow); their experience of aloneness at night; their confrontation with the hostility of nature in the shark; and, finally, their recognition that death might be a welcome release from toil and suffering. They respond by drawing together in a communion that sustains them, sharing their labor and their body heat, huddled together in their tiny, helpless dinghy. Even their strong bond of comradeship, however, cannot withstand the onslaught of the waves. When the boat is swamped, it is every man for himself: Each individual must face death alone. Because of the fellowship that has grown up among them, however, when Billie dies, each of the others feels the oiler's death as his own. The reader, whom Crane's narrative has caused to share thirty hours at sea in an open boat, may recognize the implication in what is spoken by "the sound of the great sea's voice to the men on shore."

WILLIAM E. SHEIDLEY

Questions for Discussion

1. Contrast the imagery and the tone of the first paragraph with those of the second. Why does Crane continually seek to magnify nature and to belittle the men who are struggling with it? Find other instances of Crane's reductive irony, and discuss their effects.
2. How does Crane convey the men's concentration on keeping the boat afloat?
3. Explain Crane's use of the word "probably" in the first paragraph of section II.
4. Why does the seagull seem "somehow gruesome and ominous" to the men in the boat? Compare and contrast the seagull with the shark that appears later.
5. Comment on the imagery Crane uses to describe changing seats in the dinghy (stealing eggs, Sèvres).
6. What is it that the correspondent "knew even at the time was the best experience of his life"? Why is it the best?
7. What is the purpose of Crane's understatement in the line "neither the oiler nor the correspondent was fond of rowing at this time"?
8. What is the effect on the reader of the men's lighting up cigars?
9. Discuss the meaning of the correspondent's question "Was I brought here merely to have my nose dragged away as I was about to nibble the sacred cheese of life?"
10. What do you think the man waving a coat means? Why is it impossible for him to communicate with the men in the boat?
11. "A night on the sea in an open boat is a long night," says Crane. How does he make the reader feel the truth of that assertion?

12. At one point the correspondent thinks that he is "the one man afloat on all the oceans." Explain that sensation. Why does the wind he hears sound "sadder than the end"? Why does he later wish he had known the captain was awake when the shark came by?
13. Why does the correspondent have a different attitude toward the poem about the dying soldier in Algiers from the one he had as a boy?
14. Examine the third paragraph of section VII. How important are the thoughts of the correspondent to our understanding of the story? What would the story lose if they were omitted? What would the effect of this passage have been if Crane had narrated the story in the first person? If he had made these comments in the voice of an omniscient third-person narrator?
15. Define the correspondent's physical, mental, and emotional condition during his final moments on the boat and during his swim to the beach.
16. Characterize and explain the tone of Crane's description of the man who pulls the castaways from the sea.
17. Why does Crane make fun of the women who bring coffee to the survivors?

Topics for Writing

1. Consider Crane's handling of point of view in "The Open Boat."
2. Discuss the importance of repetition in Crane's narrative.
3. Analyze imagery as a key to tone in "The Open Boat."
4. After reading the story once rapidly, read it again with a pencil in hand, marking every simile and metaphor. Then sort them into categories. What realms of experience does Crane bring into view through these devices that are not actually part of the simple boat-sea-sky-beach world in which the story is set? Why?
5. **RESPONDING CREATIVELY**   Write an eyewitness account of some experience you have undergone that would be suitable for newspaper publication. Then note the changes you would make to turn it into a fictional narrative with broader or more profound implications — or write that story.

Related Commentary

Stephen Crane, The Sinking of the *Commodore*, p. 1482.

Suggested Readings

Adams, Richard P. "Naturalistic Fiction: 'The Open Boat.' " *Stephen Crane's Career: Perspectives and Evaluations.* Ed. Thomas A. Gullason. New York: New York UP, 1972. 421–29. Originally published in *Tulane Studies in English* 4 (1954): 137–46.

Cady, Edwin H. *Stephen Crane.* Twayne's United States Authors Series 23. Rev. ed. Boston: G. K. Hall, 1980. 150–54.

Colvert, James B. *Stephen Crane.* New York: Ungar, 1987.

Follett, Wilson, ed. *The Work of Stephen Crane.* New York: Knopf, 1925.

Fryckstedt, O. W., ed. *Stephen Crane: Uncollected Writings.* Uppsala: Studia Anglistica Upsaliensia, 1963.

Hagemann, E. R. "'Sadder Than the End': Another Look at 'The Open Boat.'" *Stephen Crane in Transition: Centenary Essays.* Ed. Joseph Katz. DeKalb: Northern Illinois UP, 1972. 66–85.

Johnson, Glen M. "Stephen Crane." *American Short-Story Writers, 1880–1910. Dictionary of Literary Biography,* vol. 78. Detroit: Gale, 1989.

Katz, Joseph, ed. *The Portable Stephen Crane.* New York: Viking, 1985.

Kissane, Leedice. "Interpretation through Language: A Study of the Metaphors in Stephen Crane's 'The Open Boat.'" Gullason, cited above. 410–16. Originally published in *Rendezvous* (Idaho State U) 1 (1966): 18–22.

Knapp, Bettina L. *Stephen Crane.* New York: Ungar, 1987.

Stallman, R. W. *Stephen Crane: A Critical Bibliography.* Ames: Iowa State UP, 1972.

———. *Stories and Tales/Stephen Crane.* New York: Vintage, 1955.

Wolford, Chester L. *Stephen Crane: A Study of the Short Fiction.* Boston: Twayne, 1989.

EDWIDGE DANTICAT

Night Women (p. 424)

This powerful story is a complex portrait of a woman whom we would consider to be a prostitute but who justifies her way of life to herself by using the word *lovers* for the two men who visit her regularly and pay her for their nights together and objectifies her casual customers with the word *suitors.* The subject of the story, however, is her relationship with her young son, the child of one of her lovers, "who disappeared with the night's shadows a long time ago." The boy lives with her in a one-room shack and sleeps on a mat in the corner. At night he wraps her blood-red scarf around his neck so that he will have something of hers with him when his eyes close. There is the low buzz of the transistor radio he plugs into his ears as he sleeps. It was the gift of a lover who wanted him to continue sleeping while his mother, in her word, "worked."

Although the woman in the story is without education, the author presents her as describing herself in a language that has none of the educational deficiencies we would expect from someone caught in her life. Danticat has convinced us that the woman experiences what is happening to her in rich, vivid imagery, and the story is told as an expression of this inner consciousness. It is as though instead of listening to her speak, we are hearing her thoughts, and what we hear is the partly real, partly dreamed record of everything the woman is feeling and seeing as she perceives it — not as she would struggle to tell it in any ordinary way of speaking. The woman says of herself in the story's second sentence, "I feel as bare as open flesh," and the phrase convinces us. The second paragraph is a startling image of the shadows that move on the wall as her boy goes to bed on his mat. The light stretches his shadow until he becomes man-sized, and then he sleeps. She tells us, in another vivid image, about her son's face in the mornings when he wakens. He has learned to slap the mosquitoes in his sleep: "In the morning he will have bloody spots on his forehead, as though he had spent the whole night kissing a woman with wide-open flesh wounds on her face." Danticat has presented her so powerfully that we accept the levels of symbolism in her narrative.

Students reading the story quickly might not notice what the woman tells us in her description of her son's sleep: "He shifts his small body carefully so as not to crease his Sunday clothes." It is this detail, however, that is the most touching of the complicated revelations she presents to us about her way of life. To justify the fact that she is still dressed and wearing make-up when he goes to sleep, she has told him that angels come to them in the night, and that he must be dressed in his best clothes, as she is, to be ready for them. If he wakes when she is with a customer she will tell him that it was only a mirage that he saw, and when he is older she will tell him that it was an angel. "I will tell him that his father has come, that an angel brought him back from heaven for awhile."

In the morning, when she wakes him, his first words are, "Mommy, have I missed the angels again?" Perhaps it is a dream fantasy that she half-believes herself. It is clear that because the woman's daily reality is so despairing, she retreats into a world of dreams. She is conscious that the boy will grow older, and the stories she tells him will no longer be believed, but when the morning comes and she slips into the boy's bed to sleep for a moment beside him, we understand that the moment itself is the only future she will allow herself. Danticat's portrait stirs our heart, and it is unforgettable.

Questions for Discussion

1. What are the two kinds of women the central character in the story finds in the world? What is the difference she sees between herself and these other women?
2. Why does she choose not to tell her boy about love?
3. What is she telling us about the prostitutes of Ville Rose in the image beginning "they ride the crests"?
4. What is the implication of her phrase "mountain stories"?
5. She describes women in the night undoing patches of cloth that they spent the day weaving. What classical reference comes to mind with this image? Is it this allusion the woman is making, or do we suspect that the classic tale has become a part of folk legend?
6. The country of the story is Haiti, which means the language is French. As the boy falls asleep she hears him singing a song she calls "Kompe Jako." What is the title as we know it? What does the linguistic shift tell us about the boy's school?
7. What do the stars seen through the holes in her roof represent? Why don't the suitors want the holes to be fixed?

Topics for Writing

1. Discuss the deception the woman practices with her son and decide if it is justified.
2. List some of the woman's most striking figures of speech and discuss their meaning in terms of her life. How is this use of language justified in the story?
3. Many of the details of the story relate to its setting in Haiti. Could the story have been set in some other country? Why or why not?
4. Some of the woman's expressions and attitudes have obvious roots in her native folk culture. Discuss their meaning in terms of her everyday life.
5. As the story ends the woman watches other women going to work in a factory and says to herself, "I thank the stars that at least I have the days to myself." Comment on what this tells us about the woman.

Suggested Reading

Danticat, Edwidge, ed. *The Beacon Best of 2000: Great Writing by Women and Men of All Colors*. Boston: Beacon, 2000.

Junot Díaz

The Sun, the Moon, the Stars (p. 428)

Junot Díaz is one of a young generation of talented writers who are giving us a clear insight into the realities of American life today as they are experienced by an immigrant who has only partially completed the inevitable assimilation process. The protagonist of his story still thinks in Spanish, and there is a strong emotional attachment to his old home in Santo Domingo. Díaz himself is of Dominican background, and there is much in the story that can be read as autobiographical. Some students may be familiar with other examples of writing in this particularly American genre. For several generations there have been American writers who have written about these shared perceptions of their immigrant experience, although the racial and cultural backgrounds are dissimilar. For many readers the example that will come immediately to mind is the American Jewish community, with authors like I. B. Singer, Henry Roth, Saul Bellow, and Philip Roth. Gifted authors from countries such as Ireland, Italy, Great Britain, and Spain have also contributed their voice to this strong chorus. All of them, like Díaz, colored their narratives with expressions from their native language, and for most of them their subject was their struggle to fit themselves into the new personality that the experience in the new homeland was steadily creating, whether or not they were conscious of the changes taking place within themselves. Often their narratives were a response to something that was entirely ordinary within the American context but, as virtual outsiders, seemed to be invested with a much larger significance.

Like many of these narratives Díaz's story is, on its surface, simple and uncomplicated, but as students look at it more closely they will see that it inevitably finds its themes within the larger frame of experience. The narrator of the story, who is never named, realizes that he has fallen in love with a woman with whom he has been having a physical relationship. They met when they were both students at Rutgers, the New Jersey university across the river from New York City, but that is all we are told about him, and we learn only little more about the woman. As the result of a casual infidelity on his part she has decided to end their relationship, but she agrees to go with him back to his family's home in the Dominican Republic for a short vacation. From what we are told about the relationship it seems that she only agreed to the trip because it was something they had planned when she still was emotionally involved with him, and she has decided she wants a vacation.

There are no complications in the presentation of the story — the trip is a fiasco and their relationship ends, just as the reader expects. It is in the story's subtext, however, that students will find the larger themes of assimilation and racial stereotyping that give the story narrative weight. The narrator refers to himself several times as a "nigger," and she is described as an "octoroon." An octoroon is a person of mixed race who is one-eighth black. She is, in other words, much lighter-skinned than he is. This has been a recurring theme in the various literatures of the African diaspora — the tension between dark-skinned men and light-skinned women. The tension here is palpable, particularly when they travel to the Dominican Republic, where with her light skin she is an immediate object of interest for every man they encounter.

What is even more evident in the tensions between them is a social difference that in their first attraction to each other hadn't seemed as crucial. We are told she has Cuban relatives, and although her father works as a baker and her mother sells children's clothing door to door, her parents live in a house, and they clearly consider themselves part of the middle class. They have taken many more steps along the path to assimilation than the young man, who finds himself suspended between his affection for the life he knows from Santo Domingo and the uncertainties of his new life in New York. All of their differences become glaringly obvious when she finds herself confronted with his relative lack of sophistication. She moves steadily away from him, changing her style of dress and makeup and turning more and more to a group of women friends who shun him, just as his friends are hostile to her. The tensions that are present in the story's underlying themes should be immediately obvious.

As an example of this literary genre, however, the story does present some problems in interpretation. One characteristic of such narratives is that the protagonist generally seems conscious of his or her predicament. Díaz's young man, however, seems oblivious of anything other than his obsessive sexuality. Díaz has also created some uncertainty in the mind of the reader through the melding of vocabulary and incident. His young man sometimes expresses himself in coarse street dialect and sometimes in grammar and diction that seem advanced, even for someone with a Rutgers background. He does not seem to be conscious of his own racial attitudes or the effects of his crude insensitivity not only toward women, but toward the realities of everyday life. It is left to the reader to decide who the young man is and how to respond to his story.

Questions for Discussion

1. In the usual sense of the word *plot,* the story seems to revolve around the young woman's response to the man's act of infidelity. By the end of the story do you still feel that this is the motivation for her decision to end the relationship?
2. How would you describe the function of "his boys" and "her girls" in the story? What do they represent to the protagonists?
3. What does the man mean by the phrase "She Bartlebys me," and how does this phrase fit into the context of his presentation of himself? Is it what we would expect?
4. His reaction to Santo Domingo as they drive from the airport seems to be strongly negative, but he also feels a strong emotional attachment to the streets and the neighborhoods where he grew up. How is this conflict resolved in his conduct toward her, and what does it tell us about him?
5. The young man obviously has no difficulty with money, but we are never told that he works or anything about his family. What can we infer about his circumstances? Has the author given us enough information to make a decision?

6.   Does this story depend on its setting in New York City for its sense of versimilitude, or could it take place in any large American city?

Topics for Writing

1.   The syntax of the story is weighted with many contemporary colloquialisms. Some examples are: "real fly," "chill," "nerd," "a done deal," "homegirl," "knickknacks." Discuss whether these terms will present difficulties for future readers or whether they help lend the story a stronger sense of versimilitude.
2.   The author's linguistic idiom sometimes seems to present contradictions, and the young man, who generally expresses himself in street obscenities, at one point tells us that the woman was not "too hot on the rapprochement at first, but I had the momentum of the past on my side." Discuss his use of the term "rapprochement" here, and relate it to what we have been told about him.
3.   **CONNECTIONS**   Discuss the racial attitudes that we can infer from the man's comments on the woman's skin color and his own background. Develop this discussion with a comparison to another story in the collection that also presents the American racial dilemma, such as Charles Chesnutt's "The Wife of His Youth." (p. 312)
4.   Discuss this story in the context of other immigrant literature and the themes of assimilation and loss of identity.

Suggested Reading

Díaz, Junot. *Drown*. New York: Riverhead, 1996.

ISAK DINESEN

Sorrow-Acre (p. 440)

Readers of the great stories by Isak Dinesen generally are aware that in her everyday life she was the Baroness Karen Blixen-Finecke. She was born into an old Danish aristocratic family but spent almost twenty years as the struggling owner of a primitive coffee plantation in the newly colonized British East African territory of Kenya, living in semi-isolation with a drunken, unfaithful husband who infected her with an incurable case of syphilis. The inherent conflicts in her situation could have silenced her, but instead the African years only intensified her identification with her earlier background and deepened the insights she brought to her writing when she turned to this material for her subjects. It is difficult to imagine that someone who was not of "noble birth" could have understood the complex issues that are represented on the day she describes, as the peasant woman struggles to fulfill the inhuman test the old lord has devised for her.

One characteristic of short stories is that they're short, and often their theme is a momentary illumination, but in this story we are presented with a larger setting. It is a measure of Dinesen's genius that she is able to present us with a serious debate about the feudal system in the complex unfolding of her story. In the silence of the peasants crowding after the woman as she works and in the tense argument between the two men looking on we sense that the system, as the older man knows it, soon will come to an end. The epiphany of the story — another measure of Dinesen's achievement — is intellectual and philosophical. The old lord, whom the young man had grown up admiring, has caused the death of the peasant woman with a challenge he set almost as a whim. The peasants who followed her all day under the hot sun, refusing to do their own work, who comforted her and gave her water but did nothing to interfere with the conditions the lord had set for her to save her son, turn to him silently after her death, and it is clear that nothing in the complex relationship between lord and servant will be the same again. The reader understands that in some real way the older man's life has ended at the same moment.

Although there may have been many local incidents like this in other countries of Europe as the old system was breaking down, there is much about this story that is intensely Danish. Students who have visited Denmark will be familiar with the gentle flatness of its fields and the soft golden sun of its summer days. There is also something quintessentially Danish in the character of the old man and his younger relative and in the attitudes of the watching peasants. There is a stubborn reasonableness to the Danish character that can quickly change into fixed attitudes that are just as unreasonable. The author not only knows her country's land and its history; the people themselves, in all their contradictions, are as close to her. This story lingers in the reader's mind long after the day it describes has passed.

Questions for Discussion

1. We understand from the references in the story that it is set in the years 1775–1776. Is this important to our understanding of the story?
2. The author tells us that language is inadequate to describe the timeless life of the countryside. Why does she suggest that there are things that can't be described? What kinds of things could they be?
3. What is the author telling us in the sentence "A child of the country would read this open landscape like a book"?
4. Although in the feudal system the peasant is a bound servant of the lord of the manor, is the manor also part of this landscape, like the cottages of the peasants?
5. What is the significance of the attitude of the king that it made no difference which individual occupied the manor house? What does that tell us about the feudal system?
6. What is the paradox of the woman's role in the manor house, as it is described in the story? Is there anything similar to this in American history of this period?
7. The young man has been changed by his experience in England. What is it there that has changed him?
8. What allows the lord to set the test for the woman? Why doesn't he simply free the boy?

Topics for Writing

1. Although Danish was Dinesen's first language, she wrote her stories in English. Comment on the syntax and the vocabulary of this story, paying special attention to any elements that might suggest that English is a second language for her.
2. Discuss the nature of the feudal contract as we see it worked out in the field on the day this story takes place.
3. Discuss the image of America in European society at this time, and compare it to the image of America in today's more complex world.
4. In his conversation with the young man the lord explains why the boy is so important to the woman: "He means to her her daily bread and support in old age." Discuss the implication of this statement and comment on its relevance or lack of relevance to modern social structures.

Suggested Readings

Dinesen, Isak. *Winter's Tales.* New York: Random, 1942, 1970.
Hannah, Donald. "In Memoriam Karen Blixen: Some Aspects of Her Attitude to Life." *Sewanee Review* 71 (1963): 585–604.
Landry, M. "Anecdote as Destiny: Isak Dinesen and the Story-Teller." *Massachusetts Review* 19 (1978): 389–406.

RALPH ELLISON

Battle Royal (p. 464)

In the headnote to his comments on "Battle Royal" reprinted in Part Two (p. 1486), Ellison is quoted expounding on the importance of "converting experience into symbolic action" in fiction. One of the major triumphs of "Battle Royal" (and of *Invisible Man* as a whole) is Ellison's success in the realistic rendering of experiences that are in themselves so obviously significant of larger social, psychological, and moral truths that explication is unnecessary. From the small American flag tattooed on the nude dancer's belly to the "rope of bloody saliva forming a shape like an undiscovered continent" that the narrator drools on his new briefcase, Ellison's account of the festivities at the men's smoker effectively symbolizes the condition of blacks in America while remaining thoroughly persuasive in its verisimilitude. Both the broader structure of the evening and the finer details of narration and description carry the force of Ellison's theme. The young blacks are tortured first by having the most forbidden of America's riches dangled before them, then by being put through their paces in a melee in which their only victims are their fellows and the whites look on with glee, and finally by being debased into groveling for money (some of it counterfeit) on a rug whose electrification underlines their own powerlessness. In one brief passage, the nightmare of such an existence appears in a strange subaqueous vision of primitive life: "The boys groped about like blind, cautious crabs crouching to protect their midsections, their heads pulled in short against their shoulders, their arms stretched nervously before them, with their fists testing the smoke-filled air like the knobbed feelers of hypersensitive snails."

Because his actual experience forms itself into such revealing images, the narrator's dream of his grandfather seems all the more credible as a statement of his position. "Keep This Nigger-Boy Running," he dreams the message of his brief-case says — not far from "You've got to know your place at all times." The narrator's grandfather knew his place and played his role, but he never believed a word of it. It is this assurance of an inner being quite different from the face he turned toward the world that makes him so troubling to his descendants. In his effort to please the white folks and in so doing to get ahead, the narrator seeks alliance rather than secret enmity with his antagonists. As a result he subjects himself to the trickery and delusions the white community chooses to impose on him. Dependent for his sense of himself on his ability to guess what they want him to do, the narrator finds himself groping in a fog deeper than the swirls of cigar smoke that hang over the scene of the battle royal. When the smoke clears and the blindfold comes off, he will recognize, as he puts it at the start, that he is invisible to the whites and may therefore discover his own identity within himself.

The first episode of a long novel does not accomplish the narrator's enlightenment, but it constitutes his initiation into the realities of the world he must eventually come to understand. Ellison says (in the Commentary in Part Two, p. 1486) that the battle royal "is a ritual in preservation of caste lines, a keeping of taboo to appease the gods and ward off bad luck," and that "it is also the initiation ritual to which all greenhorns are subjected." This rite of initiation bears a revealing relation to the primitive initiation ceremonies known to anthropologists. The battle royal, for example, separates the boys from their families, challenges them to prove their valor, and subjects them to instruction by the tribal elders in a sort of men's house. The boys are stripped and introduced to sexual mysteries. But the hazing of women that is a frequent feature of such initiations is not carried on here by the boys but by the gross elders, whose savagery is barely under control; the ritual ends not with the entry of the initiates into the larger community but with their pointed exclusion; and the sacred lore embodied in the narrator's recital of his graduation speech makes explicit the contradictions inherent in the society it describes. To cast down his bucket where he is forces him to swallow his own blood. The narrator is delighted with the scholarship to "the state college for Negroes" that he wins by toeing the line and knowing his place, and he does not object that the "gold" coins he groveled for are fraudulent. His education in the meaning of his grandfather's troubling injunctions will continue, but the reader has already seen enough to recognize their validity.

WILLIAM E. SHEIDLEY

Questions for Discussion

1. In the opening paragraph the narrator says, "I was naive." In what ways is his naiveté revealed in the story that follows?
2. Why does the narrator feel guilty when praised?
3. What is the message to the narrator behind the suggestion "that since I was to be there anyway I might as well take part in the battle royal"? Explain his hesitation. What is the most important part of the evening for the whites?
4. Who is present at the smoker? Discuss the role of the school superintendent.

5.   What techniques does Ellison use to convey to the reader the impact that seeing the stripper has on the boys?
6.   What does the stripper have in common with the boys? Why are both a stripper and a battle royal part of the evening's entertainment?
7.   During the chaos of the battle, the narrator worries about how his speech will be received. Is that absurd or understandable?
8.   Does the deathbed advice of the narrator's grandfather offer a way to handle the battle royal?
9.   Why does Tatlock refuse to take a dive?
10. Explain the narrator's first reaction to seeing the "small square rug." In what sense is his instinct correct?
11. What is the meaning of the electric rug to the whites? What do they wish it to demonstrate to the blacks?
12. Explain Mr. Colcord's reaction when the narrator tries to topple him onto the rug.
13. Analyze the narrator's speech. What is the implication of his having to deliver it while swallowing his own blood?
14. Why is the school superintendent confident that the narrator will "lead his people in the proper paths"?
15. Why does the narrator stand in front of his grandfather's picture holding his briefcase? Who gets the better of this confrontation?

Topics for Writing

1.   Make a study of seeing and understanding in "Battle Royal."
2.   Analyze the role of sex, violence, and power in Ellison's "Battle Royal."
3.   Write an essay exploring the battle royal and black experience in America.
4.   Describe the "permanent interest" of "Battle Royal." (See Ellison's Commentary in Part Two, p. 1486.)
5.   Examine the blonde, the gold coins, and the calfskin briefcase in "Battle Royal."
6.   Select a passage of twenty lines or less from this story for detailed explication. Relate as many of its images as possible to others in the story and to the general ideas that the story develops. To what extent does the passage you chose reflect the meaning of the story as a whole?
7.   **RESPONDING CREATIVELY**   Recall an experience in which you were humiliated or embarrassed. What motives of your own and of those before whom you were embarrassed put you in such a position? Narrate the incident so these underlying purposes become evident to the reader.
8.   **RESPONDING CREATIVELY**   Write a description of a game or ceremony with which you are familiar. What set of principles or relationships (not necessarily malign) does it express?

Related Commentary

Ralph Ellison, The Influence of Folklore on "Battle Royal," p. 1486.

Suggested Readings

Blake, Susan L. "Ritual and Rationalization: Black Folklore in the Works of Ralph Ellison." *PMLA* 94 (1979): 121–26, esp. 122–23.

Horowitz, Ellin. "The Rebirth of the Artist." *Twentieth-Century Interpretations of Invisible Man.* Ed. John M. Reilly. Englewood Cliffs, NJ: Prentice, 1970. 80–88, esp. 81. (Originally published in 1964.)

O'Meally, Robert G. *The Craft of Ralph Ellison.* Cambridge, MA: Harvard UP, 1980. 12–14.

Vogler, Thomas A. "*Invisible Man:* Somebody's Protest Novel." *Ralph Ellison: A Collection of Critical Essays.* Ed. John Hersey. Englewood Cliffs, NJ: Prentice, 1974. 127–50, esp. 143–44.

LOUISE ERDRICH

The Red Convertible (p. 475)

The story takes place in 1974, when Henry Junior comes back to the Chippewa Indian reservation after more than three years as a soldier in Vietnam. He is mentally disturbed by his experiences in the war, and, as his brother Lyman (who narrates the story) says laconically, "the change was no good."

Erdrich has structured her story in a traditional manner. It is narrated in the first person by Lyman, who uses the past tense to describe the finality of what happened to his brother and the red Oldsmobile convertible they once shared. The plot moves conventionally, after a lengthy introduction giving the background of the two brothers and their pleasure in the car. They are Indians who work hard for what they earn, but they also enjoy their money. As Lyman says, "We went places in that car, me and Henry." An atmosphere of innocence pervades this part of the story. They enjoy sightseeing along the western highways, going when and where they please, spending an entire summer in Alaska after they drive a female hitchhiker with long, beautiful hair home.

The story moves forward chronologically (although it is told as a flashback after the opening frame of four paragraphs), organized in sections usually several paragraphs long. Its structure is as loose and comfortable as the brothers' relationship. Then, midway, the story darkens when Henry goes off to Vietnam. For three sections, Lyman describes Henry's disorientation after the war. Then Henry fixes the convertible, the boys get back behind the wheel, and it seems briefly as if the good times are again starting to roll. But Henry feels internal turmoil similar to that of the flooded river they park alongside. The story reaches its climax when Henry suddenly goes wild after drinking several beers, deteriorating into what he calls a "crazy Indian." Lyman stares after him as he jumps into the river, shouting, "Got to cool me off!" His last words are quieter, "My boots are filling," and then he is gone.

The last paragraph of the story is its final section, Lyman describing how he drove the car into the river after he couldn't rescue Henry. It has gotten dark, and he is left alone with the sound of the rush of the water "going and running and running." This brings the story full circle, back to the beginning, where Lyman told us that now he "walks everywhere he goes." His grief for his brother is as understated as the rest of his personality. Erdrich has invented a natural story-teller in Lyman. We feel his emotional loss as if it were our own.

Questions for Discussion

1. In the opening paragraph, Lyman says that he and Henry owned the red convertible "together until his boots filled with water on a windy night and he bought out my share." When does the meaning of this sentence become clear to you? What is the effect of putting this sentence in the first paragraph?
2. Also in the opening paragraph, Erdrich writes: "his youngest brother Lyman (that's myself), Lyman walks everywhere he goes." If Lyman is narrating this story, why does he name himself? Does speaking of himself in the third person create any particular effect?
3. What is the function of the third section of the story? Why does the narrator tell us about their wandering, about meeting Susy? What associations does the red convertible carry?
4. Watching Henry watching television, Lyman says, "He sat in his chair grip-ping the armrests with all his might, as if the chair itself was moving at a high speed and if he let go at all he would rocket forward and maybe crash right through the set." How would you describe the diction in this sen-tence? What effect does the sentence's length — and its syntax — create? What is the tone? What does this line, and the paragraphs around it, tell you about Lyman's reaction to Henry's change?
5. Where do Lyman and Henry speak directly to each other in this story? Where do they speak indirectly? How do they communicate without speech? De-scribe how Erdrich presents the moments of emotion in this story.
6. Why is Lyman upset by the picture of himself and his brother? When does the picture begin to bother him? Do we know if it's before or after Henry's death? Does it make a difference to our interpretation of the story? What burden of memory does this picture carry?
7. Consider the tone of the final paragraph, in which Lyman is describing how he felt when he gave his car to his dead brother. Look at the diction sur-rounding the red convertible here: It plows into the water; the headlights "reach in . . . go down, searching"; they are "still lighted. . . ." What attribute does the diction give the car? How is the car different now from the way it's been in the rest of the story? Does this transformation of the car invoke a sense of closure in the story?
8. The closing sentence says "And then there is only the water, the sound of it going and running and going and running and running." How does this statement comment on the relationship between the two brothers?

Topics for Writing

1. Write an essay considering brotherhood in "The Red Convertible."
2. Discuss Erdrich's use of setting to determine tone.
3. **RESPONDING CREATIVELY**   Rewrite the story from the third-person point

of view.
4. **CONNECTIONS**   Compare and discuss Lyman's initiation into maturity with that of Julian in Flannery O'Connor's "Everything That Rises Must Converge."

Suggested Readings

Erdrich, Louise. "Excellence Has Always Made Me Fill with Fright When It Is Demanded by Other People, but Fills Me with Pleasure When I Am Left to Practice It Alone." *Ms.* 13 (1985): 84.
———. "Where I Ought to Be: A Writer's Sense of Place." *New York Times Book Review* 28 (July 1985): 1+.
Howard, J. "Louise Erdrich." *Life* 8 (1985): 27+.

WILLIAM FAULKNER

A Rose for Emily (p. 484)

Few stories, surely, differ more on a second reading than does "A Rose for Emily," which yields to the initiate some detail or circumstance anticipating the ending in nearly every paragraph. But Faulkner sets the pieces of his puzzle in place so coolly that the first-time reader hardly suspects them to fit together into a picture at all, until the curtain is finally swept aside and the shocking secret of Miss Emily's upstairs room is revealed. Faulkner makes it easy to write off the episodes of the smell, Miss Emily's denial of her father's death, the arsenic, and the aborted wedding (note the shuffled chronology) as the simple eccentricities of a pathetic old maid, to be pitied and indulged. The impact of the final scene drives home the realization that the passions of a former generation and its experience of life are no less real or profound for all their being in the past — whether we view them through the haze of sentimental nostalgia, as the Confederate veterans near the end of the story do, or place them at an aesthetic distance, as the townspeople do in the romantic tableau imagined in section II.

In his interviews with students at the University of Virginia (excerpted in Part Two, p. 1490), Faulkner stressed Miss Emily's being "kept down" by her father as an important factor in driving her to violate the code of her society by taking a lover, and he expressed a deep human sympathy for her long expiation for that sin. In the narrative consciousness of the story, however — the impersonal "we" that speaks for the communal mind of Jefferson — Miss Emily Grierson is a town relic, a monument to the local past to be shown to strangers, like the graves of the men slain at the battle of Jefferson or the big houses on what long ago, before they put the sidewalks in, was the "most select street." Because all relics are to a degree symbolic, one should not hesitate to take up the challenge found in Faulkner's ambiguous claim quoted in the headnote, that "the writer is too busy ... to have time to be conscious of all the symbolism that he may put into what he does or what people may read into it." Miss Emily, for example, may be understood to express the part of southern culture that is paralyzed in the present by its inability to let go of the past, even though that past is as dead as Homer Barron, and even though its reality differed from the treasured memory as greatly as the Yankee paving contractor — "not a marrying man" — differs from the husband of Miss Emily's desperate longings. Other details in Faulkner's economical narration fit this reading: the prominence of Miss Emily's iconic portrait of her father; her refusal to acknowledge changing laws and customs; her insistence that the privilege of paying no taxes, bestowed on her by the chivalrous Colonel Sartoris, is an inalienable right; her dependence on the labors of her Negro servant, whose patient silence renders him an accomplice in her strange crime; and, not least, her relationship of mutual exploitation with Homer, the representative of the North — a relationship that ends in a morbid and grotesque parody of marriage. In this context, the smell of death that reeks from Miss Emily's house tells how the story judges what she stands for, and the dust that falls on everything brings the welcome promise of relief.

But Faulkner will not let it lie. Seen for what she is, neither romanticized nor trivialized, Miss Emily has a forthright dignity and a singleness of purpose that contrast sharply with those representatives of propriety and progress who sneak around her foundation in the dark spreading lime or knock on her door in the ineffectual effort to collect her taxes. And as the speechless townsfolk tiptoe aghast about her bridal chamber, it is Miss Emily's iron will, speaking through the strand of iron-gray hair that lies where she has lain, that has the final word.

WILLIAM E. SHEIDLEY

Questions for Discussion

1. The story begins and ends with Miss Emily's funeral. Trace the chronology of the intervening sections.
2. Emily is called "a fallen monument" and "a tradition." Explain.
3. Why does the narrator label Miss Emily's house "an eyesore among eyesores"?
4. Define the opposing forces in the confrontation that occupies most of section I. How does Miss Emily "vanquish them"?
5. Discuss the transition between sections I and II. In what ways are the two episodes parallel?
6. Apart from her black servant, Miss Emily has three men in her life. What similarities are there in her attitudes toward them?
7. Why is Homer Barron considered an inappropriate companion for Miss Emily?
8. Consider Faulkner's introduction of the rat poison into the story in section III. What is the narrator's avowed reason for bringing it up?
9. At the beginning of section IV, the townspeople think Emily will commit suicide, and they think "it would be the best thing." Why? What is the basis of their error regarding her intentions?
10. Why do you think Miss Emily gets fat and develops gray hair when she does?
11. Why does Miss Emily's servant disappear after her death?
12. Describe Miss Emily's funeral before the upstairs room is opened. In what way does that scene serve as a foil to what follows?
13. Discuss the role of dust in the last few paragraphs of the story.
14. Why does Faulkner end the story with "a long strand of iron-gray hair"?

Topics for Writing

1. Contrast the various attitudes toward the past in "A Rose for Emily."
2. Discuss the meaning of time and Faulkner's handling of chronology in "A Rose for Emily."
3. Construct a profile of Emily Grierson: Is she a criminal, a lunatic, or a heroine?
4. Explain the title of "A Rose for Emily."
5. Consider the relationship between "A Rose for Emily" and the history of the South.
6. What can you discern about the narrator of "A Rose for Emily"?
7. Were you surprised by the story's ending? On a second reading, mark all the passages that foreshadow it.
8. **RESPONDING CREATIVELY** Imitate Faulkner by telling the events that lead up to a climax out of chronological order. What new effects do you find it possible to achieve? What problems in continuity do you encounter?

Related Commentary

William Faulkner, The Meaning of "A Rose for Emily," p. 1490.

Suggested Readings

See page 98.

WILLIAM FAULKNER

That Evening Sun (p. 491)

"That Evening Sun" is one of a handful of American short stories that have been so frequently anthologized and discussed that they almost define the style and the method of American short fiction. For the instructor the question may not be so much presenting the story for its literary qualities, but in seeing how well the story still relates to the political and social attitudes of students today, more than sixty years since it was first published. It isn't as acceptable now for a white writer to deal with themes of African American life, and for many feminists there can be questions about a white male author's presentation of a black woman's experience. Does the story still have the powerful effect on its readers that it had in the harsh years of the Great Depression and the cruelest decades of legalized segregation?

The answer is that the narrative device that gave the story so much of its first impact still is as effective today. By weaving through the story the uncomprehending chorus of children's voices, Faulkner succeeds in making the brutal violence of the story frighteningly real. There is no more desperate moment in American literature than when Nancy's attempt to keep the children amused in her lonely cabin ends with the broken popcorn popper. The reader's realization that the children don't understand what is happening only sharpens the effect. For women readers the story perhaps will reflect some of their own emotions and responses as the society is ready now to listen to the stories of battered wives and of women threatened by lovers or friends. The terror that is stalking Nancy is no different from the fear that a woman feels when she knows that a restraining order issued by a distant judge won't protect her from the rage of a disturbed ex-husband.

From the perspective of sixty years, it is also possible to see the racial dimensions of the story in a different way. Perhaps part of what gave Faulkner his great international reputation — and his Nobel Prize — was an understanding that what he was describing was the bitter reality of life for any underclass. The black underclass outside the white neighborhoods of this southern town has been forced into the way of life of the peasants of the older European societies. Faulkner's Nancy could have been a servant in a renter's cottage outside the manor walls in nineteenth-century England, or a woman forced outside the social framework — as she would be by her unwed pregnancy — in any European small town before World War I. Faulkner's story still forces us to face this very real inhumanity in a world we realize has not left this legacy of violence behind.

Questions for Discussion

1. Compare the ages of the children with the responses to Nancy's fear. How much more awareness do the older children have?
2. How does Faulkner describe the small town's ability to help someone like Nancy?
3. Why is Jesus still able to go free, despite the awareness of the children's father of what is happening?

Topics for Writing

1. Faulkner describes the uneasy boundary where the white and the black societies of this small town meet. What are the real effects of this boundary?
2. Compare the situation Nancy faces with a similar situation today.
3. The children's father acts in a way that he would consider sympathetic and protective but would be considered paternalistic today. Discuss his character and role in the story.

Suggested Readings

Basset, John E. *Vision and Revisions: Essays on Faulkner.* West Cornwall, CT: Locust Hill, 1989.

Bloom, Harold. *William Faulkner.* New York: Chelsea House, 1986.

Blotner, Joseph. *Faulkner: A Biography.* New York: Random, 1991.

Brooks, Cleanth. *A Shaping Joy.* New York: Harcourt, 1971.

Gwynn, Frederick, and Joseph Blotner, eds. *Faulkner in the University.* Charlottesville: U of Virginia P, 1959.

Hall, Donald. *To Read Literature: Fiction, Poetry, Drama.* New York: Holt, 1981. 10–16.

Heller, Terry. "The Telltale Hair: A Critical Study of William Faulkner's 'A Rose for Emily.' " *Arizona Quarterly* 28 (1972): 301–18.

Hoffman, Frederick J. *William Faulkner, Revised.* Boston: Twayne, 1990.
Howe, Irving. *William Faulkner: A Critical Study.* 2nd ed. New York: Vintage, 1962. 265.
Leary, Lewis. *William Faulkner of Yoknapatawpha County.* Twentieth-Century American Writers. New York: Crowell, 1973. 136.
Millgate, Michael. *The Achievement of William Faulkner.* New York: Random, 1966.

F. Scott Fitzgerald

Babylon Revisited (p. 505)

"Babylon Revisited" develops a paradox about the past: It is irretrievably lost, but it controls the present inescapably. Charlie Wales revisits the scenes of "the big party" carried on by stock-market rich Americans in Paris during the 1920s — a party at which he was one of the chief celebrants — and shakes his head over how much things have changed. His memories of those times come into focus only gradually, and as they do his nostalgia modulates to disgust. His guilt-ridden desire to repudiate his past behavior reaches a peak *not* when his negotiations to get his daughter back remind him that he brought on his wife's pneumonia by locking her out in the snow, but only when Lorraine's *pneumatique* reminds him that for several years his life was given over to trivial foolishness. For a man trying to reestablish himself as a loving and responsible father, the memory of harming his wife in wild anger at her flirtation with "young Webb" is less embarrassing than the memory of riding a stolen tricycle all over the Étoile with another man's wife.

The problem for Charlie Wales is that his past — for the moment embodied in the pathetic relics Duncan and Lorraine — clings to him despite his efforts to repudiate it. The reader (like Marion) is inclined to fear that Charlie might return to his past ways, but Charlie is not tempted by Lorraine or by the lure of alcohol. His lesson has been learned, but that does not prevent the past from destroying his plans for the future. Or perhaps, as David Toor argues, it is Charlie who clings to the past; perhaps he ambivalently punishes himself out of a guilt he refuses to acknowledge, as when he sabotages his campaign to get Honoria from the Peterses by leaving their address for Duncan with the bartender at the Ritz. As the story ends, history is repeating itself. Just as Charlie caused Helen's sickness, the inopportune arrival of his old friends has sickened Marion. As a result he loses Honoria, at least for six months of her fast-waning and irretrievable childhood — just as he has lost Helen for good.

WILLIAM E. SHEIDLEY

Questions for Discussion

1. Why does Fitzgerald begin the story with what seems to be the end of a conversation that then begins when Charlie walks into the bar in the next paragraph?
2. As Charlie rides through Paris on his way to see his daughter, he thinks, "I spoiled this city for myself." What reason might Fitzgerald have for treating this subject so mildly and in such vague terms here?

3. Characterize the Peters family. To what extent are we to approve of their attitudes?
4. What is the effect of Charlie's repeatedly taking "only one drink every afternoon"? Does the reader expect him to regress into alcohol abuse?
5. What does Charlie's brief encounter with the woman in the *brasserie* contribute to the story?
6. Why does Charlie identify the fine fall day as "football weather"?
7. Discuss the impact of the appearance of Duncan and Lorraine after Charlie's lunch with Honoria.
8. Why is Marion reluctant to release Honoria to her father? Why is Charlie able to win her consent, temporarily?
9. When Marion suggests that Charlie may have caused Helen's death, "an electric current of agony surged through him," but Lincoln says, "I never thought you were responsible for that." Was he? What does Charlie himself think? Explain his reaction.
10. Explain Charlie's reaction to Lorraine's *pneumatique*. Why does he ignore it? Why does that tactic fail?
11. Why does Fitzgerald introduce the arrival of Duncan and Lorraine precisely where he does, and in the way he does?
12. What does Paul mean when he supposes that Charlie "lost everything [he] wanted in the boom" by "selling short"? What does Charlie mean when he replies, "Something like that"?
13. Explain the irony of Charlie's present financial success, apparently unique among his old friends.
14. What does the title mean?

Topics for Writing

1. Analyze Fitzgerald's use of recurring motifs and foreshadowing in "Babylon Revisited."
2. Consider Charlie Wales as a study of remorse.
3. Write an essay describing the techniques of characterization in "Babylon Revisited" of the secondary characters.
4. Consider Charlie's daughter's name as the key to his underlying motives.
5. **RESPONDING CREATIVELY**   After reading each of the five sections of the story, write a paragraph giving your assessment of Charlie Wales and your prediction of what will happen to him. Is there consistency, or a progression, in your judgments?

Suggested Readings

Gallo, Rose Adrienne. *F. Scott Fitzgerald.* Modern Literature Monographs. New York: Ungar, 1978. 101–05.

Gross, Seymour. "Fitzgerald's 'Babylon Revisited.' " *College English* 25 (1963): 128–35.

Male, Roy R. " 'Babylon Revisited': The Story of the Exile's Return." *Studies in Short Fiction* 2 (1965): 270–77.

Toor, David. "Guilt and Retribution in 'Babylon Revisited.' " *Fitzgerald/Hemingway Annual 1973.* Ed. Matthew J. Bruccoli and C. E. Frazer Clark, Jr. Washington, D.C.: Microcard Eds., 1974. 155–64.

GUSTAVE FLAUBERT

A Simple Heart (p. 522)

Students may find Flaubert's long narrative boring and pointless, its central character too narrow and insignificant for such extended treatment, and its plot lacking the qualities of conflict, suspense, and climax customary in well-structured fiction. Rather than assuring them of the work's recognized perfection or quoting Ezra Pound's judgment that "A Simple Heart" embodies "all that anyone knows about writing," you might try placing the work in contexts that will make it more interesting and accessible.

That the tale is an autobiographically intimate recollection of the people and places of Flaubert's childhood, some of them revisited while it was being written, underlines the degree to which his objective narration controls strong personal feelings. Add that Félicité is run down by the mail coach at precisely the same spot on the road where Flaubert suffered the first onset of the epilepsy that led him to choose a life of retirement and dedicated labor at his art — a life in many ways comparable to Félicité's own obscure and laborious existence — and students may find themselves ready to give the story a second look.

Flaubert wrote "A Simple Heart" during the last years of his life as one of three interrelated tales, the *Trois Contes*, on religious themes. By this time Flaubert had suffered the humiliation of seeing Normandy and his own home occupied by the invading Prussians; he had lost most of his money through misguided generosity to the husband of an ungrateful niece; and he had watched his friends die off. One of them was the novelist George Sand, for whom he was writing "A Simple Heart" in response to her chiding him for insensitivity in his detached style of fiction. The *Trois Contes*, each in a different way, embody Flaubert's reaction to these losses. Each subjects pride and worldliness to a devastating confrontation with humility and self-abnegation.

The genre of "A Simple Heart" is the saint's life; its deceptively simple chronological structure traces the stages by which the protagonist throws off selfishness and worldly desires and, in the process, attains the spiritual purity requisite for miracles, martyrdom, and assumption into bliss. With the loss of Théodore, Félicité leaves ordinary erotic love behind her and enters upon a lifelong devotion to selfless labor. She does this not as a self-conscious and would-be heroic rejection of the world but only because she knows of nothing else to do. The love she feels subsequently, however, is as selfless as her labor. It goes virtually unrewarded by Paul, Virginie, and Victor, but it is in a sense its own reward, for it enables Félicité to experience a vicarious life of the imagination seemingly more real than her own, as in Virginie's first communion or Victor's trip to Havana. As the world relentlessly strips her of each beloved person and finally even of the very senses by which to apprehend them, Félicité can resort to the power of her imagination, unrestrained by any conventional critical intellect. Imagination blooming into faith allows her not only to find the answer to her loneliness in a parrot but also to endow the dead, stuffed bird with spiritual life and to experience her final beatific vision of the parrotlike Holy Ghost spreading over her from heaven.

Flaubert worried that his tale would seem ironic and Félicité's confusion of the parrot Loulou with the deity absurd. On the contrary, he insisted, "it is in no way ironic, as you may suppose, but . . . very serious and very sad" (quoted by Stratton Buck, p. 105). The question of tone should lead a class discussion straight to the fundamental issues raised by the story. Félicité's utter lack of pretension, as Jonathan Culler argues, defeats the impulse toward irony because it allows nothing for irony to deflate, while Flaubert, by avoiding commentary and committing himself to the pure and precise rendering of the facts of the case, presents the reader with the necessity, in order to give meaning to Félicité's life, of imagining a sacred order in which her vision of the parrot is not a mockery but a divine blessing and a fit reward.

WILLIAM E. SHEIDLEY

Questions for Discussion

1. One critic (Peter Cortland) remarks that in a way Félicité's life is "entirely covered" by Flaubert's opening sentence. How is that so? In what sense does that sentence miss everything?

2. Why does Flaubert introduce his second section by defeating any excitement or special interest the reader might feel about Félicité's affair with Théodore?

3. What is the effect of Flaubert's detailed descriptions of the Norman countryside as well as the other settings and circumstances of the story?

4. Explain the purpose of Félicité's musings about the Holy Ghost in the third section.

5. Why is Virginie's first communion more meaningful to Félicité than her own reception of the sacrament?

6. Compare the reactions of Félicité and Mme Aubain to the death of Virginie. What do the differences reveal about their characters?

7. What is the effect on the reader's attitude toward Félicité of the passage that begins when she is whipped by the coachman?

8. Why does Flaubert have Mère Simon tell herself, as she sponges the sweat from the dying Félicité's temples, "that one day she would have to go the same way"?

9. *Félicité* means happiness, good fortune, or bliss. Is the name of Flaubert's heroine ironic?

Topics for Writing

1. Examine the episode of Loulou's disappearance and return, and the consequences of Félicité's search for him as an epitome of the story.

2. Discuss the circumstances of Félicité's death as a key to Flaubert's theme.

3. Analyze the function of the brief, one-sentence paragraphs that punctuate the text at certain points.

4. Review the story and make a list of everything Félicité loses. Is it possible to make a corresponding list of things she gains?

5. Study Flaubert's description of Mme Aubain's house in the first section and write a similar description of a house you know.

6. **RESPONDING CREATIVELY** Write an obituary for Félicité such as might have been published in the Pont-l'Évêque newspaper. Are you satisfied with the result?

Suggested Readings

Buck, Stratton. *Gustave Flaubert.* Twayne's World Authors Series 3. New York: Twayne, 1966. Esp. 103–08.

Cortland, Peter. *A Reader's Guide to Flaubert.* New York: Helios, 1968. 127–46.

Cross, Richard K. *Flaubert and Joyce: The Rite of Fiction.* Princeton: Princeton UP, 1971. 17–25.

Culler, Jonathan. *Flaubert: The Uses of Uncertainty.* Ithaca: Cornell UP, 1974. Esp. 11–19, 208–11.

MARY E. WILKINS FREEMAN

The Revolt of "Mother" (p. 547)

In "The Revolt of 'Mother,'" Freeman draws a sharp but subtle portrait of a woman character whom most students will find appealing, although she acts in a devious, underhanded way to assert her will over her husband. Freeman is careful to enlist our sympathies for the wife in the beginning of the story, yet she is presented in humorous terms at the end to minimize the implications of her domestic rebellion. A close reading of the opening paragraphs will reveal the skillful ways Freeman makes Mrs. Penn a sympathetic character in the conflict with her husband.

The story opens with an exchange of dialogue between the husband and wife. Really, though, *dialogue* is not quite the term, since Mr. Penn tries to avoid his wife's direct question: "What are them men diggin' over there in the field for?" He is silent until his wife repeats the question. Then he tells her to go back in the house and mind her own business. Implacable, she stands her ground.

The dialect used in the conversational exchange is colloquial, and Freeman takes pains to make us *hear* the characters. The husband "ran his words together, and his speech was almost as inarticulate as a growl." Freeman's language as narrator is more sophisticated than her fictional characters' speech. Reading the story, we accept her view of the situation as an informed bystander, even if we suspect that she is not an impartial one.

The characters in these opening paragraphs are defined by what they do as well as what they say and how they say it. The husband's face drops at his wife's question, and he jerks the collar roughly over his bay mare and slaps on the saddle. Mrs. Penn is less physically aggressive than her husband, but her will is at least as strong as his. Freeman takes pleasure in describing her inner strength as she waits for her husband to answer her. "Her eyes, fixed upon the old man, looked as if the meekness had been the result of her own will, never of the will of another." She is like John's sister in Gilman's "The Yellow Wallpaper," a conventional woman who is (as Gilman wrote) a "perfect and enthusiastic housekeeper, and hopes for no better profession."

"The Revolt of 'Mother'" is a realistic local-color story, but the New England landscape and lives depicted in it have symbolic overtones too. It is spring, a time of growth and renewal. Mrs. Penn's will is like the dandelions in the vivid green grass, determined to survive even if unencouraged by her husband. Mr. Penn sees his wife in symbolic terms: "She looked as immovable to him as one of the rocks in his pasture-land, bound to the earth with generations of blackberry vines." In due time, Mrs. Penn, a "perfect and enthusiastic housekeeper," will be preserving these blackberries and baking her family delicious berry pies. She is no infertile rocklike earth goddess or unconventional rebel girl. She is the living spirit of the domestic hearth, and she deserves a home larger than the "infinitesimal" one her husband has provided for her, "scarcely as commodious for people as the little boxes under the barn eaves were for doves."

Mrs. Penn's actions at the end of the story continue on the larger-than-life level introduced so carefully with the symbolism in these early paragraphs, only now Freeman shifts her tone to suggest burlesque. Mother's feat moving into the new barn "was equal in its way to Wolfe's storming of the Heights of Abraham," an allusion to the war between the English and the French in Quebec, when the British general James Wolfe led his troops to victory on the Plains of Abraham. Mrs. Penn's action has "a certain uncanny and superhuman quality" when she takes over her husband's new barn. Its threshold "might have been Plymouth Rock from her bearing." Freeman meant her readers to find this symbolism and hyperbole funny, but today's readers (even if they aren't feminists) may see the revolt of "mother" in a different light. Was Freeman too sympathetic toward her heroine in the early pages of the story or too heavy-handed in the later ones? Don't let students miss the ambivalence in the treatment of Mrs. Penn.

Questions for Discussion

1. What does the opening scene of this short story establish about the character of Sarah Penn? How does her husband, Adoniram, view her? Is this view similar to or different from the narrator's presentation of her?
2. How would you describe Adoniram Penn? Based on the opening scene of the story, what would you say is the nature of the relationship between the Penns?
3. Are the characters defined only by their conversations, or by their actions as well? Give examples.
4. Note the colloquial dialect used by Sarah and Adoniram Penn. How does this differ from that used by the narrator of the story? What devices does Freeman employ to make us "hear" the conversation of the characters?
5. What is the point of view of this story? In your opinion, can we trust the judgment of the narrator? Why or why not? How impartial do you feel the narrator is?
6. What is the setting of the story? How is it one of the main sources of conflict?
7. Note the fact that only the narrator refers to Sarah and Adoniram by name. Within the story itself, these characters are referred to, and refer to each other, only as "mother" and "father." To what extent do the characters fulfill these symbolic roles? Has Freeman given them any individuality outside these roles?

8. What is the function of Sammy and Nanny? Are they necessary to the story?
9. Toward the end of the story, Sarah Penn becomes larger than life and almost superhuman. Where does this shift of treatment take place? How does Freeman accomplish it? What problems does this ambivalent treatment of Sarah Penn create in the story?
10. Freeman's treatment of Adoniram Penn also changes. How would you describe this shift, and what does it contribute to your understanding of Adoniram as an individual?
11. What significance would you attach to Freeman's putting the word "mother" in quotation marks in the title of the story?

Topics for Writing

1. Examine the dilemma of individuality versus societal expectations and roles as shown in the characters of the story.
2. What is the importance of the relationship of children to parents and the tendency of children to emulate their parents as elements in "The Revolt of 'Mother'"?
3. Discuss the importance of setting to the conflict of the story.
4. State the themes of Freeman's story as they relate to philosophy and social criticism.
5. **RESPONDING CREATIVELY** Try to rewrite the story from the point of view of Adoniram Penn; from the point of view of Nanny or Sammy.

Suggested Readings

Pryse, M. "An Uncloistered New England Nun." *Studies in Short Fiction* 20 (1983): 289–95.
Toth, S. A. "Defiant Light: A Positive View of Mary Wilkins Freeman." *New England Quarterly* 46 (1973): 82–93.

MARY GAITSKILL

Tiny, Smiling Daddy (p. 559)

Gaitskill explains the meaning of her title at the end of the story, when the "daddy" who is her protagonist thinks about his relationship with his dead father and contrasts his devastating memories with the psychological phrase "the good parent in yourself," which he considers a cliché: "What did the well-meaning idiots who thought of these phrases mean by them? When a father dies, he is gone, there is no tiny, smiling daddy who appears, waving happily, in a secret pocket in your chest." Gaitskill uses third-person narration to tell her story, which explores the feelings of Stew, a father who feels himself wronged because his daughter Kitty has left home to live an independent life as a lesbian. As a boy, Stew's own father was insensitive to him, and Stew retaliates by being brutal to his daughter after she tells her parents that she is a lesbian. He says to her, "And if you ever try to come back here I'm going to spit in your face. I don't care if I'm on my deathbed, I'll still have the energy to spit in your face."

Stew is presented in a harsh light as a father, deliberately offending his daughter by acts of coarseness. In his own eyes he has been a "good daddy," but Gaitskill lets us understand the way his daughter has experienced his love. He never physically abused her, but Kitty has felt that he emotionally dominated the household. She resents the way that he devalued her feelings and left her without self-respect by treating her and her mother Marsha as if the two women formed a small harem for his pleasure alone. Stew can only see a situation in terms of good and bad, with no shadings in between. Since his daughter is a lesbian, she is not normal in his eyes. A normal woman would grow up, get married, and give him a son-in-law and grandchildren. She would stay "his beautiful, happy little girl" all her life, instead of turning into a "glum, weird teenager" who leaves home in rebellion. When Kitty publishes an article in a national magazine, he asks himself, "How could she have done this to him? She knew how he dreaded exposure of any kind."

The reader asks, "Exposure of what?" What were his hidden feelings toward his daughter? Was incest at the back of his mind while she was growing up in his house? Is he genuinely sorry for brutally rejecting her when she told him she was a lesbian, and for being incapable of accepting her as his daughter after that? Or is he fiercely protective of his privacy because he believes that she is still emotionally immature, and that her feelings toward him will change as she grows older? Or is Stew's fear of exposure based on his experience as an astute student of the media, understanding the vulgar commercial exploitation fueling "feel-good" talk shows on television and "true-story" articles based on pop psychology in national magazines? Stew isn't critical of the society he lives in, except to mourn the passing of the good old days of his boyhood. There is no bridging the gulf between him and his daughter, as everyone in his "tiny" family is sadly aware.

Questions for Discussion

1. What is Gaitskill suggesting about Stew in her opening sentence, when she tells us that "the phone rang five times before he got up to answer it"?
2. Define the basic conflict in the story between Stew and Kitty. Is either one of them a sympathetic character?
3. What role does Marsha play in her marriage with Stew? What details in the story tell you how well he understands her? Does Marsha share Stew's hostility toward their daughter?
4. In what way would you call the family in this story dysfunctional? In what way is it functional?
5. How would the story have been different if Gaitskill had chosen a first-person instead of a third-person narrator?

Topics for Writing

1. Write an essay analyzing Gaitskill's characterization of Kitty in the story.
2. **RESPONDING CREATIVELY** Continue Gaitskill's narrative by imagining a devastating telephone conversation between Stew and Kitty about her magazine article, after which Marsha persuades him to go to a family therapist to explore the reasons he is so angry with his daughter.

Suggested Reading

Gaitskill, Mary. *Because They Wanted To.* New York: Simon & Schuster, 1997.

GABRIEL GARCÍA MÁRQUEZ

A Very Old Man with Enormous Wings (p. 570)

The word "allegories" in the headnote presents a challenge to readers of this story, and the inevitable failure of any simple scheme of interpretation to grasp fully the mystery at its heart, reflects García Márquez's central theme exactly. Like the crabs, which come into the human world from an alien realm, the "flesh-and-blood angel" constitutes an intrusion of something strange and unfathomable into the comfortable world of reality as we choose to define it. Everybody, from the "wise" woman next door to the pope, takes a turn at trying to find a slot in which to file the winged visitor, but no definition seems satisfactory, and even Pelayo and Elisenda, whom the angel's presence has made wealthy, spend their money on a house "with iron bars on the windows so that angels wouldn't get in." When at last the old man flies away, Elisenda feels relief, "because then he was no longer an annoyance in her life but an imaginary dot on the horizon of the sea."

In discussing how he receives artistic inspiration, García Márquez says, "There's nothing deliberate or predictable in all this, nor do I know when it's going to happen to me. I'm at the mercy of my imagination." Without intending to limit the story's implications, one might associate the angel with this sort of unpredictable intrusion of the visionary and wonderful into everyday life. As an old man with wings, the angel recalls the mythical symbol of the artist, Daedalus, except that his wings are "so natural on that completely human organism that [the doctor] couldn't understand why other men didn't have them too." Bogged down in the mud, the angel seems less an allusion to Daedalus's son, the overreacher Icarus, than a representation of the difficulty of the artistic imagination in sustaining its flight through the unpleasant circumstances of this "sad" world. True artists are often misunderstood, ill treated, and rejected in favor of more practical concerns or of the creators of ersatz works that flatter established prejudices. Just so, nobody can understand the angel's "hermetic" language, and when he performs his aggressively unpractical miracles, no one is delighted. Exploited by his keepers, to whom he brings vast wealth, the angel receives as royalties only his quarters in the chicken coop and the flat side of the broom when underfoot. Popular for a time as a sideshow attraction, the angel is soon passed over in favor of the horrible "woman who had been changed into a spider for having disobeyed her parents," a grotesque and slapdash creation of the lowest order of imaginative synthesis, whose "human truth" gratifies both sentimentality and narrow-mindedness. But the artistic imagination lives happily on eggplant mush, possesses a supernatural patience, and though functionally blind to the bumping posts of ordinary reality, ever again takes wing. The angel has, perhaps rightly, appeared to his human observers "a cataclysm in repose," but near the end, as he sings his sea chanteys under the stars, he definitely comes to resemble "a hero taking his ease," preparing to navigate the high seas beyond the horizon.

WILLIAM E. SHEIDLEY

Questions for Discussion

1. Why are there crabs in the house? Is it for the same reason the old man with enormous wings has fallen in the courtyard? What other associations does the story make between the old man and the crabs?
2. Pelayo first thinks the old man is a nightmare. What other attempts are made to put this prodigy into a familiar category?
3. How does the old man differ from our usual conceptions of angels? What is the essential difference?
4. Explain Father Gonzaga's approach to the angel. What implications — about the angel and about the church — may be derived from his failure to communicate with him effectively?
5. Comment on the angel's career as a sideshow freak. Who receives the benefit of his success? Why does he fall? Compare what he has to offer with what the spider-woman has. What reasons might people have to prefer the latter?
6. Why do you think the angel tolerates the child patiently?
7. What are the implications of the angel's examination by the doctor?
8. How do we feel as the angel finally flaps away at the end? Does Elisenda's response adequately express the reader's?

Topics for Writing

1. Consider the ordinary and the enormous in "A Very Old Man with Enormous Wings." (Consider the etymological meaning of "enormous.")
2. Is García Márquez's fallen angel a fairy tale, a myth, or an allegory?
3. Recharging the sense of wonder: How does García Márquez make the reader believe in his angel?
4. Read the story aloud to a selected spectrum of people (at least three) of various ages and educational levels. Tabulate their responses and opinions, perhaps in an interview. Combining this evidence with your own response to the story, try to define the basis of its appeal.
5. **RESPONDING CREATIVELY** Select a supernatural being from a fairy tale or other familiar source (the cartoons involving talking animals that wear clothes and drive cars might be worth considering), and imagine the being as a physical reality in your own ordinary surroundings. Write a sketch about what happens.
6. **CONNECTIONS** Compare "A Very Old Man with Enormous Wings" with other presentations of the supernatural (Hawthorne's, for example).

Suggested Readings

Bell-Villada, Gene H. *García Márquez: The Man and His Work.* Chapel Hill: U of North Carolina P, 1990.

Byk, John. "From Fact to Fiction: Gabriel García Márquez and the Short Story." *Mid-American Review* 6.2 (1986): 111–16.

Fau, Margaret Eustella. *Bibliographic Guide to Gabriel García Márquez 1979–1985.* Westport, CT: Greenwood, 1986.

García Márquez, Gabriel. *Collected Stories.* New York: Harper, 1984.

———. *Strange Pilgrims: Twelve Stories.* New York: Knopf, 1993.

McMurray, George R. *Gabriel García Márquez.* New York: Ungar, 1977. 116–19.

McNerney, Kathleen. *Understanding Gabriel García Márquez.* Columbia: U of South Carolina P, 1989.

Morello Frosch, Marta. "The Common Wonders of García Márquez's Recent Fiction." *Books Abroad* 47 (1973): 496–501.

Oberhelman, Harley D., ed. *Gabriel García Márquez: A Study of the Short Fiction.* Boston: Twayne, 1991.

Ortega, Julio. *Gabriel García Márquez and the Powers of Fiction.* Austin: U of Texas P, 1988.

Williams, Raymond L. *Gabriel García Márquez.* Boston: Twayne, 1984.

Zhu, Jingdong. "García Márquez and His Writing of Short Stories." *Foreign Literatures* 1 (1987): 77–80.

CHARLOTTE PERKINS GILMAN

The Yellow Wallpaper (p. 576)

Gilman wrote "The Yellow Wallpaper" between 1890 and 1894, during what she later recalled were the hardest years of her life. She had left her first husband and child to live alone in California after a nervous breakdown, and she was beginning to give lectures on socialism and freedom for women while she kept a boardinghouse, taught school, and edited newspapers. During this time, her husband married her best friend, to whom Gilman relinquished her child. The emotional pressures and economic uncertainties under which Gilman lived contributed to the desperate tone of this story.

Early readers of "The Yellow Wallpaper" compared it with the horror stories of Edgar Allan Poe (William Dean Howells said it was a story to "freeze our . . . blood" when he reprinted it in 1920 in *Great Modern American Stories*). Like Poe's homicidal narrators, Gilman's heroine tells her story in a state of neurotic compulsion. But she is no homicidal maniac. Unlike Poe, Gilman suggests that a specific social malady has driven her heroine to the brink of madness: the bondage of conventional marriage.

Her husband is her physician and keeper, the father of her beloved but absent child, the money earner who pays the rent on the mansion where she is held captive for her "own good." When she begs to get away, he replies practically, "Our lease will be up in three weeks, and I can't see how to leave before." Insisting that he knows what is best for her, he believes that the cure for her mysterious "weakness" is total rest. The husband is supported in his view by the opinion of the foremost medical authority on the treatment of mental illness, Dr. S. Weir Mitchell, a name explicitly mentioned in the story. Gilman had spent a month in Dr. Mitchell's sanitorium five years before. In her autobiography she later reported that she almost lost her mind there and would often "crawl into remote closets and under beds — to hide from the grinding pressure of that profound distress."

Gilman transferred the memory of her physical debilitation and "absolute incapacity" for normal (read "conventional") married life into her heroine's state in "The Yellow Wallpaper." The story dramatizes Gilman's fear while living with her first husband that marriage and motherhood might incapacitate her (as it apparently had Gilman's mother) for what she called "work in the world." She felt imprisoned within her marriage, a victim of her desire to please, trapped by her wedding ring. Gilman left her husband, but in "The Yellow Wallpaper" her heroine is sacrificed to the emotional turmoil she experiences.

As a symbolic projection of psychological stress, "The Yellow Wallpaper" has resemblances to Kafka's "The Metamorphosis," although it is more specific in its focus on social injustice to women. Like Gregor Samsa, Gilman's heroine is victimized by the people she loves. The yellow wallpaper surrounding her is "like a bad dream." It furnishes the central images in the story. The reader can use it like a Rorschach test to understand the heroine's experience of entrapment, confinement, and sacrifice for other family members. Like Gregor Samsa, she regresses to subhuman behavior as a self-inflicted punishment following her psychological rebellion — the wallpaper's bad smell, its bars and grid, its fungus and toadstools, and its images of the creeping (dependent, inferior) woman. But unlike Gregor Samsa, Gilman's heroine thinks she is freed from the "bad dream" by telling her story, not to a "living soul," but to what she calls (nonjudgmentally) "dead paper."

Telling her story enables her to achieve her greatest desire — the symbolic death of her husband. The story ends, "Now why should that man have fainted? But he did, and right across my path by the wall, so that I had to creep over him every time!" The central irony of the story, however, is that by the time she realizes the twisted ambition fostered by obediently following "like a good girl" her passive role as a conventional member of the "weaker sex," she has been driven insane.

Questions for Discussion

1. Why have the narrator and her husband, John, rented the "colonial mansion"? What is its history, and what is the reaction of the heroine to this estate? Does she feel comfortable living in the house?

2. Give a description of John. Why does the heroine say that his profession is "*perhaps* . . . one reason I do not get well faster"? How does the narrator view her husband? Does she agree with John's diagnosis and treatment? Who else supports John's diagnosis? What effect does this have on the heroine?

3. What clue does the narrator's repeated lament, "what can one do?" give us about her personality? Describe other aspects of the woman's personality that are revealed in the opening of the story. What conflicting emotions is she having toward her husband, her condition, and the mansion?

4. How would you characterize the narrator's initial reaction to, and description of, the wallpaper?

5. Describe the narrator's state after the first two weeks of residence. Has John's relationship with his wife changed at all?

6. Who is Jennie? What is her relationship to the narrator, and what is her function in the story?

7. How has the narrator changed in her description of the wallpaper? Is it fair to say that the wallpaper has become more dominant in her day-to-day routine? Explain.

8. By the Fourth of July, what does the narrator admit about the wallpaper? What clues does Gilman give us about the education of the narrator and her

increasingly agitated state? Is she finding it more and more difficult to communicate? Explain.

9. As the summer continues, describe the narrator's thoughts. What is her physical condition? Is there a link between her symptoms and psychological illness?

10. How does the narrator try to reach out to her husband? What is his reaction? Is this her last contact with sanity? Do you think John really has no comprehension of the seriousness of her illness?

11. Why do you think Gilman briefly changes the point of view from first person singular to the second person as the narrator describes the pattern of the wallpaper? What effect does the narrator say light has on the wallpaper?

12. Who does the narrator see in the wallpaper? How have her perceptions of John and Jennie changed from the beginning of the story?

13. Abruptly the narrator switches mood from boredom and frustration to excitement. To what does she attribute this change? How does John react to this? What new aspects of the wallpaper does she discuss?

14. By the final section of the story, what is the narrator's relationship to her husband? to Jennie? to the wallpaper? How has the narrator's perspective changed from the start of the story? What change do we see in her actions?

15. Identify what has driven the narrator to the brink of madness. How does she try to free herself from this element? What is her greatest desire? What is the central irony of the story?

Topics for Writing

1. Compare and contrast the husband-wife relationship and its outcome in Gilman's "The Yellow Wallpaper" and Henrik Ibsen's play "A Doll's House."

2. **CONNECTIONS** Compare and contrast the monologue in Gilman's "The Yellow Wallpaper" with that in Poe's "The Cask of Amontillado" or "The Tell-Tale Heart."

3. **CONNECTIONS** Compare and discuss the concept of marriage in Gilman's "The Yellow Wallpaper" and Carver's "What We Talk About When We Talk About Love."

Related Commentaries

Sandra M. Gilbert and Susan Gubar, A Feminist Reading of Gilman's "The Yellow Wallpaper," p. 1493.
Charlotte Perkins Gilman, Undergoing the Cure for Nervous Prostration, p. 1496.
Charlotte Perkins Gilman, Why I Wrote "The Yellow Wallpaper," p. 1498.

Suggested Readings

Bader, J. "The Dissolving Vision: Realism in Jewett, Freeman and Gilman." *American Realism: New Essays*. Ed. Eric J. Sundquist. Baltimore: Johns Hopkins UP, 1982. 176–98.
Delaney, Sheila. *Writing Women: Women Writers and Women in Literature, Medieval to Modern*. New York: Schocken, 1983.

Feminist Papers: From Adams to de Beauvoir. Ed. Alice S. Rossi. New York: Columbia UP, 1973.

Hanley-Peritz, J. "Monumental Feminism and Literature's Ancestral House: Another Look at 'The Yellow Wallpaper.'" *Women's Studies* 12.2 (1986): 113–28.

Hill, Mary A. "Charlotte Perkins Gilman: A Feminist's Struggle with Womanhood." *Massachusetts Review* 21 (1980): 503–26.

———. *Charlotte Perkins Gilman: The Making of a Radical Feminist, 1860–1896.* Philadelphia: Temple UP, 1980.

Lane, Ann J. "Charlotte Perkins Gilman: The Personal Is Political." *Feminist Theorists.* Ed. Dale Spender. New York: Pantheon, 1983.

Nies, Judith. *Seven Women.* New York: Viking, 1977. 127–45.

Shumaker, C. "'Too Terribly Good to Be Printed': Charlotte Gilman's 'The Yellow Wallpaper.'" *American Literature* 57 (1985): 588–99.

Nikolai Gogol

The Overcoat (p. 590)

"The Overcoat," like Gogol's work in general, has been the subject of widely differing critical responses, some of which will surely be replicated in class discussion. A humanitarian view that sees the story as the vindication of a downtrodden little man coordinates fairly well with an interpretation that stresses the story's satiric attack on the rigid Czarist bureaucracy. Readers who note the grim joke with which the story ends, however, find its report on the destruction of a being too paltry even for contempt to be harrowingly cynical and heartless, while those who closely attend to the shifting narrative tone praise Gogol for producing a masterpiece of that combination of comedy and horror that we designate as the grotesque.

In some ways an obverse of romantic or Laforguian irony, which expresses a self-conscious revulsion from one's own emotional enthusiasms, the grotesque vision dissolves in grim laughter the appalled revulsion from a world devoid of any positive value. Neither Akaky Akakievich Bashmachkin (whose name in Russian alludes to dung on a shoe) nor the social and physical world with which he is at odds offers anything admirable, and the narrator's continuously shifting understatements, overstatements, verbal ironies, and bathetic juxtapositions repeatedly prevent the reader from any mistaken investment of esteem. Nonetheless, the possibility that Akaky Akakievich is our brother in ways not considered by his sentimental young colleague remains the source of the story's grip on our imagination.

Before time, which ages his coat, and the chill of the St. Petersburg winter combine to impose a need on him, Akaky Akakievich lives in a static and self-contained world of meaningless alphabetic letters, which he finds fulfillment and delight in replicating. He is a "writer" of sorts, but a writer who — like Gogol himself, according to Charles C. Bernheimer — hesitates to express himself in what he writes. With his fall from this undifferentiated condition into his struggle to acquire an overcoat, he is born into temporal human existence. His isolation breaks down, and so does his innocence: He makes a friend; he participates in a creative act; he experiences stirrings of sensuality; and he eventually manages to assert himself in words. He also becomes guilty of vanity, pride, lust, and deception. Having gained an identity as a man with a new coat, he becomes vulnerable to the destruction of that identity and consequently of the self it defines, which happens in three rapid stages.

Because we have seen him emerge from a state approximating nonexistence, Akaky Akakievich's brief history as a suffering human being does not appear to be much different from the radically reduced quintessence of the fate we imagine to be our own. That the retribution carried out by the shade of Akaky Akakievich — which suggests his vindication and the exaltation of his overcoat-identity to the stature of a myth — can finally be nothing more than a fantasy or a joke only serves to underline the inescapable dilemma that the story propounds between the meaninglessness of remaining locked within the circle of the self and the danger of aspiring beyond it.

WILLIAM E. SHEIDLEY

Questions for Discussion

1.   Characterize the narrative mode of the opening paragraphs. Can you define a consistent tone?
2.   In what sense was it "out of the question" to give Akaky Akakievich any other name?
3.   Does Gogol share the feelings of "the young man" who thinks Akaky Akakievich's complaints mean "I am your brother"?
4.   Describe Akaky Akakievich's life before his coat wore out.
5.   Why does Gogol bother to make Petrovich such an unsavory character?
6.   Describe Akaky Akakievich's feelings about his new overcoat once he decides to acquire it.
7.   What possible attitudes might one take toward Akaky Akakievich's experience at the party? about his visit to the "Person of Consequence"?
8.   Near the end, the narrator speaks of how "our little story unexpectedly finishes with a fantastic ending." What is the effect of this and the narrator's other implicit acknowledgments of the fictionality of his story — made as implausible assertions of its veracity — on the reader?
9.   Consider Nabokov's commentary on "The Overcoat." What "gaps and black holes in the texture of Gogol's style" seem to you to "imply flaws in the texture of life itself"?

Topics for Writing

1.   Discuss satire as a diversionary tactic in "The Overcoat."
2.   Consider the "Person of Consequence" and a person of little consequence: two sides of the same coin?
3.   Write an essay arguing that disappointed expectation is the goal of Gogol's style.
4.   **RESPONDING CREATIVELY**   Study the long sentence on page 593 that begins "Even at those hours . . ." and continues nearly to the end of the paragraph it opens. Write a similar sentence about a community with which you are familiar (e.g., college students on a campus; the residents of your neighborhood). Try to follow Gogol as closely as possible: clause for clause,

phrase for phrase. How would you define the tone of what you have written? Is it the same as Gogol's tone?

5.   **RESPONDING CREATIVELY**   Nabokov concludes his commentary on this story (p. 1543) by suggesting that "after reading Gogol one's eyes may become gogolized and one is apt to see bits of [Gogol's irrational] world in the most unexpected places." Write a sketch in which, by manipulating style and diction, you cause your reader to glimpse a darker world beyond the surface appearances of things.

6.   **Connections**   Compare and discuss Gogol's Akaky Akakievich and Melville's Bartleby as versions of the artist.

Related Commentary

Vladimir Nabokov, Gogol's Genius in "The Overcoat," p. 1543.

Suggested Readings

Bernheimer, Charles C. "Cloaking the Self: The Literary Space of Gogol's 'Overcoat.' " *PMLA* 90 (1975): 53–61.
Erlich, Victor. *Gogol*. Yale Russian and East European Studies 8. New Haven: Yale UP, 1969. Esp. 143–56.
Karlinsky, Simon. *The Sexual Labyrinth of Nikolai Gogol*. Cambridge, MA: Harvard UP, 1976. 135–44.
Lindstrom, Thaïs S. *Nikolay Gogol*. Twayne's World Authors Series 299. New York: Twayne, 1974. Esp. 88–96.

NADINE GORDIMER

The Ultimate Safari (p. 613)

Nadine Gordimer is one of today's most honored authors, having been awarded the Nobel Prize for literature for the compassion of her writing and for her passionate concern for human dignity and racial justice. This story is an unforgettable example of her power to evoke the social conditions of modern Africa and to force us to consider the effects on people of the changes that have been set in motion in Africa by our economic system. For many students the context of the story will be the popular children's television programs they have seen documenting the life cycles of the animals of the African game parks. In these films, the struggle for existence is waged tirelessly between animal predators and their prey, and if human beings are seen they are presented as interlopers whose primitive farms and ragged cattle threaten the natural environment of the park. As we read the story we experience not only the terrors of the journey that Gordimer describes, we also experience our appalled realization that at some level we have been participants.

As we become quickly aware, the title of the story is bitterly ironic. We never see the "ultimate safari" that is described so alluringly in the advertisement that is the story's epigraph. We hear its sounds, we see traces of its presence — but most disturbingly, we are aware of the effect of the safari's carefully staged glimpse of animal life on the human life at the edges of the park. Gordimer has tightened the focus of her indictment of the economic forces shaping the life of the villagers by telling the story through the eyes of a child. This long-established literary device can present the risk of asking the reader to believe the words of a child who is too wise or too mature for the knowledge imparted. Gordimer's control of her material, however, is carefully sustained throughout her narrative. The child's helplessness is emphasized by her complete ignorance of the circumstances that have led to the death of her mother and her own flight with her grandmother across the park. It is our own knowledge of the reality of the girl's plight that extends the dimensions of the story. It is that context that the reader supplies.

Although we experience the story through the girl's eyes, it is her grandmother who emerges as the central figure. It is obvious that the situation in which the girl and the old woman find themselves is so elemental that their only chance of survival lies in strength and resourcefulness. The necessity of maintaining silence as they traverse the park makes it impossible for them to ask for help or even to make what use they can of the park's resources. One of the strengths of the story is that Gordimer is careful not to personalize the forces that have driven the group into flight. The village's attackers are described only as "bandits," and the people enjoying the safari are heard only as distant voices. We are left with the consciousness that an impersonal economic and social system controls the story's events, a system in which each of us has a role, however unwillingly or unknowingly. As the girl says reasonably, "the bandits had long ago taken the sheep and the cow, because they were hungry, too." It is only when the party of refugees comes to the other side of the park and they meet other people that their survival is assured, and they survive only because the people they encounter are of their own tribe. We have long ago given up the reassuring concept that the human race itself is a single, multivoiced tribe that sustains and nurtures all of its peoples.

Questions for Discussion

1. Although the people of the story are not specifically identified, the place where the story takes place is made clear. Where is the game park?
2. Can you describe the circumstance that led to the flight of the people of the village? What do you know about the bandits?
3. The girl herself does not blame anyone for what is happening to her. Is this because she knows so little about the world she lives in? Is it because there is nowhere for her to place the blame for the tragedy?
4. Are the people on the safari, presumably wealthy white tourists, presented as evil? Are the two worlds, the refugees' and the tourists', close enough for the girl to make a judgment about them?
5. The language of the story is simple, like a child's. How does this limit what the girl can tell us? How does it intensify the effect of her descriptions?
6. How does she experience the animals of the park, in contrast to the presentation we see of the animals through nature films?
7. What can the reader know about the fate of the grandfather? What was the reason for Gordimer to leave it unclear?

Topics for Writing

1.   Often stories told from a child's viewpoint trouble the reader with the child's precociousness or moral maturity. Discuss Gordimer's presentation of the story through the child's eyes, and comment on how this affects our perception of the events.
2.   Discuss the complex interaction of the animals in the game park, the safari guests, and the fleeing refugees.
3.   It is the members of her own tribe who shelter the refugee when they have crossed the park. Discuss the historical background for this tribal identification, and compare it to the multicultural societies that are being formed in today's nations.

Suggested Readings

Clayton, Cherry, ed. *Women and Writing in South Africa: A Critical Anthology.* Marshalltown: Heinemann Southern Africa, 1989, 183ff.

Cooke, J. "African Landscapes: The World of Nadine Gordimer." *World Literature Today* 52 (1978): 533–38.

Eckstein, B. "Pleasure and Joy: Political Activism in Nadine Gordimer's Short Stories." *World Literature Today* 59 (1985): 343–46.

Gordimer, Nadine. *Jump and Other Stories.* New York: Farrar, 1991.

Gray, S. "Interview with Nadine Gordimer." *Contemporary Literature* 22 (1981): 263–71.

Heywood, Christopher. *Nadine Gordimer.* Windsor, ONT: Profile, 1983.

Hurwitt, J. "Art of Fiction: Nadine Gordimer." *Paris Review* 25 (1983): 83–127.

Jacobs, J. U. "Living Space and Narrative Space in Nadine Gordimer's 'Something Out There.'" *English in Africa* 14.2 (Oct. 1987): 31–43.

Lazar, Karen. "Feminism as 'Piffling'? Ambiguities in Some of Nadine Gordimer's Short Stories." *Current Writing* 2.1 (Oct. 1990): 101–16.

Mazurek, Raymond A. "Nadine Gordimer's 'Something Out There' and Ndebele's 'Fools' and Other Stories: The Politics of Literary Form." *Studies in Short Fiction* 26.1 (Winter 1989): 71–79.

Newman, Judie. *Nadine Gordimer.* New York: Routledge, 1988.

Ross, Robert L., ed. *International Literature on Major Writers.* New York: Garland, 1991. 762ff.

Smith, Rowland. *Critical Essays on Nadine Gordimer.* Boston: G. K. Hall, 1990.

Smyer, R. I. "Africa in the Fiction of Nadine Gordimer." *Ariel* 16 (1985): 15–29.

Trump, Martin. "The Short Fiction of Nadine Gordimer." *Research in African Literature* 17.3 (Fall 1968): 341–69.

Nathaniel Hawthorne

The Birthmark *(p. 622)*

"The Birthmark" was written by Hawthorne in the spring of 1843, and made its first appearance in *Pioneer,* a new magazine launched by his friend, the poet James Russell Lowell. Three years later Hawthorne included the story in his collection *Mosses from an Old Manse,* opening the first volume with it. During this period Hawthorne was trying to support himself and his family with his writing, and this was one of many stories that he created for the ephemeral magazine market of the time.

The story is carefully written, and for Hawthorne it is somewhat of a departure from his usual physical settings, since there is no tie in the characters or the action to his more familiar New England background. For the modern reader the narrative is a complicated presentation of myth and symbol, and for students the story offers innumerable themes for discussion and writing. In its simplest outline "The Birthmark" presents a young loving couple, who typify the emotional attitudes of the time. The man worships his wife for her beauty, both of soul and body, and the woman regards herself as the passive embodiment of her husband's love. The distinctive element of the story is the husband's commitment to what was then modern science. He becomes obsessed with a vivid birthmark on his wife's cheek and conceives a method using chemical preparations to remove it — not only its surface manifestation, but whatever inner stains it might have left on his wife's soul. As the reader anticipates, the potion he has his wife drink removes the mark, but at the same moment causes her death.

For the reader of Hawthorne's time, the story represented the dangers of the new science, and, for many of his readers, embodied a familiar journalistic formula. On a psychological level, these popular magazine stories represented a frightened response to the flood of scientific knowledge that was overtaking much conventional wisdom and weakening the intricate structure of morality and myth that had been supported by the established religious beliefs. Readers encountering one of these genre stories in a contemporary magazine could read it with the assurance that they would be disturbed by the tragedy that would inevitably result, but at the same time be reassured by the failure of the new science, once again, to upset what was conceived as the natural order of the universe.

The best known of these contemporary tales was, of course, Mary Shelley's *Frankenstein,* but critic Lea Bertani Vozar Newman, in her useful introduction to Hawthorne's short fiction, *A Reader's Guide to the Short Stories of Nathaniel Hawthorne* (Boston, G. K. Hall & Co., 1979) also suggests the influence of Goethe's *Faust* and two dramas of Shakespeare, *Cymbeline* and *The Tempest,* which Hawthorne and his wife read aloud to each other over the weeks that he was writing the story (31). Newman points out the similarities in the relationship between the characters of Aminidab and the scientist, Aylmer, in the story and Prospero and Caliban of *The Tempest.* The theme of the indelible mark on the skin that reflects an inner blemish of the soul is also familiar to any reader of Hawthorne's later novel *The Scarlet Letter.*

The story also has implications that have been discussed by feminist critics of Hawthorne, in particular Judith Fetterley, in her 1978 essay "Women Beware Science: 'The Birthmark'" (Reprinted in *Critical Essays on Hawthorne's Short Stories,* Boston, G. K. Hall & Co., 1991, p. 164). Her examination of the story suggests, among other insights, that "'The Birthmark' demonstrates the fact that the idealization of women has its source in a profound hostility toward women and it is at once a disguise for this hostility and the fullest expression of it." This response to the story will be of considerable interest to many students and could be a useful introduction to a class discussion.

Questions for Discussion

1. Could the story be placed in a specific place or time? Why or why not? Is this something to be expected of an American story of this time?
2. How would you describe Aylmer's scientific methods? Does Hawthorne seem to have a strong grasp of current scientific principles?
3. Does Aylmer's attitude toward his wife seem to represent a typical concern with the Victorian obsession with perfect beauty? Does it have any counterpart in our modern attitudes toward women and beauty?
4. How would a student compare this story to the theme of Mary Shelley's *Frankenstein?* Why does this theme continue to be relevant today?
5. Why does Hawthorne insist that Georgina finally comes to share her husband's revulsion at her disfiguring mark? Why did she accept the mark when she was younger?
6. Could the birthmark be a metaphor for what many people of the period regarded as the imperfection, both physical and moral, of women? Why or why not?
7. Could this story be related to a story like "Snow White and the Seven Dwarfs," with its description of the witch's potion that has the ability to alter the appearance of anyone eating or drinking it?

Topics for Writing

1. The audience for Hawthorne's story would have been a woman of a typical middle-class family. Discuss what she might have expected from a story dealing with this theme, and suggest her reaction to its conclusion.
2. Discuss the attitudes toward women implicit in the story, and compare these attitudes with other stories in which women are similarly idealized. Students should also discuss a feminist critical approach to the story, with their own response to the story's theme of sexual dominance.
3. If students read the pages of popular magazines today they will find many advertisements for chemical solutions, ointments, tablets, and pills that are guaranteed to produce some of the same results as Aylmer's elixir. Discuss these advertisements and compare the effects advertised with the effect that Aylmer was attempting to achieve.
4. Compare the birthmark of this story with Hawthorne's letter "A" in *The Scarlet Letter*, discussing the concept that the physical mark on the skin symbolizes an inner moral taint.

Related Commentary

Edgar Allan Poe, The Importance of the Single Effect in a Prose Tale, p. 1692.

Suggested Readings

See page 120.

Nathaniel Hawthorne

Young Goodman Brown (p. 633)

Teaching "Young Goodman Brown," you should encourage students to read "The Elements of Fiction" (p. 1739) carefully, since different aspects of Hawthorne's story are analyzed throughout the discussion of the elements of short fiction. "Writing about Short Stories" (p. 1752) also has student essays developing different ideas about "Young Goodman Brown."

Students often need help recognizing stories that are not intended to be read as realistic narrative. Some readers tend to take every word in the story literally; Hawthorne, however, meant "Young Goodman Brown" to be a moral allegory, not a realistic story. While most students will be able to recognize the use of symbolism, you might have to introduce them to the idea of allegory, in which the entire story is an extended metaphor representing one thing in the guise of another.

An allegory is a story that has a dual meaning — one in the events, characters, and setting; and the other in the ideas they are intended to convey. At first, "Young Goodman Brown" holds our interest on the level of the surface narrative. But the story also has a second meaning, which must be read beneath, and concurrent with, the surface narrative. This second meaning is not to be confused with the theme of the story — all stories have themes, but not all stories are allegories. In an allegory, the characters are usually personifications of abstract qualities (faith) and the setting is representative of the relations among the abstractions (Goodman Brown takes leave of his "Faith" at the beginning of the story).

A story is an allegory only if the characters, events, and setting are presented in a logical pattern so that they represent meanings independent of the action described in the surface story. Most writers of allegorical fiction are moralists. In this moral allegory, Hawthorne is suggesting the ethical principle that should govern human life. The *unpardonable sin* for Hawthorne is a "want of love and reverence for the Human Soul" and is typified by the person who searches the depths of the heart with "a cold philosophical curiosity." The result is a separation of the intellect from the heart, which is fatal in relationships among human beings, as shown in what happens to Goodman Brown when he returns to Salem village at the end of the story.

Questions for Discussion

1. When is a careful reader first aware that Hawthorne intends this story to be read as a moral allegory?
2. One of the characters in a Hawthorne story says, "You know that I can never separate the idea from the symbol in which it manifests itself." Hawthorne's flat characters — such as Deacon Gookin, Goody Cloyse, and the minister — represent social institutions. Why does Hawthorne include them in the story?
3. On page 635, Hawthorne writes, "But the only thing about him that could be fixed upon as remarkable was his staff, which bore the likeness of a great black snake, so curiously wrought that it might almost be seen to twist and wriggle itself like a living serpent. This, of course, must have been an ocular

deception, assisted by the uncertain light." What is the assertion contained in the first sentence? What effect do the words "might almost" have on that assertion? Why does Hawthorne immediately qualify the first sentence in the second? On page 640, Hawthorne writes: "Either the sudden gleams of light flashing over the obscure field bedazzled Goodman Brown, or he recognized a score of the church members of Salem village famous for their especial sanctity." Discuss the function of this sentence and find others like it throughout the story. What is their cumulative effect?

4. Why is it important that most of the action in this story takes place in the forest? Looking through Hawthorne's story, isolate the particular words that are associated with the woods. Consider the paragraph on page 639 that begins "And, maddened with despair." List the characteristics of forests that are responsible for this long literary tradition. Consider, too, whether the idea of wilderness remains static throughout history. In the late nineteenth century, with industrialization such a potent force, would people have conceived of the forest in the same way the early settlers did? Why or why not?

5. Where does this story take place (besides in the forest)? On page 634 a man addresses the protagonist, saying, "You are late, Goodman Brown. . . . The clock of the Old South was striking as I came through Boston, and that is full fifteen minutes agone." What does this detail — that the traveler was in Boston fifteen minutes ago — mean to our interpretation of the story?

6. On page 641, "the dark figure" welcomes his listeners to "the communion of your race." What is usually meant by the word "communion"? How is it meant here? What does the speaker mean by the phrase in which he uses it? What kinds of powers does the "sable form" promise the crowd? Discuss the kinds of knowledge that will henceforth be accessible to his listeners' senses. Who is speaking in this passage on pages 641–42: "Herein did the shape of evil dip his hand and prepare to lay the mark of baptism upon their foreheads, that they might be partakers of the mystery of sin, more conscious of the secret guilt of others, both in deed and thought, than they could now be of their own"? How does this sentence guide your judgment of Young Goodman Brown in the closing paragraph of the story? How does the sable figure's sermon comment on the closing paragraph?

7. How much time does this story cover? Where do the first seven paragraphs take place? How many paragraphs are set in the forest? What do the final three paragraphs address? What might be some reasons for the story to be built this way?

Topic for Writing

1. Show how a knowledge of seventeenth-century New England history and Puritan theology can enhance a reading of the story.

Related Commentaries

Herman Melville, Blackness in Hawthorne's "Young Goodman Brown," p. 1535.
Edgar Allan Poe, The Importance of the Single Effect in a Prose Tale, p. 1692.

Suggested Readings

Arvin, Newton. *Hawthorne*. New York: Russell and Russell, 1961.

Bloom, Harold. *Nathaniel Hawthorne*. New York: Chelsea House, 1990.

Cowley, Malcolm, ed. *Portable Hawthorne*. New York: Penguin, 1977.

Crowley, J. Donald, ed. *Centenary Edition of the Works of Nathaniel Hawthorne*. Columbus: Ohio State UP, 1974. Vol IX, *Twice-Told Tales;* Vol. X, *Mosses from an Old Manse;* Vol. XI, *The Snow Image and Uncollected Tales*.

Ferguson, J. M., Jr. "Hawthorne's 'Young Goodman Brown.' " *Explicator* 28 (1969): Item 32.

Fetterley, Judith. *The Resisting Reader*. Bloomington: Indiana UP, 1978.

Gallagher, Edward J. "The Concluding Paragraph of 'Young Goodman Brown.' " *Studies in Short Fiction* 12 (1975): 29–30.

McIntosh, James, ed. *Nathaniel Hawthorne's Tales*. New York: Norton, 1987.

Newman, Lea Bertani. *A Reader's Guide to the Short Stories of Nathaniel Hawthorne*. Boston: G. K. Hall, 1979.

Robinson, E. Arthur. "The Vision of Goodman Brown: A Source and Interpretation." *American Literature* 35 (1963): 218–25.

Von Frank, Albert J., ed. *Critical Essays on Hawthorne's Short Stories*. Boston: G. K. Hall, 1991.

Whelan, Robert E. "Hawthorne Interprets 'Young Goodman Brown.' " *Emerson Society Quarterly* 62 (1971): 3–6.

BESSIE HEAD

Woman from America (p. 643)

This story could be considered as much a character sketch as it is a story. The only "event" is the effect of the newly arrived American woman on the African village where she has come to live. This event, however, has already had an influence on the lives of the people there, and we can anticipate that there will be major changes if she remains. The woman represents the wave of change that is already sweeping over Africa as the old societies give way to new patterns of life that may be, in the beginning, less successful than the traditional self-sufficient way of life. As the author describes her, "She is a new kind of American or even maybe will be a new kind of African." Head tells us the village is isolated, but already a man has left, traveled to the United States, and returned with an American wife. As the author expresses it, "The whole world is crashing and interchanging itself and even remote bush villages in Africa are not to be left out!"

Head is conscious that there are as many surprises in her new life for the American woman as there are for the village women she meets, but the narrator finds that the woman is more capable of handling her unfamiliar situation than she would have expected. She couldn't expect that the woman could give up the things that Head imagines were part of her everyday life in America: "chicken, hamburgers, TV, escalators." To the village woman it seems that what the woman has found is the traditional woman's role. The American woman, with her "wild carefree laugh," is "as busy as women the world over about things women always entangle themselves in — a man, a home." The woman would probably be disappointed to find herself stereotyped in the classic woman's role, especially since she has made the long journey to Africa in what would seem to be a repudiation of this role in the United States. She may be immersed in the daily effort to keep family life going, but she doesn't seem to be dependent on a husband, especially since we never hear anything about him. However, her laughter and her excitement are a stimulation and a challenge to the village woman, and in their long conversations, when the children "fall asleep on the floor, dazed by it all," there are the first stirrings of a new consciousness that will finally change the village forever.

Questions for Discussion

1. This is a story about an American black woman, but the author makes it clear that she is of mixed racial ancestry. Is this part of her exoticism for the African woman?
2. What are some of the images from nature that the African woman uses to describe the American woman? What do the images tell us about the African woman's experience?
3. Head tells us that the woman is American, but she uses an English expression, "I'm all fagged out," to express her exhaustion. Why does the woman remember her using an English term instead of an American one?
4. How would you describe the things that Head feels the woman has left behind her when she moved to the village? Are any of these things part of the village's life?
5. What is the woman telling us when she says that what the woman is doing "is a most strenuous and difficult thing to do"?

Topics for Writing

1. Discuss the statement in the story that "authority carries the weight of an age pressing down on life," and show how it relates to the way of life in the village.
2. Head's view of life in the United States as she expresses it through the woman's viewpoint might not seem to some Americans to be an accurate depiction. Discuss what seems to be right or what isn't right in the village woman's perceptions
3. Comment on the statement, "Black people in America care about Africa." Discuss the historical and emotional implications of the statement.
4. Discuss the African woman's perception that the woman "is a new kind of American or maybe will be a new kind of African."

Suggested Readings

Head, Bessie. *The Collector of Treasures and Other Botswana Village Tales.* London: Heinemann, 1977.
————. *Tales of Tenderness and Power.* Portsmouth, NH: Heinemann International, 1990.

ERNEST HEMINGWAY

Hills Like White Elephants (p. 647)

Hemingway wrote this story in May 1927, while on his honeymoon in the Rhône delta with his second wife, Pauline. According to his biographer Kenneth Lynn, the story was a dramatization of a fantasy he had about his first wife, Hadley: "[I]f only the two of them had not allowed a child to enter their lives they would never have parted." Throughout his biography, Lynn interprets the fiction in terms of Hemingway's relationships. How much this approach sheds light on the fiction each reader must judge.

This story is an early example of a minimalist technique. Characterization and plot are mere suggestions, and it is possible for some young readers to finish the story for the first time with no idea that the couple are discussing an abortion. The setting Hemingway chooses for the couple's conversation is more richly developed. The symbolism of the "two lines of rails" at the station (the choice either to end the pregnancy or have the child); the fields of grain and trees along the Ebro River, which the girl sees on the other side of the station (fertility, a settled life) compared with the barren hills, long and white like white elephants (something considered unlucky, unwanted, and rejected); the bar and the station building (the temporary escape offered by alcohol, the sense of people in transit) — one can interpret these details in perfect harmony with the couple's emotional and physical dilemma.

The man's bullying of the girl drives the story. His ignorance about abortion and his insensitivity to what she is feeling or will have to endure physically ("It's not really anything. It's just to let the air in") are not presented as weakness. They are simply part of his insistence on persuading Jig to do what he wants her to do. The girl is also worthy of discussion. Her vulnerability is idealized, yet she is not stupid. Without the suggestion of her intelligence, there would be no story.

Hemingway regarded "Hills Like White Elephants" as one of his best stories, reserving a prominent place for it in his second collection, *Men Without Women*, published in the fall of 1927. Lynn states that in choosing this title for the book, Hemingway meant to suggest "that the alienation of women from men (as well as vice versa) was one of his themes."

Questions for Discussion

1. In what ways could you categorize this story as a minimalist work?
2. What do we know about the man? About the girl? Why isn't Jig called "a woman" in the story?
3. What is a "white elephant"? How does this expression suit the story?
4. What do you think will happen to this couple after the story ends?
5. Read the story aloud in class, assigning two students the roles of the man and the girl. Is the story as effective read as dialogue as it is on the page as a literary text?

Topic for Writing

1. **RESPONDING CREATIVELY**   Rewrite the story in a different setting to dis-
    cover the importance of the railroad station and the Spanish landscape in
    "Hills Like White Elephants."

Related Story

Russell Banks, Black Man and White Woman in Dark Green Rowboat, p. 115.

Suggested Readings

Baker, Carlos, ed. *Ernest Hemingway: A Life Story.* New York: Macmillan, 1976.
———. *Ernest Hemingway: Selected Letters 1917–1961.* Scribner's, 1981.
Beegel, Susan F., ed. *Hemingway's Neglected Short Fiction: New Perspectives.* Ann
    Arbor: UMI Research Press, 1989.
Benson, Jackson. *The Short Stories of Ernest Hemingway: Critical Essays.* Durham,
    NC: Duke UP, 1975.
———, ed. *New Critical Approaches to the Short Stories of Ernest Hemingway.* Durham,
    NC: Duke UP, 1990.
Brenner, Gerry, and Earl Rovit. *Ernest Hemingway, Revised Edition.* Boston: Twayne,
    1990.
Flora, Joseph M. *Ernest Hemingway: A Study of the Short Fiction.* Boston: Twayne,
    1989.
Hays, Peter L. *Ernest Hemingway.* New York: Continuum, 1990.
Lynn, Kenneth S. *Hemingway.* New York: Simon, 1987.
Martin, Terence. *Ernest Hemingway: Revised Edition.* Boston: Twayne, 1990.
Reynolds, Michael S., ed. *Critical Essays on Ernest Hemingway's* In Our Time. Bos-
    ton: G. K. Hall, 1983.

Zora Neale Hurston

The Gilded Six-Bits (p. 652)

An instructor presenting this story may find that it is difficult to reconcile
some of the contemporary commentary on the work of Zora Neale Hurston with
the realities of her short fiction. The tendency has been to idealize her and her
work, overlooking the bitter realities that she describes. It may be that she grew
up in an isolated community, and that a current writer could comment, as did
scholar Mary Helen Washington, that the community was "neither ghetto, nor
slum, nor black bottom, but a rich source of black cultural traditions . . . ," but the
violence and the near collapse of the strong familial tradition that Hurston describes in a story like "The Gilded Six-Bits" reflects a society that has been degraded by years of systematic racism and economic repression.

It is sometimes emphasized that Hurston learned much about her little community through her research into the oral folk tradition, but the story doesn't
relate to any of the characteristics of the oral folktale. Despite the muted senti-

mentality of the ending, the story is a realistic description of a clumsy infidelity on the part of a young wife. Hurston described how she loved to listen to the men of the community vying with each other as they told the old folktales on the grocery steps, but the story certainly doesn't have anything to do with Brer Rabbit.

At a point in American social consciousness when there is much concern about the effect of negative images in the portrayal of minority groups, it is interesting that the story has recently enjoyed a widespread popularity. Perhaps this is because Hurston's opening descriptions of the young couple, Joe and Missie May, present them as childlike and innocent. What she describes in the short story is almost a child marriage. Joe is so delighted with Missie May's girlishness that, when she is seduced by a newcomer to town, he punishes her the way a child would be punished, with silence and withdrawal.

Joe is almost as childlike as Missie May in his eventual acceptance of her infidelity. The newcomer had impressed him the way an adult impresses a child, with his swagger, his pretense of sophistication and wealth. For Joe this is summarized by the gold piece the man wears on his watch chain. When Joe surprises the man in bed with Missie May there is a short fight, and Joe pulls loose the man's chain with the gold piece. When he looks at it later he finds that it's only a fifty cent piece that has been gilded to look like gold, and it's obvious all the man's claims were lies. After some weeks Joe and Missie May mend their marriage, and she bears him a son. A week after the child is born Joe tells the storekeeper that he was never fooled by the other man at all, and he uses the fifty cent piece to buy candy for his wife and son. When he returns home they play again the youthful game of their marriage that opened the story.

In the real world of the dirt road, tar-paper shack communities that Hurston is describing, adultery was much more harshly punished. Perhaps the story has earned some of its popularity with student readers by describing the world as we wish it were, instead of how it is.

Questions for Discussion

1. How would you describe the economic conditions of Joe and Missie May's life?
2. Would this description only be real for the community of Eatonville, Florida, where Hurston grew up, or would it apply to black rural communities everywhere in the South?
3. How does the author make us aware of Joe's lack of sophistication? Is this presented in a negative way?
4. Why does the author make a point of Joe's being excited that the newcomer has lived in a city?
5. How is the newcomer different from the other men in the small town?
6. Hurston never tells the reader what finally happens to Slemmons. Why isn't this important to her?
7. What is likely to happen to Missie May in the future?

Topics for Writing

1. Discuss the images of coins and money that occur in the story, beginning with the title.

2. Consider the possibilities that Joe and Missie May have to change their life for the better.
3. Analyze the economic factors that make a man like Slemmons fascinating to people in the small town.
4. Describe the elements of racism that have conditioned Joe and Missie May to accept their life as it is.

Related Commentaries

Rosalie Murphy Baum, The Shape of Hurston's Fiction, p. 1657.
Robert Bone, A Folkloric Analysis of Hurston's "Spunk," p. 1656.
Zora Neale Hurston, How It Feels to Be Colored Me, p. 1648.
Zora Neale Hurston, What White Publishers Won't Print, p. 1652.
Alice Walker, Zora Neale Hurston: A Cautionary Tale and a Partisan View, p. 1661.

Suggested Readings

See page 129.

ZORA NEALE HURSTON

Spunk (p. 660)

The title of Hurston's story has a double meaning. "Spunk" refers to Spunk Banks, the giant of a man who courts the married woman Lena and who "ain't skeered of nothin' on God's green footstool — *nothin'*!" But it also refers to the quality of "spunk" (courage) shown by Lena's timid husband, Joe, the sarsaparilla-drinking "round-shouldered figure in overalls much too large," who comes back from the grave after Spunk has shot him in order to take his revenge. It took spunk for Joe to try to get Lena back from her pistol-packing lover, and Joe's courage lasts until he succeeds at what he wanted to do.

Hurston has written a ghost story based on the revenge motif in the Florida black tradition of vernacular speech and folk superstition. Joe first comes back from the dead in the figure of a "big black bob-cat" (an unearthly color for a bob-cat). In this animal form he frightens Spunk so much that Spunk can't shoot his army .45 pistol, a small revenge in itself. For the ultimate revenge, something pushes Spunk in the back onto the buzz saw. Spunk believes it's Joe's ghost and vows to get him in hell. As a storyteller, Hurston pulls out of the two men's quarrel at this point. She ends the narrative with Lena, the "small pretty woman" who is the object of the two men's affections and who holds a wake for her departed lover. Hurston's interest is firmly in this world, describing the scene with a poetic economy of detail:

> The cooling board consisting of three sixteen-inch boards on saw horses, a dingy sheet was his shroud.
>
> The women ate heartily of the funeral baked meats and wondered who would be Lena's next. The men whispered coarse conjectures between guzzles of whiskey.

Questions for Discussion

1. Why is the main part of the story told through the conversation between Elijah Mosley and Walter Thomas? They are, after all, outsiders to the intimate action, depending on hearsay for the bulk of their information.
2. Look at the final paragraph: "The women ate heartily of the funeral baked meats and wondered who would be Lena's next. The men whispered coarse conjectures between guzzles of whiskey." How does this paragraph, one of the few scenes related by the narrator, influence your interpretation of this story? Is "Spunk" about events that happen, or is it about the stories about events that happen? What's the difference?
3. This story is split into four parts, yet it's only five pages long. What is the effect of this structure? What is the narrative burden of each section?
4. In the opening paragraph of section II, Hurston writes, "Lena wept in a frightened manner." What are some other ways of saying this? What effect does this particular way have on your estimation of Lena's character? In the next paragraph Hurston writes, " 'Well,' Spunk announced calmly, 'Joe came out there wid a meat axe an' made me kill him.' " Is this statement factually true? Where does the language Spunk uses locate the responsibility for the killing?
5. What effect does the black Florida dialect have on the setting and characterization of the story? How much physical description is present in "Spunk"? How does the dialect convey the same ideas that physical detail might?
6. Analyze the final paragraph in section II: "A clear case of self-defense, the trial was a short one, and Spunk walked out of the court house to freedom again. He could work again, ride the dangerous log-carriage that fed the singing, snarling, biting circle-saw: he could stroll the soft dark lanes with his guitar. He was free to roam the woods again; he was free to return to Lena. He did all of these things." Notice the sentence lengths: three long sentences followed by a short one. What sentence gains the emphasis in this arrangement and why? What effect does the repetition of both words and syntax create? Look at the list of adjectives that precedes "circle-saw." How would you describe the style of this paragraph? How does it relate to the kind of story Hurston is telling?
7. What do you make of the supernatural elements that are introduced into sections III and IV? What kinds of stories contain supernatural elements like this? What is a "h'ant"?
8. With whom does the narrator place her sympathies in this story: Spunk, Joe, Lena, Elijah, or Walter? Discuss the passages that support your conclusion.

Topics for Writing

1. Examine country humor in "Spunk."
2. Discuss courage in "Spunk."
3. Analyze supernatural elements in "Spunk."
4. **CONNECTIONS** Compare and contrast folk elements in "Spunk" and Ellison's "Battle Royal."
5. **RESPONDING CREATIVELY** Rewrite the story from Lena's point of view.

Related Commentaries

Rosalie Murphy Baum, The Shape of Hurston's Fiction, p. 1657.
Robert Bone, A Folkloric Analysis of Hurston's "Spunk" p. 1656.
Zora Neale Hurston, How It Feels to Be Colored Me, p. 1648.
Zora Neale Hurston, What White Publishers Won't Print, p. 1652.
Alice Walker, Zora Neale Hurston: A Cautionary Tale and a Partisan View, p. 1661.

Suggested Readings

See page 129.

ZORA NEALE HURSTON

Sweat (p. 664)

"Sweat" is interesting for the modern reader on many levels. For the student familiar with the regional authors of the previous generation — writers such as Sarah Orne Jewett and Kate Chopin — the style of the story will be familiar. The story is set in a small, isolated community; the central figure is an older woman; and the story is concerned with her personal tragedy. As in most regional stories, the line of the horizon is the boundary of the action. In "Sweat" there is no suggestion that there is a world beyond the limits of the small town and the woman's cabin on a dirt road just on the outskirts. The carefully rendered dialogue is written in the colloquial speech favored by the regionalists, and, as in their work, the descriptions of the house and the dirt roads set the scene with precise detail.

For the student who has read such contemporary black women writers as Alice Walker and Toni Morrison, the theme of the story will also be familiar. Hurston presents the same bitter anger and despair between black men and women in the rural South that Walker and Morrison present later. Hurston is perhaps even more important as a precursor of current openness than she is as a writer who is simply continuing an older, regional literary style.

In reading a story like "Sweat" it is useful to forget Hurston's studies in black folklore, which in fact were done *after* the story was published. At this point in her career she was part of a very sophisticated and socially conscious movement that was attempting to give the black minority in the United States a literary voice. Unlike many of the writers of a generation before who modeled their work on Maupassant, Hurston is much closer to the French realist Émile Zola, whose grim novels of small-town life in the French provinces were widely read in the United States at this time. There is in his work, as in Hurston's, an uncompromising hardness, and he would have approved of Hurston's heroine as she creeps back in the shadows to let her husband die of the rattlesnake bite he had intended for her. It is a description that Alice Walker would appreciate.

Questions for Discussion

1. Why doesn't Delia go to the sheriff when her husband terrorizes her with the snake?
2. Why is it this "other" woman of Sykes's who finally drives Delia to try to do something to save what is left of her life?
3. What will happen to Delia now that her husband is dead?
4. Why didn't people in the community try to help Delia when they learned of her husband's open infidelities?
5. Why does Delia decide to go to a different church?
6. Why is her husband still permitted to take part in church services, even though he is not trying to hide his "sinful ways"?
7. Will there be any investigation into the circumstances of Delia's husband's death?

Topics for Writing

1. Discuss the role of the white families in the small town in making it possible for Delia to eke out her hard living. What could the community have done to make her life better?
2. Discuss the social attitudes that accept Delia's husband's right to brutalize her physically and emotionally.
3. **CONNECTIONS** Compare the description of Delia's situation in "Sweat" with Nancy's situation in Faulkner's "That Evening Sun." How do the different authors resolve their plots?

Related Commentaries

Rosalie Murphy Baum, The Shape of Hurston's Fiction, p. 1657.
Zora Neale Hurston, How It Feels to Be Colored Me, p. 1648.
Zora Neale Hurston, What White Publishers Won't Print, p. 1652.
Alice Walker, Zora Neale Hurston: A Cautionary Tale and a Partisan View, p. 1661.

Suggested Readings

Edwards, Lee R. *Psyche as Hero: Female Heroism and Fictional Form.* Middletown, CT: Wesleyan, 1984.
Gates, Henry Louis, ed. *Black Literature and Literary Theory.* New York: Methuen, 1984.
Hemenway, Robert. *Zora Neale Hurston: A Literary Biography.* Urbana: U of Illinois P, 1977.
Howard, Lillie P. *Zora Neale Hurston.* Boston: Twayne, 1980.
Hull, Gloria T. *Color, Sex, and Poetry: Three Women Writers of the Harlem Renaissance.* Bloomington: Indiana UP, 1987.
Hurston, Zora Neale. *The Gilded Six-Bits.* Minneapolis: Redpath, 1986.
———. *I Love Myself When I Am Laughing . . . and Then Again When I Am Looking Mean and Impressive.* Ed. Alice Walker. Old Westbury, NY: Feminist, 1979.
———. *Mules and Men.* Westport, CT: Greenwood, 1969.
Lupton, Mary Jane. "Zora Neale Hurston and the Survival of the Female." *Southern Literary Journal* 15.1 (Fall 1982): 45–54.

Washington, Mary Helen, ed. *Invented Lives: Narratives of Black Women, 1860–1960.* Garden City, NY: Anchor, 1987.

Yates, Janelle. *Zora Neale Hurston: A Storyteller's Life.* Staten Island, NY: Ward Hill, 1991.

Yusuf Idris

The Chair Carrier (p. 674)

In the last months of 2001 it became clear to many Americans that they understand very little about the Arab world. Students will find that this story will help them relate to some of the anomalies that shape the Arab consciousness today. Although the setting of the story is presented as a realistic street scene in modern Cairo, Egypt's capital city, it quickly becomes clear that the story is an allegory, and the scene itself is only incidental. Significantly, in the first paragraph the author tells us that it is a miracle that the incident he witnessed didn't cause a single passer-by to stop — and also that this is a not only a miracle — it is a disaster. With this qualification he suggests the troubling implications of his allegory immediately.

It is the impossibility of the scene the author describes that tells us within a few sentences not to expect a realistic narrative. The narrator of the story relates that as he was walking on a crowded Cairo street he encountered a man carrying a "vast chair." The chair is so large that the man carrying it is almost lost beneath it. Although the author doesn't make it clear, the man seems to be carrying the chair on his head, which would be an everyday occurrence in Cairo, except that the chair is so large. "In awe and amazement you almost prostrated yourself before it in worship and offered up sacrifices to it."

First the size of the chair astonishes the narrator; then he discovers it is being carried by only a single man, so thin that he seems to be only a fifth leg between the bulky legs at the four corners of the chair. His astonishment grows when he looks closely at the man and sees that he is naked except for a waistband and a loincloth made out of sailcloth. He remembers that this is the costume of Egyptians from the era of the pharaohs, many centuries before, and the man confuses him even more by addressing him in an ancient form of the Egyptian language.

In his surprise the narrator asks the man if he is an ancient Egyptian, and the man's reply is an enigmatic question of his own. "And are there ancient and modern? I'm simply an Egyptian."

As the narrator questions the man as to how long he has been carrying the chair — "Tell anyone who asks — a year and then a few thousand" is the man's answer — what we finally understand is that the chair represents the burden of the past that the Arab world is unable to relinquish. The narrator, in frustration, attempts to convince the man that he has carried the burden long enough, that he can put it down and, as the writing on the chair tells him, "seat yourself upon it your whole life long." What the narrator is trying to tell him is that this burden doesn't need to go on destroying him; it can instead become a foundation of modern Arab life. The man, however, insists that he can only relinquish his burden when someone can authorize him to put it down, and there is no authority to whom the narrator can send him. In the end the narrator questions himself: "Or should I blame myself for not knowing what the token of authorization was?" In his allegory the author has presented us with a world of contradictions and frustrated hopes. Although we, as outsiders, can do little to change the situation that he describes, this brilliant small tale can help us understand it.

Questions for Discussion

1. Why does the bearer appear as a fifth leg of the chair?
2. What in the description of the chair tells us that the story is an allegory?
3. Why are we told that no else in the street notices what is happening?
4. Why does the man respond to the question whether he is an ancient Egyptian with his own question, "And are there ancient and modern?"?
5. What is the author inferring with the man's question about Uncle Ptah Ra?
6. Why does the author describe the man as saying that only the past, or someone who can present an authorization from the past, can release him from his labors?
7. What prevents the bearer from heeding the words on the tablet?

Topics for Writing

1. Discuss the elements that constitute the burden of the chair and relate them to the present.
2. Although this story relates particularly to Egyptians and to the Arab world, each society carries with it burdens from its past. Discuss what some of these might be in our own history.
3. Comment on the statement, "Anyone capable of carrying a chair of such dimensions and weight for a single moment could equally have been carrying it for thousands of years."
4. Discuss the options the narrator presents to himself for freeing the man from his burden at the end of the story and suggest the practicality or impracticality of each alternative.

Suggested Reading

Idris, Yusuf. *The Cheapest Night and other stories*, translated from the Arabic by Wadida Wasssef. London: Heinemann; Washington, DC: Three Continents, 1978.

WASHINGTON IRVING

Rip Van Winkle (p. 680)

Class discussion of this story could center on the statement that Nachtigal's folktale "Peter Klaus the Goatherd" tends to *summarize* the action, while Irving's short story *develops* it. One of the ways that Irving developed the tale was to add more details about the protagonist's wife. In "Rip Van Winkle," Dame Winkle henpecks her husband so mercilessly that he runs off to hunt squirrel in the Catskill Mountains in order to avoid her. Feminist readers have criticized Irving for his unflattering portrait of Rip's wife. On further reflection, you can see that Irving paid a substantial price for his humorous tone in the story — including the verbal irony in his portrait of Dame Winkle. It forced him to sacrifice the tragic under- tones suggested in Nachtigal's transcription of the folktale.

Questions for Discussion

1. In what ways did Irving rewrite Nachtigal's folktale to make it an Ameri- can story?
2. Why did Irving begin his tale with the poem by Cartwright (an unidenti- fied poet) and the cumbersome explanation of the origin of the tale in Diedrich Knickerbocker's papers?
3. What different kinds of humor are present in "Rip Van Winkle"?
4. Do you think any less (or any more) of Irving's story after reading "Peter Klaus the Goatherd"? How important is evidence of an author's originality in judging the success or failure of a literary work?
5. Do you think the portrait of Dame Winkle is fair or unfair? How essential is her role in Rip's story?

Topics for Writing

1. Investigate and report on other mythical stories about a human being's en- counter with the spirit world.
2. **CONNECTIONS**   Compare and contrast the plots in "Peter Klaus the Goatherd" and "Rip Van Winkle."

Related Commentaries

J. C. C. Nachtigal, Peter Klaus the Goatherd, p. 1545.
Washington Irving, Letter to Henry Brevoort, December 11, 1824, 1504.

SHIRLEY JACKSON

The Lottery (p. 693)

The interpretive suggestions in the headnote should guide students toward a recognition of the main themes of "The Lottery." The near universality of the ritual sacrifice of year gods and scapegoats in primitive cultures to ensure fertil- ity, the continuation of life, and the purgation of society has been a common as- sumption since the publication of James G. Frazer's *The Golden Bough*. Jackson does not explore the transmutations of these old ceremonies in the accepted reli- gious practices and psychological mechanisms of modern humanity; rather, she attempts to shock her readers into an awareness of the presence of raw, brutal, and superstitious impulses within us all. A fruitful approach for class discussion might involve exploring how the story achieves its impact. Jackson's comments (included in Part Two, p. 1506) provide incontrovertible documentation of the power of "The Lottery" to stir the dark instincts dwelling below the surface of the civilized psyche, perhaps the same regions from which the story emerged fully formed — as Jackson claims — in the mind of the writer. No wonder readers, from the author's agent on, have found "The Lottery" disturbing.

But they have also found it compelling, fascinating, and irresistible, and the reason may have partly to do with Jackson's technical skill. For the inattentive first reader, the natural suspense of any drawing, contest, or lottery provides strong motivation to hurry through to the ending, and when the realization of what is at stake comes, it strikes with redoubled force because of the reader's increased velocity. For the more careful reader, or for the reader already aware of the ending, the subtle foreshadowing — the boys are gathering stones, the box is black, Tessie Hutchinson "clean forgot what day it was" — triggers an uncomfortable double awareness that also urges haste, a haste like that which spurs Mr. Summers's final, horrible remark, "All right, folks. . . . Let's finish quickly," and the cries of "Come on" and "Hurry up" by other villagers.

For Jackson has succeeded in gaining the reader's vicarious participation in the lottery. Even the backwoods New England quaintness of the setting draws not the kind of condescending laughter that would distance the reader but the warm sentimental indulgence we reserve for the cutest Norman Rockwell illustrations. Little boys are being little boys as they pick up the stones, the villagers are walking clichés, and even Tessie Hutchinson, singled out from the rest by her tardiness, is tardy for the most housewifely of reasons. (How different the story would be if she appeared nervous and flustered, a few moments ahead of, say, a disheveled Steve Adams!) The reader is drawn to sink into this warm bath of comfortable stereotypes, illusions intact. Totally off guard against the possibility that the good hearts of these neighborly folks might beat in time with an ancient and brutal rhythm, that superstitious fears of hunger and death might easily outweigh feelings of friendliness and compassion, the reader may well recoil from any previous fascination and, in an effort to deny involvement, recoil from the story, too. Except that we do not reject it; "The Lottery" continues to exert such power over the imagination of its readers that it clearly must be providing a catharsis for instincts similar to those that move the villagers to pick up stones.

WILLIAM E. SHEIDLEY

Questions for Discussion

1. What associations does the word *lottery* have for you? Are they relevant to the story?
2. Comment on the ending of the first paragraph.
3. On what other occasions might the people of the village gather in the way they do for the lottery? Mr. Summers is in charge of "civic activities." Is the lottery one of these? Explain.
4. Discuss the degree to which the tradition of the lottery has been kept. Why does no one want to make a new box? Why is the whole institution not abandoned?
5. Examine the character of Tessie Hutchinson. She claims that her fate is not *fair*. Is there any reason why she should be singled out? Is she a tragic hero-

ine? Consider her cry, "There's Don and Eva. . . . Make *them* take their chance!"

6. On your first reading, when did you begin to suspect what happens at the end of the story? How soon might it become evident? What are the most important hints?

7. One reason the ending can surprise a reader is that the villagers never speak directly of what they are about. Why not? Are they ashamed? afraid?

8. Comment on the conversation between the Adamses and Old Man Warner. What is the implication of Steve Adams's last appearance in the story?

9. Does the rhyme "Lottery in June, corn be heavy soon" adequately explain the institution of the lottery? What other reasons might people have for such behavior? What is the social function of a scapegoat?

10. After her family has received the black spot, Tessie complains, but Mrs. Delacroix tells her, "Be a good sport, Tessie." Comment on this choice of words.

11. Discuss the reaction of the Hutchinson family. Why does the lottery single out a family first, then a victim?

12. Old Man Warner says, "People ain't the way they used to be." Are they? What does he mean?

13. Why are the people in such a hurry to "finish"?

14. What is the implication of "someone gave little Davy Hutchinson a few pebbles"?

Topics for Writing

1. Discuss Jackson's techniques for building suspense in "The Lottery."

2. Write an essay exploring the usefulness of stereotypes in "The Lottery."

3. Examine the behavior of groups of people with which you are familiar. Can you find actual instances of formal or informal practices similar to the one described in "The Lottery" — even though they may not lead to such a brutal finale? Have you or has anyone you know been made a scapegoat? Write an essay showing how one such case reflects and confirms the implications of Jackson's story.

4. **CONNECTIONS**   Compare and contrast Jackson's "The Lottery" and Le Guin's "The Ones Who Walk Away from Omelas."

Related Commentary

Shirley Jackson, The Morning of June 28, 1948, and "The Lottery," p. 1506.

Suggested Reading

Freidman, Lenemaja. *Shirley Jackson.* Twayne's United States Authors Series 253. Boston: G. K. Hall, 1975. 63–67.

HENRY JAMES

The Real Thing (p. 701)

According to the narrator of this story, the *real thing*, which might be fine for representation by the mechanical means of photography, is constraining to his artistic imagination. Major and Mrs. Monarch become colossal figures crowding his canvas and blocking his creativity. By contrast, Miss Churm and Oronte, because they have to pretend to be the subject being painted, enter into "the deceptive atmosphere of art" and help its "alchemy" to take place. No master artist himself, the narrator is unable to transform the Monarchs into anything but themselves, and his effort to do so results in monstrous misrepresentations. Because he needs to produce potboilers, he does not try to paint a portrait of the Monarch — although to be a painter of portraits is his stated ambition. But, he sees them so clearly — and what he sees involves so little plasticity — that he cannot draw illustrations of fiction with them before him.

He can paint their portrait in the words of the story, however, and as he does they come to life for both artist and reader. Although the narrator first regards them as types and appraises them like animals, they have gained dignity and individuality and have become objects of compassion by the later stages of the story. If the narrator persists in blaming the defects of his art on the defects of his models, he seems willing at least to accept his limitations and to place a higher value on his human contact with the Monarchs.

The rigidity of the Monarchs may symbolize both the intractability of the real world upon which the artist struggles to work and the literal-minded insensitivity of the audience with which he seeks to communicate; but their chief interest as characters lies in how that rigidity at last dissolves. Hampered by their twenty years of inane leisure on the countryhouse circuit, the Monarchs are less "a compendium of everything (most objectionable) in the social system" of England, as Jack Hawley would have it, than they are the victims of that social system. Trained as real gentlefolk, they reveal that insofar as that *real thing* is seen as mere surface manners and physical appearance, it may appear an empty shell, devoid of sensitivity and imagination. Clinging desperately to the façade of their social status even when the money to support it no longer exists, the Monarchs find themselves unemployable at any job beneath their station. But their integrity and tenacity, epitomized in the solidity of their marriage, give them strength. The story's conclusion suggests that their experience in the studio, which is indeed for them as for the narrator "a place to learn to see," has taught them how to relinquish the self-defeating proprieties of their rank and to accept a new role as servants, a role which they can perform effectively and which will enable them to survive. The alchemy of the studio has not "sublimated" but lowered them in social rank; still, in freeing them from having to continue to be "the real thing," it may have released them to explore the myriad possibilities of being themselves.

The sympathy that the story generates for the Monarchs, and that leaves fond memories of them in the minds of the reader and of the narrator, arises from the narrative method defined in the headnote. Whatever James planned in his notebook (see Part Two, p. 1509), attention to the "nuances of perception" is as crucial to "The Real Thing" as it is to *The Ambassadors*; and it stimulates an alertness in the reader that enables him to enter sympathetically into the Monarchs' plight. Consider the opening section. Most of the information so painfully gleaned in those pages is recapitulated in summary form in the second section. The narrator's claim to have gathered so much from that first interview challenges the reader to be similarly perceptive, just as the opening paragraph, with its deliberate mystifications and plentiful clues about the narrator's profession, requires the reader to become actively engaged in deciphering the text. If he does so, the reader will be rewarded by feeling the full power of the last line of that section as it poignantly anticipates the end of the tale.

Questions for Discussion

1. Why do the Monarchs have such difficulty announcing their business when they first come to the narrator's studio? Contrast their approach with that of Oronte.
2. Why is the narrator afraid the Monarchs might prove artistic? Do they?
3. Consider your reactions to the Monarchs on one hand and to Miss Churm and Oronte on the other. Which pair deserves the greater respect?
4. Why is the narrator happiest drawing Major Monarch's trousers and Mrs. Monarch's back or *profil perdu*?
5. What is Jack Hawley's role in the story? Why does the narrator need his opinion? Why does he hesitate to take his advice?
6. Why does the narrator think it ideal to have the Monarchs as his servants rather than as his models?
7. How serious are the narrator's artistic ambitions? Do you agree with his theory of art? Does his inability to deal with *the real thing* suggest that he is not *the real thing* as an artist? As a man?

Topics for Writing

1. Discuss the steps James took beyond the plan for "The Real Thing" that he was evolving in his notebook entry (p. 1509) to arrive at the finished story.
2. Examine the four sections of the story individually, noting what is accomplished in each with regard to four processes in the story: the unrolling of the plot; the growth of the Monarchs; the growth of the narrator; and the exploration of the theme.

Related Commentary

Henry James, The Genesis of "The Real Thing," p. 1509.

Suggested Readings

Labor, Earle. " 'The Real Thing': Three Levels of Meaning." Tompkins, cited below. 29–32. Originally published in *College English* 23 (1962): 376–78.

Tompkins, Jane P. Introduction. *Twentieth Century Interpretations of "The Turn of the Screw" and Other Tales*. Ed. Tompkins. Englewood Cliffs, NJ: Prentice, 1970. 1–10, esp. 6–7.

Toor, David. "Narrative Irony in Henry James's 'The Real Thing.' " Tompkins, cited above. 33–39. Originally published in *University Review* 24 (1967): 95–99.

Winner, Viola Hopkins. *Henry James and the Visual Arts.* Charlottesville: U of Virginia P, 1970. 108–11.

GISH JEN

Who's Irish? (p. 719)

Although this troubling story is presented as a painful moment in the experience of an elderly Chinese woman attempting to adjust to life in the United States, it could have been a story of any older person who finds herself in an unfamilar situation that she can neither understand nor accept. Attempts to solve the new problem with answers from an older life experience can lead to unfortunate consequences, as it does here, and the life of the woman in the story is left empty and confused.

Gish Jen, who is herself a child of Chinese immigrants to the United States, structures the story around the polarities of the child's parentage — her Chinese American mother and her Irish American father. The older woman says that the Chinese traits she hopes to develop in the girl are obedience and self-control, since the Irish side, the Shea family, is "wild." In an interview, Jen was asked about her use of humor in her stories, in contrast to other Asian American writers who express considerable anger in their portrayal of their American experience. She responded, "Maybe humor is one way of expressing anger." Certainly the woman's problems with her daughter's life lead her into confrontations with her Irish son-in-law and his family. When the family has talked at some length about the baby's brown color the woman grows tired of the conversation, which she compares to a Christmas tree train that goes around and around in an unending circle.

"Maybe John is not her father, I say one day, to stop the train. And sure enough, train wreck."

The woman seems too unaware of the consequences of her suggestion that her daughter has been unfaithful to her husband, but we suspect that she is conscious of the consequences of her actions. When she begins to spank the daughter, and when finally she loses control and hurts the daughter after the little girl has defied her by crawling into a hole in a sand pile, we realize that the strongest element in the woman's character is anger. She is angry at a life that excludes her, a life in which the role she once played in the restaurant she owned with her husband has been taken from her. She is a woman who struggled to achieve the economic success she and her husband enjoyed, and she is contemptuous of her son-in-law and his brothers for their inability to find jobs. She rails at them: "They say they cannot find work, this is not the economy of the fifties, but I say, Even the black people doing better these days, some of them live so fancy, you'd be surprised. Why the Shea family have so much trouble? They are white people, they speak English."

And her anger finally overwhelms her. As she attacks the three-year-old girl who has hidden in the sand with a long stick, the reader is afraid that the woman may kill her. In the confrontation with her daughter and her husband that follows, the woman justifies what she has done by saying, "She is not like any Chinese girl I ever saw."

It is necessary for the daughter to move her mother away from the family before her husband divorces her. At the end of the story it is clear that the older woman is unrepentant, and the experience of living with the Irish mother of her son-in-law has not endeared her to the woman or to the Irish. She feels that the woman's words, "Permanent resident. Not going anywhere," which echo the legal term for a resident alien, strike her like the stick she used against her granddaughter. "I don't know how Bess Shea learn to use her words, but I hear what she say a long time later." There are aspects of the story the woman's telling that have elements of humor, but the reader's final impression is that Jen has used the humor, as she said, to express a deep and continuing anger.

Questions for Discussion

1. The woman's description of herself is "fierce." What confirms the reader in this impression of her? Does she seem conscious of the implications of the word?
2. What is her opinion of the Irish? Would you describe her as prejudiced?
3. What does the daughter mean when she tells her mother not to say "Irish this, Irish that"?
4. Are the mother's attitudes representative of newly arrived immigrant groups?
5. What is the difference between her and her daughter in their understanding of words like "supportive" and "creative"? Is the mother making an effort to understand these differences? Is the daughter sympathetic to her mother's attitudes?
6. Are the differences between the two women only a misunderstanding of certain words, or do their differences reflect their new life experience in the United States?
7. What does the woman's statement that "Chinese people don't think a daughter is so great" tell us about her?
8. Do the two old women in the story have any deeper understanding of each other? Has their age made them any closer?

Topics for Writing

1. The old woman feels justified in her physical punishment of her granddaughter. Discuss her attitudes toward child rearing, in contrast to what she perceives as the American attitudes toward discipline and obedience.
2. Some of the woman's strong temperament must be a necessary element of a new immigrant's character if the individual is to survive the wrenching changes in her life. Discuss this statement and relate it to the woman's memories of her life in the restaurant with her husband.
3. Relate the comments the woman makes about the Irish, and her comparisons with African Americans, to the larger problems of immigrant assimilation, using one additional group as an example.
4. Many of the woman's comments about her granddaughter's behavior reflect differences between generations as much as they characterize the Chinese attitude toward childrearing. Discuss the unrealistic expectations that some older people have toward newer ideas as you have experienced them.

Suggested Readings

Chin, Marilyn. *Dwarf Bamboo*. Greenfield Center, NY: Greenfield Review Press, 1987.

———. *The Phoenix Gone, the Terrace Empty*. Minneapolis: Milkweed Editions, 1994.

Hagedorn, Jessica, ed. *Charlie Chan Is Dead: An Anthology of Contemporary Asian American Fiction*. New York: Penguin, 1993.

SARAH ORNE JEWETT

A White Heron (p. 729)

Jewett portrays Sylvia, whose very name associates her with the woodland, as torn between the natural world in which she is so fully at home and the first stirrings of the "great power" of love in her "woman's heart." Her project of pleasing the young hunter and winning the treasure of his gratitude, in the form of ten dollars, leads her out of her shyness and into the heroic adventure of climbing the great pine tree. As a result of her efforts, Sylvia grows within herself. The reader worries that she may be tempted into betraying the white heron and thus into surrendering something essential to her own integrity, but Sylvia, in her vision from the top of the tree and her face-to-face meeting with the heron, has gained the perspective necessary to hold firm.

Jewett's rich evocation of the landscape and the emotional intensity with which she narrates the climactic action contribute to the story's deeper resonances. If Sylvia recalls the woodland goddess Diana — and similarly guards her chastity — she also resembles those heroes and heroines of myth and folklore who must go to some symbolic world-navel or towering height in quest of wisdom, or who must suffer an initiation that involves mastering their fear of the (sometimes phallic) *other* and reintegrating their identities in order to cope with it. Sylvia rejects the destructive gun and mounts the pine tree, "a great main-mast to the voyaging earth," electing the fecund life of a natural world she is still discovering over the destructive promises of the "ornithologist," whose grounds are populated with dead, stuffed birds. While the narrator ends fretting over Sylvia's having consigned herself to loneliness and love-longing, nothing in the story suggests that she would be better off having sold herself for ten dollars and a whistle.

Students may find it easier to approach the story through its autobiographical dimensions. According to Eugene Hillhouse Pool, who builds on F. O. Matthiessen's early study, Jewett remained childlike and single all her life, treasuring the love of her father, who used to take her on long rambles through the countryside when she was a girl. "As Sylvia elects to keep her private and meaningful secret, so is she choosing for Miss Jewett too. . . . She chooses, psychologically, to remain a child, with Sylvia." But if Jewett chose to remain a child, it is a child in terms she met in reading Wordsworth, whom she admired: as one privy to the indwelling spirit of the natural world.

The imagery that surrounds Sylvia is uniformly associated with *mother* nature until she ventures up the tree and meets the heron. Her adventure enables her to reject assertively the young man and the advancing modern world of science and machinery with which he is associated. This is a step forward from her original strategies of withdrawal and concealment. The antinomy, however, is not resolved. The only perfect marriage in the story is between the nesting herons; and Jewett offers no key to a satisfactory union between the world of nature and the civilization that threatens to despoil it.

WILLIAM E. SHEIDLEY

Questions for Discussion

1. Jewett is known as a local colorist. To what extent is the locale of this story its subject? To what extent does the story transcend its specific Maine setting?
2. Discuss the presentation of the cow Sylvia is driving as the story opens. What does her "loud moo by way of explanation" actually explain?
3. Comment on the men, apart from the hunter, mentioned in the story. Is the absence of men from Sylvia's world a significant factor in the story?
4. As a child in town, Sylvia has the reputation of being "afraid of folks." Is she? Does she have reason?
5. Explain Sylvia's reaction when she hears the hunter's whistle. Why does Jewett briefly switch to the present tense here? Does she do so elsewhere?
6. Comment on the omniscient-narrative point of view in this story. How is it controlled? What does the narrative voice contribute?
7. Describe the character and appurtenances of the young hunter, and contrast them with those of Sylvia. How important are his evident gentleness and good intentions?
8. How does Jewett charge the pine tree and Sylvia's climb to the top of it with special meaning? What does Sylvia see up there that she has never seen before?
9. What do Sylvia and the heron have in common?
10. Analyze the last paragraph. What has Sylvia lost? What has she preserved? What has she gained?

Topics for Writing

1. Research elements of folk and fairy tale in "A White Heron."
2. Analyze Sylvia's nighttime excursion as a journey into the self.
3. Examine maternal and sexual imagery in "A White Heron."
4. Consider "A White Heron" as a rejection of modern industrial society.

Related Commentary

Sarah Orne Jewett, Looking Back on Girlhood, p. 1513.

Suggested Readings

Brenzo, Richard. "Free Heron or Dead Sparrow: Sylvia's Choice in Sarah Orne Jewett's 'A White Heron.' " *Colby Library Quarterly* 14 (1978): 36–41.
Cary, Richard. *Sarah Orne Jewett*. Albany, NY: New Collections UP, 1962.
Donovan, Josephine L. *Sarah Orne Jewett*. New York: Ungar, 1980.

Hovet, Theodore R. "America's 'Lonely Country Child': The Theme of Separation in Sarah Orne Jewett's 'A White Heron.'" *Colby Library Quarterly* 14 (1978): 166–71.

———. "'Once Upon a Time': Sarah Orne Jewett's 'A White Heron' as a Fairy Tale." *Studies in Short Fiction* 15 (1978): 63–68.

Keyworth, Cynthia, et al. *Master Smart Women: A Portrait of Sarah Orne Jewett.* Belfast, ME: North Country, 1988.

Nagel, Gwen. *Critical Essays on Sarah Orne Jewett.* Boston: G. K. Hall, 1984.

Pool, Eugene Hillhouse. "The Child in Sarah Orne Jewett." *Appreciation of Sarah Orne Jewett.* Ed. Richard Cary. Waterville, ME: Colby College P, 1973. 223–28, esp. 225. Originally published in *Colby Library Quarterly* 7 (1967): 503–09.

Westbrook, Perry D. *Acres of Flint: Sarah Orne Jewett and Her Contemporaries,* Rev. Ed. Metuchen, NJ: Scarecrow, 1981.

Ha Jin

The Bridegroom (p. 738)

This story traces a twisting path through a labyrinth of unfamiliar social customs. As we follow the path's twists and turns we react to many of its unfamiliarities with the same startled surprise we experience on a carnival ride through a garish funhouse where things jump out at us from the darkness. In this story the social context is so different from our own that there is no way for us to anticipate many of the attitudes and responses of its characters. The situation itself would be unexpected, although perhaps in an earlier century it would not have seemed unusual. An older man living in a small city in modern China has agreed to look after the daughter of a friend following the friend's death, and he takes the responsibility seriously enough to give the girl special privileges in the factory where he is head of the security section. As the story opens his concern is with finding her a husband, since she is shy and unattractive. At twenty-three there is a danger that she will not be married.

When a man who has stirred the interest of many of the young women in the factory asks her to marry him, the older man is uncomfortable and then disappointed with the meager engagement gifts the man brings, but he chooses to ignore his misgivings so that the girl can be married. A Chinese reader perhaps would notice enough signs in the opening pages to anticipate the tragedy that is to come, but most students will find themselves a step behind the author as they try to absorb the situation that the author presents. The discovery that the man is a homosexual is only the beginning of a series of revelations that lead us to understand how profoundly different Chinese society is from ours. The story's power comes from the twists we encounter in the story's path as we are confronted with situations that the characters in the story interpret in one way and that we interpret in another.

When the elderly official is first presented with charges against his son-in-law, he fears that it will be a political case and that there will be nothing he can do to help him. Then to his bewilderment he is told that the young man is guilty of something called homosexuality. The father-in-law is confused. "We had heard of the term, but didn't know what it meant exactly." The officials discussing the accusations squirm with discomfort when they are asked to say specifically what this means. The old man is told that it is "a social disease, like gambling, or prostitution, or syphilis." It is a product of Western capitalism and the bourgeois lifestyle. The Chinese government treats it as a crime, "a kind of hooliganism," and there will be a long, indefinite prison sentence.

Again, for the Chinese reader this labeling of homosexuality as a criminal act will not be unexpected, but sexual preferences have been a private matter in the United States long enough for students to be surprised by this turn in the path. Then we learn of the medieval "cures" that the prison officials inflict on the prisoners to cure them of their "disease." Almost with disbelief we read of the man's willing immersion in "electric baths," in which he lies in water that is gradually charged with electricity. The man submits to the physical torture in the hope that he can be released, but again the reader comes to another twist of the path. The doctor who is responsible for the so-called treatments admits to the old man that homosexuality isn't a criminal act, it isn't an illness, it is a sexual preference, and the electric baths will do nothing to "cure" the man. When the older man asks why the doctor goes ahead with the painful treatments, the doctor admits that he does it because of the government's regulations. The treatment is required by the Department of Public Health. The story's somber resolution, in which the man is found in a physical embrace with another man in prison, admits that the act took place, and finally is labeled a criminal and given a jail sentence, is the one turn in the story that the Western reader could have anticipated.

Ha Jin, who has left China and does not expect to return, has given Western readers a complicated view of his society, and perhaps for us what is the most surprising of all we have learned is the public nature of every act. The other workers, the officials, the doctors, the police — each has a role to play in the social situation that the "crime" has created, and the resolution of every act is determined by its effect on the social order. For those who live in a society that regards a measure of privacy for personal acts as a right, the world that the author describes is as different from ours as the shadows on the moon.

Questions for Discussion

1. The elderly official must balance the duties of his job with his desire to help his friend's daughter. What are some of the things he has been able to do to help her? Is this unusual in a factory?
2. How would you characterize the activities of Men's World, the social gathering where the young husband was beaten and arrested? Would this be considered a homosexual gathering in our society? Is the statement of one of the men that "[o]nly in here can I stop living in hypocrisy" still be something that might be said in the United States in a situation with some similarities?
3. Although much of what happens in the story is public knowledge the older man is stunned by the secret agreement between the young man and the woman he is helping. How might you interpret this marriage compact between them?
4. Do the reasons that both Baowen and Beina give him for their marriage seem reasonable? Does the old man seem to understand their reasons?
5. Is there a contradiction between Baowen's sexual preferences and his skill as a kung fu fighter?

6. Is the attitude of the other workers toward the predicament of the young bride sympathetic in any way? Will this attitude continue unchanged, do you think?
7. Why is the labeling of the act as a crime so decisive in the society?
8. Although the marriage is clearly a sham, all three of the protagonists — the elderly man, the young husband, and the young woman — share a desire to continue the marriage, at least in form. What is it in the society that causes them to feel this way?

Topics for Writing

1. Discuss whether the shock of the elderly man and the government officials at their discovery of homosexuality in their community is a reflection of their lack of sophistication and whether a broader understanding of the world might lead to a more understanding attitude. Is it possible for a modern American student to believe that the men were as unknowledgeable about homosexuality as the author tells us?
2. Marriage is presented as the single desirable state for men and women in this society. Comment on the social factors that might lead to this conclusion and discuss whether this is a historical custom that could change in the future.
3. A Chinese factory, with its workers living together in barracks, their communal morning exercises, meals taken together, joint discussions of every issue, and a wildly flourishing climate of gossip and innuendo, is similar to the life of a Chinese village. Compare these two social situations and comment on their role in changes in Chinese society.
4. There has been a tradition of punishment for homosexual acts in nearly every society. Study some of them and comment on the reasoning behind the punishments and why they have gradually fallen into disfavor in the western democracies.

Suggested Readings

Jin, Ha. *Between Silences: A Voice from China.* Chicago: U of Chicago P, 1990.
———. *The Bridegroom: Stories.* New York: Pantheon, 2000.
———. *Under the Red Flag: Stories.* Athens: U of Georgia P, 1997.

CHARLES R. JOHNSON

Menagerie, a Child's Fable (p. 754)

Despite the subtitle of "Menagerie" ("A Child's Fable"), Johnson's interest in psychology, philosophy, religion, history, and folk and popular culture contributes such a wealth of references to people, ideas, images, and events in this story that it jumps out of the category of Children's Literature to become a story for adults (or precocious children). Yet Johnson's writing is so clear, steady, and lucid that his references, far from seeming obscure, explain themselves with little fuss or fanfare. Of course a flighty aerobic dance teacher would own a flirtatious little female poodle. Of course a cruel pet shop owner with a heart condition would live alone and fail to show up one fine Monday morning. By the time readers finish "Menagerie," there's a good chance they will have empathized so closely with the narrator Berkeley, the German shepherd, that they will feel that they are also on his intellectual wavelength: "Not the smartest, but steady."

Children's stories with fabulous talking animals that dramatize a moral are not unusual (Aesop's fables come immediately to mind), but adult stories "peopled" with talking animals instead of human beings are rare indeed. Johnson's irrepressible sense of humor — and his unwavering moral sense — underpin the narrative, but it is his ability to create realistic "human" characters in the bodies of dog, monkey, turtle, fish, rabbit, and Siamese that holds our interest.

Take Monkey, for example. We're told right from the start that Berkeley didn't care "a whole lot" for him, and then we're shown his uninhibited wickedness: He is "a comedian always grabbing his groin to get a laugh, throwing feces, or fooling with the other animals." He's the Freudian amoral id in action, doing just as he pleases, totally devoid of any higher instincts of conscience, justice, or gratitude, entirely capable of biting the hand that feeds him. Tortoise, on the other hand, is at the other extreme, so repressed by his dizzying week of freedom after escaping from his cage that "he hadn't spoken in a year."

"Menagerie, A Child's Fable" is included in Johnson's collection of what he calls "tales and conjurations," *The Sorcerer's Apprentice*. (*Webster's Dictionary* defines "conjuration" as the act of conjuring, or practicing magic; the word also has a second meaning, "a solemn appeal.") Johnson uses as an epigraph a quotation from chapter XXIII of Herman Melville's *The Confidence Man*: "It is with fiction as with religion; it should present another world, and yet one to which we feel the tie." "Menagerie" presents a fictional world that has such clear ties to our own muddled state of humanity that students should understand the allegory without much explanation. If they need help interpreting the chaos of the last scene, a suggestion that they watch the evening news on television or read the front page of their local newspaper might help to illuminate Johnson's meaning for them.

Questions for Discussion

1. When do you become aware that the story will be narrated solely from the point of view of the animals in the pet shop?
2. What is the larger point Johnson is making when he tells us that Berkeley mistakes the gunfire on television for the real thing?
3. What is the basic conflict in the story?
4. How does Johnson make you sympathetic to some of the animals and hostile to others?
5. Is Monkey right in saying that Berkeley is being a fascist by keeping the animals locked up? In what ways is Monkey smarter than Berkeley? In what ways is Monkey less intelligent?
6. Why is Berkeley unsympathetic to Rabbit's organization of the females into a radical group hostile to the males? What does Berkeley suggest to smooth relations between the sexes? Why does his rational suggestion fall upon deaf ears?
7. Why does Berkeley fret over the idea that "truth was decided in the end by those who could be bloodiest in fang and claw"? How does this idea reflect

Darwin's theory of evolution? Does Monkey's use of the store owner's gun challenge nineteenth-century evolutionary theory?

8. Why does Johnson give Tortoise the last grim word in the story?

Topics for Writing

1. **RESPONDING CREATIVELY** Create a story in which animals who think and speak and interact are the only characters.
2. **RESPONDING CREATIVELY** Write an essay in which you discuss the implications of Johnson's fable as a moral allegory.
3. Rewrite "Menagerie" as a comic strip.

Suggested Reading

Johnson, Charles. *The Sorcerer's Apprentice.* New York: Penguin, 1987.

JAMES JOYCE

Araby (p. 762)

The rich texture of imagery and allusion that Joyce weaves into "Araby" may delight the sophisticated reader, but for the classroom instructor it represents a temptation comparable to the temptation that may be brought to mind by the apple tree in the "wild garden" mentioned in the second paragraph. Students should not be asked to contemplate the story's symbolism until they grasp its plot. To begin class discussion of "Araby" with the question What happens? may well be to discover that, for a novice reader, no meaningful action seems to have been completed. When the confusion arising from this sense of anticlimax is compounded by the difficulties presented by the unfamiliarity of florins, bazaars, hallstands, and other things old and Irish, "Araby" may strike students as pointless and unnecessarily obscure.

Once it is seen, however, that the narrator's disappointment at the bazaar resolves the tension built up by his attraction to Mangan's sister and his quest to fetch her a symbol of his love, the many specific contrasts between the sensuous and romantic world of the narrator's imagination and the banal and tawdry world of actual experience become meaningful keys to understanding what has happened. The opposition between fantasy and reality continues throughout: "Her image accompanied me even in places the most hostile to romance." The story's pivotal paragraph ends with the narrator cooling his forehead against the window in one of the empty upper rooms, staring out not really at Mangan's sister but at "the brown-clad figure cast by my imagination." Before this moment, his excited fancy has transformed the "decent" and somewhat dilapidated neighborhood of North Richmond Street into a fitting backdrop for such a tale as one might find in a yellow-leaved romance. Mangan's sister, kissed by lamplight, becomes in his view a work of art like a painting by Rossetti. The narrator's soul luxuriates in a dream of exotic beauty soon to be possessed by means of a journey to Araby: "I imagined that I bore my chalice safely through a throng of foes." But after the protracted visit from the tedious Mrs. Mercer and the even longer delayed return of the narrator's uncle with the necessary coin, the limitations of the romantic imagination begin to emerge. The "chalice" is replaced by a florin, held "tightly in my hand"; the quest is made by "third-class carriage"; and the bazaar itself, its potential visionary qualities defeated by failing illumination, turns out to be an ordinary market populated by ordinary shop girls from no farther east than England. At Araby, what matters is not purity of heart but hard cash.

The pitiful inadequacy of the narrator's two pennies and sixpence to master "the great jars that stood like eastern guards" at the door of the bazaar stall completes his painful disillusionment, but Joyce allows his hero one last Byronic vision of himself "as a creature driven and derided by vanity." When the lights go out in Araby, its delusive magic collapses, and the bazaar becomes as "blind" as North Richmond Street. Well might the narrator's eyes burn, for they have been working hard to create out of intractable materials a much more beautiful illusion than Araby. This imaginative power cannot be entirely vain, however, since in the mind that tells the story it is capable of evoking experiences like those described in the story's third paragraph, against which even the hoped-for transports of Araby would have paled.

WILLIAM E. SHEIDLEY

Questions for Discussion

1. Why does the narrator want to go to the bazaar?
2. Why does he arrive so late?
3. Why doesn't he buy anything for Mangan's sister?
4. Enumerate the activities taking place at Araby. To what extent do they sustain its "magical name"?
5. What had the narrator expected to find at Araby? What was the basis of his expectation?
6. Define the narrator's feelings for Mangan's sister. To what extent is she the cause of those feelings? What, as they say, does he *see* in her?
7. What purpose might Joyce have had in choosing not to mention the object of the narrator's affections until the middle of the third paragraph? Describe the context into which she is introduced. In what ways is she part of the world of North Richmond Street?
8. What is the role of the narrator's uncle in the story? What values and attitudes does he represent? Are they preferable to those of the narrator?

Topics for Writing

1. Make a study of light, vision, and beauty in "Araby."
2. Compare "Araby" and the quest for the Holy Grail.
3. Analyze the function of nonvisual sense imagery in "Araby."
4. Explore Joyce's control of tone in "Araby."
5. On a second reading of the story, keep two lists. In the first record ideas, images, and allusions that suggest contexts remote from the immediate situation, jotting down associations that they bring to mind. In the second list note anything mentioned in the story with which you are unfamiliar. Look some of these items up. Then write an informal paragraph or two showing

to what extent tracking Joyce's mind in this fashion helped you to understand and enjoy the story.

6. **RESPONDING CREATIVELY** Using the first three paragraphs of "Araby"
   as a model, write a recollection of the way you spent your evenings at some
   memorable period of your childhood. Use specific sensory images to evoke
   the locale, the activities, and the way you felt at the time.

7. **RESPONDING CREATIVELY** Narrate an experience in which you were disappointed. First show how your erroneous expectations were generated;
   then describe what you actually encountered in such a way that its contrast
   with your expectations is clear.

Suggested Readings

See page 149.

JAMES JOYCE

The Dead (p. 766)

"The Dead" is an apprehension of mortality. Joyce's carefully detailed scru-
tiny of the party, with all its apparent vivacity, serves only to reveal the triviality,
transience, and emptiness of what passes for life in Dublin. The story involves a
series of supersessions. Miss Ivors's friendliness is superseded by rigid politics,
and she departs. Her kind of fervor is superseded by the "hospitality" of the dinner table that Gabriel feels so good about and that he celebrates in his speech.
That conviviality, however, is exposed as mostly hypocritical, as each person reveals a selfish preoccupation — including Gabriel, who uses his oration to reas-
sure himself after his self-esteem has been wounded by Miss Ivors. The long
evening, however, generates in the heart of Gabriel a strong surge of love for
Gretta that supersedes his selfishness. It is edged with jealousy and self-contempt,
Gabriel's habitual weaknesses; nonetheless, the reader feels for a while that out of
the waste of the soiree at least this rejuvenation has been salvaged. But Gabriel is
longing for something just as dead as Michael Furey, and Gretta's devastating
disclosure of a dead lover's power over her mind brings the "thought-tormented"
Gabriel to his final recognition of the predominance of death. Like the monks of
Mount Melleray, all people in Ireland, dead or alive — from the aged Aunt Julia
on down — seem to be sleeping in their coffins.

While Gabriel's vision is triggered by the revelation of a dead man's sway
over the emotions of his wife and of his consequent power to thwart Gabriel's
desire, it is supported by the pervasive imagery of snow, chill, and death that
comes to fulfillment in the last paragraph. The snow has been falling intermit-
tently throughout the story. Gabriel is blanketed with it when he arrives on the
scene, and images of cold and dampness pervade the narration. Last year "Gretta
caught a dreadful cold"; Bartell D'Arcy has one this year. The girl in the song he
sings holds her death-cold infant in a soaking rain. Not only are the physical descriptions of some characters so vivid that one almost sees the skulls beneath the
flesh; even the warm, lively, cheerful elements of the story contribute to the final
impression of morbidity. The Misses Morkan are giving what may be their final

dance. The alcoholic antics of Mr. Browne and Freddy Malins consist only of er-satz good humor. And Gabriel himself, on whom everyone depends, can barely sustain his nerve and perform his function as master of the revels, keeper of or-der, and sustainer of life.

In the moribund and sterile world presided over by his three spinster aunts, Gabriel is called upon to play a role not unlike that of a year god at this Christmas season. (The party probably takes place on Epiphany, January 6.) From the outset he is willing, but in three sequential encounters he fails. Each failure strikes a blow at his naiveté, his self-confidence, and his sense of superiority. His first two defeats are followed by accomplishments (handling Freddy, his performance at dinner), but their effect on him is cumulative. Gabriel's cheerful banter with the pale, pale Lily does not suit her, as one who has been hurt in love, and his Christ-mas gift of a coin can do little to ease her "great bitterness." Afterward, his pre-tensions to take care of people are subjected to merciless ridicule in the "goloshes" passage. With Miss Ivors, Gabriel is more circumspect than with Lily, but that does not prevent him from being whipsawed between her political hostility and her personal affection. This confusing interaction not only causes Miss Ivors to abandon the company and Gabriel in his speech to reject the entire younger gen-eration of Ireland, it also sets the stage for his ultimate failure with Gretta. Gretta's favorable response to Miss Ivors's plan for a trip to Galway now seems to Gabriel a betrayal, and the association of this trip with Gretta's love for the long-dead Michael compounds the feelings of alienation and self-contempt that Miss Ivors's disapproval fosters in him.

Gabriel's failures and self-doubts should not diminish him unduly in the reader's eyes: Joyce portrays him as aesthetically sensitive, charitable, and lov-ing. The "generous tears" he sheds out of sympathy for Gretta's sorrow may not redeem anyone in a world devoted to death, but they are the distillation of a compassion quite opposite to the self-serving hypocrisy that has passed for friendly conversation at the Misses Morkan's ball. By the end of the story Gabriel no longer feels superior to his compatriots. He recognizes that when Aunt Julia dies his speechifying will be useless. He turns his mind away from the past and toward a future in which, as he feels his old identity fade and dissolve, at least the theoreti-cal possibility of growth and change exists. The ambiguity of Gabriel's much-debated "journey westward" reflects the uncertainty of any future, but Gabriel's readiness to embrace it represents a major step forward from his rejection of Miss Ivors's proposition in favor of cycling the European continent again.

WILLIAM E. SHEIDLEY

Questions for Discussion

1. Contrast the mood of the first paragraph with that of the second. Why does Joyce move from anticipation to rigidity?
2. Why are the Misses Morkan so eager for Gabriel to arrive?
3. What is the basis of Gabriel's error with Lily?
4. Explain Gabriel's hesitation to quote Browning.
5. What does Gabriel's interest in galoshes reveal about him?
6. Comment on the men present at the dance besides Gabriel. Why does Joyce limit his cast so narrowly?
7. Discuss the reception of Mary Jane's "Academy piece."

8. What does Miss Ivors want from Gabriel? Why is he so upset by his conversation with her? Why does she leave early? Figuratively, what does she take with her when she goes?
9. Explain Gabriel's longing to be out in the snow. Is Gabriel "thought-tormented"?
10. Explain the irony of Julia's singing "Arrayed for the Bridal" to Mary Jane's accompaniment. What, in this regard, is the effect of the subsequent conversation?
11. Comment on the relevance of the dinner-table conversation to the themes of the story.
12. Why is Gabriel so cheerful when carving and when proposing his toast? Is he justified? Why does he imagine people standing in the snow before he begins to speak?
13. What is the effect of Joyce's ending the tribute to the Misses Morkan with a glimpse of Freddy conducting the singers with his fork?
14. Comment on Gabriel's anecdote about "the never-to-be-forgotten Johnny." Can it be read as a summation in a minor key of the party now ending? of the life of the Morkan family? of their society?
15. Discuss the scene in which Gabriel watches Gretta listening to D'Arcy. What is Gabriel responding to? What is Gretta responding to? What do they have in common? Trace their moods as they proceed to the hotel.
16. Why is Gabriel so humiliated when he learns that Michael Furey is dead? What other effects does this revelation have on him? Explain what he realizes in the last section of the story.
17. Discuss the final paragraph. What does its poetic beauty contribute to the story? What is our final attitude toward Gabriel?

Topics for Writing

1. Discuss the relationship between Gabriel Conroy and women in general.
2. Would you say "The Dead" is a Christmas story? Why or why not?
3. Comment upon Gabriel Conroy's death wish.
4. Consider Gabriel Conroy as a failed redeemer.
5. Explore habit and hypocrisy in "The Dead."
6. After your first reading of the story, scan it again, marking the following: all references to cold, dampness, and snow; all references to death, illness, or people dead at the time of the story; all references to warmth, light, fire, and the like; all references to youth, young people, children, and the like. Catalog your findings and write a paragraph on the importance of these elements in the story.
7. **RESPONDING CREATIVELY** For a specific occasion, plan and compose an after-dinner speech with several headings like Gabriel's. Then analyze your speech, explaining what you were trying to accomplish for your audience — and for yourself. Compare your intentions with Gabriel's.

Related Commentaries

Richard Ellmann, A Biographical Perspective on Joyce's "The Dead," p. 1487.
Frank O'Connor, Style and Form in Joyce's "The Dead," p. 1554.

Suggested Readings

Anderson, Chester G. *James Joyce*. New York: Thames Hudson, 1986.

Attridge, Derek, ed. *The Cambridge Companion to James Joyce*. New York: Cambridge UP, 1990.

Beck, Warren. *Joyce's "Dubliners": Substance, Vision, and Art*. Durham, NC: Duke UP, 1969. 303–60.

Beckett, Samuel, et al. *An Examination of James Joyce*. Brooklyn: Haskell, 1974.

Benstock, Bernard, ed. *Critical Essays on James Joyce*. Boston: G. K. Hall, 1985.

Brugaletta, J. J., and M. H. Hayden. "Motivation for Anguish in Joyce's 'Araby.'" *Studies in Short Fiction* 15 (1978): 11–17.

Cronin, E. J. "James Joyce's Trilogy and Epilogue: 'The Sisters,' 'An Encounter,' 'Araby,' and 'The Dead.'" *Renascence* 31 (1979): 229–48.

Ellmann, Richard. *James Joyce. New and Revised Edition*. New York: Oxford UP, 1982.

Levin, Harry. *James Joyce: A Critical Introduction*. New York: New Directions, 1960.

Loomis, C. C., Jr. "Structure and Sympathy in 'The Dead.'" *Twentieth Century Interpretations of "Dubliners."* Ed. Peter K. Garrett. Englewood Cliffs, NJ: Prentice, 1968. 110–14. Originally published in *PMLA* 75 (1960): 149–51.

Mason, Ellsworth, and Richard Ellmann, eds. *The Critical Writings of James Joyce*. Ithaca, NY: Cornell UP, 1989.

Morrissey, L. J. "Joyce's Narrative Struggles in 'Araby.'" *Modern Fiction Studies* 28 (1982): 45–52.

Riqueline, John P. *Teller and Tale in Joyce's Fiction: Oscillating Perspectives*. Baltimore: Johns Hopkins UP, 1983.

Roberts, R. P. "'Araby' and the Palimpsest of Criticism, or Through a Glass Eye Darkly." *Antioch Review* 26 (1966–67): 469–89.

San Juan, Epifanio, Jr. *James Joyce and the Craft of Fiction: An Interpretation of "Dubliners."* Rutherford, NJ: Fairleigh Dickinson UP, 1972, 209–23.

Scott, Bonnie. *James Joyce*. Atlantic Highlands, NJ: Humanities P International, 1987.

Stone, H. "'Araby' and the Writings of James Joyce." *Antioch Review* 25 (1965): 375–410.

FRANZ KAFKA

A Hunger Artist (p. 797)

This "brief but striking parable of alienation" (to quote Kafka biographer Ernst Pawel) was probably written in February 1922, shortly before Kafka began *The Castle*. He had just returned to Prague after a four-week winter vacation prescribed by his doctor as a sort of "shock treatment" to arrest his advancing tuberculosis and deepening depression. Back at his desk, in his room in his parents' apartment, Kafka described his activities in a letter to a friend: "In order to save myself from what is commonly referred to as 'nerves,' I have lately begun to write a little. From about seven at night I sit at my desk, but it doesn't amount to much. It is like trying to dig a foxhole with one's fingernails in the midst of battle."

"A Hunger Artist" was among the few works Kafka allowed to be published in his lifetime. Ironically, he read the galley proofs only a few days before his death. Pawel describes the scene:

On May 11, [his friend Max] Brod came for what he knew would be his last visit, pretending merely to have stopped off on his way to a lecture in Vienna so as not to alarm his friend. Kafka, by then quite unable to eat, was wasting away, dying of starvation [because of throat lesions] and immersed in the galley proofs of "A Hunger Artist." Fate lacked the subtle touch of Kafka's art.

The effort drained him. "Kafka's physical condition at this point," Klopstock [a medical student] later wrote, "and the whole situation of his literally starving to death, were truly ghastly. Reading the proofs must have been not only a tremendous emotional strain but also a shattering kind of spiritual encounter with his former self, and when he had finished, the tears kept flowing for a long time. It was the first time I ever saw him overtly expressing his emotions this way. Kafka had always shown an almost superhuman self-control."

As a parable, "A Hunger Artist" may be interpreted in as many ways as there are readers finding words to describe their response to the text. Kafka created in his fiction a metaphorical language akin to music, touching emotions at a level beyond the denotations of the words he used to dramatize his imaginary characters' situations. The title is significant: "*A* Hunger Artist," not "*The* Hunger Artist." There are many kinds of hungers, and many kinds of artists expressing different needs for substance. Students may define the "hunger" as a desire for religious certainty and the "fasting" as the stubborn abstention from a faith without God. Or the key to the parable may lie in the Hunger Artist's statement at the end of the story: "I have to fast. I can't help it. . . . Because I couldn't find the food I liked. If I had found it, believe me, I should have made no fuss and stuffed myself like you or anyone else." Kafka was tormented by a failure of nourishment — from his faith, his family, his talent, his art.

Questions for Discussion

1. What is a parable? Is "A Hunger Artist" a parable?
2. Is it possible to read Kafka's story literally, as a realistic tale? What gives you the sense that there is more to "A Hunger Artist" than its plot and characters?
3. Is Kafka describing an unimaginable situation? Explain.
4. Gaping spectators, butchers, theatrical managers, circus people — the world of the Hunger Artist is mercenary and materialistic. He is described as a "martyr." A martyr to what?
5. As the Hunger Artist loses his popularity, he joins the circus, and his cage is put on display near the animal cages. What does this symbolize? What does this action foreshadow?
6. Explicate the last paragraph of the story. Analyze the function of the panther and his "noble body."

Topics for Writing

1. **RESPONDING CREATIVELY** Write a parable of your own.
2. Agree or disagree with this statement by Primo Levi, the Italian author who translated Kafka's *The Trial*:

Now I love and admire Kafka because he writes in a way that is totally unavailable to me. In my writing, for good or evil, knowingly or not, I've always strived to pass from the darkness into the light. . . . Kafka forges his path in the opposite direction: he endlessly unravels the hallucinations that he draws from incredibly profound layers, and he never filters them. The reader . . . never receives any help in tearing through the veil or circumventing it to go and see what it conceals. Kafka never touches ground, he never condescends to giving you the end of Ariadne's thread.

But this love of mine is ambivalent, close to fear and rejection: it is similar to the emotion we feel for someone dear who suffers and asks us for help we cannot give. . . . His suffering is genuine and continuous, it assails you and does not let you go.

3.   CONNECTIONS   "It was not the hunger artist who was cheating, he was working honestly, but the world was cheating him of his reward." Compare and contrast "A Hunger Artist" and "The Metamorphosis," taking this statement as the theme of both stories.

Suggested Readings

See page 154.

Franz Kafka

The Metamorphosis (p. 803)

This story admits the broadest range of explications — biographical, psychoanalytical, religious, philosophical. Here is one way it might be read: As the sole supporter of his family after the collapse of his father's business, Gregor Samsa has selflessly devoted himself to serving others. Bringing home "hard cash that could be plunked down on the table at home in front of his astonished and delighted family" has given him great satisfaction, and his only ambition has been to send his sister, "who, unlike him, loved music," to study at the Conservatory. After his metamorphosis, Gregor can no longer justify his existence by serving others. Instead, he must come to terms with himself *as* himself, an alien being whose own nature and needs are perhaps only by a degree more strange to Gregor than those of the human Gregor Samsa would have been, if somehow he had confronted them rather than deferring to the version of himself projected by the supposed needs of his family.

Kafka simultaneously traces Gregor's painful growth to self-willed individuality and the family's liberation from dependence upon him, for the relationship of dependence and exploitation has been crippling to both parties. Gregor learns what food he likes, stakes his sticky claim to the sexually suggestive picture of the woman with the fur muff (which may represent an objectification of his libido), and, no longer "considerate," at last *comes* out, intruding his obscene existence upon the world out of a purely self-assertive desire to enjoy his sister's music and to be united with its beauty. With this act Gregor has become fully himself; his death soon after simply releases him from the misery of his existence.

It is also a final release of the family from dependence and from the shame and incompetence that it entails. As an insect, Gregor becomes quite obviously the embarrassment to the family that they allowed him to be when he was human. Step by step they discover their ability to support themselves — taking jobs, coping with what is now merely the troublesome burden of Gregor, and learning finally the necessity of escaping from the prison that his solicitousness has placed them in. Gregor's battle with his father strangely transmutes the Oedipal conflict. It is triggered by Gregor's becoming a being for whom there is no longer room in the family, just as if he were a youth growing to sexual maturity, but the result is that the father, who has previously been reduced to a state of supine inertia by Gregor's diligent exertions, returns to claim his full manhood as husband and paterfamilias.

Emerging from their apartment, "which Gregor had picked for them," the family members grow into an independent purposiveness that Gregor himself is never able to attain. The story may be said to end with a second metamorphosis, focused in the image of Grete stretching her young body — almost like a butterfly newly emerged from her cocoon. Gregor, left behind like the caterpillar whose demise releases her, is denied all but a premonitory glimpse of the sexual and reproductive fulfillment for which his sister seems destined.

WILLIAM E. SHEIDLEY

Questions for Discussion

1. Describe the effect of Kafka's matter-of-fact assertion of the bizarre incident with which the story begins. Are you very interested in how it came to pass? How does Kafka keep that from becoming an issue in the story?
2. What are Gregor's concerns in section I? To what degree do they differ from what would matter to him if he had *not* been transformed into an insect?
3. When Gregor is trying to get out of bed, he considers calling for help but then dismisses the idea. Why?
4. What seems most important to the members of Gregor's family as he lies in bed? his health?
5. Describe the reaction of Gregor's parents to their first view of the metamorphosed Gregor. What circumstances in ordinary life might elicit a similar response?
6. Discuss the view from Gregor's window.
7. Trace Gregor's adaptation to his new body. In what ways do the satisfactions of his life as an insect differ from the satisfactions of his life as a traveling salesman?
8. When Gregor's father pushes him back into his room at the end of section I, Kafka calls it "truly his salvation." Comment on the possible implications of that description.
9. Describe Grete's treatment of Gregor in section II. Is Gregor ill?
10. What are Gregor's hopes for the future? Is there anything wrong with those hopes?
11. For a time, Gregor is ashamed of his condition and tries to hide from everyone. In what way might this be called a step forward for him?

12. Discuss the conflicting feelings Gregor has about the furniture's being taken out of his room. Why does he try to save the picture? What might Kafka's intention be in stressing that it is on this occasion that Grete calls Gregor by his name for the first time since his metamorphosis?
13. "Gregor's broken out." What does Gregor's father do? Why? Explain the situation that has developed by the end of section II.
14. How does the charwoman relate to Gregor? Why is she the one who presides over his "funeral"?
15. Compare the role of the lodgers in the family with that of Gregor. Have they supplanted him? Why does Gregor's father send them away in the morning?
16. Why does Gregor, who previously did not like music, feel so attracted to his sister's playing? What change has taken place in his attitude toward himself? What might Kafka mean by "the unknown nourishment he longed for"?
17. Comment on Grete's use of the neuter pronoun "it" to refer to Gregor.
18. What is the mood of the final passages of the story?

Topics for Writing

1. Write an essay describing how Kafka gains the reader's "willing suspension of disbelief."
2. Consider Gregor Samsa's metamorphosis as a triumph of the self.
3. Analyze Kafka's "The Metamorphosis" as a study of sublimated incest.
4. **RESPONDING CREATIVELY** Consider Kafka's use of apparently symbolic images whose complete meaning seems impossible to state in abstract terms — the apples, the fur muff, or the hospital beyond the window, for example. Write a vignette in which symbolic objects play a role without becoming counters in a paraphrasable allegory. Some examples of symbols: a candle, a cup, the sea, broken glass, ants.
5. **CONNECTIONS** Compare and discuss Tolstoy's "The Death of Ivan Ilych" and Kafka's "The Metamorphosis" as two studies of dying.

Related Commentaries

Gustav Janouch, Kafka's View of "The Metamorphosis," p. 1511.
Jane Smiley, Gregor: My Life as a Bug, p. 1581.
John Updike, Kafka and "The Metamorphosis," p. 1588.

Suggested Readings

Anderson, Mark. *Reading Kafka*. New York: Schocken, 1990.
Canetti, Elias. *Kafka's Other Trial: Letters to Felice*. New York: Schocken, 1988.
Greenberg, Martin. "Kafka's 'Metamorphosis' and Modern Spirituality." *Tri-Quarterly* 6 (1966): 5–20.
Gross, Ruth V. *Critical Essays on Franz Kafka*. Boston: G. K. Hall, 1990.
Kafka, Franz. *The Diaries of Franz Kafka*. New York: Schocken, 1988.
———. *The Metamorphosis*. Trans. and ed. Stanley Corngold. New York: Bantam, 1972. (Contains notes, documents, and ten critical essays.)
Levi, Primo. "Translating Kafka." *The Mirror Maker*. New York: Schocken, 1989.

Moss, Leonard. "A Key to the Door Image in 'The Metamorphosis.'" *Modern Fiction Studies* 17 (1971): 37–42.

Nabokov, Vladimir. *Lectures on Literature.* New York: Harcourt, 1980. 250–83.

Pascal, Roy. *Kafka's Narrators: A Study of His Stories and Sketches.* New York: Cambridge UP, 1984.

Pawel, Ernst. *The Nightmare of Reason: A Life of Franz Kafka.* New York: Farrar, 1984.

Spann, Meno. *Franz Kafka.* Boston: G. K. Hall, 1976.

Tauber, Herbert. *Franz Kafka: An Interpretation of His Works.* Brooklyn: Haskell, 1969.

Taylor, Alexander. "The Waking: The Theme of Kafka's 'Metamorphosis.'" *Studies in Short Fiction* 2 (1965): 337–42.

Wolkenfeld, Suzanne. "Christian Symbolism in Kafka's 'The Metamorphosis.'" *Studies in Short Fiction* 10 (1973): 205–07.

JAMAICA KINCAID

Girl (p. 839)

Kincaid's one-paragraph story is a dialogue between a mother and a daughter, consisting mostly of the mother's litany of advice about how to act in a ladylike manner. Students might enjoy reading it aloud. The West Indian prose rhythms are subtly beautiful, and the humor of the mother's advice is revealed in the audible reading process for anyone who has missed it by scanning too quickly. The conflict between the girl and her mother is evident in the mother's fears that her daughter will grow up to be a "slut." Everything the mother says is twisted in light of that fear. The daughter wonders, *"But what if the baker won't let me feel the bread?"* And the mother replies, "You mean to say that after all you are really going to be the kind of woman who the baker won't let near the bread?" The speech rhythm is reminiscent of James Joyce's interior monologues. In fact, we are not amiss to ask whether the mother is actually speaking to her daughter in the story, or whether the daughter has internalized her mother's voice and written it down for us to read to the accompaniment of our own laughter.

Questions for Discussion

1. What are the major subjects in this litany of advice? What kind of life do they describe?
2. The title of the story is "Girl," yet the girl seems to have only two lines of her own, one a protest and the other a question. Why might the author have decided to call the story "Girl" rather than "Mother" or "Woman" or "Advice" or "Memory"?
3. Identify and discuss Kincaid's use of humor in "Girl." What contribution does it make to the story?
4. What is the effect of fairly precise household rules alternating with comments such as "on Sundays try to walk like a lady and not like the slut you are so bent on becoming." String together the lines that admonish the potential slut. What do we think of the mother? What connection is there between the subjects the mother is speaking of and the idea of a slut? Why

does it keep popping up from the most innocuous of items? What does this refrain make us think of the daughter? Is the slut refrain a joke or is the author making a suggestion about the construction of self?

5.   Some of the advice seems like it could never have been spoken, but only inferred: "this is how you smile to someone you don't like too much; this is how you smile to someone you don't like at all; this is how you smile to someone you like completely." Throughout the whole piece, do you think the mother is speaking to her daughter? What other possibilities could underlie the story's composition?

6.   On page 839 the kind of advice changes: "this is how to make a good medicine to throw away a child before it even becomes a child," says the mother. Surely she's not speaking to a young girl here. In the final line, the mother calls her a "woman," the only direct address in the story; earlier the listener has been addressed as a potential slut and been told she's "not a boy." What's the difference between the advice that precedes and follows the reference to aborting a child? Which is more concrete? More abstract? Why does the advice change because of the listener's age? What kinds of knowledge is her mother able to offer?

Topics for Writing

1.   Analyze Kincaid's use of humor to indicate conflict in "Girl."
2.   **RESPONDING CREATIVELY**   Expand the story through the use of descriptive prose. Is the result more or less effective than Kincaid's original?
3.   **RESPONDING CREATIVELY**   Write a short story in which you use only dialogue.

Related Commentary

Jamaica Kincaid, On "Girl," p. 1518.

Suggested Readings

Kincaid, Jamaica. *At the Bottom of the River.* New York: Vintage, 1985.
———. Interview. *New York Times Book Review* 7 Apr. 1985: 6+.

IVAN KLÍMA

The White House (p. 842)

Students who have visited Prague as tourists in recent years will be able to visualize the scene of the castle entrance where the blind girl stands playing her flute. The crowds surge across the Peter Paul Bridge, with its unforgettable rows of statues, and they come to the base of the hill where the castle stands. The castle's heavy ramparts and the thrusting shapes of roofs loom over the road, and along the bridge and on the way to the castle there are many people like the girl, some performing small scenes, others singing, occasionally tap dancing, all of them hoping that someone in the passing crowd will stop for a moment, listen or watch, and leave something for the performer.

Much about this narrative presents the reader with a reasonable story about a university student who finds himself attracted to a musician playing at the entrance to the castle. Although the young woman is described as beautiful, with red hair and a pale complexion, it is her blindness that somehow interests him. The reader is reminded of the Chaplin film *City Lights*, in which Chaplin's tramp falls hopelessly in love with the blind girl he sees on the street. In "The White House," the girl's response is careful and self-protective, and it is only over a period of time that the student is able to convince her of his seriousness and they become lovers. He begins to understand that her world is different from his but that there are strengths and revelations that she experiences and he can only intuit. As the story develops the student begins to lose interest in their relationship. He begins to feel the restrictions of her blindness. However, he has also been described as possessing youthful irresolution. He has only recently broken off with a young woman from his class.

It is during what he conceives as a last trip together before he tells her that their relationship is over that the story takes on the symbolic dimension that is suggested in the story's title. He takes her to a mountain forest and in his carelessness gets them lost in a storm, vainly following paths that lead nowhere. It is only when she tells him that she "sees" a white house on a hilltop above them, when he can see nothing, that his own decisions about their relationship are brought into question. As a sign of his impatience he drags her up the muddy slope, and she stumbles helplessly after him. When he finds at the top of the hill that what she has "seen" is a white building that is part of a cemetery, he understands that what has happened to them has been a test of his love. As the story ends, he turns to her and asks her never to leave him.

The reader is conscious that one thread of the story's symbolism is her leading him to a cemetery. She asks him if it is a cemetery they have come to and when he tells her that it is, she says, "Then there must be a path leading to it," and he answers, "All paths lead to it." The other thread is the white house itself. We are never told precisely what it represents, but she tells him that what caused her to imagine it was that she sensed her love for him. The author has left it for his readers to decide for themselves.

Questions for Discussion

1. The song the girl is playing when he first sees her, "El Condor Pasa," had a special significance in the 1960s, when it was first popular. Does it still have this significance?
2. What is it about her that attracts him? Is this something he entirely understands himself?
3. What is it that makes him try walking a few steps with his eyes closed?
4. How does he perceive her world of sensations?
5. Can the author, with words, convey images that we cannot see?
6. Is our sight a learned experience? What do we learn from the girl and her perceptions that would suggest that it is or is not learned?
7. How can she follow him on the path when they begin their walk? Is this something we would expect?
8. What causes him to say to her, "Don't leave me"?

Topics for Writing

1. Discuss the statement in the story that "[l]ove can only be repaid with love."
2. Comment on the paragraph that begins, "Sometimes it struck him that her world, which lacked colours and clearly defined shapes, was no poorer than his own."
3. The young man tells himself that "People who worried too much about the future were incapable of experiencing the here and now." Discuss the implications of this statement.
4. Define the term *symbolism* as a literary term, and describe the use of symbolism in the last pages of the story. Certain aspects of the author's description of the young woman's sensitivities have prepared us for the possibility of the white house. Discuss them and relate them to the plot of the story.
5. If you have seen the film *City Lights,* compare it to the story, commenting on the elements of the film and the story that prepare us for their very different endings.

Suggested Readings

Klíma, Ivan. *My Golden Trades,* trans. by Paul Wilson. New York: Scribner, 1994.
———. *My Merry Mornings: Stories from Prague,* trans. by George Theiner. London; New York: Readers International, 1985.
———. *The Spirit of Prague and Other Essays,* trans. by Paul Wilson. New York: Granta Books, 1995.

JHUMPA LAHIRI

Interpreter of Maladies (p. 850)

Although the central figure in the story, the person through whose eyes we observe the action, works as an interpreter, the narrative presents us with a encounter between an Indian man and an Americanized Indian woman that ends in misunderstanding. At the moment when the woman reveals the secret of her past to the man, expecting him to answer her with understanding and sensitivity, the interpreter finds that the differences between their cultures cannot be bridged by words, even words that they each understand. It is not only their failure to understand each other that becomes a painful factor in the story, however. The reader is conscious that the story itself is woven out of patterns of misunderstanding.

Although it is the misunderstanding between the older guide and the young wife that is the central event, we are conscious that the relationship between the man and the wife is based on their misunderstanding of each other's emotional needs. After a crowded and exciting adolescence, Mrs. Das has found herself isolated in a surburban house with first one child, then two children more, one of them the son of a near stranger who spent a few days as a guest in their home. As she tells the guide, "I have terrible urges, Mr. Kapasi, to throw things away. One day I had the urge to throw everything I own out the window, the television, the children, everything."

The almost total misunderstanding that yawns wide as a gulf between the middle-aged guide and the young woman has its roots in their inability to understand each other's cultures. He has no set of standards by which to judge their concept of childraising, and to him the children are hopelessly pampered and out of control. He is probably more accustomed to women wearing casual blouses and short skirts than most Indian men of his generation, but he also misunderstands what he conceives as a sexual invitation in her style of dress. Each of them, however, also brings a desire into the confusions of the afternoon. She chooses to misunderstand his interest in her because she desperately needs someone to tell her secret, and the guide, who seems sympathetic and, more important, is someone she'll never see again, becomes the listener she has sought for many years. The guide has been taken by surprise by his sexual interest in the woman, and he chooses to misunderstand her need simply to talk with someone. He interprets it as the beginning of what he fantasizes will be a long and fulfilling relationship.

During the drive the woman, obviously as much out of boredom as from any real interest, has been questioning the guide about his other work as an interpreter in a doctor's office. He is, as the title of the story indicates, an "interpreter of maladies." It is his job to listen to the doctor's patients as they explain their illness in languages that the doctor doesn't understand. The irony of the story is that when the guide is presented with the woman's pain, which is as real as the illnesses of many of the doctor's patients, he has no words to explain it and he feels insulted that the woman has asked him to respond to her "common, trivial little secret." At the end of the day's outing, as the family leaves the car and returns to the frustrations of their daily life, he knows that she has already forgotten him.

Questions for Discussion

1. Although the couple are of Indian background, like the author, they have adopted many of the mannerisms of typical American tourists. What are some of these mannerisms? How do they affect the Indians who are observing them?
2. The driver has had experience with foreigners, but is he upset by some of the family manners he observes. What upsets him, in particular?
3. There are references in the story to things about the United States that they have all learned about through television. How much could a foreigner learn about the country by watching television programs? What gives us the impression that Indian viewers have only a tentative understanding of what they are watching?
4. What do the monkeys represent? Are they also related somehow to the past that the ruins symbolize?
5. Who is right about the importance of his job — the man, who within himself is dismayed at what he feels is the meaninglessness of what he does, or the woman, who finds his work "romantic"?
6. How do you account for the guide's tailored clothes? Do you really understand him by the story's end?
7. What does the guide's surprise at being asked to share lunch with the family tell us about India?
8. Do you think that the author means the title of the story to be taken ironically?

Topics for Writing

1. Discuss the behavior of the children and explain why it would be difficult for someone from India to understand.
2. Comment on the difference between the two cultures that are revealed when the woman tells the guide her secret. Suggest different circumstances for a meeting between them that might end differently.
3. Does the story tell us about a failure of language or a failure of cultural understanding? Discuss the failure in communication that we perceive, and comment on how it could, or could not, have been avoided.

Suggested Reading

Lahiri, Jhumpa. *Interpreter of Maladies: Stories.* Boston: Houghton Mifflin, 1999.

MARY LAVIN

The Widow's Son (p. 866)

This story will be a useful reminder to students that the readings in this class are not historical documents or psychological case studies. They are stories, which have taken form in the mind of a writer, and although writers like to describe the independent spirit of the characters they have created, the truth is that the writer has created the story and can alter its shape and outcome at any point. This story, with two different endings, both tragic but each tragic in its own way, also reminds us that if the writer does choose to change a story's ending, the consequences may be more complicated than we expect.

After she has narrated the first version, Lavin tells us very specifically that she is taking advantage of her privileges as a writer to end the story differently. With her statement she makes it clear to us that the subject of the story is not a boy and his mother and a bicycle accident that did or didn't occur — the subject of her narrative is storytelling itself. Lavin's statement is particularly useful as a way for students to understand the creative process that has produced the narratives that fill this anthology. As she writes, "Knowing the whole art of storytelling . . . I lean no heavier now on your credulity than I did by telling you what happened in the first instance."

If students read the story carefully, they will notice that each of the possible endings of the story is followed to its ultimate conclusion, and each of them is a reasonable presentation of what we could regard as the facts of the story. It is the storyteller's responsibility not to disappoint the reader, and each possibility must be equally plausible. Lavin's art is to convince the reader of either possibility, and she has slyly suggested that one of the stories is an invention. "In fact, it is sometimes easier to invent than to remember, and were this not so, the art of the storyteller and the art of gossip would wither in an instant." The reality that Lavin pretends to hide from her readers is, of course, that she has made up everything about the stories, and neither one is more true than the other.

In each of the story's variations the characters and the situation are the same, but one of the characters makes a crucial decision that determines the outcome. In the first version, the woman only intended to frighten the chickens out of the way of her son's bicycle by flapping her apron, but one of the chickens flew into the bicycle, and the crash was inevitable. In the second version, the woman is sweeping the road and not flapping her apron, but the chickens still have scattered in fright at the approach of the bicycle, and the clucking hen is still on the road. Although her beloved son manages to brake in time to save himself from injury, the mother has been boasting of his skills and talents to an old neighbor and she becomes enraged, shouting that he could have avoided the accident by swerving. She accuses him of taking a safer course and killing the chicken. The reader cannot help but be relieved that in this version the boy is alive, but Lavin chooses not to let us have a happier ending. The most vivid image of the story is the widow's angry beating of her son with the bloody carcass of the bird he has accidentally run over. The next morning he has left the house, never to return. The most haunting effect of the story is the realization that either of the two versions has the dark inevitability of tragedy. In her retelling the author has only lifted the reader's expectations for a moment and then dashed them again. It is a brilliant, and harrowing, demonstration of the storyteller's art.

Questions for Discussion

1. Although there is nothing in the story that tells us where it is set, we can judge the approximate period when it takes place. When does the story happen, and what are the details that help us know this?
2. What are some differences in the rural society at the time of the story and in the modern era?
3. What is the meaning of the comparison of "her few bald acres" and "their great bearded meadows"?
4. Are the old man and the boy's mother having a real conversation as she waits for him to come home, or are they simply setting the scene for the reader?
5. In her talk about her boy, the widow exaggerates his abilities. What causes her to do this? Will it have an effect on the events that will soon happen?
6. Why doesn't she accept some blame for the accident in either version of the story, instead of placing it all on her son?
7. Does her sudden attack on her son in the second version of the story cause us to change our judgment of her character?

Topics for Writing

1. Compare the two versions of the story and decide which one is "true." Defend your decision by referring to details in the story.
2. Discuss the sense of illusion that a writer tries to create and analyze why we trust the narration we are reading, even though we know that it is only illusion.
3. Compare the economic situation of the widow and a widow like her in our own time, and discuss the role of the community in each situation.

4.   **RESPONDING CREATIVELY**   Write a version of the story presenting a similar accident but set in today's world, in which nearly everything about the
events would be different.

Suggested Readings

Kelly, Angeline A. *Mary Lavin, Quiet Rebel: A Study of Her Short Stories.* New York:
 Barnes & Noble, 1980.
Peterson, Richard F. *Mary Lavin.* Boston: Twayne, 1978.
Lavin, Mary. *Collected Stories.* Introd. by V. S. Pritchett. Boston: Houghton, 1971.
———. *In a Cafe: Selected Stories.* Ed. Elizabeth Walsh Peavoy, foreword by Tho-
    mas Kilroy. London: Penguin, 1999.
———. *Selected Stories.* New York: Macmillan, 1959.
———. *The Stories of Mary Lavin.* London: Constable, 1974.

D. H. Lawrence

Odour of Chrysanthemums (p. 875)

Because of its unusual vocabulary and emotional complexity, this can be a
difficult story for many students to understand. Before they read it, their attention should be directed to the first paragraph of the headnote, which suggests an
approach. Elizabeth Bates, the protagonist, is bitter because she feels trapped in
her marriage. She is caught between her attempt to relate to her husband and her
struggle to break free from her marital bondage. Her husband drinks away most
of the meager wages he earns at the coal mine, leaving her to tend the children in
a dark, squalid cottage she calls a "dirty hole, rats and all." She is fiercely protective of their two children — daughter, Annie, and young son, John. There is another baby on the way. Consumed with anger toward her husband, Elizabeth chan-
nels her love and tenderness toward her children. She feels herself "absolutely
necessary for them. They were her business."

Recognizing the pattern of Lawrence's use of symbolism in the story may
be one of the best ways to approach it. In the opening paragraph, Elizabeth's
emotional situation is prefigured in the image of the nameless woman forced back
into the hedge by the oncoming train. The female-male opposition in the story is
symbolized here: marriage and home (the hedge) versus the mine and the pub
(the train). A little later on, Lawrence has Elizabeth comment explicitly on the
symbolism implied in the title of the story. When her young daughter is charmed
to see her mother wearing the chrysanthemums — "You've got a flower in your
apron" (pregnancy = flowering), Elizabeth tells her that she's speaking nonsense.
To the mother, the flowers are not beautiful anymore. Most emphatically she does
not treasure them as a hardy symbol of fertility in her otherwise bleak existence.
To her, they are a symbol of death: "It was chrysanthemums when I married him,
and chrysanthemums when you were born, and the first time they ever brought
him home drunk, he'd got brown chrysanthemums in his button-hole."

Ironically, near the end of the story, when Elizabeth lays out her dead husband on the parlor floor, she smells "a cold, deathly smell of chrysanthemums in

the room." One of the miners coming in with the stretcher knocks the vase of flowers to the floor, and she mops up the spilled water. In this action she is a servant of death, "her ultimate master" at the end of the story.

For most of the story, however, her master is her husband. The word "master" is the common name for husband among the village wives, but Elizabeth has refused to submit to her destiny. The line between female and male is clearly drawn in her world, where the sight of twelve children living at home on a miner's salary is not uncommon. But Elizabeth feels herself apart from the other housewives and miners. She judges everyone she comes in contact with, except herself. Then, as she begins to wash the naked body of her dead husband, she feels herself "countermanded. She saw him, how utterly inviolable he lay in himself. She had nothing to do with him. She could not accept it."

The final scene of "Odour of Chrysanthemums," the description of the mother and the wife laying out the body of the dead man, is one of the most unforgettable moments in Lawrence's fiction. The physicality of the dead man is unmistakable, and it affects the two women differently. Now Elizabeth fully accepts the reality of her individuality, her separate existence in the world. Before, she felt herself apart as an emotional defense against her disappointment with her marriage. Now she knows "the utter isolation of the human soul." The husband she hated existed only in her mind. With his death, she is free to ask, "Who am I? What have I been doing? . . . What wrong have I done? . . . There lies the reality, this man." The story ends with her horrified by the distance between them. Yet she is at peace.

Questions for Discussion

1. "Odour of Chrysanthemums" is set in the kind of mining village Lawrence grew up in. The first four paragraphs "pan in" on the social world of the story, establishing a relationship among the industrial landscape, wild nature, and human beings. Read the opening carefully, noting the diction of the passage, and try to state Lawrence's vision of the relationship among these elements.

2. Note how Elizabeth Bates appears on the scene merely as "a woman." How does the author go on to establish a closer relationship to her? What is she like when we first meet her? Describe the world she inhabits.

3. When Elizabeth sets out to find Walter, she notes "with faint disapproval the general untidiness" of the Rigleys. Consider the use of dialect in this passage. Who uses it? Can you determine Elizabeth's relationship to her neighbors and her class position? Might it be connected to her general satisfaction with her marriage?

4. In section I the family awaits Walter Bates's return from the mines — and yet his presence seems to haunt the family. What influence does even his absence exert on his wife and children?

5. Elizabeth's mother-in-law arrives, and the two women discuss Walter. How does Lawrence subtly and comically establish their relationship to each other and to Walter?

6. Miners stripped down to work underground; half-naked, white Walter is strangely beautiful as he is brought home. Her husband's body is a revelation to Elizabeth: "And she knew what a stranger he was to her." Try to

explain the epiphany Elizabeth undergoes; what does she now understand about her marriage?

7.   Lawrence said of literary symbols, "You can't give a symbol a meaning anymore than you can give a cat a 'meaning.' Symbols are organic units of consciousness with a life of their own, and you can never explain them away because their value is dynamic, emotional, belonging to the sense-consciousness of the body and soul, and not simply mental. An allegorical image has a *meaning*" (from an essay that appears in *Dragon of Apocalypse: Selected Literary Criticism,* ed. Anthony Beal [New York: Viking, 1966]). Trace the meaning that chrysanthemums take on in each stage of this story. Is it possible to give them a "full" meaning? According to Lawrence, are the flowers symbolic or allegorical?

8.   Given the portrait of the social world in the story and the portrayal of this unhappy marriage, how might the two be related? Is Lawrence explicit about the relationship or might you like to argue with him about the causes of feeling in it?

9.   One of the difficulties in understanding "Odour of Chrysanthemums" is its vocabulary. Consult a good dictionary to discover the meanings of words such as "gorse," "coppice," "hips," "spinney," "cleaved," "whimsey," "reedy," "pit-pond," "alders," "tarred," "pit-bank," "headstocks," and "colliery." How does this increase your understanding of Lawrence's story?

Topics for Writing

1.   Analyze light and dark imagery in "Odour of Chrysanthemums."
2.   Discuss the use of sound and silence in "Odour of Chrysanthemums."
3.   **CONNECTIONS**   Compare the isolation and alienation of marriage in Lawrence's "Odour of Chrysanthemums" and Bobbie Ann Mason's "Shiloh."

Related Commentaries

D. H. Lawrence, Draft Passage from "Odour of Chrysanthemums," p. 1519.
D. H. Lawrence, On "The Fall of the House of Usher" and "The Cask of Amontillado," p. 1694.
Jay Parini, Lawrence's and Steinbeck's "Chrysanthemums," p. 1560.

Related Story

John Steinbeck, The Chrysanthemums, p. 1269.

Suggested Readings

See page 167.

D. H. Lawrence

The Rocking-Horse Winner (p. 889)

Lawrence's masterful technical control wins the reader's assent to the fantastic premise on which the story is built; without that assent, the thematic statement the story propounds would lack cogency. Rather than confronting us boldly with his improbable donnée, as Kafka does in "The Metamorphosis," Lawrence edges up to it. The whispering voices in the house that drive Paul to his furious rocking begin as a thought in the mother's mind and then become a figure of speech that crystallizes imperceptibly into a literal fact — or rather, into an auditory hallucination heard by the children that expresses their perception of their mother's unquenchable need for funds. Paul's ability to pick a winner by riding his rocking horse to where he is lucky requires even more circumspect handling. Like the family members, we learn about it after the fact, putting together bits of information to explain a set of peculiar but at first not at all implausible circumstances — Paul's claim, "Well, I got there!", his familiarity with race horses, Bassett's reluctance "to give him away" to Oscar, Paul's giving Oscar a tip on a long shot that comes in a winner, and only then, with Oscar's skepticism always preempting that of the reader, the revelation of how much he has won. It is not until the very end that we, with his astonished mother, actually witness Paul in the act of receiving revelation — just as he slips beyond the world of everyday probability for good and into the uncharted supernatural realm from whence his "luck" seems to emanate.

Although no explanation, supernatural or otherwise, is necessary to account for good fortune at the race track, Lawrence persuades the reader that Paul's success is caused by his exertions and therefore has a moral meaning. In Paul's household the lack of love is perceived as a lack of money and the lack of money is attributed to a lack of luck. Since luck is by definition something that happens *to* one, to blame one's troubles on luck is to deny responsibility for them and to abandon any effort to overcome them. As the event makes clear, Paul's mother will never be satisfied, no matter how much money falls her way, because no amount of money can fill the emptiness left by the absence of love. The "hard little place" in her heart at the beginning of the story has expanded until, at the end, she feels that her whole heart has "turned actually into a stone." Paul sets out by the force of will to redefine luck as something one can acquire. He places belief before evidence and asserts, "I'm a lucky person. . . . God told me," and then makes good on his promise by riding his rocking horse to where luck comes from. " 'It's as if he had it from heaven,'" Bassett says, "in a secret, religious voice."

In his single-minded devotion to winning money for his mother at the racetrack by riding his rocking horse (which W. D. Snodgrass has likened to masturbation as Lawrence understood it), Paul diverts his spiritual and emotional forces to material aims, and Lawrence symbolically represents the effect of this *materialization* in the process of petrification by which the mother's heart and Paul's blue eyes, which have throughout the story served as an emblem of his obsession, turn to stone. At the end Oscar states the case with epigrammatic precision: Hester's son has been transformed into eighty-odd thousand pounds — a tidy sum, but of course it will not be enough.

William E. Sheidley

Questions for Discussion

1. How is Paul's mother portrayed at the outset? Does Lawrence suggest that she is blameworthy? Why or why not?
2. Explain the family's "grinding sense of the shortage of money." Why do the voices get even louder when some money becomes available? What would it take to still the voices?
3. Discuss the implications of Paul's confusing *luck* with *lucre*. How accurate is his mother's definition of luck? What would constitute true good luck for him?
4. Explain Paul's claim to be lucky. In what sense is he justified? In what sense is he very unlucky?
5. What function do Oscar and Bassett play in the story, beyond providing Paul with practical access to the racetrack and the lawyer?
6. "Bassett was serious as a church." Is this a humorous line? Does it suggest anything beyond the comic?
7. What is the effect on the reader of the episode in which Oscar takes Paul to the track and Paul's horse Daffodil wins the race?
8. Explain the mother's response to her birthday gift. What is its effect on Paul? Why?
9. Before the Derby, Paul does not "know" for several races. Can this dry spell be explained? What brings it to an end?
10. Analyze Paul's last words in the story. What does he mean by *"get there"*? Where, in fact, does he go? Is *absolute* certainty possible? How? Why is Paul so proud to proclaim that he is lucky to his mother? Finally, comment on her reaction.
11. Evaluate Oscar's remarks, which end the story. Was Paul a "poor devil"? In what senses?

Topics for Writing

1. Describe the handling of the supernatural in Lawrence's "The Rocking-Horse Winner."
2. Explore the religious theme of "The Rocking-Horse Winner."
3. Consider luck, will, and faith in "The Rocking-Horse Winner."
4. Analyze the realistic elements and the social theme of Lawrence's supernatural tale.
5. **RESPONDING CREATIVELY**   Consider luck, lucre, and love in "The Rocking-Horse Winner."
6. **RESPONDING CREATIVELY**   Look up a newspaper story about some unexplained phenomenon, ghost, or poltergeist, and work it into a narrative whose meaning is finally not dependent on an interest in the supernatural.

Related Commentaries

Janice H. Harris, Levels of Meaning in Lawrence's "The Rocking-Horse Winner," p. 1499.
D. H. Lawrence, On "The Fall of the House of Usher" and "The Cask of Amontillado," p. 1494.

Suggested Readings

Boulton, J. T., ed. *The Letters of D. H. Lawrence*. New York: Cambridge UP, 1989.

Clayton, J. J. "D. H. Lawrence: Psychic Wholeness through Rebirth." *Massachusetts Review* 25 (1984): 200–21.

Harris, Janice. *The Short Fiction of D. H. Lawrence*. New Brunswick, NJ: Rutgers UP, 1984.

Hyde, G. M. *D. H. Lawrence*. New York: St. Martin's, 1990.

Jackson, Dennis, and Felda Jackson. *Critical Essays on D. H. Lawrence*. Boston: G. K. Hall, 1988.

Kalnins, M. "D. H. Lawrence's 'Odour of Chrysanthemums': The Three Endings." *Studies in Short Fiction* 13 (1976): 471–79.

Lawrence, D. H. *Portable D. H. Lawrence*. New York: Penguin, 1977.

Meyers, Jeffry. *D. H. Lawrence: A Biography*. New York: Knopf, 1990.

Olson, Charles. *D. H. Lawrence and the High Temptation of the Mind*. Santa Barbara, CA: Black Sparrow, 1980.

Rice, Thomas Jackson. *D. H. Lawrence: A Guide to Research*. New York: Garland, 1983.

Rose, S. "Physical Trauma in D. H. Lawrence's Short Fiction." *Contemporary Literature* 16 (1975): 73–83.

Sager, Keith. *D. H. Lawrence: Life into Art*. Athens: U of Georgia P, 1985.

San Juan, E., Jr. "Theme versus Imitation: D. H. Lawrence's 'The Rocking-Horse Winner,'" *D. H. Lawrence Review* 3 (1970): 136–40.

Schneider, Daniel J. *The Consciousness of D. H. Lawrence: An Intellectual Biography*. Lawrence: UP of Kansas, 1986.

———. *D. H. Lawrence: The Artist as Psychologist*. Lawrence: UP of Kansas, 1984.

Shaw, M. "Lawrence and Feminism." *Critical Quarterly* 25 (1983): 23–27.

Snodgrass, W. D. "A Rocking Horse: The Symbol, the Pattern, the Way to Live." *D. H. Lawrence: A Collection of Critical Essays*. Ed. Mark Spilka. *Twentieth Century Views*. Englewood Cliffs, NJ: Prentice, 1963. Originally published in *Hudson Review* 11 (1958).

Squires, Michael, and Keith Cushman. *The Challenge of D. H. Lawrence*. Madison: U of Wisconsin P, 1990.

Widmer, Kingsley. *The Art of Perversity: D. H. Lawrence's Shorter Fictions*. Seattle: U of Washington P, 1962. 92–95, 213.

Ursula K. Le Guin

The Ones Who Walk Away from Omelas (p. 902)

The tone of Le Guin's story deserves special mention, because it supports the humane wisdom of her theme. Rational, unhurried, calm, and composed, her words flow in long paragraphs like the deep bed of a river. She subtitles her story "Variations on a theme by William James." Read her explanation of the source of her story in Part Two (p. 1524), where she quotes two paragraphs by James, the American philosopher and experimental psychologist (1842–1910) and older brother of the writer Henry James. Students will recognize that Le Guin's tone is similar to James's in his philosophical discourse, which she so admires.

The tone of Le Guin's story is animated by her choice of narrator. Simultaneously certain and uncertain, she is both assured and tentative in her description of the happy, peace-loving community. (Remember *Omelas* means "O-peace," as well as Salem, Oregon, spelled backward.) Le Guin is too modest in her assertion of writing about "fortune cookie ideas." She possesses great authority in her definitions: "Happiness is based on a just discrimination of what is necessary, what is neither necessary nor destructive, and what is destructive." Perhaps students need to discuss this philosophical point to make sure they understand it. Major themes of the story — that ideals are the probable causes of future experience, and that what you touch, touches you — are based on this definition of happiness. The ones who walk away from Omelas have used it in formulating their decision to leave the utopian community.

Le Guin is also wise in matters of human psychology. She purposely leaves the details of the good life in Omelas vague, so that readers can imagine their own utopias, complete with as many or as few drugs and as much or as little sex as they are comfortable with. She also knows that her readers will find her vision of the good life more believable after her description of the tormented child on whom everything depends. For human beings, the ideal becomes real only with the introduction of pain and loss, "the terrible justice of reality." The destination of those who leave Omelas is less imaginable than the city of near-perfection. The ones who leave are unwilling to be bound by the terrible laws of this "utopia"; they must create their own futures. Le Guin's fantasy isn't escapist literature. It's as real and inescapable as life itself.

Questions for Discussion

1. What is the tone of this story?
2. What is the point of view in the story? Who is the narrator? Briefly discuss the dual attitudes of the narrator.
3. How accurate is Le Guin's contention that "happiness is based on a just discrimination of what is necessary, what is neither necessary nor destructive, and what is destructive"? How central is this idea to the themes of the story?
4. What type of society is Omelas? Did you find the narrator's description substantive or vague? Discuss possible reasons the author constructed the story in this manner.
5. What role does the tormented child play in the story? How does it affect the citizens of Omelas?
6. Why do some citizens desert Omelas? What is the place that is "even less imaginable to most of us than the city of happiness"?
7. What is the source of conflict in the story? Who is the protagonist? the antagonist?
8. Discuss the major themes of the story.
9. How would you characterize Le Guin's narrative style? Do you feel her use of the short question is effective? Why?
10. What is your reaction to the story?

Topics for Writing

1. Analyze the idea of the utopian society in "The Ones Who Walk Away from Omelas."
2. **CONNECTIONS** Compare and contrast the societies and philosophies in Omelas and in the small town in Jackson's "The Lottery."

Related Commentary

Ursula K. Le Guin, The Scapegoat in Omelas, p. 1524.

Suggested Readings

Cogell, E. C. "Setting as Analogue to Characterization in Ursula Le Guin." *Extrapolation* 18 (1977): 131–41.
Manlove, C. N. "Conservatism in the Fantasy of Le Guin." *Extrapolation* 21 (1980): 287–97.
Moylan, T. "Beyond Negation: The Critical Utopias of Ursula K. Le Guin and Samuel R. Delany." *Extrapolation* 21 (1980): 236–53.
Wood, S. "Discovering Worlds: The Fiction of Ursula K. Le Guin." *Voices for the Future: Essays on Major Science Fiction Writers*. Ed. J. D. Clareson. Bowling Green: Bowling Green U Popular P, 1976–79. 2:154–79.

DORIS LESSING

A Sunrise on the Veld (p. 908)

In this story, Doris Lessing describes a teenager taking a step toward becoming an adult. In each of the stories the step involves the realization that the protagonist bears some responsibility for the things that are happening around him. The character begins to understand the role he also plays in the destruction of the Africa he grew up in. He begins to be aware of his own guilt. In "A Sunrise on the Veld" a boy is forced to realize that the scene he has just witnessed, the death of a wounded antelope devoured by a horde of ants, could have been caused by his own careless hunting on any previous morning when he shot but made no effort to pursue and kill the animal he wounded.

In "A Sunrise on the Veld" the cruel revelation is made even more intense by a fifteen-year-old boy's ecstatic response to nature and the dawn. The boy arises in the dark, takes his rifle and the family's two hunting dogs, and goes out to greet the dawn. Lessing makes it clear that he is not thinking about hunting, but simply absorbing the experience of the new day — the emerging light symbolizing his adolescence.

Again, Lessing has only needed to conceive a character and a story emerges. With her powerful gift of empathy she is able to immerse herself in the character of the teenage boy. It is youth and its excitements that Lessing presents to us here, and this aspect of adolescence has no gender boundaries. To give us an image that would be so strong that the boy must react — even with his years of wandering in the bush around his family's farms — Lessing confronts the boy, and the reader, with by appalling image of a struggling horned buck engulfed with a black sheet that half covers its white and bleeding skin. The boy for a moment can't even see what it is, and Lessing lets us stand beside him, trying to understand what is happening, until we suddenly are aware that it is a wave of ants. The boy's being forced to confront his own complicity in a death that is happening in the world is a situation that can be appreciated by all readers.

Questions for Discussion

1. Why doesn't the boy want his parents to know he's slipping out of the house?
2. Why does the boy take his rifle and the dogs?
3. Why does he walk with his shoes hung around his neck?
4. Why don't the ants attack him?
5. When he doesn't follow an animal he has perhaps only wounded he is disobeying one of the first rules of hunting. How does he justify this to himself?

Topics for Writing

1. Compare this boy's life with your own adolescence.
2. Discuss the role of hunting in a boy's coming of age in tribal African societies.
3. Discuss what the ferocity of the ants tells us about the African landscape.
4. **CONNECTIONS**   Compare and contrast the white teenager's African experience in "A Sunrise on the Veld" with Dave's experience in rural Mississippi in Wright's story "The Man Who Was Almost a Man."

Suggested Readings

Dembo, L. S., and Anis Pratt, eds. *Doris Lessing: Critical Essays.* Ann Arbor, MI: Books Demand UMI, 1988.

Fishburn, Katherine. *The Unexpected Universe of Doris Lessing: A Study in Narrative Technique.* Westport, CT: Greenwood Press, 1985.

Hakac, John. "Budding Profanity in 'A Sunrise on the Veld.' " *Doris Lessing Newsletter 10(1)* (Spring 1986): 13.

Hanson, Clare. "Each Other: Images of Otherness in the Short Fiction of Doris Lessing, Jean Rhys, and Angela Carter." *Journal of the Short Story in English* 10 (Spring 1988): 67–82.

Hanson, Clare, ed. *Re-Reading the Short Story.* New York: St. Martin's Press, 1989.

Knapp, Mona. *Doris Lessing.* New York: Ungar, 1984.

Lessing, Doris. *The Doris Lessing Reader.* New York: Knopf, 1989.

Pickering, Jean. *Understanding Doris Lessing.* Columbia: U of South Carolina P, 1990.

Pruitt, Virginia. "The Crucial Balance: A Theme in Lessing's Short Fiction." *Studies in Short Fiction 18(3)* (Summer 1981): 281–285.

Sprague, Claire, and Virginia Tiger, eds. *Critical Essays on Doris Lessing.* Boston: Hall, 1986.

Watson, Irene G. "Lessing's 'To Room Nineteen' " *Explicator 47(3)* (Spring 1989): 54–55.

Whittaker, Ruth. *Doris Lessing.* New York: St. Martin's, 1988.

CLARICE LISPECTOR

The Smallest Woman in the World (p. 914)

An idea that sheds light on Lispector's theme has been provided by the critic Giovanni Pontiero, who recognized that Lispector's characters — like the smallest woman in the world — are "free from psychological conflicts, [so] they show a greater participation in what is real, the greater space that includes all spaces." This is perhaps Little Flower's possession of "the most perfect feeling," her knowledge that "not to be devoured is the secret goal of a whole life."

Questions for Discussion

1. Lispector has framed the beginning and ending of her story by setting it "in the depths of Equatorial Africa," where the French explorer Marcel Pretre has discovered the smallest woman in the world. In the middle of the story, Lispector dramatizes the responses of the "civilized world" to the newspaper reports of Little Flower. How does Lispector keep our interest in the story despite her unconventional organization of her plot?
2. In the fifth paragraph, Lispector refers to "the heart of Africa," which the white explorer has penetrated to find Little Flower. What is Lispector's view of "the heart of Africa" in this story? How does it compare to conventional views of Africa, as in Joseph Conrad's story "Heart of Darkness"?
3. What kinds of humor do you find in "The Smallest Woman in the World"?
4. Why do the people reading about Little Flower in the newspaper react so differently to her? What is Lispector trying to show about our so-called civilized life?
5. How does Lispector shape the conclusion of her story by giving the last word to "one old lady, folding up the newspaper decisively"?

Topic for Writing

1. **CONNECTIONS** Compare and contrast "The Smallest Woman in the World" with Gabriel García Márquez's "A Very Old Man with Enormous Wings" as examples of magical realism.

Suggested Readings

Cixous, Helene. *Reading with Clarice Lispector.* Ed. and trans. Verena Andermatt Conley. Minneapolis: U of Minnesota P, 1990.

Peixoto, Marta. *Passionate Fictions: Gender, Narrative, and Violence in Clarice Lispector.* Minneapolis: U of Minnesota P, 1994.

JACK LONDON

To Build a Fire (p. 920)

While the protagonist of "To Build a Fire" lacks sufficient imagination to concern himself with "significances" or to "meditate upon . . . man's place in the universe," London's story leads us directly to these issues. Its setting and structure strip man's confrontation with death in an alien and indifferent or even hostile universe down to a starkly simple example, while its slow and detailed pace brings home the reality of that confrontation with all the force of actual experience.

The nameless traveler across the blank Arctic landscape is as well equipped as any man for coping with his situation. He is resourceful, cautious, tenacious, and able to tolerate a great deal of discomfort. More experience in the Yukon would not have improved his ability to cope: It would simply have supplied him with such wisdom as is propounded by the old-timer: Don't try it, or don't try it alone. But avoidance can only be temporary. Man must face death, and face it alone. London places his character on "the unprotected tip of the planet," exposed to the frigid emptiness of the universe, and the story details how it overcomes him.

London defines the man's condition by contrasting it with that of the dog, which is at home in the hostile environment. Fitted by nature with adequate defenses against the cold and guided by unfailing instinct in deciding what to do, the dog provides an unsentimental perspective on the man's struggles. Although the man's judgment is a poor substitute for canine instinct and although his improvised technology, despite its provision of fire, proves disastrously less reliable than husky fur, the man's consciousness of his situation, his errors, and his eventual dignity in accepting his death earn him a heroic stature impossible for the dog, which London portrays *as* a dog, not as a person deserving credit for his decisions and hence his survival. At the end, the husky has more in common with "the stars that leaped and danced and shone brightly in the cold sky" than with the human spirit that has passed from the frozen corpse, leaving behind its mark in the dignity of the posture that the corpse retains.

Readers may disagree over whether the story — which, as Earle Labor has shown, corresponds remarkably with Greek tragedy as defined by Aristotle — conveys a tragic sense of order or the black pessimism characteristic of the mature London. Surely all readers will, however, acknowledge the powerful effect that the story creates, thanks to London's artful use of foreshadowing, repetition, and close observation of authentic detail. As numbness and frost invade and gradually seize the body of the man, the metaphysical chill accompanying the recognition of mortality creeps irresistibly into the reader's mind. Each detail of the story contributes to this single impression — the atmosphere; the cold ironic voice of the narrator; and most poignantly, perhaps, the contrasting moments of warmth by the fire at lunch, the remembered comfort of which is strangely echoed in the repose of the dying man's last thoughts.

Questions for Discussion

1. Describe the atmosphere established in the first two paragraphs.
2. What techniques does London use to impress the reader with the man's solitude? Why does he refrain for so long from mentioning the dog?
3. How cold is it? How does London make clear what such cold is like? Why is it important for him to do so?
4. London tells us that the man lacks imagination. What good would imagination have done him?
5. Why is the dog reluctant to follow the man? Why does it follow him anyway? Trace the dog's attitudes throughout the story.
6. The man keeps close track of time and distances. Why are they important to him? What significance might they have for the reader?
7. What is the reason for London's careful introduction of the hazards of the hidden spots of water in such detail before the man actually slips into one? What would be the difference if he withheld these explanations until afterwards?
8. What does the man do at half past twelve when he arrives at the forks? What does his behavior reveal about his character? In what way are those traits important to the subsequent action?
9. The words of an old-timer from Sulphur Creek enter the man's memory at intervals in the story. Trace the changes in his response to them. What does the old-timer have in common with the dog?
10. Several times London associates the cold with outer space. Consider the possible implications of this connection.
11. Why does London wait until after lunch to have the man fall into the water?
12. What mistake does the man make in building his second fire? Why does he commit that error?
13. While his second fire is getting started, the man indulges in some distinctly prideful thoughts. Is pride his downfall? Explain.
14. How do we feel about the man as he struggles to build his third fire?
15. What is wrong with the man's plan to kill the dog, warm his hands in the dog's body, and then start another fire?
16. At one point the man crawls after the dog on all fours, like an animal; at another he feels that he is flying like the god Mercury. What do you think London means to imply by these comparisons?
17. Although the man readily accepts the likelihood that he will lose parts of his body to the frost, he refuses to acknowledge that he is going to die until nearly the end. Contrast his behavior before and after he makes that recognition.
18. By the end, does the man still lack imagination?
19. Explain the effect of the last paragraph's being narrated from the dog's point of view.

Topics for Writing

1. Write an essay contrasting the use of instinct and judgment in "To Build a Fire."
2. Discuss London's use of foreshadowing and repetition.

3. Discuss London's treatment of the partial source of the story, Jeremiah Lynch's *Three Years in the Klondike* (London, 1904). (Quoted in Franklin Walker, *Jack London and the Klondike*, pp. 256–57; see Suggested Readings, below.)
4. After reading the story, make a list of the elements that compose it, such as *man, dog, cold, old-timer, fire, water*, and so on. Read it again, classifying each passage into the appropriate category or categories. Invent new categories as needed, but keep your list as short as possible. Draw a diagram showing how the elements are related. Does your diagram reveal or confirm anything about the meaning of the story?
5. **RESPONDING CREATIVELY**   Write a story or vignette involving a human being and an animal. Imitate London by telling part of it from the animal's point of view but without anthropomorphizing the animal in any way.

Related Commentary

Jack London, Letter to the Editor on "To Build a Fire," p. 1526.

Suggested Readings

Labor, Earle. *Jack London.* Twayne's United States Authors Series 230. New York: Twayne, 1974. 63–70.
McClintock, James I. *White Logic: Jack London's Short Stories.* Grand Rapids, MI: Wolf House, 1975. 116–19.
Walker, Franklin. *Jack London and the Klondike: The Genesis of an American Writer.* San Marino, CA: Huntington Library, 1966. 254–60.

KATHERINE MANSFIELD

Bliss (p. 932)

The life that blooms in Bertha Young presses against the restraints of "idiotic civilization" like a blossom bursting out of its bud case. Through all the incidents leading up to the devastating revelation of the liaison between Harry and Pearl, Mansfield develops Bertha's flowerlike vulnerability. We are attracted by her tolerant and amused appreciation of her husband and guests, the delight she takes in her "absolutely satisfactory house and garden," and her love for Little B. But at the same time we must feel a growing anxiety for this young woman, who herself knows that she is "too happy — too happy!" She is so little in command of her life that she must beg Nanny for a chance to feed her own daughter; her catalog of the wonderful things in her life dwindles off into trivia ("their new cook made the most superb omelettes"); and her husband and "modern, thrilling friends" look to the skeptical eye of the reader more like *poseurs* and hypocrites than the charming and sincere eccentrics Bertha takes them for.

Mansfield defines Bertha's condition and the danger to which it exposes her in the explicit symbol of the pear tree in bloom, to which Bertha likens herself, and in the unsettling glimpse of the cats, a gray one and its black shadow, that creep across the lawn beneath it. On the telephone to Harry, Bertha tries and fails to communicate her state of bliss, but she hopes that her fascinating new "find," Pearl Fulton, with whom she feels a mysterious kinship, will somehow be able to understand. In the moonlight the pear tree resembles the silvery Pearl, just as in the daylight it matched Bertha's green and white apparel, and as the two women gaze at it together, Bertha feels that the ecstatic communion she has desired is taking place. And in a sense it is, for the moment seems to release in Bertha for the first time a passionate sexual desire for her husband that, as she too soon learns, is shared by Pearl.

The reader winces as the long-anticipated blow falls at last, and Eddie Warren intones the line that might end a more cynical version of the story: "'Why Must it Always be Tomato Soup?' It's so *deeply* true, don't you feel? Tomato soup is so *dreadfully* eternal." But Mansfield will not leave it there. As the gray cat Pearl and the black cat Eddie slink off into the night, Bertha returns to the window to find the pear tree, an embodiment of the same energy and beauty that wells up within herself, standing "as lovely as ever and as full of flower and as still."

WILLIAM E. SHEIDLEY

Questions for Discussion

1. Define the impression of Bertha given by the opening section. What is the source of her bliss?
2. What is the function of the scene in which Bertha feeds Little B? Comment on the way the section ends.
3. What does Bertha try and fail to say to Harry on the telephone?
4. What explains Pearl Fulton's limited frankness?
5. Do you agree that Harry's use of phrases like "liver frozen, my dear girl" or "pure flatulence" is an endearing, almost admirable quality? Why or why not?
6. Comment on the juxtaposition of the cats and the pear tree.
7. Can one be "too happy"? Explain.
8. Evaluate Bertha's summary of her situation. Does she indeed have "everything"?
9. Explain the line "Her petals rushed softly into the hall."
10. What techniques does Mansfield use to characterize the Knights and Eddie Warren? What do you think of these people?
11. Comment on the possible implications of Harry's delayed arrival, followed shortly by that of Pearl Fulton.
12. Why is Bertha eager for Pearl to "give a sign"?
13. What transpires as Bertha and Pearl look at the pear tree?
14. Explain Harry's way of offering a cigarette to Pearl and Bertha's interpretation of it.
15. Why does Bertha feel "that this self of hers was taking leave of them forever" as she bids farewell to her guests?
16. What is the effect of Eddie Warren's quoting a poem about tomato soup while the climax of the story takes place?
17. What *is* going to happen now?

Topics for Writing

1. Comment on the names in "Bliss."
2. Discuss the rebirth of Bertha Young.
3. Write an essay analyzing Mansfield's use of light and color in "Bliss."
4. The story is divided by white spaces into a number of sections. On your first reading, stop at each one of these spaces and write a few sentences addressed to Bertha Young. What would you say to her at each of those moments? When you have finished the story, review your previous advice and write one more letter to Bertha in response to her concluding question.
5. **RESPONDING CREATIVELY**   Study the way Mansfield characterizes Harry, the Knights, Eddie, and Pearl. Then write a character sketch of your own using some of the same techniques and devices.

Related Commentaries

Willa Cather, The Stories of Katherine Mansfield, p. 1467.
Katherine Mansfield, Review of Woolf's "Kew Gardens," p. 1529.

Suggested Readings

See page 178.

KATHERINE MANSFIELD

The Garden-Party (p. 942)

"The Garden-Party," like its protagonist, Laura Sheridan, is brimming with life. Mansfield's lush, sensual descriptions of the sights, sounds, smells, and tastes that are observed by Laura throughout the party preparations help to create a vibrant character filled with a childlike wonder and anticipation. Posed on the brink of adulthood, Laura sees and feels everything so intensely that we feel uneasy for her, sensing that some calamity, or at the very least some major disappointment, is waiting to shake her innocent dream of life's perfection.

For all her sensitivity and good nature, Laura appears, in the opening scenes, to be a typical upper-class young woman, delighted by the prospect of a party, and rather egocentric in her vision of such things as the cooperation of the weather and the blooming of the roses, and of the "absurdity" of the class distinction between herself and the workmen. She naively imagines that taking a bite of her bread and butter in front of these men makes her "just like a work-girl," but, as she will be reminded before the end of the story, there is a much greater difference between her life and that of a workgirl than a simple relaxation of stuffy manners and conventions. Laura is clearly glamorizing the lives of the working class in these imaginings, although it seems that she should know better. Later on, we discover that she and her brother have walked many times through the lane of cottages just below their home, where the poor live, because "one must go everywhere; one must see everything." While this is a perfect description of Laura's enthusiastic willingness to embrace life, we have to wonder what these excursions have really shown her, if she is so easily able to envision herself as a "work-girl."

It is the fate of the cottages that brings Laura's awakening to some of life's realities. The news of the accidental death of a young man from the lane intrudes on Laura's beautiful day. She reacts with characteristically intense emotion to the news, insisting that the party "must be called off." But she quickly discovers that she is the only one of her family and friends who is at all disturbed by the knowledge of the young man's death. In her exchanges with her sister and mother, she begins to discover just how deep are the class distinctions that she had scoffed at earlier. Her mother calmly states "people like that don't expect sacrifices from us," and that she "can't understand how they keep alive in those poky little holes" (as if they had any choice). Laura's sensitivity, which allows her to imagine the pain of the widow, and to recoil at the impropriety of the band playing and people laughing just yards from where a tragedy is occurring, is obviously not shared by her family. She is shaken and confused by the vast difference between her own instinctive sympathy and the cold lack of concern displayed by her mother and sister, but concludes that her mother "must be right," that it would be selfish and silly for her to "spoil the party" for everyone else, and decides to "think about it all later."

After the party, when Laura's mother, Mrs. Sheridan, is reminded of the unpleasant subject of the dead man by her husband, she has the "brilliant idea" of sending some of the leftover party food to the widow. Laura is repelled by this idea, which she finds too patronizing. But, after her own "extravagant" display of sympathy, she can't refuse when she is chosen to take the basket to the dead man's house. There, she has her first unromanticized view of the lives of the lower class, and an acutely painful realization of her own difference from them, as well as her first close-up view of death. However, it is in Laura's "encounter" with the dead man that the truly remarkable strength and beauty of her character emerges. For she is even able to empathize with the dead, to feel death from the man's point of view, a "marvelous" state of peace, rest, and beauty. Laura sees death, in a very realistic but highly unusual way for one so young, as just another aspect of the wondrous, overwhelming beauty and mystery of life.

Questions for Discussion

1. How would you characterize Laura after reading the scene where she "supervises" the workmen?
2. Does your vision of Laura change as the story progresses? Trace the development of her character through the major incidents of the story.
3. How do you think Laura's mother and sisters see her? What do you think creates the close bond between her and her brother Laurie?
4. What is the effect of the detailed, highly sensual description of the setting? How does it contribute to your understanding of Laura as a character?
5. Do you think the party should have been canceled? Why or why not?
6. How do you react to Laura's mother and sister Jose as characters? Compare them to Laura.

7. How do you think the mourners feel about Laura's visit to deliver the food basket? Is the sense that she was "expected" all in Laura's mind? Do the people show any resentment?
8. Were you surprised by Laura's reaction to the dead man? Discuss her attitude toward death. Is it consistent with other things that you have learned about her character?

Topics for Writing

1. Analyze "The Garden-Party" as a story of maturation and development.
2. Discuss Laura's desire to be just like "a work-girl."
3. **CONNECTIONS**   Compare and discuss the imagery in "The Garden-Party" and "Bliss."

Related Commentaries

Willa Cather, The Stories of Katherine Mansfield, p. 1467.
Katherine Mansfield, On "The Garden Party," p. 1528.
Katherine Mansfield, Review of Woolf's "Kew Gardens," p. 1529.

Suggested Readings

Boddy, Gill. *Katherine Mansfield: The Woman and the Writer.* New York: Penguin, 1988.
Fullbrook, Kate. *Katherine Mansfield.* Muskogee: Indiana UP, 1986.
Hanson, Clare, ed. *The Critical Writings of Katherine Mansfield.* New York: St. Martin's, 1987.
Kobler, Jasper F. *Katherine Mansfield: A Study of the Short Fiction.* Boston: G. K. Hall, 1990.
Mansfield, Katherine. *Journal of Katherine Mansfield.* New York: Ecco, 1983.
O'Sullivan, Vincent, and Margaret Scott. *The Collected Letters of Katherine Mansfield.* New York: Oxford UP, 1987.
Rohrberger, Mary H. *The Art of Katherine Mansfield.* Ann Arbor, MI: UMI, 1977.

BOBBIE ANN MASON

Shiloh (p. 954)

The trip to Shiloh is supposed to be a second honeymoon for Leroy and Norma Jean Moffitt, a chance for them to start their marriage all over again, as Leroy says, "right back at the beginning." The trouble is, as Norma Jean is quick to point out to her husband, they had already started all over again after his tractor-trailer accident brought him home for good, and "this is how it turned out."

It's a topsy-turvy world in Mason's story. Husbands are hurt so they take up needlepoint; housewives are self-reliant so they study composition at community college when they aren't working at the drugstore. Thirty-four-year-old "girls" like Norma Jean irrationally turn on their mothers after years of obedience just because their mothers catch them smoking cigarettes. And yet it's a familiar world to readers of fiction by women authors about women's domestic rebellion these past fifteen years: Erica Jong's *Fear of Flying*, Sue Kauffman's *Diary of a Mad Housewife,* and Lisa Alther's *Kinflicks,* for example. Norma Jean might scoff at her husband's suggestion that she has been influenced by the feminist movement — he asks her, "Is this one of those women's lib things?" — but he's no fool. She probably wouldn't have told him she was going to leave him if Betty Friedan hadn't published *The Feminine Mystique* and helped bring a feminist consciousness back to America about the time Norma Jean married her high school sweetheart, Leroy Moffitt.

The old patriarchal consciousness still permeates the story, of course, since this consciousness has a tight hold on the mate and the older fictional characters. Norma Jean is introduced in the first sentence as "Leroy Moffitt's wife, Norma Jean." The story is told in the present tense, making the reader aware of the slow passage of time for the characters caught in a static way of life, as mother Mabel says, "just waiting for time to pass." But Norma Jean feels the need for change. The opening of "Shiloh" is one of the most exhilarating first sentences in contemporary American short fiction. "Leroy Moffitt's wife, Norma Jean, is working on her pectorals." Used to be only boys lifted weights to build up their muscles. Now opportunity beckons even for a thirty-four-year-old married woman who bakes cream-of-mushroom casseroles. She doesn't want to be known as somebody's wife, a hackneyed first name between two commas evoking the more famous "real" name of a departed sex goddess from an era before Betty Friedan.

We don't know much about what she's thinking, this fictional Norma Jean, because Mason has structured the story so that her husband's consciousness and feelings are in the forefront. Through his confusion about what's happening with his wife, the reader senses that probably at this point Norma Jean doesn't know exactly what she wants herself, beyond wanting to break free. On their trip to Shiloh she walks rapidly away from Leroy to stand alone on a bluff by the river. He sees her waving her arms, and he can't tell if she's beckoning him or doing another exercise for her pectorals. One thing they both know is that she won't be needing the dust ruffle his mother-in-law made for their marital bed. If this Wonder Woman has her way, she won't be pushing her jogging shoes under her husband's couch or hiding the dust under his bed one day longer than she has to.

Questions for Discussion

1. After reading the story, look back at the first five paragraphs. What do they say about Norma Jean and Leroy's relationship? Does the rest of the story bear out the opening moment?
2. On the first page we discover that, through building an array of kits, "Leroy has grown to appreciate how things are put together." How does his fascination with building comment on Leroy's marriage? What is the impulse behind building the log cabin? How would you compare Leroy's hobby with Norma Jean's interests?
3. In this passage Mason introduces the background of the Moffitts' marriage: "Perhaps he reminds her too much of the early days of their marriage, before he went on the road. They had a child who died as an infant, years ago.

They never speak about their memories of Randy, which have almost faded, but now that Leroy is home all the time, they sometimes feel awkward around each other, and Leroy wonders if one of them should mention the child. He has the feeling that they are waking up out of a dream together — that they must create a new marriage, start afresh. They are lucky they are still married. Leroy has read that for most people losing a child destroys the marriage." The figure of a dead child might be expected to haunt the couple in this story. Does the child control their present actions? We discover later that Randy would be sixteen now, so Leroy has been away from home, basically, for sixteen years. What difference does his sudden presence make to the marriage?

4. "When the first movie ended, the baby was dead. . . . A dead baby feels like a sack of flour." Usually, a subject like the death of infants evokes a particular kind of rhetoric, laden with sentimentality and tragedy. How would you describe these two sentences? Why doesn't the narrator use some euphemisms for death? What effect do these perceptions create? How do these sentences influence your assessment of Leroy's character?

5. Although the title emphasizes the importance of "Shiloh," we don't hear anything about it until page 957, when Mabel Beasley says, "I still think before you get tied down y'all ought to take a little run to Shiloh." What does Shiloh represent for Mabel? What does history itself mean to Leroy and Norma Jean? Can they articulate their shared history? Consider the passage about the baby on page 956.

6. When Norma Jean tells Leroy she's leaving him, he asks her, "Is this one of those women's lib things?" Is this a story about feminism? Consider the point of view; discuss the ideology apparent in the opening line of the story. What do we know about Norma Jean's feelings? Consider how a descriptive sentence such as "She is doing goose steps" gives us some access into her emotional life. How would you describe Mabel Beasley within a feminist framework?

7. How does Leroy's opinion that "nobody knows anything. . . . The answers are always changing" comment on the themes of this story?

8. Leroy concludes that "the real inner workings of a marriage, like most of history, have escaped him." This seems like a poignant realization in the face of Norma Jean's departure. Does Leroy assign blame for the dissolution of his marriage? Does this knowledge imply that he will be able to forge a new, vital marriage with Norma Jean? Is the final paragraph hopeful? What do you make of Leroy's inability to distinguish between Norma Jean's exercise and her signals?

Topics for Writing

1. In an interview Bobbie Ann Mason gave to Lila Havens, she said she's more interested in the male characters in her stories than in the females. How has she selected the details of "Shiloh" to portray Norma Jean's husband, Leroy Moffitt, with compassion?

2. Discuss Mason's use of details to enrich the story's reality.

3. **CONNECTIONS** Compare and contrast the theme of alienation in Mason's "Shiloh" and Lawrence's "Odour of Chrysanthemums."

Related Commentary

Bobbie Ann Mason, On Tim O'Brien's "The Things They Carried," p. 1531.

Suggested Readings

Reed, J. D. "Postfeminism: Playing for Keeps." *Time* 10 Jan. 1983: 61.
Ryan, Maureen. "Stopping Places: Bobbie Ann Mason's Short Stories." *Women Writers of the Contemporary South.* Ed. Peggy Whitman Prenshaw. Jackson: UP of Mississippi, 1984. 283–94.
Smith, W. "Publisher's Weekly Interviews." *Publisher's Weekly* 30 Aug. 1985: 424–25.

GUY DE MAUPASSANT

The Necklace (p. 966)

"The Necklace" has long been one of the most popular of Maupassant's stories, and one of the most interesting aspects of the story is this popularity, since artistically it is far from his best. The story is little more than an anecdote. Mme. Loisel, a woman from the lower middle class, is deeply dissatisfied with her station in life. As she sits down to dinner with her husband — a "little clerk at the Ministry of Public Instructions" — she thinks of "dainty dinners, of shining silverware, of tapestry which peopled the walls with ancient personages and with strange birds in the middle of a fairy forest."

Her husband, sensing her unhappiness, gets a ticket for a grand ball, and, when she is miserable at not having a fine dress, he gives her money he has been saving for a gun and a shooting holiday with his friends. When she is still unhappy at not having jewels, he suggests she borrow some from a wealthy friend, Mme. Forestier. Mme. Loisel borrows what she thinks is a diamond necklace, is a great success at the ball, but loses the necklace on the way home.

Too ashamed to tell the friend what has happened, the couple borrow money to buy a diamond necklace like the one that was lost. They return the necklace and slowly repay the loan. After ten years, during which the wife has become "the woman of impoverished households — strong and hard and rough," she accidentally meets Mme. Forestier and learns that she had lent her only a paste copy of a diamond necklace. Mme. Loisel and her husband have destroyed their lives for nothing.

Unlike in his finest stories, Maupassant here stays on the surface of the characters. Mme. Forestier and Mme. Loisel's husband are only faintly sketched; they seem to exist merely to act out roles. The anecdote itself is so implausible that a single question — why didn't Mme. Forestier notice that a different necklace had been returned to her? why did M. Loisel allow his life to be destroyed without a protest? — would bring it to earth. But most readers are willing to suspend their disbelief.

When we place the story in the time it was written, its themes stand out even more sharply. On its most obvious level this is one of the tales of moral instruction that were so widespread in nineteenth-century popular literature. Mme. Loisel's dreams of clothes and jewels represent the sin of vanity, and someone who has such dreams must be punished. The punishment inflicted on the woman and her husband is memorably out of proportion to their sin, the better to serve as a warning to those reading the story for moral instruction.

A second theme, which may be less obvious to the contemporary reader, is that Mme. Loisel has dreamed of moving to a higher social level. French society was rigidly structured, and Mme. Loisel's ambitions represented a threat, however vague, to the story's privileged audience. They would, of course, want to see her punished for this ambition.

These facts help to explain why the story was so widely read when it was written — but for today's readers other factors seem to be at work. For example, to one young student the necklace became the symbol for everything the world of adults represents. Perhaps it is the story's weaknesses — its implausible simplicities, the lack of definition of its minor characters, the trite obviousness of Mme. Loisel's yearning, and the pious cruelty of her punishment — that make it possible for other generations to give "The Necklace" their own interpretation.

Questions for Discussion

1. Do we use anecdotes like "The Necklace" to point out moral lessons today? What other examples of this kind of moral instruction can you think of in popular literature?
2. How did an evening at a ball offer Mme. Loisel a chance to present herself in a new guise?
3. What do we learn from the story about the structure of French society at the time "The Necklace" was written?
4. What symbols for wealth and station could be used in a story like this written for today?

Topics for Writing

1. Analyze the symbolic implications of the necklace.
2. Consider the contrast between the lives of Mme. Loisel and her friend Mme. Forestier.

Related Commentaries

Kate Chopin, How I Stumbled upon Maupassant, p. 1474.
Guy de Maupassant, The Writer's Goal, p. 1533.

Suggested Readings

Fusco, Richard A. "Maupassant and the Turn of the Century American Short Story." *Dissertation Abstracts International* 51.5 (Nov. 1990): 1612A.

James, Henry. *Tales of Art and Life.* Schenectady, NY: Union College P, 1984.

Lohafer, Susan, ed. *Short Story Theory at a Crossroads.* Baton Rouge: Louisiana State UP, 1989. 276–98.

Los Angeles Public Library Staff. *Index to the Stories of Guy de Maupassant.* Boston: G. K. Hall, 1970.

McCrory, Donald. "Maupassant: Problems of Interpretation." *Modern Languages: Journal of the Modern Language Association* 70.1 (Mar. 1989): 39–43.

Poteau-Tralie, Mary L. "Voices of Authority: The Criminal Obsession in Guy de Maupassant's Short Works." *Dissertation Abstracts International* 52.4 (Oct. 1991): 1353A.

Traill, Nancy Helen. "The Fantastic for the Realist: The Paranormal Fictions of Dickens, Turgenev, and Maupassant." *Dissertation Abstracts International* 50.9 (Mar. 1990): 2891A.

Troyat, Henri. *Maupassant.* Paris: Flammarion, 1989.

Guy de Maupassant

Clochette (p. 972)

Although Maupassant's stories caused a stir in the United States when they first appeared in the late nineteenth century, they were sensational in ways that may be difficult for students today to comprehend. Not only was his writing considered lacking in taste and decorum but several of his stories were singled out by critics as obscene, and it was many years before his work became acceptable reading for American students. At the same time, other writers understood that not only had Maupassant opened the way for a freer depiction of the sexual implications of our social relationships, but he had also given writers an entire new set of characters to set in motion.

The magazines and newspapers where stories were first published during this period were produced for a middle-class audience, and to appeal to this audience the characters in the stories were generally themselves middle-class. The plots of the stories centered on their concerns — marriage, legitimacy, inheritance, social duty, religious faith. In contrast, many of Maupassant's finest stories focused on society's simple people, the servants and the workers who made the lifestyle of the middle-class families possible. "Clochette" is the story of one of the many heroines of his writings who come from this lower class. We could say that Maupassant gave to other writers an understanding of the drama of the insignificant. In his greatest work, he lent to this lowest group of his society a dignity and a respect that they had seldom been accorded before.

As though he wanted to make certain that we would understand his moral attitude of unquestioning acceptance toward his central figure, Masupassant describes Clochette as ugly. He writes about her heaviness and her limp in unforgettable images: "She walked with a limp, not an ordinary limp, but a limp which made her rock like a ship at anchor. When she put the full weight of her large, crooked, bony frame on her good leg, she seemed to be gathering herself up to crest some monstrous wave and then, suddenly plummeting as though about to disappear into a deep trough, she would sink into the ground." To make his readers even more conscious of the poor woman's condition, he also describes the tufts of hair that cover her face and arms, which are perhaps even more of an obstacle to an ordinary life than her limp. "[N]o, hairy, rather, for she had whiskers all over her face, astounding, unexpected whiskers sprouting in unbelievable bunches and curly tufts which seemed to have been sown by some madman all over her large face and made her look like a policeman in skirts."

In the balance scale that a work of moral intent automatically posits, the reader understands that there will be some justification for Clochette's disabilities. The child in the story adores her, and in the world of stories children's moral instincts are infallible. We learn the circumstances of her tragedy, as the narrator of the tale learned himself in the story within the story. The narrator, while still a child, overheard the village doctor telling his parents her story when he had completed his examination of her body after a fatal heart attack. She had been one of the village's beauties, and briefly, as a teenager, she had given in to a moment of temptation from a new, handsome schoolteacher. Before anything could happen beyond a hurried kiss in the hayloft of the school building they were interrupted by the school director, who came up the stairs declaring that he heard voices. She jumped from the window, breaking her leg in three places, and she lay silently against the wall where she fell, refusing to cry for help and reveal her presence. The doctor, new to the village, treated her, and she would only say, "It's a judgement. I got what was coming to me."

In his short narrative, Maupassant has shown us the much larger drama of the insignificant. What has happened to her has implications that go beyond the simple banalities of her accident. We accept her refusal to be bitter in her simple belief that she has been punished as a judgment for what she regarded as her moment of sin. Despite her ugliness and her isolation, the doctor's judgment of her is also the reader's: "She was a martyr, a soul of great price, sublime and faithful to the end! If I did not have the greatest admiration for her, I should not have told you this story which I would never have divulged to anyone as long as she was alive."

It was only a relatively short time before Maupassant's stories became widely read everywhere in the world, and they became a dominant influence on today's short narrative. Where in the beginning some readers saw only degradation, ultimately it was widely recognized that the true force behind his writing was compassion.

Questions for Discussion

1. What do we mean when we describe this tale as a "story within a story"?
2. What is the device the author uses to tell the story?
3. The doctor tells the story to the child's parents. Would he have told the story to the child? How did the child hear?
4. What is the source of the moral decision Clochette makes for herself? Could this system of moral judgment be considered too demanding? Does Clochette think so herself?
5. If she had told the truth at the moment of the accident, would the villagers also have shared her judgment that she had only gotten what was coming to her?
6. What is it about Clochette's stories that fascinates the child?

7. Have we lost this mode of communication in our modern society? If we have, what has taken its place?

Topics for Writing

1. **CONNECTIONS** Compare this story to another story in the anthology such as "The Ultimate Safari" that is also told from a child's viewpoint, and examine the ways in which a child's experience is shaped and utilized as a literary device by the author in each story.
2. Discuss the concept of sin that would cause Clochette to say that her punishment was justified, with some comment on the modern interpretation of this moral question.
3. Discuss what the attitude of the villagers might have been if she had told the truth, relating this to the main characters in the story, including the teacher and the doctor.
4. Discuss the importance to a child of the stories Clochette told to the narrator, and examine the possible sources for such stories in our own society today.

Related Commentary

Guy de Maupassant, The Writer's Goal, p. 1533.

HERMAN MELVILLE

Bartleby, the Scrivener (p. 977)

Many students have trouble reading this story because they cannot accept what they consider the weirdness of Bartleby's character. On first reading, the story seems to yield this interpretation. Shortly after it appeared in the November and December issues of *Putnam's Monthly Magazine* in 1853, for example, Richard Henry Dana Sr. wrote to Melville's friend Evert Duyckinck saying that he admired the skill involved in creating the character of Bartleby because "the secret power of such an inefficient and harmless creature over his employer, who all the while has a misgiving of it, shows no common insight." Dana's interpretation will probably also be the way 99 percent of present-day college students will respond to the story, sharing his lack of sympathy for Bartleby.

The question is: Did Melville intend the readers of his story to feel this way? Why did he conclude his tale with the lines "Ah, Bartleby! Ah, humanity!"?

Most sympathetic literary critics see this story as Melville's attempt to dramatize the complex question of an individual's obligation to society. Like the dead letters that Bartleby burned in his previous job after they were no longer needed, his life ends when he is no longer useful to his employer. What standards should we use to judge someone's worth? How should we view those who no longer accept the world they are offered?

Questions for Discussion

1. How does the narrator's viewpoint affect your feelings toward Bartleby? What details particularly influence you one way or the other?
2. Do your feelings toward Bartleby change when the narrator reveals Bartleby's previous job in the Dead Letter Office?
3. How does Melville's humorous description of the two other clerks in the law office relieve his heavy presentation of the Wall Street setting? How do these minor characters set off each other, the lawyer, and Bartleby?
4. Do you ever feel like saying "I would prefer not to" in reply to figures of authority? What do you do when you feel a bit of Bartleby in you?

Topics for Writing

1. Explicate the paragraph beginning "For the first time in my life a feeling of overpowering stinging melancholy seized me." A close reading of this passage may bring you closer to realizing the complexity of Melville's portrayal of the lawyer's relationship to Bartleby.
2. Analyze the conclusion of the story. How can Bartleby's life be compared to a dead letter?
3. This story has an unusually prolonged and discursive exposition before the title character is introduced. Also, Melville doesn't motivate his behavior until the end of the story, after he is dead and the lawyer finds out about his previous job. Breaking the customary rules of starting a short story with a brief exposition and motivating the characters as they are introduced, Melville might be accused of writing a poorly structured tale. Argue for or against this accusation, remembering that the short-story genre was in its infancy when Melville wrote "Bartleby, the Scrivener."

Related Commentaries

Herman Melville, Blackness in Hawthorne's "Young Goodman Brown," p. 1535.
J. Hillis Miller, A Deconstructive Reading of Melville's "Bartleby, the Scrivener," p. 1537.

Suggested Readings

Boswell, Jeanetta. *Herman Melville and the Critics: A Checklist of Criticism.* Metuchen, NJ: Scarecrow, 1981.
Budd, Louis J., and Edwin H. Cady, eds. *On Melville.* Durham, NC: Duke UP, 1988.
Dillingham, W. B. *Melville's Short Fiction, 1853–1856.* Athens: U of Georgia P, 1977.
Fogle, R. H. *Melville's Shorter Tales.* Norman: U of Oklahoma P, 1960.
Freeman, John. *Herman Melville.* Brooklyn, NY: Haskell, 1974.
Higgins, Brian. *Herman Melville: A Reference Guide, 1931–1960.* Boston: G. K. Hall, 1987.
Inge, M. Thomas, ed. *Bartleby the Inscrutable: A Collection of Commentary on Herman Melville's Tale "Bartleby, the Scrivener."* Hamden, CT: Shoe String, 1979.
McCall, Dan. *The Silence of Bartleby.* Ithaca, NY: Cornell UP, 1989.

Melville, Herman. *Correspondence.* Evanston, IL: Northwestern UP, 1991.

———. *Pierre, The Piazza Tales and Uncollected Prose.* New York: Library of America, 1984.

Vincent, H. P., ed. *"Bartleby, the Scrivener": Melville Annual for 1965.* Kent, OH: Kent State UP, 1967. Includes Henry Murray's "Bartleby and I," 3–24.

Whitehead, Fred A. "Melville's 'Bartleby, the Scrivener': A Case Study." *New York State Journal of Medicine* 90 (Jan. 1990): 17–22.

SUSAN MINOT

Lust (p. 1004)

This story may be difficult for students to discuss in class, since it describes personal feelings about a subject (sexual intercourse) that they may consider more appropriately discussed with friends of the same sex, or not at all. To overcome their reluctance, you might ask students to write down their thoughts about the story, which could lead into a discussion of how the class as a whole has responded.

Such a questionnaire (not a quiz) could consist of statements from the story that students are asked to "strongly agree . . . strongly disagree" with. For example, 1. "The less they [boys] notice you, the more you got them on the brain." 2. "My parents had no idea. Parents never really know what's going on." 3. "If you go out with them, you sort of have to do something." 4. "Teenage years. You know just what you're doing and don't see the things that start to get in the way." 5. "Lots of boys, but never two at the same time." 6. "The more girls a boy has, the better. . . . For a girl, with each boy, it's as though a petal gets plucked each time." 7. "After the briskness of loving, loving stops."

The narrative form of "Lust" might be another way to approach the story's content. How does Minot present her material? The theme is dramatized episodically, in short paragraphs, bringing about an effect of intense compression. The reader has as brief an encounter with the story of each boyfriend as the narrator appears to have with the boy himself. Leo, Roger, Bruce et al. appear and disappear so rapidly that it's as if the girl is picking the boys like the petals of a daisy. Yet, as she makes clear, she — unlike the boys she dates — is experiencing emotional vulnerability as her dominant feeling. Minot has effectively dramatized the differences in sexual maturity between adolescent males and females. "Postcoital melancholy" pervades her narrative from beginning to end.

Questions for Discussion

1. How do we know that the narrator is a girl?
2. What is your impression of the narrator? How old is she? What is her social background? Does she have a conscience?
3. What direction and guidance does the narrator get from the adults in her life, her parents and the headmaster at her school? Does she want more advice from them about how to live?
4. What is the narrator's primary interest in boys? How is she vulnerable?

5.   How does the short, fragmented paragraph structure of "Lust" contribute
     to its mood and meaning?
6.   Characterize the style of Minot's sentences.

Topics for Writing

1.   **RESPONDING CREATIVELY**   Rewrite "Lust" in the same form, but from a
     boy's point of view.
2.   **RESPONDING CREATIVELY**   Continue "Lust" beyond Minot's ending to
     bring the narrator to an awareness that she wants to try a different approach
     to relationships with the boys in her life.
3.   Analyze the section with the housemother, Mrs. Gunther. What does it con-
     tribute to the story?
4.   **CONNECTIONS**   Compare the voice of Updike's adolescent narrator in
     "A & P" with that of Minot's narrator in "Lust."

YUKIO MISHIMA

Patriotism (p. 1013)

This obsessive, powerful story has long been one of the author's most successful works, perhaps in part because it provides his readers with a disturbing
presentiment of his own ritual suicide. In his native Japan, the story aroused such
strong sentiments that it has been filmed, reprinted many times, and been published in an edition illustrated with photographs that follow the story to its grisly
climax. In each of its many versions the story is as painfully drawn, and its obsessions remain intact. Clearly in Japan it is read as a complex symbol of the country's
lost militarist traditions, which could justify what to a non-Japanese reader may
be its excessive violence. The traditions have still some resilience, although there
is less consciousness of ritual suicide. At the time Mishima wrote the story, Japanese newspapers occasionally carried stories about businessmen or lower-level
government officials who committed *sepuko* to atone for a failure to perform their
work in what they conceived as an honorable manner. In Japan today the president of a multinational corporation might appear before the company's stock-
holders, weep, and ask forgiveness as he announces the dismissal of several thousand life-long employees, but there is no Mishima to demand that he perform the
honored ceremony.

For most people in Western culture, and to many students, the story is appalling. It is usually read with the same kind of horrified fascination that is given
to accounts of mass rape or ritual strangulation. For Mishima, however, the act he
describes in the story is a kind of sacrament. As he writes at the story's beginning,
"The last moment of this heroic and dedicated couple were such as to make the
gods themselves weep." To a non-Japanese reader it is difficult to respond to
Mishima's obvious delight at the young bride's presentation of her own dagger
to assure her husband that she is also prepared to commit suicide: "Returning to
her place, she laid the dagger without a word on the mat before her, just as her
husband had laid his sword. A silent understanding was achieved at once, and
the lieutenant never again sought to test his wife's resolve."

For its readers, both Japanese and non-Japanese, an element of the fascination with the story is certainly its linking of the erotic nature of the couple's relationship to their almost mystical celebration of their own death. This was a connection that Mishima made many times in his writings, and it is no surprise that the group of young men whom he trained to be the vanguard of a new dedication of the Japanese spirit practiced a group sexuality and that the man who assisted him by attempting to sever his head as Mishima disemboweled himself was one of his lovers.

It has sometimes been suggested that this story could be defined as an expression of the pornography of violence. The sexual elements in the narration are subsumed in the overriding obsession with the act of ritual suicide, and there is the same concentration — to the exclusion of everything outside the story — on a single physical act, an act that takes on ecstatic overtones. In the Christian world suicide is considered a sinful act, and suicides cannot be buried in hallowed ground. As they read the story, students should continue to think about these contradictory attitudes and decide for themselves if the power of the story is sufficient justification for the views its author presents.

Questions for Discussion

1. What is the author referring to when he speaks of an "eight mat" room? Would a Japanese person be able immediately to visualize what he means?
2. Mishima gives a strong emotional character to his couple, but he never suggests that there is any humor in their relationship. Is their overwhelming seriousness a sign of the tragedy that is to come?
3. Do we feel that the couple have a real identity, or do we feel that the author has idealized them?
4. How do we understand the wife's immediate decision to begin preparing for her own suicide? Is she acting on her own emotions, or is she being led by what she perceives will be her husband's decision?
5. What is our perception of her decision to leave the small animal figures she has loved behind? How would we define in our own terms her idea that "Now she merely loved the memory of having once loved them"?
6. Do the circumstances which the lieutenant uses to justify his suicide — the mutiny of other young officers who were friends — convince us that he has a real reason for his act, or does this seem only an excuse for something that he had long contemplated?
7. How should we interpret the author's concept of the "usual" suicide pact — "If the lieutenant had been a suspicious husband, he would doubtless, as in the usual suicide pact, have chosen to kill his wife first"?

Topics for Writing

1. The title of the story is "Patriotism." Discuss various definitions of the word and analyze why the author thought the word was a proper title for his story.
2. Discuss how this story could be thought of as an example of the pornography of violence, considering the many definitions of *pornography*.

3. Analyze the arguments Mishima presents for the inevitability and the beauty of the couple's suicide pact, and contrast them with the Western ideal of the inviolability of life.

4. Discuss the problem of reading a story like Mishima's on its own terms, and present arguments why or why not we can read it without reconsidering our own attitudes.

5. As the lieutenant contemplates the act they are both about to commit he tells himself, "There was some special favor here. He did not understand precisely what it was, but it was a domain unknown to others; a dispensation granted to no one else had been permitted to himself." Discuss this conclusion and its moral implications.

Suggested Readings

Boardman, Gwenn R. "Greek Hope and Japanese Samurai: Mishima's New Aesthetic." *Critique* 12 (1970): 103–15.

Enright, D. J. "Mishima's Way." *Encounter* 36 (1971): 57–61.

Falk, Ray. "Yukio Mishima." *Saturday Review* 16 May 1959: 29.

Mishima, Yukio. *Acts of Worship.* Trans. and with an introduction by John Bester. Tokyo: Kodansha International, 1989.

———. *Death in Midsummer and Other Stories.* New York: New Directions, 1966.

Seidensticker, Edward. "Mishima Yukio." *Hudson Review* 24 (1971): 272–82.

Spurling, J. "Death in Hero's Costume: The Meaning of Mishima." *Encounter* 44 (1975): 56+.

Ueda, Makoto. "Mishima Yukio" *Modern Japanese Writers and the Nature of Literature.* Stanford: Stanford UP, 1976. 219–59.

RICK MOODY

Boys (p. 1032)

As Moody has told us in his own comment on the story, it was written at the slow speed of two sentences a day, and he had no plan of any kind when he began. He had only the four words "Boys enter the house." Perhaps because he let the story grow as he added his day's assignment of sentences, the simple phrase grew unchecked into a moving portrait of two boys — twins — growing up and experiencing dislocation and the death of their father. He takes his readers on a fast-forward, jerky, careening trip through an emotional landscape that many will recognize. The story is told in a roller-coaster ride of verbal imagery, a mosaic in which each fragment is a glimpse of life lived, of life experienced. Although the story on the page seems modest, it assumes much larger dimensions than many more conventional short narratives with their moment of epiphany summing up a fragment of our experience. Moody's story is the experience of life itself.

The story is an ordinary one. Although the lives of the two boys are unique, as any life is unique, we all have some familiarity with what Moody describes — the sicknesses, boyish battles, school sex, acne, struggles with parents; even the death of a younger sister that is part of the pattern. At the same time he has communicated the extraordinariness of their lives in vivid images that spin past us on the page. "Boys enter the house with girls efflorescent and homely," blue jeans lie on the floor "coiled like asps," one boy writes home "and thereby enters the house through the mail slot."

For today's students, however, the story can present a problem. It is only boys who enter the house. We are so accustomed to the older attitudes that it is only after we have gotten off the author's dizzying ride that we realize he hasn't taken all of us along with him. In some other version of the story perhaps he will also tell us what will happen when girls enter the house.

The story Moody presents us could become banal, since it follows a well-trampled path, a path on which we are all walking ourselves. "Boys," however, renews a story that we are continually telling ourselves, although without the daring and the imagination of his telling.

Questions for Discussion

1. Why did the author begin with the motif "enter the house"? How does it function as a motif for the story?
2. What does he mean by the image in the first paragraph of "kettles on the boil"?
3. He places the story in Edison, New Jersey, but does it have a specific location for us? Why has he deliberately chosen a place that we can consider as generic?
4. Is there anything specific in the story relating to the fact that the boys are twins? Would two brothers of different ages have had similar experiences?
5. What do we learn of their relationships with their mother, father, and sister?
6. How would we characterize the family members' changing relationships to each other? Are these changes typical?
7. Will the cycle of life begin again with them entering a new house?
8. Many things in the story are humorous, but would we characterize it as a funny story?

Topics for Writing

1. Discuss how the author achieves the fast-forward effect of the story.
2. Discuss what is usual or unusual about the boys.
3. **CONNECTIONS** Compare this story with Alice Munro's "Family Furnishings," which also tells the story of a child growing up but with a different narrative style and a girl as the narrator.
4. Discuss the language of the story and analyze how the imagery conveys the emotional setting of the boys' lives.
5. **RESPONDING CREATIVELY** Write a page of the story in the author's style, but this time beginning, "Girls enter the house."

Suggested Readings

Moody, Rick. *Demonology: Stories.* Boston: Little, 2000.
————. *The Ring of Brightest Angels Around Heaven: A novella and stories.* Boston: Little, 1995.

LORRIE MOORE

How to Become a Writer (p. 1036)

Students reading this humorous story may regard it as a mirror reflecting a "sitcom" version of themselves. It is as familiar as an empty Diet Coke can. The setting of the story is both nonexistent and omnipresent: parents on the verge of divorce, a son in the armed services, a kid sister who's good with little kids. Life swirls around, full of plot action, and what's a crazy girl who wants to become a writer to do? The answer for this affluent family: Advance one painless step — go on to college.

The girl attends college as a child psychology major. Nothing much happens there except a fateful accident: A computer erroneously assigns the girl to a creative writing class instead of "The Ornithological Field Trip" on Tuesdays and Thursdays at 2 P.M. So begins her apprenticeship to her craft, for which she shows more enthusiasm than talent. She apparently never reads short fiction, yet she tries very hard to write it. After graduation, she flirts briefly with the idea of law school before settling for slow starvation at home. Her kind, divorced mother is resigned: "Sure you like to write. Of course. Sure you like to write."

Moore's decision to tell the story in the second person gives her narrative its sense of immediacy. Her sense of humor does the rest, as she carves and serves up her tender victim, a sacrifice to the creative spirit that lives within us all.

Questions for Discussion

1. What is the irony involved in the girl's inability to find good plots for her stories, in the light of her parents' troubled marriage and her brother's military service in Vietnam?
2. Judging from the girl's behavior in her writing classes, does she show any talent? Are creative writing classes in college a good place to find out if one can write?
3. What does Moore gain by organizing her story chronologically?
4. Do you think that the fragments the girl keeps in a folder can be developed into good stories?
5. How does the detail the girl notices about her date at the end of the story suggest that she might have the talent to become a writer after all?

Topic for Writing

1. **RESPONDING CREATIVELY** Moore's story is a goldmine of possibilities for writing other stories. For example, experiment with the point of view of her narrative — rewrite it in the first or the third person. Or, develop her fragments into short stories of your own, humorous if possible, tragic if not.

Suggested Reading

Moore, Lorrie. *Self-Help.* New York: Knopf, 1985.

BHARATI MUKHERJEE

The Management of Grief (p. 1043)

Bharati Mukherjee cites Moghul miniature painting, with "its insistence that everything happens simultaneously, bound only by shape and color," as a model for her fiction. This "sense of the interpenetration of all things" informs "The Management of Grief," which initially situates the reader among a rather bewildering array of characters and actions. Gradually we become aware that Shaila Bhave, who narrates the story, has recently lost her husband and two sons in a plane crash. The disoriented quality of her narrative ("A woman I don't know is boiling tea the Indian way in my kitchen") mirrors the state of her mind as she struggles to make sense of her loss, focusing on memories and odd details. The abruptness of our entry into the story suggests the abruptness of tragedy itself. Kusum, the similarly bereaved neighbor, voices the question that might occur to anyone afflicted with such loss: "Why does God give so much if all along He intends to take it away?"

Mukherjee asks us to consider the manner in which various characters cope with grief. The community looks toward Mrs. Bhave as "a pillar" because she has "taken it more calmly," but she is troubled by her inability to grieve outwardly, referring to herself as "a freak." Her equanimity, we learn, is due as much to Valium as to inner strength. With the help of the drug she is able to "manage" her grief in a way that may be ultimately less healthy than that of the relatives who express their grief more openly. While in Ireland waiting to identify bodies, she admits, "I haven't eaten in four days, haven't brushed my teeth." By the end of the story Shaila experiences a visitation on the streets of Toronto by her departed husband and sons, who urge her, "Go, be brave." While the experience may be interpreted in a positive light, a transition in her grieving process, it also may be seen as an aural hallucination, the result of her mixing tranquilizers in her distraught emotional state. Her dropping her package and directionless walking suggest purposelessness and lack of direction.

While personal tragedy commands center stage in this story, cultural vectors play out across the background. The crash may have been caused by a Sikh bomb. Judith Templeton, the culturally naive social worker, persuades Shaila to try to convince a grieving Sikh couple to take advantage of available aid. Templeton, while meaning well, has little sensitivity to the cultural and political complications of the situation, and she overlooks the difficulty of the position for which she recruits Shaila — that of helping a potential enemy. The plane crash pulls the relatives, now well assimilated into Canada, back to India and the old ways, which cling with more tenacity than they may have realized.

Questions for Discussion

1. At one point, Shaila observes, "Like my husband's spirit, I flutter between worlds." What does she mean?
2. Review the India section of the story. In what ways have the characters changed in moving from India to Canada?
3. Do you detect a pattern of inhibited emotional response in Shaila? If so, to what extent may this pattern be culturally induced?

Topic for Writing

1. Discuss the grieving processes and coping mechanisms of the various characters. Is Shaila as healthy and calm as she outwardly appears to be? What does Dr. Ranganathan mean when he says, "We've been melted down and recast as a new tribe"? Do the relatives experience successive stages of grief?

Suggested Readings

Boxill, Anthony. "Women and Migration in Some Short Stories of Bharati Mukherjee and Neil Bissoondath." *Literary Half Yearly* 32.2 (July 1991): 43–50.
Mukherjee, Bharati. *The Middleman and Other Stories.* New York: Grove, 1988.
Nelson, Emmanuel S. *Bharati Mukherjee: Critical Perspectives.* New York: Garland, 1993.
———. "Kamala Markandaya, Bharati Mukherjee and the Indian Immigrant Experience." *Toronto South Asian Review* 9.2 (Winter 1991): 1–9.

ALICE MUNRO

Family Furnishings (p. 1056)

The title of the story, "Family Furnishings," is itself enigmatic, since when we think of *home* furnishings or *office* furnishings, we know exactly what we mean. But in the title Munro is asking the reader to take an oblique step with her and consider the family itself as having some of the qualities of furniture — that the people in the rooms can be placed in the mind of the reader like the *things* in the room. We learn late in the story that by the title she means family furniture, which she uses as symbolic of the lives she is describing, but our first impression of the story stays with us.

Munro is one of the modern period's most accomplished writers of short fiction, and this story is a brilliant example of her skills. Students perhaps will find it necessary to read it with closer attention than many other stories, but they will find that in the detail and clear focus of her narrative she has presented them with a complex portrait of not only the narrator but also the other major characters. Munro has devoted her life to writing short fiction, and we sense her skill and experience in the first few lines, which with confident strokes sketch the setting and suggest the boundaries of her story. We learn that it is memory we will be tracing, since how could she recall something that her father experienced? And we have a suggestion of the time, since it is the father's memory of the end of World War I she says she remembers. Finally, with the physical details of the road and the ice and the joy in the distant town over the news of the armistice we have a social context.

Within the first paragraphs, just as she clarified the specifics of the story in the first lines, she moves from the generalities of the scene to the specifics of one family by describing the newspaper columns that her distant relative Alfrida writes. Through the materials of the columns we understand the isolation of the farm families and the provincialism of the small community. The daughter of the family, who narrates the story, doesn't give us a detailed description of herself, but Munro allows us to see her through her mother's responses to her daughter's tentative attempts to broaden her own horizons. Alfrida is the contrasting presence against which the other family members are measured, and we see her effect on the narrator as the narrator's view of the older woman undergoes continual shifts — from a young girl's awestruck admiration, to her increasing awareness of the older woman's prejudices and limitations, and finally to her realization that Alfrida no longer has a role to play in her life. Her realization (from what her father tells her of the letter that Alfrida had already withdrawn from her because of her use in one of her stories of something Alfrida had told her) signals the end of the bright contrast that Alfrida had presented at the story's beginning. Then, with a completely unexpected development of the story's plot, Munro allows us to see that Alfrida, by giving birth to a child, had showed herself to be truly further along on the path to self-realization than the younger woman understood. In place of what might have been the story's simple resolution Munro leaves us with a portrait of a challenging woman whom the narrator cannot dismiss and at the same time is not able to accept within the narrow, work-driven limits she has set for her own life.

Within the framework of the story we experience much that has the bright ring of reality, but at the same time we are conscious that there is a shift of larger symbols below the story's surface. "Family furnishings" can be simply that, the family's old furniture. We have seen the furnishings as things, and we know where each of the things would be placed in the house that is the life of the people in the story. The furnishings are the metaphor for what we bring with us from the past — and it is significant that Alfrida is left with the furnishings that she finally can't use or bring herself to sell. She simply walks away from them. It is the narrator who is ultimately left with the metaphoric furnishings that she can't shed — her memories of her now distant family.

Questions for Discussion

1. When does the story takes place? How do we know?
2. The narrator casually mentions that her father had beaten her. Is her lack of emotion about this an indication that it was something common for the time? How do we interpret it today?

3. Would the family be described as friendly? Are their social customs presented as unusual for the time and place of the story?
4. How do we interpret the narrator's imitation of her older relative: "Looks like the groundworms have got into the hogs. Yup"?
5. The family uses the word "smart" as a pejorative. How does this affect the narrator's decisions later in life?
6. How does she find out about Alfrida's income? Why does it surprise her that the older woman doesn't have a great deal of money?
7. Do newspapers today still make use of writers like Alfrida? What is the role that they play in the newspaper's service to its readers?
8. We are given several examples of Alfrida's jealousy. What causes it? Is it justified?
9. Why has no one spoken to the younger woman about Alfrida's child?

Topics for Writing

1. The narrator describes something she calls her mother's "inner tone." Discuss what she means by this, and examine the sources for her mother's assurance.
2. Explain how a figure like Alfrida could present such a strong challenge to a family like the one in the story.
3. Analyze the descriptions Munro gives us of the family conversations, and discuss possible reasons for the pattern of inarticulate remarks and uncomfortable silences. Include some conclusions about the isolation of rural families during this period.
4. There is a conflict of memory when the narrator meets Alfrida's daughter. Use this disparity to comment on the reliability of memory as a guide to the past.
5. Comment on Alfrida's anger that something she told the narrator was used in a story, and discuss the ways writers make use of the sources of material around them.
6. In the story, Tennessee Williams presents too much of a challenge even to someone who has been presented as sophisticated and worldly. Discuss how the writing of someone like Williams could have been perceived as threatening by some readers at that time.

Related Commentary

Alice Munro, How I Write Short Stories, p. 1541.

Suggested Readings

Bardolph, Jacqueline, ed. *Short Fiction in the New Literature in English: Proceedings of the Nice Conference of the European Association for the Common Wealth Literature and Language Studies.* Nice: Faculté des Lettres et Sciences Humaines de Nice, 1989. 141–51.
Blodgett, E. D. *Alice Munro.* Boston: Twayne, 1988.
Carrington, Ildiko de Papp. *Controlling the Uncontrollable: The Fiction of Alice Munro.* DeKalb: Northern Illinois UP, 1989.

Hanson, Clare, ed. *Rereading the Short Story.* New York: St. Martin's, 1989. 65–85.

Jansen, Reamy. "Being Lonely: Dimensions of the Short Story." *Crosscurrents* 39.4 (Winter 1989–90): 391–401, 419.

MacKendrick, Louis K., ed. *Probable Fictions: Alice Munro's Narrative Acts.* Downsview, ONT: ECW, 1983.

Martin, W. R. *Alice Munro: Paradox and Parallel.* Edmonton: U of Alberta P, 1987.

Miller, Judith. *The Art of Alice Munro: Saying the Unsayable: Papers from the Waterloo Conference.* Madison: U of Wisconsin P, 1984.

Munro, Alice. *Selected Stories.* New York: Knopf, 1996.

Nischik, Reingard M., ed. *Modes of Narrative: Approaches to American, Canadian, and British Fiction.* Wurzburg: Konigshausen, 1990. 110–18, 141–52.

Rasporich, Beverly J. *Dance of the Sexes: Art and Gender in the Fiction of Alice Munro.* Edmonton: U of Alberta P, 1990.

Stich, K. P., ed. *Reflections: Autobiography and Canadian Literature.* Ottawa: U of Ottawa P, 1988. 176.

Haruki Murakami

The Seventh Man (p. 1078)

Although we think of Japan as a densely populated, highly industrialized island nation, the response to nature is still such an important part of the Japanese character that natural occurrences play a central role in Japanese writing and art. To Westerners the quintessential Japanese artwork is the landscape scroll painting, and as they read this vivid story many students will be reminded of the devastating waves depicted in the woodblock prints of artists such as Hiroshige and Hokusai. It is interesting that Murakami is considered one of the modern Japanese authors who has been strongly influenced by Western writers, in particular Raymond Carver, whose work he translated into Japanese and whom he interviewed in 1984, but the story is an expression of what we in the West would consider the essence of the Japanese spirit.

It is clear that the story is only one of a linked group, and students might be confused by the reference to the seventh man and to his explanation that "[I]n my case it was a wave." We can assume that the context is a group of people telling each other stories that reveal some decisive moment or experience in their lives. We are not told who the other people in the group may be, and they seem, at least in regard to the seventh man, to be strangers. We are told that "[n]one of those assembled there knew his name or what he did for a living." What we note most strongly about him is that "[h]is face had the look you see on people when they can't quite find the words they need." The intimation is that there is something he has experienced for which he has been trying to find some meaning, and this story is what he relates to the others.

It becomes clear, as he describes the typhoon and the moment when his closest friend is seized by the wave and drowns, that what he has been struggling against for most of his life are his overwhelming feelings of guilt that he simply shouted to K. to tell him the wave was approaching and then ran to safety. Although no one accuses him of any complicity in the other boy's death, he is haunted by nightmares. "I knew the truth. I knew that I could have saved K. if I had tried."

It is only when he forces himself to look at the bundle of the other boy's water-color paintings that his brother has sent to him after their father's death that he begins to see that there could be some other cause that lay deeper than his childhood understanding. What he learns from his contemplation of the paintings is that he had shared his friend's responses to the world around them: "I realized that his eyes were my eyes, that I myself had looked upon the world back then with the same lively, unclouded vision as the boy who had walked by my side."

With that realization he comes finally to the understanding that what he had interpreted as accusing anger in K.'s face as the wave swirled his body close to the beach again was only a farewell. As his friend drowned he had felt no anger toward the man telling the story. The reader could even interpret the drowning as the boy's embrace of the waves that he has studied so passionately. Certainly the man felt that in the moments before the accident the waves had assumed a human consciousness:

> The waves that had approached me were as unthreatening as waves can be — a gentle washing of the sandy beach. But something ominous about them — something like the touch of a reptile's skin – had sent a chill down my spine. My fear was totally groundless — and totally real. I knew instinctively that they were alive. The waves were alive. They knew I was here and they were planning to grab me.

As the man tells the group, it was at the moment when he understood his friend's emotions that the nightmares that had haunted his life dissipated, and he was able to return to the beach. The waves again felt alive to him, but this time there was no threat: "Almost in reconciliation, it seemed, the same waves that had washed up on the beach when I was a boy were now fondly washing my feet, soaking black my shoes and pant cuffs."

It is this mystical identification with the forces of the waves and the storm that tells the reader that the story is by a Japanese writer — or at least that it is by someone who is not closely linked to the Western storytelling tradition, with its emphasis on the realistic and the comprehensible. An American writer could evoke the force of a typhoon — or a hurricane, as the author would term it — but we would be surprised if to the American the waves would become a living presence on which the writer could bestow the gift of memory.

Questions for Discussion

1. This is another example of a story within a story. Do we need the context of the place and the scene where the story is told in order to respond to what the man tells us?
2. What is the author telling us when he describes the man by saying, "His face had the look you see on people when they can't quite find the words they need"?
3. Are typhoons and hurricanes considered "a wonderful source of excitement" by children in every part of the world? What is the American experience of them?
4. As the wind rises the air is filled with tiles. What is the writer telling his readers about Japanese villages?

5. What do we call the figure of speech the author is using in his description of the storm; "The wind kept up its savage howling as it tried to uproot everything that stood on land"?
6. Do the adults have the same sense of relaxed pleasure as the children when they are in the eye of the storm?
7. What is it about the storm that allows the two boys to go so far from shore?
8. What could explain the fact that K. and his dog fail to hear the wave, while to the narrator the sound is overwhelming?
9. Is there anything in the story to suggest that the glimpse the narrator has of his friend's drowned body could be a hallucination?

Topics for Writing

1. Discuss the imagery and figures of speech that the writer uses to describe the waves. Comment on the importance of these descriptions to the effect of the story.
2. Discuss the reverence toward nature that we associate with Japanese art and literature, commenting on the boy's paintings in this story. Include some comment on the relation between the Japanese reverence for nature and the religions of the country.
3. The nature of tidal waves is still not entirely understood, and they continue to cause mass destruction in many areas of the world. Write a paper about tidal waves and relate the scientific knowledge to more imaginative depictions of them in art and literature.

JOYCE CAROL OATES

Where Are You Going, Where Have You Been? (p. 1089)

Pointing to Oates's remark that she usually writes "about real people in a real society" should help to keep discussion away from premature allegorization or mythologizing, which — for all its eventual value and interest — smothers the story's impact by diverting attention from its realism. Her further observation that she understands Connie to be "struggling heroically to define personal identity in the face of incredible opposition, even in the face of death itself," may suggest how to go about answering the main question the story poses when considered in naturalistic terms: Why does Connie go out to Arnold Friend?

Connie's life as Oates depicts it takes place in two realms. Within her home and family Connie feels condemned and rejected, and she returns the disapproval. Outside these familiar precincts lies a world defined by movies, the drive-in restaurant, and the ever-present popular music. It is *not* the music of Bob Dylan, as Tom Quirk assures us, but the comparatively mindless, sentimental, and romantic music against which in the early 1960s Dylan stood out in such bold contrast. Connie's idea of the world into which, at the age of fifteen, she is beginning to make her first tentative forays is shaped by these songs and occupied by *boys*: boys who can be snubbed with impunity, boys who merge into one undifferentiated and safe blur in her mind, boys who offer hamburgers and "the caresses of love." And that love is "not the way someone like June would suppose but sweet, gentle, the way it was in movies and promised in songs." To these boys Connie presents herself as undifferentiated *girl,* and she is concerned that she look attractive to them.

The world, however, is occupied not only by frank and tentative boys but also by determined and deceitful men, by evil as well as by innocence, by hypocrisy, perversion, and violence — an exponent of all of which Connie attracts in Arnold Friend. Although in the course of their interview Connie sees through his disguise, the impoverishment of her world provides her no way to resist his advances. Her home offers no refuge, her father does not come when she needs him (he has always been essentially absent anyway), and she is unable to manipulate the telephone because of her panic. Meanwhile, Arnold, who presents himself in the guise of a movie hero, a teenage "boy," and her lover, offers to take charge of her. He places his mark upon her and gives her a role to play in a world of his devising. Because she is cut off from her past and has no idea of a future, she is at his mercy in determining what to do in the present. Like her cultural cousin, Vladimir Nabokov's Lolita, sobbing in Humbert's arms, she simply has nowhere else to go. Not only does Arnold show Connie that she is desired, he also provides her a way to be "good": By going with him she will save her undeserving family from getting hurt. Connie does not so much decide to go out to Arnold as she watches an alien being that Arnold has called into existence in her body respond to his desires. The final ironic horror, of course, is that she will be raped and murdered and buried in the desert not as brown-eyed Connie but as the imaginary "sweet little blue-eyed girl" of Arnold's sick imagination.

Oates acknowledges that her inspiration for the story came in part from reading about an actual case, and Tom Quirk has demonstrated at length the degree to which the circumstances of "Where Are You Going, Where Have You Been?" seem to be derived from an article in *Life* (4 Mar. 1955) by Don Moser titled (in a reference to some lyrics from a popular song) "The Pied Piper of Tucson." Even some of the most apparently allegorical details, such as Arnold's trouble with his boots, which has been attributed to his having cloven hooves or wolf paws, reflect the facts about Charles Schmid, a wiry gymnast of twenty-three who stuffed things in his boots, wore makeup, and drove around Tucson in a gold car playing the hero to a group of high-school kids until he was arrested for raping and murdering three young girls. Quirk's argument that Oates followed the magazine article's theme in relating this horror in the "golden west" to the emptiness of "the American dream" points out an important dimension of the story, and his emphasis keeps the real horror of the incident in focus.

Gretchen Schulz and R. J. R. Rockwood are aware of the *Life* article, but they focus instead on another acknowledged source of Oates's inspiration, the folktale. Their discussion of the story's allusions to and affinities with "The Pied Piper of Hamelin," "Cinderella," "Little Red Riding Hood," and other tales suggests why "Where Are You Going, Where Have You Been?" is such a disturbing work. Their article offers detailed interpretations of the psychological crises Connie passes through, based on psychoanalytic interpretations of the meaning and developmental function of the analogous tales. (They use Bruno Bettelheim as their chief authority.) But whereas folktales most often smooth the passage of their readers through Oedipal conflicts and reintegration of the childhood identity into the adult by working through to a happy ending, "Where Are You Going, Where Have You Been?" taps these powerful psychic forces in the reader only to pour them out on the sand.

WILLIAM E. SHEIDLEY

Questions for Discussion

1. Define Connie's relationships with her mother, sister, and father. What is missing from this family? Why does Connie wish "her mother was dead and she herself was dead and it was all over"?

2. What are Connie's "two sides"? In your opinion, is Connie's case unusual for a girl her age in our society? In what ways is she atypical? What about June?

3. The girls enter the drive-in with "faces pleased and expectant as if they were entering a sacred building," and the popular music in the background seems "like music at a church service." Explore the drive-in religion further. What are its creeds, its mysteries? Is it a true religion? a guide to the good life? Does Connie believe in anything else?

4. Discuss the similarities between Eddie, who rotates on a counter stool and offers "something to eat," and the emblem of the drive-in on its bottle-top roof. What else does Eddie offer? Compare Eddie with Arnold Friend as we first see him at the drive-in.

5. What does Oates accomplish by returning briefly to Connie's relationship with her family before narrating what happens "one Sunday"?

6. Discuss Connie's daydreams, in which "all the boys fell back and dissolved into a single face that was not even a face, but an idea, a feeling, mixed up with the urgent insistent pounding of the music," and in which she associates sunbathing with the "sweet, gentle" lovemaking "in movies and promised in song." What is the source of the sexual desire reflected in these dreams? What is its object?

7. Asbestos was formerly used as a noninflammable insulating material. Trace the images of heat and fire associated with it in the story.

8. Compare Connie's gentle breathing as she listens to the "XYZ Sunday Jamboree" with her breath "jerking back and forth in her lungs" when she tries to use the telephone at the climax of the story.

9. Why does Connie whisper "Christ. Christ" when she hears a car coming up the driveway? Does the effort to see Arnold Friend as a Christ figure find further substantiation in the text? Does it yield any meaningful insights?

10. Where does Connie stand during the first part of her conversation with Arnold? Is Oates's blocking of the scene realistic? symbolic?

11. Describe Arnold's car and clothing. What purpose is served by his transparent disguise? Why does it take Connie so long to penetrate the disguise?

12. Does Arnold have supernatural knowledge about Connie, her family, and her friends? Can his apparent clairvoyance about the barbecue be explained in naturalistic terms?

13. Account for Connie's idea that Arnold "had driven up the driveway all right but had come from nowhere before that and belonged nowhere and that everything about him and even the music that was so familiar to her was only half real." Explain the importance of that idea for understanding what happens to Connie.

14. Why does Connie's kitchen seem "like a place she had never seen before"? How has Arnold succeeded in making Connie feel cut off from her past and unprotected in her home? What is the implication of "the echo of a song from last year" in this context?

15. What is the role of Ellie in Arnold's assault on Connie?

16. Arnold implies that Connie can protect her family from harm by coming with him. How important a factor is this in his winning her over to his will?

17.   Examine the passage in which Connie tries to telephone her mother and then collapses in panic and hysteria. Notice its associations with sex and birth. What is taking place in Connie at this moment?
18.   Arnold asks rhetorically, "What else is there for a girl like you but to be sweet and pretty and give in?" In what sense is this true?
19.   Explain Connie's feeling that she is watching herself go out the door. What has caused this split in her consciousness?

Topics for Writing

1.   Discuss Arnold Friend's obvious masquerade, and why it succeeds.
2.   Comment on popular music and religion in "Where Are You Going, Where Have You Been?"
3.   Read the story once while bearing in mind that it is "based on fact" — something very much like this is known to have actually happened. After finishing the story, write a personal essay giving your reaction. What does this account imply about human nature? About the society reflected in the story?
4.   Reread the story with an eye to its allusions to folktales and fairy tales with which you are familiar. Arnold's "coach" has a pumpkin on it; Connie is nearly asleep when he awakens her; he has big teeth; and so forth. What are the tales alluded to about? Is this story a fairy tale, too?
5.   **RESPONDING CREATIVELY**   Select an item from the news that grips your imagination, and ask yourself why it does. Does it have affinities with folktales or myths? Does it suggest disturbing ideas about human nature and society? Write a narrative of the event, perhaps from the point of view of one of the participants, that incorporates these larger implications.
6.   **CONNECTIONS**   Compare technique and theme in Oates's "Where Are You Going, Where Have You Been?" and Jackson's "The Lottery."
7.   **CONNECTIONS**   Compare and contrast Arnold Friend and Flannery O'Connor's Misfit.
8.   **CONNECTIONS**   Study the allusions to religion in the story. How would Flannery O'Connor have handled this material?

Related Commentary

Joyce Carol Oates, *Smooth Talk:* Short Story into Film, p. 1548.

Suggested Readings

Bloom, Harold. *Joyce Carol Oates.* New York: Chelsea House, 1981.
Friedman, Ellen G. "Joyce Carol Oates." *Modern American Women Writers.* Ed. Elaine Showalter. New York: Macmillan, 1991.
Gardner, John. *On Writers and Writing.* Reading, MA: Addison-Wesley, 1994. 75.
Gillis, Christina Marsden. " 'Where Are You Going, Where Have You Been?': Seduction, Space, and a Fictional Mode." *Studies in Short Fiction* 18 (1981): 65–70.
Johnson, Greg. *Understanding Joyce Carol Oates.* Columbia: U of South Carolina P, 1987.

Oates, Joyce Carol. *New Heaven, New Earth.* New York: Vanguard, 1974.

———. *(Woman) Writer: Occasions and Opportunities.* New York: NAL-Dutton, 1989.

Milazzo, Lee. *Conversations with Joyce Carol Oates.* Jackson: UP of Mississippi, 1989.

Pearlman, Mickey, ed. *American Women Writing Fiction: Memory, Identity, Family, Space.* Lexington: U of Kentucky P, 1989. 9–44.

Plimpton, George. *Women Writers at Work: The* Paris Review *Interviews.* New York: Penguin, 1989.

Quirk, Tom. "A Source for 'Where Are You Going, Where Have You Been?' " *Studies in Short Fiction* 18 (1981): 413–19.

Rozga, Margaret. "Threatening Places, Hiding Places: The Midwest in Selected Stories by Joyce Carol Oates." *Midwestern Miscellany* 18 (1990): 34–44.

Schulz, Gretchen, and R. J. R. Rockwood. "In Fairyland, without a Map: Connie's Exploration Inward in Joyce Carol Oates's 'Where Are You Going, Where Have You Been?' " *Literature and Psychology* 30 (1980): 155–67.

Urbanski, Marie Mitchell Olesen. "Existential Allegory: Joyce Carol Oates's 'Where Are You Going, Where Have You Been?' " *Studies in Short Fiction* 15 (1978): 200–03.

Wegs, Joyce M. " 'Don't You Know Who I Am?': The Grotesque in Oates's 'Where Are You Going, Where Have You Been?' " *Journal of Narrative Technique* 5 (1975): 66–72.

Wesley, Marilyn Clarke. "Transgression and Refusal: The Dynamic of Power in the Domestic Fiction of Joyce Carol Oates." *Dissertation Abstracts International* 49.11 (May 1989): 3365A.

Winslow, Joan D. "The Stranger Within: Two Stories by Oates and Hawthorne." *Studies in Short Fiction* 17 (1980): 263–68.

Tim O'Brien

The Things They Carried (p. 1102)

In "The Things They Carried," O'Brien has found a brilliant solution to one of the most common problems a writer faces: how to find a new way to approach a subject that has been written about many times before. His subject is men at war, a topic that has occupied writers since remotest antiquity. The earliest epic in the European tradition is Homer's account of the siege of Troy, and the earliest griot narratives from the empires of Africa recount battles fought along the banks of the Niger River.

The Vietnam War has been treated in a stream of stories, books, articles, studies, and debates. O'Brien's innovation is to tell us directly not about the soldiers, or about the meaningless war they find themselves in, but about the things they are carrying on their shoulders and in their pockets. This simple device is startling and effective. The things his "grunts" are carrying are one way to identify them, to bring them to life, and the author also tells us about the things they carry under different circumstances.

This use of the small detail to illuminate the whole picture would not be as effective if it were limited to a simple description of what each of the men is carrying. But as he discusses the items — their use, their importance to the assignment the men are carrying out, and the significance of each thing to each man — O'Brien

tells us about the war itself, and the soldiers' attitudes toward what they are doing. By presenting each of these objects as a microcosm of the reality of the war,
the author makes the experience more comprehensible. He has found a dimension that shows us the soldiers as human beings, and that is the most important
task for a writer who wants to make us face this cruel reality again.

Questions for Discussion

1. What is the effect of O'Brien's use of abbreviations and acronyms: R & R,
    SOP, M & Ms, USO, Psy Ops, KIA?
2. When the author writes, "Afterward they burned Than Khe," what is he
    telling us about the attitude of the men toward the people in the villages
    around them?
3. Why is it important to specify the weight of the equipment each man is
    carrying?
4. Does the language of the soldiers sound "real"? Do the descriptions of the
    weapons have the feeling of reality?
5. Why does the lieutenant burn the letters he has been carrying?

Topics for Writing

1. Soldiers from both sides are fighting the war, but the author only tells us
    about the men from one side. Why doesn't he describe the North Vietnam-
    ese soldiers?
2. Discuss the attitudes toward the war in the United States as they are re-
    flected in the attitudes of the soldiers in "The Things They Carried."
3. Stories about men at war usually emphasize heroism and heroic acts; these
    are completely absent in this story. What has caused this change in atti-
    tude?

Related Commentaries

Bobbie Ann Mason, On Tim O'Brien's "The Things They Carried," p. 1531.
Tim O'Brien, Alpha Company, p. 1551.

Suggested Readings

Bonn, Maria S. "A Different World: The Vietnam Veteran Novel Comes Home."
    Fourteen Landing Zones: Approaches to Vietnam War Literature. Ed. Philip K.
    Jason. Iowa City: U of Iowa P, 1992.
Calloway, Catherine. "Pluralities of Vision: *Going after Cacciato* and Tim O'Brien's
    Short Fiction." *America Rediscovered: Critical Essays on Literature and Film of
    the Vietnam War.* Ed. Owen W. Gilman, Jr. New York: Garland, 1990.
———. "Tim O'Brien (1946–): A Primary and Secondary Bibliography." *Bulletin of
    Bibliography* 50.3 (Sept. 1993): 223–29.

Flannery O'Connor

Everything That Rises Must Converge (p. 1117)

"Everything That Rises Must Converge" is one of O'Connor's most power-ful stories. Although they are emotionally linked as closely as Siamese twins, Julian and his mother are in such fundamental disagreement that only death can bring their souls together, since "everything that rises must converge." O'Connor goes to great lengths to spell out the differences between mother and son. They are so extreme that humor is the one thing that makes them bearable to the sensitive reader. Julian asserts that "true culture is in the mind." His mother says, "It's in the heart." He insists that "nobody in the damn bus cares who you are." She re-plies, "I care who I am." She always looks on the bright side of things. He glories in scenting out impending disasters. He tells himself he isn't dominated by his mother. She knows he's both financially and emotionally dependent on her, and she gets him to do whatever she asks.

Contrasts and opposites rule this unlikely pair, but the world they inhabit is also in a state of opposition to their sense of themselves. Blacks no longer know their place in the back of the bus; mother and son are exiled from the destroyed family mansion; Julian wants to be a writer after his college education, but he's selling typewriters instead. The only constant is his mother's ridiculous hat. It reappears on the head of the black lady sitting with her little son next to Julian and his mother on the bus. This sight amuses his mother, who hasn't lost her sense of humor, her spirit refusing to be worn down by the remarks and behavior of her critical, hostile son. As a character she is partially redeemed (despite her racial bigotry) by her humor and her fundamental generosity. In contrast, Julian is damned by his sense of pride.

O'Connor makes certain of this damnation by subtly shifting the point of view to Julian's mental outlook during his journey on the bus, when he with-draws "into the inner compartment of his mind where he spent most of his time." He will be alone there, feeling smugly superior to his mother, until he realizes that he has lost her, at which time he will be forced to include her in his emotional state by entering "the world of guilt and sorrow."

Students may enjoy discussing the humor in this story as well as O'Connor's sublime ear for the ridiculous in her characters' speech. "Everything That Rises Must Converge" also lends itself well to different critical perspectives. Since O'Connor wrote from a Christian orientation, the religious implications of the narrative can be traced: the references to Saint Sebastian, or the Negro mother's threat to her little boy, "Quit yo' foolishness . . . before I knock the living Jesus out of you!" Or O'Connor's quiet comment about "guilt and sorrow" at the end. Stu-dents who are budding social historians, psychologists, or feminists can also find abundant material in this story to explore from their orientations.

Questions for Discussion

1. O'Connor writes that Julian's mother's eyes, "sky-blue, were as innocent and untouched by experience as they must have been when she was ten." Again, when she turns her eyes, now a "bruised purple," on Julian, he gets

an "uncomfortable sense of her innocence." What are we to make of her innocence? How do we reconcile this attribute with her racism?

2.   Julian seems to hate almost everything about his mother. Does she hate anything about her son? Why does he despise her? Why does she love him?

3.   The idea of family mansion implies family ties. How do family ties appear in this story? Does the "decayed mansion" mean more to Julian or to his mother? What does it mean to him? to her?

4.   What point of view controls "Everything That Rises Must Converge"? At which points in the story do we have the most intimate access to Julian's thoughts?

5.   Describe Julian's relationships with people other than his mother. Consider the paragraphs beginning "He began to imagine" and "He imagined his mother." Who would he like to be friends with and why? Does his acknowledgment of his mother's racism imply positive things about Julian's own character?

6.   On page 1121 we discover that Julian's mother doesn't think Julian knows "a thing about 'life,' that he hadn't even entered the real world" yet. Does the narrator agree with her? Discuss this sentence and the closing sentence of the story together. What does this imply about the characteristics that belong to "real life"?

7.   After his mother's stroke, Julian looks "into a face he had never seen before." What is different about her face now? What metaphor is O'Connor sustaining behind the description of the literal differences brought on by neurological devastation?

8.   O'Connor, a devout Catholic, said her stories were meant to be more like parables than true to life. What elements of this story are Christian? Is the preoccupation central to this story available only to Christians?

Topics for Writing

1.   Compare and contrast the two mothers and the two sons in the story.
2.   Analyze the symbolism of the hat at the convergence of two apparent opposites — the two mothers.
3.   Discuss the role of pride and the response to charity in Julian and the black mother.
4.   Write an examination of the changing social order between the generations of Julian's mother and Julian.
5.   Explore the role of irony in "Everything That Rises Must Converge."

Related Commentaries

Wayne C. Booth, A Rhetorical Reading of O'Connor's "Everything That Rises Must Converge," p. 1685.
Robert H. Brinkmeyer Jr., Flannery O'Connor and Her Readers, p. 1676.
Flannery O'Connor, From Letters, 1954–55, p. 1663.
Flannery O'Connor, Writing Short Stories, p. 1666.
V. S. Pritchett, Flannery O'Connor: Satan Comes to Georgia, p. 1674.

Suggested Readings

See page 212.

FLANNERY O'CONNOR

Good Country People (p. 1128)

In the world of Flannery O'Connor's fiction, characters are seldom who we think they are or even who they think they are. "Good Country People" provides an intriguing twist on the archetypal theme: Events and people are seldom as simple as they seem.

O'Connor revels in the idiosyncrasies of personality, peopling this story with three strong characters in Joy (Hulga), Mrs. Hopewell, and Manley Pointer, as well as an interesting subsidiary character, Mrs. Freeman, with her "special fondness for the details of secret infections, hidden deformities," and "assaults upon children." O'Connor's choice of names figures prominently. Joy changes her name to Hulga to symbolize her sense of her own ugliness. Mrs. Hopewell continually hopes well of things, blathering a stream of banal platitudes that reveal her own lack of depth. The name Manley Pointer strikes the reader as almost humorously phallic and predatory-sounding, given the surprising turn of events in the storage barn.

We don't see how "right" the details of this story are until we reach its sardonic conclusion, Pointer going Hulga's intellectual atheism one better, disappearing with her leg in his "Bible" valise, Mrs. Hopewell in her ignorance commenting on "that nice dull young man." Looking back, we see the clever meticulousness of Pointer's con — the feigned heaviness of his satchel, his feigned simplicity (as in mistaking the name of the house for its owner), the rube suit. It turns out that this specimen of "good country people" reads people better than the highly educated Hulga or the self-aggrandizing Mrs. Hopewell.

The experience of losing her artificial limb to the perverted Manley Pointer is the loss of a certain kind of virginity for Hulga, and however harrowing the experience, we sense that it will be a valuable one. Prior to her victimization, we feel mainly revulsion for Joy/Hulga. We sympathize with her hunting accident, but O'Connor highlights the unpleasant abrasiveness of her personality; clearly Hulga's psyche, as well as her body, has been damaged. Hulga's low self-esteem is exacerbated by her mother's implications of Hulga's abnormality, which focus on her intellectualism as much as on her disfigurement. For all Mrs. Hopewell's assertions that "it takes all kinds to make the world go 'round," she resents her daughter's interest in philosophy (female education is for a "good time") as well as Hulga's individuation: "It seemed to Mrs. Hopewell that every year she grew less like other people and more like herself."

In this multifaceted story of moral blindness, Hulga experiences a physical intimacy with Pointer that forces her into a new mode of reacting and out of her customary detached intellectualism: "Without the leg she felt entirely dependent on him. Her brain seemed to have stopped thinking altogether and to be about some other function that it was not very good at." However dastardly Pointer's actions, he forces Hulga to feel and acknowledge her emotions for the first time. We go away from the story feeling that Hulga will be a changed — and humbled — person less presumptuous and closer to psychic wholeness.

Questions for Discussion

1. What does Mrs. Hopewell mean by "good country people"?
2. Why does Joy change her name to Hulga?
3. In what ways do you expect Joy/Hulga will change after her experience in the barn with Manley Pointer?
4. Discuss O'Connor's choice of names for the characters in this story.
5. Is Manley Pointer a believable character? Have you in your own experience encountered people who are entirely other than they seem? What is Pointer really interested in? Why does he carry off Hulga's leg?
6. Discuss the dramatic function of Mrs. Freeman and her two daughters.
7. Discuss the effects on characterization of O'Connor's choosing to give Joy a Ph.D. in philosophy and an artificial leg. How do these details predispose our expectations?

Topics for Writing

1. Discuss the function of Christianity in "Good Country People."
2. **CONNECTIONS**   Compare "Good Country People" with "Everything That Rises Must Converge." What similarities and differences do you find among mother, son or daughter, and stranger in these stories? What can you infer from this comparison about Flannery O'Connor's attraction to certain types of characters?

Related Commentaries

Robert H. Brinkmeyer Jr., Flannery O'Connor and Her Readers, p. 1676.
Dorothy Tuck McFarland, On "Good Country People," p. 1681.
Flannery O'Connor, From Letters, 1954–55, p. 1663.
Flannery O'Connor, Writing Short Stories, p. 1666.

Suggested Readings

See page 212.

FLANNERY O'CONNOR

A Good Man Is Hard to Find (p. 1142)

O'Connor's comments (included in Part Three, p. 1671) direct attention to the climax of her story and suggest how she intended the central characters to be viewed and what she meant the story to imply. Students may benefit, however, from struggling at first to interpret the text unassisted by authorial explanation. The effort should reveal dimensions of O'Connor's art that might otherwise be overlooked.

The grandmother's reawakening to reality, which leads to her gesture of grace as she reaches out to The Misfit as one of her own children, may be triggered by the violence of the murders going on just offstage and the extremity of her own case, but her conversion has been carefully prepared for. Throughout the story this old woman longs in various ways to go back *home* — to Tennessee, to the days of her youth, to the mansion with the imaginary secret panel, which is as much in heaven as it is down a hilly back road in Georgia. Death is seldom far from her thoughts, though for a long time she does not apprehend its reality. Her initial worries about The Misfit are disingenuous, but encountering him or returning to east Tennessee come to the same thing in the end. On the road, the grandmother dresses up in nice clothes so that "anyone seeing her dead on the highway would know at once that she was a lady," observes a graveyard, and remembers her mansion at a town named Toombsboro. The Misfit and his men approach in a "hearse-like automobile"; the family awaits them in front of the woods that "gaped like a dark open mouth." The grandmother is at odds with present times. She squabbles with the children (whose behavior even the reader may find unusually improper), easily upstages the cabbage-headed, slacks-wearing woman who is their mother, joins Red Sammy in deploring the state of world affairs, and disastrously deludes Bailey by smuggling the cat into the car. But she loves the world as well, in a selfish, childish way. She *will* have the cat along; she admires the scenery (including a picturesque "pickaninny" for whose poverty she is not yet ready to feel compassion); she wishes she had married Mr. E. A. Teagarden, who courted her with watermelon and would have supplied all her worldly needs from the proceeds of his Coca-Cola stock; and she even makes a play for Red Sammy, the only tycoon in sight.

These desires may be misdirected, but just as it takes very little to upset the valise, release the cat, flip the car off the road, and carry the story into an entirely new set of circumstances, so, under the intensifying presence of death, it takes only a moment for the grandmother's selfish love for and alienation from the world to flip over into the selfless love that leads her to open her heart to The Misfit. After all, she at least rationalizes bringing the cat to protect it; she supportively asserts that Red Sammy is "a good man" in face of his own cynicism and despair; and she offers the same praise to The Misfit from the moment she recognizes him. Without a doubt the grandmother's motive in insisting that The Misfit is "a good man" and in urging him to pray is to divert him from his evident intention and so to save her skin. But as the bullets ring out in the background and the grandmother's maternal instincts burst forth in her repeated cries of "Bailey Boy!" she begins to act charitably in spite of herself. She offers The Misfit one of Bailey's shirts, listens to his confession (although she is the one who is about to die), and when he *is* wearing Bailey's shirt, she reaches out to him in his anguish. A good man *is* hard to find; Jesus may have been the only one who was intrinsically good. But when she loves and pities the radically fallen Misfit, the grandmother becomes for the moment a *good woman* through her Christlike action, as The Misfit himself acerbically recognizes.

As O'Connor mentions in her commentary, The Misfit has evoked widely differing responses from readers and critics, who have associated him with the devil, the modern agnostic existentialist, or "the prophet he was meant to become," in O'Connor's own phrase. Perhaps The Misfit's daddy provides the best way of distinguishing him from the rest of the characters with his remark "It's some that can live their whole life out without asking about it and it's others has to know why it is, and this boy is one of the latters." Unlike O'Connor, whose vision of the world was grounded in *belief*, The Misfit wants to *know*. With Faustian presumption, he seeks to comprehend the divine mysteries in terms of his own intellect and demands a kind of justice in life that he can understand. When he cannot find the answers to his questions, but only the implication of inexplicable guilt (like Original Sin) in the punishment he receives, The Misfit sees the world not as the charming place it has appeared to the grandmother but as a prison whose empty sky resembles the blank walls of his cell in the penitentiary. In his own calculus of guilt, The Misfit feels he has been excessively punished, and he seems to be going about the world committing crimes in order to right the balance. His most perverse principle, "No pleasure but meanness," is sustained surprisingly well by the world O'Connor portrays. (Is *this* the reason for the story's lack of anything or anyone to admire and its unremittingly ironic tone?) But it gives way after he has been touched by the grandmother to his first true prophecy: "It's no real pleasure in life" — no *real* pleasure in *this* life, though true goodness sometimes appears in those made conscious of death.

WILLIAM E. SHEIDLEY

Questions for Discussion

1. What is the grandmother's reason for bringing up The Misfit at the beginning of the story?
2. Describe "the children's mother." Why does O'Connor make her such a nonentity?
3. What about John Wesley and June Star? What would have been the result had O'Connor characterized them as something other than totally obnoxious?
4. Discuss the grandmother's reasons for her fatal decision to bring Pitty Sing on the trip.
5. Why does the grandmother dress so nicely for the trip?
6. Compare the grandmother's response to the scenery and the trip with that of the children. What does O'Connor accomplish by means of this distinction?
7. Just before the stop at The Tower, the grandmother reminisces about her old suitor, Edgar Atkins Teagarden. Specify the connections between the two episodes.
8. What tower might O'Connor have had in mind in choosing the name for Red Sammy's establishment? Why is there a monkey in a chinaberry tree feasting on fleas posted outside The Tower? What do we learn about the world at Red Sammy's?
9. Contrast The Tower with the mansion the grandmother awakens to remember "outside of Toombsboro."
10. What factors cause the accident? Consider its meaning as a consequence of the grandmother's choices and desires.
11. Describe the manner in which The Misfit arrives on the scene. What effect does his appearance have on the reader?
12. The grandmother's response to The Misfit's remark "it would have been better for all of you, lady, if you hadn't of reckernized me," is "You wouldn't shoot a lady, would you?" Evaluate her question.

13. To what extent is the grandmother correct in her praise of The Misfit? In what ways is he a gentleman?
14. Describe the grandmother's reaction to Bailey's departure. Is her response consistent with her previous behavior?
15. Define The Misfit's experience of the world. To what extent can his criminality be blamed on the conditions of his life? Does The Misfit feel any more free outside the penitentiary than in it?
16. How can the logic of The Misfit's position that "the crime don't matter. . . . because sooner or later you're going to forget what it was you done and just be punished for it" be attacked? To what extent does The Misfit's description of himself apply to everyone? Bear in mind that the whole family is being punished with death for no ascertainable crime.
17. Explain how, to The Misfit, "Jesus thown everything off balance."
18. What is the effect of O'Connor's comparing the grandmother to "a parched old turkey hen crying for water"?
19. Does The Misfit do or say anything to deserve the grandmother's gesture of concern?
20. Explain The Misfit's final evaluation of the grandmother: "She would of been a good woman . . . if it had been somebody there to shoot her every minute of her life."
21. Contrast The Misfit's remark "No pleasure but meanness" with his last words in the story.

Topics for Writing

1. What is the function of tone in O'Connor's story?
2. Describe techniques of characterization in "A Good Man Is Hard to Find."
3. **RESPONDING CREATIVELY** Write a parable or short tale designed to illustrate a religious or philosophical truth. Following O'Connor's example, portray your characters ruthlessly as embodiments of what you want them to represent.
4. **CONNECTIONS** Compare and contrast O'Connor's "A Good Man Is Hard to Find" and Tolstoy's "The Death of Ivan Ilych."
5. **CONNECTIONS** Comment upon the relationship between the grandmother and The Misfit in "A Good Man Is Hard to Find" and the relationship between Connie and Arnold Friend in Oates's "Where Are You Going, Where Have You Been?"

Related Commentaries

Robert H. Brinkmeyer Jr., Flannery O'Connor and Her Readers, p. 1676.
Sally Fitzgerald, Southern Sources of "A Good Man Is Hard to Find," p. 1688.
Flannery O'Connor, From Letters, 1954–55, p. 1663.
Flannery O'Connor, Writing Short Stories, p. 1666.
Flannery O'Connor, A Reasonable Use of the Unreasonable, p. 1671.

Suggested Readings

Asals, Frederick. *Flannery O'Connor: The Imagination of Extremity.* Athens: U of Georgia P, 1982. 142–54.

Brinkmeyer, Robert H., Jr. *The Art and Vision of Flannery O'Connor.* Baton Rouge: Louisiana State UP, 1989.

Browning, Preston M., Jr. *Flannery O'Connor.* Crosscurrents/Modern Critiques. Carbondale: Southern Illinois UP, 1974. 54–59.

Burke, John J. "Convergence of Flannery O'Connor and Chardin." *Renascence* 19 (1966): 41–47, 52.

Church, Joseph. "An Abuse of the Imagination in Flannery O'Connor's 'A Good Man Is Hard to Find.'" *Notes on Contemporary Literature* 20.3 (May 1990): 8–10.

Clark, Beverly Lyon, and Melville J. Friedman. *Critical Essays on Flannery O'Connor.* Boston: G. K. Hall, 1985.

Esch, Robert M. "O'Connor's 'Everything That Rises Must Converge.' " *Explicator* 27 (1969): Item 58.

Feeley, Sister Kathleen. *Flannery O'Connor: Voice of the Peacock.* New Brunswick, NJ: Rutgers UP, 1972.

Gatta, John. "*The Scarlet Letter* as Pre-Text for Flannery O'Connor's 'Good Country People.'" *The Nathaniel Hawthorne Review* 16.2 (Fall 1990): 6–9.

Giannone, Richard. *Flannery O'Connor: A Study of the Short Fiction.* Boston: Twayne, 1988.

Grimshaw, James A. *The Flannery O'Connor Companion.* Westport, CT: Greenwood, 1981.

Hendin, Josephine. *The World of Flannery O'Connor.* Ann Arbor, MI: Books Demand UMI, 1986.

Kane, Patricia. "Flannery O'Connor's 'Everything That Rises Must Converge.' " *Critique: Studies in Short Fiction* 8 (1965): 85–91.

Maida, Patricia Dinneen. "Convergence in Flannery O'Connor's 'Everything That Rises Must Converge.' " *Studies in Short Fiction* 7 (1970): 549–55.

Martin, W. R. "The Apostate in Flannery O'Connor's 'Everything That Rises Must Converge.'" *American Notes and Queries* 23 (1985): 113–14.

McDermott, John V. "Julian's Journey into Hell: Flannery O'Connor's Allegory of Pride." *Mississippi Quarterly* 28 (1975): 171–79.

Nisly, P. W. "Prison of the Self: Isolation in Flannery O'Connor's Fiction." *Studies in Short Fiction* 17 (1980): 49–54.

Ochshorn, Kathleen G. "A Cloak of Grace: Contradictions in 'A Good Man Is Hard to Find.'" *Studies in American Fiction* 18.1 (Spring 1990): 113–17.

O'Connor, Flannery. *The Habit of Being.* Letters edited and with an introduction by Sally Fitzgerald. New York: Farrar, 1979.

———. *Mystery and Manners.* New York: Farrar, 1969.

Orvell, Miles. *Invisible Parade: The Fiction of Flannery O'Connor.* Philadelphia: Temple UP, 1972.

Paulson, Suzanne. *Flannery O'Connor.* Boston: G. K. Hall, 1988.

Petry, Alice Hall. "Miss O'Connor and Mrs. Mitchell: The Example of 'Everything That Rises.'" *The Southern Quarterly: A Journal of the Arts in the South* 27.4 (Summer 1989): 5–15.

Pyron, V. "'Strange Country': The Landscape of Flannery O'Connor's Short Stories." *Mississippi Quarterly* 36 (1983): 557–68.

Frank O'Connor

Guests of the Nation (p. 1154)

O'Connor's story draws exceptional power from its concern with a betrayal of the most primitive basis of human society, the host-guest relationship. The English prisoners, billeted with their guards in a cottage so thoroughly rooted in the land that its occupant still bears traces of indigenous paganism, earn the status of guests and come to feel at home. Belcher's contributions to the household chores call attention to the simple satisfactions of the peaceful, cooperative labor that is disrupted by the war, and Hawkins's learning Irish dances implies the underlying brotherhood of men, in contrast to which the scruples of "our lads" who "at that time did not dance foreign dances on principle" seem absurd — and ominous. The futility of Hawkins's debates with Noble on theology calls further into question the reality of the issues that divide the English from the Irish, and his international socialist politics provide a hint that there are issues of at least equal importance that would not polarize the two pairs of men but unite them against a common enemy.

The inhumanity of the conflict that orders Belcher and Hawkins to be executed by their "chums," their brothers, appears clearer for O'Connor's skillful portrayal of the prisoners as distinct from each other, individualized and consistent in their personalities. Further, by opening the story with a plunge into what seems an ongoing state of affairs, O'Connor shows that it is the war that interrupts the natural friendly interaction among the men rather than their fellowship interrupting a "normal" condition of bitter hostility between the English and the Irish. Even Jeremiah Donovan, who eventually brings down the cruel warrant and carries it out, forms part of the circle around the card table and scolds Hawkins for poor play "as if he were one of our own."

Bonaparte, the narrator, embraces the Englishmen as comrades and chafes at his official duties as their guard. With Noble, he imagines that the brigade officers, who also "knew the Englishmen well," will treat them as men rather than as enemies. But when the moment of decision arrives, Noble's resistance only extends to accepting the secondary role of gravedigger, and Bonaparte, though he hopes the prisoners will run away, finds himself powerless to aid them. Belcher and Hawkins are most fully themselves at the moment of their deaths, Hawkins talking on about his larger cause, Belcher finally revealing the fullness of his loving and generous nature. To Bonaparte and Noble the execution conveys a shock of revelation that changes the world for them. As Noble prays with the old woman in the doorway of the cottage — now become a shrine to the communion that took place within it, the only holy place in a world that seems to Noble composed entirely of the grave of his friends — Bonaparte, made profane in the literal etymological sense ("outside the shrine") and figuratively as well by his participation in the killing, feels himself cast out, alone, cut off from all atonement.

WILLIAM E. SHEIDLEY

Questions for Discussion

1. Describe and explain the pacing of the story. Contrast the movement of sections II and III with that of section IV.

2.   What is the effect of the abrupt beginning of the story? Why does O'Connor introduce the characters before specifying that they are prisoners and guards in a war?
3.   Why does O'Connor trouble to introduce the message from Mary Brigid O'Connell about her brother's socks?
4.   Distinguish between the two Englishmen. Are they more different from the Irishmen or from each other?
5.   Explore the significance of the old woman's superstitions about Jupiter Pluvius and "the hidden powers." Compare her interest in religion with that of Noble and Hawkins.
6.   Why is Bonaparte so shocked when he learns what may happen to the hostages?
7.   What is the relevance to the story of Hawkins's political beliefs? Do we think less of him when he volunteers to become a traitor and join the Irish cause?
8.   What is the effect of Belcher's last-minute confidences? of his apparently sincere repetition of the word *chum* throughout his ordeal?
9.   Discuss Bonaparte's role in the execution. Is he culpable? Does he feel guilty?
10. Define the symbolic implications of the final scene. Why do Noble and Bonaparte have contrasting visions? Do their visions have anything in common? Why does Bonaparte burst out of the cottage where Noble and the old woman are praying?

Topics for Writing

1.   What is the meaning of the old woman and her cottage in "Guests of the Nation"?
2.   Summarize the conflict and the action of this story on personal, public (national, historical, political), and eternal (philosophical, religious, mythical) levels. Could these levels be reconciled so that the polarities of value would be parallel?
3.   **CONNECTIONS**   Compare and contrast O'Connor's "Guests of the Nation" and Babel's "My First Goose" — introductions to war.
4.   **CONNECTIONS**   Compare and contrast executions in O'Connor's "Guests of the Nation" and Borowski's "This Way for the Gas, Ladies and Gentlemen."

Related Commentaries

Frank O'Connor, The Nearest Thing to Lyric Poetry Is the Short Story, p. 1553.
Frank O'Connor, Style and Form in Joyce's "The Dead," p. 1554.

Suggested Readings

Bordewyk, Gordon. "Quest for Meaning: The Stories of Frank O'Connor." *Illinois Quarterly* 41 (1978): 37–47, esp. 38–39.
Matthews, James. *Voices: A Life of Frank O'Connor.* New York: Atheneum, 1983.
O'Connor, Frank. *The Lonely Voice: A Study of the Short Story.* Cleveland: World, 1963.

Prosky, Murray. "The Pattern of Diminishing Certitude in the Stories of Frank O'Connor." *Colby Library Quarterly* 9 (1971): 311–21, esp. 311–14.
Steinman, Michael. *Frank O'Connor at Work.* Syracuse, NY: Syracuse UP, 1990.
Tomory, William. *Frank O'Connor.* Boston: Twayne, 1980.

TILLIE OLSEN

I Stand Here Ironing (p. 1165)

One way to begin discussing this story is to look at the ending. "I will never total it all," the narrator affirms and then pronounces the summary whose inadequacy she has already proclaimed. The summarizing passage clarifies and organizes the impressions the reader may have gleaned from the preceding monologue. It is so clear that if it stood alone or came first in the story the validity of its interpretation of Emily could hardly be doubted. But since it follows her mother's "tormented" meditations, the summary seems incomplete in its clinical precision and must give way to a final paragraph of comparatively obscure and paradoxical requests focused in the startling but brilliantly adept image of the "dress on the ironing board, helpless before the iron," which links the story's end to its beginning and directs attention to the true central character.

What is mainly missing from the summary is the love and understanding that Emily's mother feels for her daughter as a result of living through the experiences bracketed by the orderly generalizations. Just as much as Emily, her mother has been the victim "of depression, of war, of fear." By virtue of having had to cope with those circumstances, she can respect Emily's response to them. Doing so enables her to counter the suggestion that "she's a youngster who needs help" with "Let her be." A good deal of the help Emily and her mother have received so far has put them in separate prisons — as when Emily was incarcerated at the convalescent home — and cut them off from love. To let Emily alone is at least to allow her some freedom to grow at her own slow pace.

Her mother is tempted to blame herself for the deficiencies in Emily's childhood, since she learned things about being a mother with her second family that she did not know with Emily. But her consideration of a characteristic incident early in the narrative suggests a crucial qualifying factor: When she parked Emily at nursery school at the age of two, she did not know what she was subjecting her daughter to, "except that it would have made no difference if I had known. . . . It was the only way we could be together, the only way I could hold a job." As much a victim of rigid and unfavorable economic and historic circumstances as her daughter, Emily's mother can speak her concluding line with feeling. In pleading that Emily somehow be made to know "that she is more than this dress on the ironing board, helpless before the iron," Emily's mother asks that her daughter be spared a condition to which she herself has been subjected. But Emily's mother, unlike Whistler's, does not sit for her portrait passively in a rocking chair; she stands there wielding the iron, controlling the very symbol of the circumstances that have not yet flattened her, painting her own self-portrait, and calling for help not in adjusting Emily to the world but in making the world a place in which Emily can thrive.

WILLIAM E. SHEIDLEY

Questions for Discussion

1. Who is "you" in the first sentence? What is the mother's first response to the request to unlock the mystery of Emily? Does her position change?
2. Does Emily's mother feel guilty about how she has cared for Emily? Why? What factors have affected her dealings with her daughter?
3. Why is the passage in which Emily throws the clock so effective?
4. Discuss the "help" Emily gets at the convalescent home. How does it compare with the help her mother calls for at the end?
5. Emily has suffered from the absence of her father, the exhaustion of her mother, poverty, asthma and other diseases, sibling rivalry, and unpopularity, among other complaints. What is the effect of these hardships on the young woman she has become? What is the effect of her discovery of a talent?
6. What has her mother learned from Emily?
7. Does Emily's mother love her daughter? How can we tell?

Topics for Writing

1. Compare and contrast Emily's talent and her mother's.
2. Discuss the function of the interruptions in "I Stand Here Ironing."
3. Consider "I will never total it all" — the importance of indeterminacy in Olsen's analysis of Emily.
4. Analyze the politics of "I Stand Here Ironing."
5. **RESPONDING CREATIVELY** Write a summary statement in general terms about the personality of a sibling, relative, or friend you have known closely for a long time. Put it aside and cast your memory back to three or four specific incidents involving your subject. Narrate them briefly but in specific and concrete terms. Read over your sketches and compare the personality of your subject as it emerges with what you wrote in your generalized summary. Do you still think your summary is accurate? What are its limitations?

Related Commentary

Robert Coles, Tillie Olsen: The Iron and the Riddle, p. 1478.

Suggested Readings

Frye, Joanne S. "'I Stand Here Ironing': Motherhood as Experience and Metaphor." *Studies in Short Fiction* 18 (1981): 287–92.
O'Connor, William Van. "The Short Stories of Tillie Olsen." *Studies in Short Fiction* 1 (1963): 21–25, esp. 21–22.

CYNTHIA OZICK

The Shawl (p. 1172)

The yellow Star of David sewn into Rosa's coat identifies the people on the march as Jews whose destination is a Nazi concentration camp. The prosaic details of Ozick's story are horrible. Rosa's inability to save her baby, Magda, when the prison guard throws her against the electric fence is the grim conclusion to a hopeless situation. Ozick's poetic language and skillful pacing of her narrative transform the nightmarish details of her fiction into art.

The title of the story suggests its blend of fact and poetry. "The Shawl" is on the one hand a prosaic linen shawl that Rosa uses to wrap her baby and carry her under her coat during the forced march to the camp. On the other hand, Ozick tells us that "it was a magic shawl." It nourishes Magda after Rosa's breast milk dries up. It hides the baby in the women's barracks in the camp for many months. It smothers Rosa's scream after she sees Magda thrown against the fence. The shawl appears to have a life of its own, drying like Rosa's breasts; yet before drying it nourishes Rosa: "Rosa drank Magda's shawl until it dried." That is, perhaps, until the memory of her baby's death is bearable.

The narrative develops through two conflicts, the Jewish-Aryan conflict dramatized through the camp setting and the personal conflict between the two sisters, the baby Magda and the fourteen-year-old Stella. The resolution of Stella's jealousy toward the baby — when Stella takes the shawl to cover herself against the cold and Magda totters outside the women's barracks looking for it — precipitates the climax of the story. There is no resolution to the larger Jewish-Aryan conflict, except that Rosa's will endures. She smothers her screams and survives the death of her baby.

The blend of fact and poetry is reinforced by Ozick's use of sound and silence in "The Shawl." Most of the time, the events described are unvoiced, evoking the eerie echo of silence in the black-and-white documentary films shot by the Allies liberating the concentration camps. Many students will have seen these films on TV programs about the Holocaust and will remember the images of the prison barracks, the hundreds of emaciated prisoners, the mounds of skeleton corpses.

Ozick suggests these familiar images by her use of poetic language to describe the malnutrition of her characters in "The Shawl." Stella's knees are "tumors on sticks, her elbows chicken bones." For the baby, death is a kind of deliverance. She makes a noise for the first time since her scream on the road. But the noises of the baby's scream and her cry "Maaaa" are subhuman, like the chicken-bone elbows. They reinforce the terror of the situation, people degraded into subhuman forms. In a way, silence is a relief. Rosa swallows the shawl to smother her howl so the prison guard won't shoot her. Silence is a means of survival in this story. Ironically, the silence of Ozick's words on the printed page is a testimony to the endurance of her people.

Questions for Discussion

1. How does Ozick use details to allude to the plot situation without naming it specifically? What mood does she create by her method of introducing details?
2. What two conflicts are evident throughout the story? How is the shawl central to these oppositions?
3. In what ways is the shawl "magic"? Whom does it nourish? How?
4. Discuss Ozick's use of poetic language to present the images of the story. Give examples of this use.
5. Who is the protagonist of the story? the antagonist? Is there more than one possible answer to these questions? Explain.
6. Sound and silence are integral to the total effect of the story. Discuss.
7. What is the climax of the story? Are any of the conflicts resolved? What is Ozick protesting? What human qualities does the story commemorate?

Topics for Writing

1. Discuss Ozick's use of sensory images and their contribution to the overall story.
2. **RESPONDING CREATIVELY** Rewrite the story from the point of view of Stella.
3. **CONNECTIONS** Compare and contrast the quality of endurance in O'Brien's "The Things They Carried" and Ozick's "The Shawl."
4. **CONNECTIONS** Compare and discuss the theme of quiet desperation in Ozick's "The Shawl," Gilman's "The Yellow Wallpaper," and Steinbeck's "The Chrysanthemums."

Suggested Readings

Berg, Stephen, ed. "Cynthia Ozick: Lesson of the Master." *In Praise of What Persists.* New York: Harper, 1983. 181–87.

Epstein, J. "Fiction: Cynthia Ozick, Jewish Writer." *Commentary* 77 (1984): 64–69.

Ottenberg, E. "Rich Visions of Cynthia Ozick." *New York Times Magazine* 10 (Apr. 1983): 46–47.

Rosenberg, R. "Covenanted to the Law: Cynthia Ozick." *MELUS* 9 (1982): 39–44.

Strandberg, V. "Art of Cynthia Ozick." *Texas Studies in Language and Literature* 25 (1983): 266–312.

GRACE PALEY

A Conversation with My Father (p. 1177)

The story the narrator writes in response to her father's request is so interesting that it is easy to forget for a while that it is only an element within the larger story Paley has to tell. Confronted with the inescapable fact of the father's imminent death, the narrator and her father respond in differing ways because of their differing needs. Both use gallows humor to make the situation less intolerable, as when the father remarks, "It so happens I'm not going out this evening"; but the narrator seeks that refuge much more often, and her father chides her repeatedly for doing so. Things *matter* to a dying man, and it is not surprising that he should prefer the straight line of tragedy — in which failure and defeat are compensated for by a perception of the real value of what has been lost — to the idea of "the open destiny of life," which, by holding out hope of recovery from any disaster, implies that there is nothing indispensable, no absolute loss. A man on his deathbed knows better.

The narrator's first attempt to write a story that suits her father's taste reflects her discomfort with the assignment. Her "unadorned and miserable tale" remains so sketchy that it lacks verisimilitude and conviction, like meaningless statistics on highway deaths or counterinsurgency body counts. Challenged to try again, she partly confirms her father's complaint that "with you, it's all a joke" by writing a brilliantly comic and incontrovertibly realistic version of the story, whose merits even her father has to recognize: "Number One: You have a nice sense of humor." In a few deft strokes, Paley renders an incisive satiric portrait of two contemporary "life-styles," their hypocrisy, and their destructiveness, focused neatly in the competing periodical titles, *Oh! Golden Horse!* (heroin) and *Man Does Live by Bread Alone.* The narrator knows as well as her father how thorough a perversion of true spiritual values is embodied in each of these titles, and she dramatizes her understanding in the destruction of the mother in her story. But she cannot quite "look it in the face," and she ends her tale with one last grim joke: "terrible, face-scarring, time-consuming tears." Her father spies her desperate evasion: "Number Two: I see you can't tell a plain story. So don't waste time." Ironically, the clarity of his disillusioned vision enables the dying man to feel a purer sympathy for the mother in the story than does the narrator herself, although she claims to care so much about her characters that she wants to give them all a second chance. "Poor woman," he says. "Poor girl, born in a time of fools, to live among fools. The end. The end. You were right to put that down. The end." Not necessarily, the narrator argues, and goes on to invent the kind of future for her character that we always imagine for the dying, in the probably misguided effort to ease their anxiety. But her father, as usual, knows better: " 'How long will it be?' he asked. 'Tragedy! You too. When will you look it in the face?' "

WILLIAM E. SHEIDLEY

Questions for Discussion

1. Describe the medical condition of the narrator's father. How important is it to understanding his position in the conversation?
2. Explain the phrase "despite my metaphors" in the first paragraph. What other writerly tactics of the narrator does her father ignore?
3. The narrator says she *would* like to tell a story with the kind of plot she has always despised. Analyze her conflict.
4. What is the point of the first version of the story? What is wrong with it as a piece of fiction?
5. When her father asks for details, the narrator comes up with things he calls jokes. Are they? What makes them jokes rather than facts?
6. Why does the narrator's father consider that "it is of great consequence" whether the woman in the story is married? Is he simply old-fashioned?

7.   What does the narrator add to her story in the second version? Does the point of the story remain the same? Does her father get the point?
8.   The woman in the story "would rather be with the young." Consider that motivation and its results from the point of view of the narrator and of her father.
9.   What techniques does Paley use to satirize the woman's son and his girlfriend?
10.   Explain the term "time-consuming" at the end of the inset story.
11.   The narrator's father makes three separate responses to the story. Account for each of them. Do they cohere?
12.   What does the narrator's father mean by the statement he makes in various forms culminating in his final question?

Topics for Writing

1.   Analyze "A Conversation with My Father" as a story about writing.
2.   Evaluate the qualities of tragedy versus satire in "A Conversation with My Father."
3.   **RESPONDING CREATIVELY**   Write your own version of the narrator's story. Start from her first version and elaborate on it as you choose, without necessarily using the material the narrator includes in her second version and subsequent commentary.
4.   **CONNECTIONS**   Compare and contrast attitudes toward death and life in Paley's "A Conversation with My Father" and Tolstoy's "The Death of Ivan Ilych."

Related Commentary

Grace Paley, A Conversation with Ann Charters, p. 1556.

Suggested Readings

Aarons, Victoria. "Talking Lives: Storytelling and Renewal in Grace Paley's Short Fiction." *Studies in Jewish Literature* 9.1 (Spring 1990): 20–35.
Arcana, Judith. "Grace Paley: Life and Stories." *Dissertation Abstracts International* 50.7 (Jan. 1990): 2271A.
Baba, Minako. "Faith Darwin as Writer, Heroine: A Study of Grace Paley's Short Stories." *Studies in American Jewish Literature* 7.1 (Spring 1988): 40–54.
Halfman, Ulrich, and Philipp Gerlach. "Grace Paley: A Bibliography." *Tulsa Studies in Women's Literature* 8.2 (Fall 1989): 339–54.
Isaccs, Neil David. *Grace Paley: A Study of the Short Fiction.* Boston: Twayne, 1990.
Logsdon, Loren, and Charles W. Mayer, ed. *Since Flannery O'Connor: Essays on the Contemporary American Short Story.* Macomb: Western Illinois U, 1987. 93–100.
Lyons, Bonnie. "Grace Paley's Jewish Miniatures." *Studies in American Jewish Literature* 8.1 (Spring 1989): 26–33.
Paley, Grace. *Long Walks and Intimate Talks: Stories and Poems by Grace Paley.* New York: Feminist Press and the City U of New York, 1991.

Taylor, Jacqueline. *Grace Paley: Illuminating the Dark Lives.* Austin: U of Texas P, 1990.

———. "Grace Paley on Storytelling and Story Hearing." *Literature in Performance: A Journal of Literature and Performing Art* 7.2 (April 1987): 46–58.

Wilde, Alan. "Grace Paley's World, Investing Words." Wilde, *Middle Grounds.* Philadelphia: U of Pennsylvania P, 1987.

OCTAVIO PAZ

My Life with the Wave (p. 1182)

Although the Mexican poet Octavio Paz has published few short stories, "My Life with the Wave," which first appeared in *Arenas movedizas* (1949), established him as a master of the genre. Images of water and the sea abound in Paz's poetry, so it is not surprising that his handling of these images in a work of short fiction should also exhibit his customary brilliance and virtuosity.

Students reading "My Life with the Wave" will need no help understanding it as a work of fantasy verging on the surreal. The atmosphere and events in the story take on the intense irrational reality of a dream. Paz's incongruous imagery begins immediately, when we learn that the "tall and light" wave is a "she" dressed in "floating clothes" who leaves "that sea" to go off with the narrator. He protests, but by the author's ingenious ploy of changing a pronoun (delivered with grave finality as in a dream), the narrator's fate is sealed: "No, your decision is made. You can't go back." (A rational if uncooperative response by the wave to the narrator would have been, "No, my decision is made. I can't go back.")

How do readers understand that this unusual story is about a "she" and a "he"? The female nature of the wave is given to us in the second sentence: "She was tall and light." We don't learn the sex of the narrator until we see him on a train a short time later, when one of the passengers tells the conductor, "This man put salt in the water." At first the narrator calls the wave his "friend," but after they live together, they become lovers. For four paragraphs they share a blissful happiness, until the wave turns moody and willful. She befriends certain "repulsive and ferocious" fishes, he throws them out of the house. She attacks him, he nearly drowns and begins to hate her. In the cold of winter, the wave turns into a block of ice, and the narrator knows what he must do: in order to get rid of her, he sells her to a "waiter friend," who chops the wave into bits of ice and puts them into buckets to chill bottles.

In this fantasy story Paz presents a romantic view of woman as the goddess of love — always capricious, mysteriously unknowable, eternally beautiful, and ultimately destructive.

Questions for Discussion

1. Despite the unhappy ending of the love affair, "My Life with the Wave" is often humorous. Give examples in the story of the narrator's (and the author's) sense of humor.

2. Does this story have a reliable or an unreliable narrator? Is the narrator meant to be the same person as Octavio Paz, or a fictional character in the story?
3. In what ways does the wave resemble a human woman? What problems occur in the love affair because the narrator's lover is a wave?
4. What aspects of the story suggest the narrator's fantasies about women? To what extent are these fantasies stereotypical qualities that men often attribute to women?

Topic for Writing

1. **CONNECTIONS** Compare and contrast the fantasy story "My Life with the Wave" by Octavio Paz with "A Very Old Man with Enormous Wings" by Gabriel García Márquez.

Suggested Reading

Paz, Octavio. *Eagle or Sun.* Trans. Eliot Weinberger. New York: New Directions, 1976.

EDGAR ALLAN POE

The Cask of Amontillado (p. 1188)

Poe is the great master of the contrived suspense story, and "The Cask of Amontillado" is a model of narrative compression toward a single effect. Students should understand that Poe had a theory on the short story; its essential points are suggested in his review of Hawthorne's tales in Part Three (p. 1692).

Despite Poe's rational explanation of how a writer should compose a story, his own fiction is directed toward eliciting irrational emotions. Poe's literary style aims at using as many extravagances of character, setting, and plot as he could invent, exploiting the reader's emotional vulnerability to disturbing images of darkness and chaos. The hectic unpredictability of the carnival season, the creepy subterranean wine cellar, and the ancient family crypt with its molding skeletons all challenge us emotionally and make us want to read further.

In the reading, our own fears become the true subject matter. As in a nightmare, Fortunato finds himself being buried alive, one of the most basic human fears. On a more conscious level, we rely on a social contract to bind us together as a human family, and Montresor's lawlessness plays on our fear that any person can take the law into his or her own hands without being checked by conscience. Poe doesn't have to give us a great number of details about his characters; our imagination draws from the depths of the common human psyche to supply all that we need.

This story is a good example to use in stressing the importance of the students' close reading of a text. It's easy for readers to miss, in the last paragraph,

the sentence "My heart grew sick — on account of the dampness of the catacombs."
Yet upon this sentence rests the interpretation of Montresor's character: Can we
excuse his action on grounds of insanity? Was he insane at the time he buried
Fortunato alive, or did he go insane in the half century during which, he tells us,
his crime has remained undetected? If the reader has not paid careful attention to
that sentence, he or she will have missed an essential detail in understanding the
story.

The book *Mysterious New England,* edited by A. N. Stevens (1971), suggests
that Poe first heard the anecdote upon which he might have based this story when
he was a private in the army in 1827. Supposedly, only ten years before, a popular
young lieutenant named Robert F. Massie had also been stationed at Fort Independence in Boston Harbor; when Poe was serving there, he saw a gravestone
erected to the memory of one Lieutenant Massie, who had been unfairly killed in
a duel by a bully named Captain Green.

> Feeling against Captain Green ran high for many weeks, and then
> suddenly he vanished. Years went by without a sign of him, and Green
> was written off the army records as a deserter.

> According to the story that Poe finally gathered together, Captain
> Green had been so detested by his fellow officers that they decided to
> take a terrible revenge on him for Massie's death.

> Visiting Captain Green one moonless night, they pretended to be
> friendly and plied him with wine until he was helplessly intoxicated.
> Then, carrying the captain down to one of the ancient dungeons, the
> officers forced his body through a tiny opening that led into the subter-
> ranean casemate. His captors began to shackle him to the floor, using the
> heavy iron handcuffs and footcuffs fastened into the stone. Then they
> sealed the captain up alive inside the windowless casemate, using bricks
> and mortar that they had hidden close at hand.

> Captain Green shrieked in terror and begged for mercy, but his cries
> fell on deaf ears. The last brick was finally inserted, mortar applied, and
> the room closed off, the officers believed, forever. Captain Green undoubt-
> edly died a horrible death within a few days.

William E. Sheidley

Questions for Discussion

1. How does Poe motivate the behavior of Montresor? Does the story provide
   any hints as to the "thousand injuries" he has suffered? Are any hints necessary?
2. Why is the setting of the story appropriate?
3. What does Montresor's treatment of his house servants tell us about his
   knowledge of human psychology, and how does it prepare us for his treatment of Fortunato?
4. How does Poe increase the elements of suspense as Fortunato is gradually
   walled into the catacombs?

Topics for Writing

1. Montresor doesn't tell his story until a half century after the actual event. Analyze how Poe adapts the flashback technique to affect the reader of "The Cask of Amontillado."
2. Explicate the passage in the story in which Montresor entices Fortunato into the crypt.

Related Commentaries

Joan Dayan, Amorous Bondage: Pop, Ladies, and Slaves, p. 1712.
D. H. Lawrence, On "The Fall of the House of Usher" and "The Cask of Amontillado," p. 1694.
Edgar Allan Poe, The Importance of the Single Effect in a Prose Tale, p. 1692.
James W. Gargano, The Question of Poe's Narrators in "The Tell-Tale Heart" and "The Cask of Amontillado," p. 1701.
David S. Reynolds, Poe's Art of Transformation in "The Cask of Amontillado," p. 1708.

Suggested Readings

See page 228.

EDGAR ALLAN POE

The Fall of the House of Usher (p. 1193)

Although Edgar Allan Poe was not the first writer to work within the genre of the psychological narrative, he was so dominant in this area that his name continues to be associated with this narrative form. Through Poe, and his influence on French and then other European writers, this type of narrative assumed a steadily larger role in the development of the modern story.

In Poe's time, the contemporary designation for writing such as that represented in "The Fall of the House of Usher" was Gothic, which for many of its readers reflected simply the gloom and the cluster of symbols in Gothic architecture. Poe's own readers would have recognized his settings and the devices he used to set his tales in motion. What differentiates him from the forgotten authors of the Gothic tales and romances that filled the journals of the period is a quality of obsessiveness in the writing. With Poe there is never the sense that he is using a descriptive phrase for its literary effect. The struggle within him always seems to be the need to find the phrase or the situation that would project the psychological truth of his scene. Poe, unlike other authors, was relentless in his descriptions and his characterizations, and in all of his successful tales the final scenes fulfill the forebodings of the opening sentences. This story is one of his most celebrated psychological studies, and there could be no more powerful description of a dismal landscape than his opening sentence. "During the whole of a dull, dark, and soundless day in the autumn of the year, when the clouds hung oppressively low in the heavens, I had been passing alone, on horseback, through a singularly dreary tract of country, and at length found myself, as the shades of the evening drew on, within view of the melancholy House of Usher."

The sentence is weighted with words symbolic of despair: *dull, dark, soundless, oppressively low, alone, dreary, shades of evening, melancholy.* The term often used to describe these kinds of scenes in Poe's writing is *hallucinatory.* Also, he has emphasized the symbolic premonitions of the scene by what he has omitted. A characteristic opening for a Gothic tale would have included a suggestion of a date and a place. A typical opening might be, "During the whole of a dark and soundless day in autumn of 182—, when the clouds hung oppressively low in the heavens over the dark lands of Saxony . . ." With the device of these specific places and dates, the scene could be imagined within a familiar context. Poe, however, brings us only to a darkening, wild scene that is at once so minutely described that we can visualize every tree and cloud, and at the same time the place and time are left so vague, and the description is so exaggerated, so wildly overblown, that it is like no scene we have imagined before. He ultimately achieves a total effect of oppression and despair by the relentless repetition of images and phrases that remind the reader again and again of the barren lifelessness of the scene that greeted him at the opening of the tale.

During Poe's short and difficult lifetime, his work was extravagantly praised and as vehemently criticized, and some of the negative attitudes toward his writing focused on his unexpected imagery and unusual verbal linkages. He wrote so much, under such intense economic pressure — often writing under the influence of alcohol and laudanum, the mixture of opium and alcohol used by most of the period's cultural figures such as Coleridge and DeQuincy — that he was open to charges of carelessness and indifference to the niceties of grammar and vocabulary. Almost invariably, though, what could be considered a grammatically garbled phrase or sentence emerges as crucial to the effect he sustains so brilliantly throughout his tale. In this story he describes the furniture in the rooms with the sentence, "The general furniture was profuse, comfortless, antique, and tattered." As an example of parallelism the sentence is a catastrophe. None of the four adjectives could be said to relate to each other in any obvious interpretation. "Profuse" doesn't even seem to be an adjective that would apply to furniture — and yet we have immediately an image of a scattering of furniture, whatever it is. "Comfortless" is at a considerable distance from "profuse," but somehow it forces us to modify what we have imagined of the roomful of furniture. "Antique" presents fewer problems, and "tattered" completes our associations with the vision we now have of a great deal of uncomfortable, worn, old furniture scattered around a room. On this level of association, with his nudge to the reader to do some of his work for him, Poe's sentence becomes much more reasonable. What finally gives the sentence its power in the context is its insistent allusion to the psychological context of the narrative. Of the four adjectives, two of them, "comfortless" and "tattered," again project the despair and oppression of the story's opening. Poe will not slacken the hand that is gripping his reader's neck.

In our own day readers have found that the psychological penetration of Poe's narratives has become part of the emotional landscape. Of particular interest in this story is his careful description of Usher's small painting. It is a painting that at the time of his writing existed only in Poe's fantasy, but as a modern surrealistic canvas it would not be out of place in any contemporary art museum. For students there will also be a particular interest in the music that he describes Usher performing. The recordings made in the 1960s and 1970s by visionary guitarist-singers artists such as Berkeley's Robbie Basho sound like a fulfillment of Poe's description, although Basho was not conscious of any direct connection. Of less immediate importance will be the books that Usher and his friend read together in their last wild days in the house. The books themselves suggest the similar context today of films and videos that come under the loose heading of psychological studies, or more simply, horror films.

What the reader finally perceives, as the tale comes to its frightening conclusion, is that it has no substance as a realistic portrayal. It is "real" only in that it is a realistic projection of the author's dark fantasy. We follow the details and the narrative as though they were real — in the way that we consider all fictive writing to be real — but at the same time we understand that the house that has been destroyed was a house that never existed. As a symbol of our fears, however, the house will continue to stand in its "black and lurid tarn." In our imagination we will also continue to be disturbed at some level of emotion we barely understand by "the remodelled and inverted images of the gray sedge, and the ghastly tree-stems, and the vacant and eye-like windows" of the doomed House of Usher.

Questions for Discussion

1. The reader is not given a specific place or time in the story's setting. Is this a help or a hindrance to students' response to the story?
2. Poe mentions opium twice in the story. Does this reflect the general acceptance of the use of the drug in his time? Does opium seem to influence the narrative in any way?
3. Poe describes the recovery from opium intoxication as "the bitter lapse into every-day life." How would his readers interpret this? How would a modern reader respond?
4. Does Poe intimate that the Usher family suffers from an inbred genetic condition? How does this affect the narrative?
5. Poe writes, "There can be no doubt that the consciousness of the rapid increase of my superstition . . . served mainly to accelerate the increase itself." In psychological terms, what is he telling the reader?
6. What is the atmosphere that hangs over the house? Is this a phenomenon found in nature?
7. What is Poe suggesting in saying of the doctor that "his countenance . . . wore a mingled expression of low cunning and perplexity"? What is the meaning of the doctors' interest in the dead sister's body?
8. The account of Usher's emotional state would suggest that he suffers from what is know today as "bipolar syndrome," or manic depression. How would students interpret this analysis?
9. Does the description of Emily's illness, "transient affections of a partially cataleptic character," have any modern clinical counterpart?
10. How would we characterize the paintings of Roderick Usher today?
11. How would we characterize the music that Usher creates? Have we a modern term for this genre?
12. Poe writes of Usher, "I perceived . . . on the part of Usher of the tottering of his lofty reason upon her throne." What is Poe suggesting to the reader?
13. What is the meaning of Usher's contention that the stones of the house have become sentient?
14. What suggests to us that the house is to be taken as a symbol? Will it be destroyed by the death of the brother and sister?

Topics for Writing

1. In his writing Poe uses many little-known words, such as *sentience, trepidancy,* and *collocation,* and many words in unusual forms, such as *objectless, luminousness,* and *encrimsoned.* Discuss this aspect of Poe's syntax in this story.
2. It is unusual in a story about death from this period that there is no mention of God or of any external spiritual being. Comment on this anomaly.
3. Analyze the first sentence of the story and consider its symbolic as well as its psychological allusions.
4. In the story there are continual allusions to Usher's mental illness. Analyze the specific descriptions of his illness in relation to the modern diagnosis of bipolar disorder. Include in this analysis the description of Usher's steady rocking as he awaits the approach of his sister.
5. Discuss the opening paragraphs of the story as a prefiguring of the tragedy to come. Discuss Poe's intent in this presentation of the story's foundations in symbol and metaphor.

Related Commentaries

Cleanth Brooks and Robert Penn Warren, A New Critical Reading of "The Fall of the House of Usher," p. 1698.
Joan Dayan, Amorous Bondage: Poe, Ladies, and Slaves, p. 1712.
J. Gerald Kennedy, On "The Fall of the House of Usher," p. 1704.
Edgar Allan Poe, The Importance of the Single Effect on a Prose Tale, p. 1692.

Suggested Readings

See p. 228.

EDGAR ALLAN POE

The Tell-Tale Heart (p. 1206)

"The Tell-Tale Heart" is a story about what has been called "the demonic self" — a person who feels a compulsion to commit a gratuitous act of evil. Poe wrote explicitly about what he calls this "spirit of perverseness" in his story "The Black Cat," published in 1843, two years before "The Tell-Tale Heart":

> Of this spirit [of perverseness] philosophy takes no account. Yet I am not more sure that my soul lives, than I am that perverseness is one of the primitive impulses of the human heart — one of the indivisible primary faculties, or sentiments, which give direction to the character of Man. Who has not, a hundred times, found himself committing a vile or a silly action, for no other reason than because he knows he should *not*? Have we not a perpetual inclination, in the teeth of our best judgment, to violate that which is *Law,* merely because we understand it to be such?

According to the critic Eric W. Carlson, "The Tell-Tale Heart" was one of Poe's favorite stories. In addition to dramatizing the "spirit of perverseness" in his narrative, Poe combines other elements of the gothic tale (the evil eye, the curse), the psychorealistic (the narrator's paranoia), the dramatic (concentrated intensity of tone, gradually heightened series of dramatic events), and the moral (the compulsion to confess).

Questions for Discussion

1. How would you describe the narrator of the story? How does your description compare or contrast with what he would like to have you believe about him?
2. What disease is the narrator referring to in the first paragraph?
3. What caused the narrator to murder the old man? Was his reason valid?
4. What narrative devices does Poe use to heighten the suspense of the tale? Give examples.
5. Poe believed in the existence of the "spirit of perverseness" within every man. How is this revealed in the story?
6. Do you feel the confession at the end of the tale is necessary? Why? What is Poe's purpose in presenting this confession?

Topics for Writing

1. Discuss the significance of the light and dark imagery in "The Tell-Tale Heart."
2. Consider the effect of premeditation in "The Tell-Tale Heart."
3. Discuss the use of sight and sound as dramatic devices in "The Tell-Tale Heart."
4. Write an essay analyzing the dichotomy between the narrator's view of himself and our view of him in "The Tell-Tale Heart."
5. Explore reality versus illusion in "The Tell-Tale Heart."
6. **RESPONDING CREATIVELY** Rewrite the story from the point of view of the police officers or from the point of view of the old man.
7. **RESPONDING CREATIVELY** Consider the events that might result from the action of this story, and write a sequel presenting these developments.

Related Commentary

Joan Dayan, Amorous Bondage: Poe, Ladies, and Slaves, p. 1712.
Edgar Allan Poe, The Importance of the Single Effect in a Prose Tale, p. 1692.
James W. Gargano, The Question of Poe's Narrators in "The Tell-Tale Heart" and "The Cask of Amontillado," p. 1701.

Suggested Readings

Adler, Jacob H. "Are There Flaws in 'The Cask of Amontillado'?" *Notes and Queries* 199 (1954): 32–34.
Buranelli, Vincent. *Edgar Allan Poe.* 2nd Ed. Boston: G. K. Hall, 1977.
Baudelaire, Charles P. *Baudelaire on Poe: Critical Papers.* University Park: Pennsylvania State UP, 1952.

Carlson, Eric W., ed. *Critical Essays on Edgar Allan Poe.* Boston: G. K. Hall, 1987.

Carlson, Eric W. *Introduction to Poe: A Thematic Reader.* Glenville, IL: Scott, 1967.

Dillon, John M. *Edgar Allan Poe.* Brooklyn, NY: Haskell, 1974.

Fletcher, Richard M. *The Stylistic Development of Edgar Allan Poe.* New York: Mouton, 1974.

Gargano, J. W. "'The Cask of Amontillado': A Masquerade of Motive and Identity." *Studies in Short Fiction* 4 (1967): 119–26.

———. *The Masquerade Vision in Poe's Short Stories.* Baltimore: Enoch Pratt, 1977.

Hammond, J. R. *An Edgar Allan Poe Companion: A Guide to Short Stories, Romances, and Essays.* Savage: B and N Imports, 1981.

Knapp, Bettina L. *Edgar Allan Poe.* New York: Ungar, 1984.

Levin, Harry. *The Power of Blackness: Hawthorne, Poe, Melville.* Columbus: Ohio UP, 1980.

Mabbott, Thomas Olivle, ed. *Collected Works of Edgar Allan Poe.* Cambridge, MA: Harvard UP, 1978.

May, Charles E., ed. *Edgar Allan Poe: A Study of Short Fiction.* Boston: Twayne, 1990.

Muller, John P., and William J. Richardson, eds. *The Purloined Poe: Lacan, Derrida, and Psychoanalytic Reading.* Baltimore: Johns Hopkins UP, 1988.

Pitcher, E. W. "Physiognomical Meaning of Poe's 'The Tell-Tale Heart.' " *Studies in Short Fiction* 16 (1979): 231–33.

Robinson, E. A. "Poe's 'The Tell-Tale Heart.' " *Nineteenth Century Fiction* 19 (1965): 369–78.

Symons, Julian, ed. *Selected Tales.* New York: Oxford UP, 1980.

Tucker, B. D. "Tell-Tale Heart and the Evil Eye." *Southern Literary Journal* 13 (1981): 92–98.

KATHERINE ANNE PORTER

The Jilting of Granny Weatherall (p. 1211)

Porter's title suggests the following interpretation of the theme of her story: Regardless of our chronological age and the circumstances of our life, we always remain young at heart. Granny Weatherall, nearly eighty, is physically worn out after a lifetime of serving her family — bedridden, just hours away from her fatal stroke and heart attack — yet emotionally she is still twenty and still betrothed to the bridegroom who will jilt her on her wedding day. As a young woman, then, she lost her innocence. Some time later she entered into a successful marriage with another man, John, and had four children with him, but as an old woman on her deathbed, she stubbornly fantasizes the return of a bridegroom — Jesus (although he is not named in the story) — who will take her to heaven. The playwright and screenwriter Corinne Jacker understood that since Granny is a Catholic, in this she exhibits a "sin of pride — if not sacrilege. It's an enormous act of hubris, to assume that God is going to send you a sign that you'll be received by Christ. Or that you're immortal."

Porter's conflation of two kinds of bridegroom — the secular and the divine — is the central drama of her story. Porter narrates it in the third-person from the perspective of the dying woman, brilliantly joining Granny Weatherall's stream-of-consciousness with descriptions of her physical sensations as she lies in her bed amid the growing crowd of people who attend her in her last hours — Doctor Harry, her loving daughter Cornelia, Father Connolly, and her other grown children, Jimmy and Lydia.

"The Jilting of Granny Weatherall" was included in Porter's first collection of stories, *Flowering Judas*. In an introduction to a Modern Library edition of the book ten years after its original appearance, she stated that she had "no notion of what [the stories'] meaning might be to such readers as they would find." She believed "that all our lives we are preparing to be somebody or something, even if we don't do it consciously." This element of preparation is evident in Granny Weatherall's actions in the story. The irony is that after being jilted the first time she has lived an active life as wife and mother for more than half a century, yet on her deathbed she feels the emotions she felt as a young girl, waiting for a sign that she has been especially chosen by her bridegroom. This time death itself is the disappointment.

Questions for Discussion

1. What is the setting of the story? Why has Granny Weatherall moved to her daughter's house?
2. What are her feelings toward Cornelia? What are Cornelia's feelings toward her mother?
3. How does Porter establish the failing health of her protagonist?
4. Does Granny Weatherall develop as a character during the narrative?
5. What is the climax of the story?
6. How does Porter use light in the story as a symbol of the protagonist's state of mind?
7. What is the plot of the story? How much of the action relates to this plot?
8. Do you think Porter is making a statement about religious belief in the ending of her story?

Topics for Writing

1. Does the sequence of flashbacks in Granny Weatherall's stream-of-consciousness dramatize her valiant attempts to live her life fully, or do the flashbacks suggest her inability to get over the shock of being jilted as a young woman? Support your argument with references to specific details in the story.
2. Compare and contrast Porter's story and the film version by Corinne Jacker.
3. **CONNECTIONS** Compare and contrast the value of a life lived serving others in Porter's story with Tolstoy's "The Death of Ivan Ilych."
4. **CONNECTIONS** Compare and contrast the dramatizations of a woman's life in Porter's story and in Chekhov's "Angel" [The Darling].

Related Commentary

Carolyn G. Heilbrun, A Feminist Perspective on Katherine Anne Porter and "The Jilting of Granny Weatherall," p. 1501.

Suggested Readings

Bayley, Isabel. *Letters of Katherine Anne Porter.* New York: Atlantic Monthly P, 1990.

Bruccoli, Matthew J., ed. *Understanding Katherine Anne Porter.* Columbia: U of South Carolina P, 1988.

Demouy, Jane Krause. *Katherine Anne Porter's Women: The Eye of Her Fiction.* Austin: U of Texas P, 1983.

Hendrick, Willene, and George Hendrick. *Katherine Anne Porter.* Boston: Twayne, 1988.

Mooney, Harry J. *The Fiction and Criticism of Katherine Anne Porter.* Rev. ed. Pittsburgh: U of Pittsburgh P, 1990.

Nance, William L. *Katherine Anne Porter and the Art of Rejection.* Chapel Hill: U of North Carolina P, 1964.

Plimpton, George, ed. *Women Writers at Work: The* Paris Review *Interviews.* New York: Penguin, 1989.

Porter, Katherine Anne. *The Collected Essays and Occasional Writings.* New York: Harcourt Brace, 1970.

———. *Flowering Judas.* New York: Harcourt Brace, 1930, 1958.

Stout, Janis P. *Strategies of Reticence: Silence and Meaning in the Works of Jane Austen, Willa Cather, Katherine Anne Porter, and Joan Didion.* Charlottesville: UP of Virginia, 1990.

Tanner, James T. F. *The Texas Legacy of Katherine Anne Porter.* Denton: U of North Texas P, 1990.

Unrue, Darlene H. *Truth and Vision in Katherine Anne Porter's Fiction.* Athens: U of Georgia P, 1985.

WILLIAM SYDNEY PORTER (O. HENRY)

The Last Leaf (p. 1219)

Although this could perhaps be considered a slight sketch if we compare it to the richly detailed stories of writers such as Alice Munro and Isak Dinesen, we can see within a few paragraphs why O. Henry was one of the most successful authors of his time. With the gifts he demonstrates so abundantly in these few pages, he would have achieved the same success if he had been writing today. We are immediately presented with characters whose situation intrigues us at a moment when there is a complication in their lives that must be resolved. In story after story he achieved this effect almost without seeming effort. In the many instances when the stories have been adapted by Hollywood studios or for television they have been just as immediately effective. This narrative was one of a group of O. Henry stories made into an omnibus film that included the finest Hollywood performers of the early 1950s, when the film was made. "The Last Leaf" was as simply and directly unforgettable on screen as it is on the page.

The point of departure that draws us into the story in a few sentences is the author's presentation of what was then the "new woman." In 1907, when the story was first published, the idea of two idealistic young women living in Greenwich Village and struggling to begin successful careers as artists was sufficiently exciting to his readers that he could have written almost anything about them. Although we now live in an era that is as distant from the Greenwich Village he describes as the young women were from China or Peru, there is still something inherently intriguing in the stories of women like Sue and Johnsy. The story is told so directly that it is only the social situation that requires any discussion. Obviously the young women are daughters of middle-class families, since they can pay their rent before they become self-supporting professional artists. Also, since they have the same tastes in fashion — the "bishop sleeves" — as well as in art and salads, they must both have gone to one of the few colleges such as Vassar or Mt. Holyoke that at this time admitted women. By the term "Eighth Street 'Delmonico's'" O. Henry is sharing a joke with his readers. Delmonico's was a famous and expensive New York restaurant — but there would be nothing like it along Eighth Street, which at that time was a slum.

The story also revolves around accepted beliefs that can be confusing for today's students. O. Henry shared the popular idea of that time that one way to cure an illness was to change the attitude of the person who was suffering from it. In the story he has found a way to demonstrate the truth of the idea. Since at this time there was no effective drug available to fight pneumonia, it is perhaps reasonable that anything that might have some possible benefit was seized upon. There is some of the same advice about the importance of the patient's attitudes today for someone suffering from cancer — again, in the absence of effective medication.

Students may be less convinced by the character of the painter Behrman, who lives downstairs and supports himself by posing for some of the poorer younger artists, than by the portrayals of the two young women. It does seem more than a coincidence that there is a painter living below them who has the skills to paint a realistic ivy leaf on a dark wall at night in a downpour and who is also devoted to protecting the women from the city's tribulations. For modern readers who have difficulty accepting O. Henry's stories, however, the difficulty isn't with the sentimentality of some of the depictions of his characters and his situations — like the drunken painter in this story who dies from pneumonia himself after saving the life of the sick girl. Modern films, and certainly popular romance novels, are just as sentimental, and in some of the new romance films from Hollywood the sentimentality is applied even more thickly. What causes more difficulty for the modern reader is that O. Henry's stories are such a faithful mirror of their time — not only of the physical aspects of the rooms and the streets and clothes, but of the attitudes, the prejudices, and the enthusiasms. So much has changed in our society since the stories were written that we sometimes find that we can't share the ambitions and dreams of the characters. Without ambitions and dreams, a story by O. Henry is sometimes also left without the accompanying optimism that was his greatest strength.

Questions for Discussion

1. What is the author telling us in the first paragraph — that someone coming to collect a bill could find himself entering and leaving a street without the bill being paid?
2. Is the author being patronizing in the depiction of the women coming to an agreement over a studio because they shared a taste in dress sleeves, salad, and art?
3. Would we describe a woman today, as he writes of Johnsy, "a mite of a little woman"?

4. Is the doctor sympathetic or unsympathetic to Johnsy's artistic ambitions? How do we know?
5. The author uses the phrase "jew's-harp twang" to describe the tone of Sue's voice. Would his readers be expected to know what he meant? Is he necessarily being pejorative?
6. What is the doctor saying about his patient when he says, "If you will get her to ask one question about the new winter styles in coat sleeves, I will promise you a one-in-five chance for her"? Would he have said the same thing about a male patient?
7. Can we regard the painter Behrman as a realistic character? Do we care? In the situation in the story would we be willing to accept almost any intrusion that would save Johnsy's life?

Topics for Writing

1. Discuss the method of cure that the doctor has turned to in this instance, and discuss situations today where it might still be effective.
2. Discuss the symbolism of the falling leaves, and relate it particularly to painters and their use of leaves as a symbol in their work.
3. The author's attitudes toward his women characters are representative of the more adventurous of his readers, but his description of the women's pet names for each other could be a token of their affection or they could be a sign that the author considers the women to be children. Discuss the pet names of the women in this context.
4. It is no longer considered an essential part of the artistic process to have models posing for realistic representation. Comment on the changes in the way art is created in our own period, and, using the story, comment on how much is unchanged about the lives of those who create the art.

Suggested Reading

Henry, O. *The Complete Works.* Garden City, NY: Doubleday, 1953.

ANNIE PROULX

The Blood Bay (p. 1225)

There is nothing more exciting than observing an author pull off a stylistic sleight of hand. The reader hopes, in one breath, that the writer won't be quite skilled enough to do it, and with the next breath silently cheers the writer on, hoping that wherever the writer is going the reader will be brought there safely. Proulx, a successful, honored novelist and author of short stories who spent years in the demanding apprenticeship of local news writing before her breakthrough when she was in her fifties, is one of our most practiced modern stylists — and in this story she has gone back to one of the oldest traditions of American narrative. She has consciously created for her surprised readers an example from the American frontier tradition of the "humdinger" — a whopping fib of a tall tale. If the

students find themselves confused by the story they should try to imagine themselves lying out under the stars in a sleeping bag while someone tells them the
baldly unbelievable story of Dirt Sheets and Old Man Grice's blood bay horse.
The story would certainly present no problems to them in those circumstances.

Proulx is a trickster with language, and this tall tale is a cowboy's stew of
garbled western slang and sly, learned allusions. In this terrible winter, we are
told, they have suffered through "blizzards and freeze-eye cold"; the three cowboys are "savvy and salty." One of them "a cross-eyed drinker of hair oil, was all
right on top but his luck was running muddy near the bottom." They decide to
try for Old Man Grice's because he's known to have "dried prunes or other dainties." At the cabin Grice offers them "this son-of-a-bitch stew," and to wash it
down he has "plenty conversation juice." In a single paragraph she defies us to
believe a word she is saying and presents us with a syntax that is so dizzying it
could be the subject of a student paper by itself:

> He woke half an hour before daylight, recalled it was his mother's birth-
> day and if he wanted to telegraph a filial sentiment to her he would have
> to ride faster than chain lightning with the links snapped, for the Over-
> land office closed at noon. He checked his grisly trophies, found them
> thawed and pulled the boots and socks off the originals, drew them onto
> his own pedal extremities. He threw the bare Montana feet and his old
> boots in the corner near the dish cupboard, slipped out like a falling
> feather, saddled his horse and rose away. The wind was low and the fine
> cold air refreshed him.

At the beginning of the paragraph the author is obviously dangling an absurd idea in front of us to see if we will continue to follow her increasingly unlikely tale. The plausibility of Dirt Sheets rising early to send a telegram to his
mother in the middle of the Wyoming Territory winter takes us one step too far.
Then, as if to see if we're noticing, she presents us with a slickly chosen heap of
clashing idioms to sort through. We are dragged from faux elevated language —
"filial sentiment" — to talltale hyperbole — "he would have to ride faster than
chain lightning with the links snapped" — in the same sentence. At the same time
that we are being told of his disposal of the frozen cowboy's severed feet, Sheets's
own feet become "pedal extremities" and he slips out the door "like a falling
feather." Then in a pokerfaced understatement that turns the descriptions of the
winter upside down, we are told that as he rode away "the fine cold air refreshed
him."

Like all fine stories, "The Blood Bay" can be read on several levels, and one
of the levels, of course, is as a cowboy's tall tale. It is crude, unbelievable, and
hopelessly funny, which is everything a tall tale should be. At the same time the
story is a sophisticated display of linguistic trickery. At the end of the story Proulx's
readers can only shake their heads. She has taken us for a dizzying ride, and at
the end has brought us back, perhaps chastened by her daring, but unharmed.

Questions for Discussion

1. Although the story has some realistic elements, do we believe a word of it?
2. Why is Proulx so careful to describe the winter outfits of the three cowboys?

3. The cowboys speak of riding to Grice's shack for "dried prunes or other dainties." Would any of these three be expected to use the word "dainties" or look forward to dried prunes after a winter day dragging cattle out of drifts?
4. What is the inference in the phrase "plenty conversation juice"?
5. In terms of cowboy salaries of the time, what does "three dollars and four bits" represent? (A "bit" is worth twelve and a half cents, as in "two bits, four bits, six bits, a dollar.")
6. Although a man freezes to death and has his feet hacked off, is this a tragic story? Why not?
7. What is the author suggesting with the image given as the cowboys ride off — "the grinning morning"?

Topics for Writing

1. Analyze the paragraph beginning with "He woke half an hour before daylight" in terms of its syntax and its comic intent. Consider the author's intent in taking the story a step further along its already slippery path of exaggeration.
2. Find other examples of the frontier tall tale and compare them with this example by a prize-winning modern writer.
3. It has long been understood that stories like these help people in physically difficult circumstances like the Western frontier deal more successfully with their situation. Discuss how this story, in the context of cowboy life, could help its listeners.

Suggested Readings

Proulx, Annie. *Close Range: Wyoming Stories.* New York, Scribner, 1999.
———. *Heart Songs and Other Stories.* New York: Scribner Paperback Fiction, 1995
———. *"What'll You Take for It?" Back to Barter.* Charlotte, VT: Garden Way, 1981.
Rood, Karen L. *Understanding Annie Proulx.* Columbia: U of South Carolina P, 2001.

PHILIP ROTH

The Conversion of the Jews (p. 1229)

Philip Roth has spent much of his long, productive, and richly honored literary career examining, questioning, and challenging his identity as a Jew. The intent focus of his concern is nowhere more poignantly presented than in this early story, when the questions he was posing for himself were so much closer to the surface than they became later in his writing. The story also addresses a larger issue, even though the setting is clearly the Jewish immigrant community and the events that trigger the crisis result from tensions within the confines of the Hebrew school that the boys in the story all attend. The larger the issue is that of assimilation, and the tensions within any immigrant group as the generations find themselves on opposite sides of a cultural chasm that widens steadily as the young children identify less with the immigrant values of their parents and more with the values of the new society they hope to join. This theme has continued to occupy Roth throughout his career.

Although Roth does not specifically examine the larger issue of identity in the story, many students will be aware that there are many other immigrant groups that struggle to maintain a distinct unity within the mainstream culture. For the Jewish boys in this story there is a particular focus to their studies. They are learning the requisite amount of Hebrew for their approaching Bar Mitzvah ceremony, when they will be required to read the Hebrew text before the assembled congregation. Recently it has become more and more popular for young Jewish girls to attend similar classes to prepare for their Bat Mitzvah ceremony. For other immigrant groups the goal is to maintain some tie to their cultural background. The Japanese, Chinese, and Korean communities in major American cities provide instruction for their children in their languages and traditions. There are also school systems in the United States supported by the governments of France and Germany for parents, often in the country on temporary business assignments, who wish to raise their children in their native language. Every student will be aware of some group in his or her community that steadfastly supports these ideals, even if the emotion is only nostalgia for a cultural tie that has been lost for several generations.

Roth's story, however, is about a moment in this process of assimilation when the smooth integration of a teenage boy into the mainstream culture breaks down. The uncertainties of his life with his widowed mother have led Ozzie to challenge not only his Jewish identity but also the basic tenets of the Jewish faith. What to Ozzie seems only a reasonable question — Why couldn't God have impregnated Joseph's wife Mary? — is to the rabbi and to his mother a dangerous heresy. It was precisely this point, the claims of the divinity of Christ by his supporters, that led to the schism within the Jewish faith, the rise of Christianity, and the long agony of the Jews that followed. Ozzy's question implies that for the past two thousand years the Jews have been mistaken. His friends don't seem to understand the nature of his question — his friend Itzie, already further along on the path to cultural integration, is described as comparing the achievement of God in creating the earth as being similar to his pitching a one-hit baseball game. Ozzie is left to face the tumult he has begun alone on a rooftop, and although this time there is a safe ending as he leaps into the waiting firemen's net, the questions he has raised, and his frightened act of forcing his mother and the rabbi to declare that they accept the divinity of Christ, will continue to echo in the lives of everyone who has witnessed the scene.

Although there is much in Roth's narrative that students will find humorous, it is a savage story that has no trite resolution. There has been too much death and too much brutality in the painful history of this disagreement between the Jews and the Christians for us to respond to the boy's question with a casual shrug.

Questions for Discussion

1. The lack of sophistication on the part of the boys gives the story an old-fashioned point of view. Would we expect such naivité on the part of young students in Hebrew school today?

2. Why is Itzie so excited by the possibility that the word *intercourse* would be part of the class discussion?
3. What does the comparison between God and a baseball pitcher tell us about Itzie?
4. Does Ozzie understand why his mother hit him?
5. What is Roth telling the reader in the sentence "It was the attitude of a dictator . . . whose personal valet had spit neatly in his face"?
6. What is the intimation in the description of Ozzie reading the text slowly if he wants to understand it or quickly if understanding isn't important?
7. What aspect of a rabbi's interrogation could be described as "soul battering"?
8. Why is the rabbi unwilling to call the fire department? What does this suggest about his own attitude toward assimilation? Why does Blotnik make the call?
9. Can the question Ozzie raises lead to a simpler integration within the mainstream culture for him, or could it lead to an even deeper disorientation?
10. Why does he threaten to jump? Is suicide something he has thought of before?
11. How does the presence of a group of friends affect him? Would he have acted in a similar way if they hadn't been present?

Topics for Writing

1. Roth doesn't seem to resolve any of the issues he raises in the story. Discuss his intentions in the story, and decide whether or not he has been successful in his presentation.
2. Describe an immigrant or alternative culture school and discuss the purpose of its activities.
3. Comment on the role of social acculturation that all schools play in their own communities.
4. Analyze the historical problem Roth has posed, and discuss some reasons he might have had for examining this problem.
5. A reader could say that Roth is using the character of Ozzie to advance his own social agenda. Discuss this possibility.
6. Comment on the concept of religious conversion throughout history, with reference to mass forced conversions and individual, personal conversions. Discuss the reaction of the larger community to the act of conversion.

Suggested Reading

Roth, Philip. *Beyond Despair: Three Lectures* [on the Holocaust] *and a Conversation.* New York: Fromm International, 1994.

LESLIE MARMON SILKO

Yellow Woman (p. 1241)

This story is told in the first person and presented episodically in several sections. It takes place over two days, beginning the morning Yellow Woman wakes up beside the river with Silva, the stranger she has spent the night with. The story ends at sundown the next day, when she returns to her family in the Pueblo village.

"Yellow Woman" is built on different traditions from those in the cultural background of most American students. Silko writes fiction that preserves her cultural heritage by re-creating its customs and values in stories that dramatize emotional conflicts of interest to modern readers.

As Yellow Woman narrates the story of her abduction and return to her family, the reader comes to share her mood and her interpretation of what has happened. As a girl she was fascinated by the stories her grandfather told her about Silva, the mysterious kachina spirit who kidnaps married women from the tribe, then returns them after he has kept them as his wives. These stories were probably similar to the imaginary tales passed down in an oral tradition whose origins are lost to contemporary American folklorists. Silko has created their modern equivalent, her version of how they might be reenacted in today's world. The overweight, white Arizona rancher is familiar to us, as is the Jell-O being prepared for supper, and we have no difficulty imagining the gunnysacks full of freshly slaughtered meat bouncing on the back of Yellow Woman's horse.

The dreamlike atmosphere Silko creates in "Yellow Woman" makes such realistic details protrude sharply from the soft-focus narrative. Yellow Woman doesn't think clearly. She seems bewitched by the myths her grandfather told her, and her adventure following the man she calls Silva holds her enthralled. At the end she says, "I thought about Silva, and I felt sad at leaving him; still, there was something strange about him, and I tried to figure it out all the way back home." We are not told what — if anything — she does figure out.

Instead, action takes the place of thought in the story. Yellow Woman looks at the place on the riverbank where she met Silva and tells herself that "he will come back sometime and be waiting again by the river." Action moves so swiftly that we follow Yellow Woman as obediently as she follows her abductor, mesmerized by the audacity of what is happening. There is no menace in Silva, no danger or malice in his rape of Yellow Woman. The bullets in his rifle are for the white rancher who realizes he has been killing other men's cattle, not for Yellow Woman — or for us.

Questions for Discussion

1. Why is Yellow Woman so eager to believe that she and Silva are acting out the stories her grandfather told her?
2. How does Silko structure the opening paragraphs of the story to help the reader suspend disbelief and enter the dreamlike atmosphere of Yellow Woman's perceptions?

3. Why does Silko tell the story through the woman's point of view? Describe the Pueblo Indian woman we know as Yellow Woman. Is she happy at home with her mother, grandmother, husband, and baby? Why is Yellow Woman's father absent from the story?
4. Are there any limitations to Silko's choice to tell the story through Yellow Woman's point of view? Explain.
5. Why doesn't the narrator escape from Silva when she discovers him asleep by the river as the story opens? What makes her decide to return home the next day?

Topics for Writing

1. **RESPONDING CREATIVELY** Tell the story through a third-person omniscient narration.
2. Compare "Yellow Woman" with an Indian folktale about the kachina spirit who kidnaped married women.
3. **CONNECTIONS** Compare Silko's "Yellow Woman" and Oates's "Where Are You Going, Where Have You Been?" as rape narratives.

Related Commentaries

Paula Gunn Allen, Whirlwind Man Steals Yellow Woman, p. 1452.
Leslie Marmon Silko, Language and Literature from a Pueblo Indian Perspective, p. 1575.

Suggested Readings

Allen, Paula Gunn. *The Sacred Hoop: Recovering the Feminine in American Indian Traditions*. Boston: Beacon, 1986.
————, ed. *Spider Woman's Granddaughters: Traditional Tales and Contemporary Writing by Native American Women*. Boston: Beacon, 1989.
Graulich, Melody, ed. *"Yellow Woman."* Women, Text and Contexts Series. New Brunswick, NJ: Rutgers UP, 1993.
Hoilman, Dennis. "The Ethnic Imagination: A Case History." *Canadian Journal of Native Studies* 5.2 (1985): 167–75.
Nelson, Robert M. *Place and Vision: The Function of Landscape in Native American Fiction.* New York: P. Lang, 1993.
Sands, Kathleen Mullen. "Indian Women's Personal Narrative: Voices Past and Present." *American Women's Autobiography: Fea(s)ts of Memory.* Ed. Margo Culley. Madison: U of Wisconsin P, 1992.
Silko, Leslie Marmon. *Almanac of the Dead.* New York: Simon, 1991.

SUSAN SONTAG

The Way We Live Now (p. 1249)

Most stories by contemporary authors in this anthology are told from a limited-omniscient point of view. Leslie Marmon Silko narrates her story through the perceptions of Yellow Woman; James Baldwin uses first-person narration in "Sonny's Blues." Susan Sontag does something very different in "The Way We Live Now." The story chronicles the last months of a man dying of AIDS, but we never learn directly what he sees or feels. Instead, we hear what he is suffering through the comments of his many friends. The end result is a work that deliberately treats its subject the way most people treat AIDS itself — at a distance, through hearsay, with mingled fascination and horror, as something terrible that can only happen to other people.

We never learn the name, occupation, or physical description of the AIDS victim in Sontag's story. Instead, we are told the responses of his friends, like a roll call of potential victims of the virus. These friends — more than twenty-five of them — are also not described, only presented by name as they talk to one another about the sick man. Their names follow one another so rapidly we are not given any explanation of their relationships: Max, Ellen, Greg, Tanya, Orson, Stephen, Frank, Jan, Quentin, Paolo, Kate, Aileen, Donny, Ursula, Ira, Hilda, Nora, Wesley, Victor, Xavier, Lewis, Robert, Betsy, Yvonne, Zack, and Clarice. The first-name basis is fitting, since the majority of the people know one another and inhabit the same world. We are never told what city they all live in, but we assume from the way they talk and their large numbers that they live in New York and are part of its cliques of people active in the arts, literature, and cultural journalism.

The first-name basis of the conversations is also aesthetically appropriate, because for the most part the characters are using the telephone. They repeat the latest gossip they have learned from one another; for all their sophistication, they pass along news of the stages of their friend's illness like the voices of tribal drums alerting the inhabitants of villages in Africa. The reader has the same sense of a closely knit community joined by common interests and means of livelihood. Because the community is left unspecified, the setting and the characters become mythologized into "Anyplace" and "Everyone." Sontag's implication is that we are all participants in this human tragedy. AIDS can happen to anyone.

As we read "The Way We Live Now," our rational impulses function despite the lack of specificity about the central character. The short conversational exchanges function as a literary code that we try to unlock. We attempt to trace relationships (Quentin, Lewis, Paolo, and Tanya have all been lovers of the AIDS victim); we categorize important information about lives outside the main story (Max gets AIDS too, as does Hilda's seventy-five-year-old aunt); we highlight generalizations that suggest a broader social and moral significance to this individual tragedy (the age of "debauchery" is over).

Close readers may even be able to interpret the fragments of conversations to gain psychological insights of use in other contexts. For example, Kate tells Aileen that the sick man is "not judging people or wondering about their motives" (when they come to see him in the hospital); rather, "he's just happy to see his friends." By presenting the numbers of people linked to a specific AIDS victim who appears to be well known and highly regarded in his community, Sontag is making an ironic comment about the isolation of all AIDS victims. Her story is an attempt to write about a taboo subject and encourage compassion toward those suffering from the disease.

Questions for Discussion

1. The story is developed chronologically, from the news of the patient's illness, through his first hospitalization, to his return home and rehospitalization. How does this progression give coherence to the story?
2. How do the relationships suggested among the twenty-five characters in the story give you a sense of the occupation and lifestyle of the central character?
3. Hilda says that the death of the pianist in Paris "who specialized in twentieth-century Czech and Polish music" is important because "he's such a valuable person . . . and it's such a loss to the culture." Do you think Sontag shares Hilda's opinion? Do you? Why or why not?
4. Agree or disagree with Ursula's idea at the end of the story.

Topics for Writing

1. **RESPONDING CREATIVELY** Write a review of Sontag's nonfiction work *AIDS and Its Metaphors.*
2. **RESPONDING CREATIVELY** Choose any five characters in "The Way We Live Now" and invent backgrounds for them.
3. **RESPONDING CREATIVELY** Rewrite the story from the point of view of the AIDS patient, perhaps in the form of his diary.

Suggested Reading

Sontag, Susan. *AIDS and Its Metaphors.* New York: Farrar, 1989.

GERTRUDE STEIN

Miss Furr and Miss Skeene (p. 1264)

If Samuel Beckett's "Dante and the Lobster" is an example of a modernist story weighted with symbolism and allusion, then Gertrude Stein's "Miss Furr and Miss Skeene" is an example of a modernist story set free of heavy meaning. Stein has given us a pencil sketch of the lives of two women whose names are perhaps the most suggestive things about them. Helen Furr's first name suggests her femininity and sexual allure — the Helen whose beauty caused the Trojan War. Her last name suggests animality and sensuality; the name "Furr" rhymes with *purr* if you think about it. Georgine Skeene's first name hints of masculinity; perhaps her parents hoped she would be born a little boy instead of a girl? "Skeene" suggests "skin," of course, stroked silkily under the warmth of an admiring hand. Actually the word seems like a combination of the sounds of both "skin" and "sheen." No doubt students will have other associations with these words.

The physicality of these two women is unmistakable, and yet we know nothing about their appearances — height, weight, hair, eyes, mouth, or chin. Their physicality is less important to the author of the story than the word she uses to characterize the essence of what they are looking for in life — they want to be "gay." Students will assume that this means lesbian. Stein isn't denying this assumption, but she is also careful to define the way she is using "gay" in the opening paragraph. She tells us that Helen Furr comes from a pleasant home and has pleasant parents, who support her desire to cultivate her voice, but that "she did not find it gay living in the same place where she had always been living." Here "gay" implies happiness, *joie de vivre.*

Stein's sketch is one of her most shimmering, transparent narratives. In telling the story about Miss Furr and Miss Skeene, she creates what amounts to a series of short pencil sketches suggesting the outline of their meeting as students, their life together, their study of music ("both cultivating their voices"), their eventual separation, and Miss Furr's "living well" into old age with happy memories of a fulfilled lifetime, *telling* "over and over" the "little ways one could be learning to use in being gay," after *living* them as a younger woman.

Questions for Discussion

1. What associations do you have with the names of the two women characters in the story?
2. How would you define the meaning of the word *gay* as Stein uses it here?
3. How does Stein's sketch echo the format of a fairy tale, which begins with the words "Once upon a time" and ends with "they lived happily ever after"?
4. Why does Stein introduce "some dark and heavy men" into the story?

Topic for Writing

1. Stein was interested in the use of words for their own sake, emphasizing the oral dimension of storytelling in "Miss Furr and Miss Skeene." Analyze how the *sound* of the words in her story is as important as the *sense* of the words.

Suggested Reading

Haas, Robert, ed. *A Primer for the Gradual Understanding of Gertrude Stein.* Los Angeles: Black Sparrow, 1971.

JOHN STEINBECK

The Chrysanthemums (p. 1269)

The instinctive life that Elisa Allen loves as she tends her chrysanthemum plants lies dormant under her fingers. She is good with flowers, like her mother before her. Elisa says, "She could stick anything in the ground and make it grow." But it is December, and Steinbeck tells us it is "a time of quiet and of waiting." The Salinas landscape lies peacefully, but Elisa is vaguely unfulfilled. She begins to transplant her little chrysanthemum shoots, working without haste, conscious of her "hard-swept" house and her well-ordered garden, protected with its fence of chicken wire. Everything in her little world is under control. The tension in the scene is in herself, something she vaguely senses but refuses to face: the difference between her little world and the larger one encompassing it. Elisa is strong and mature, at the height of her physical strength. Why should she lie dormant? She has no fit scope for her powers. Steinbeck suggests the contradiction between her strength and her passivity in his description of the landscape: "The yellow stubble fields seemed to be bathed in pale cold sunshine, but there was no sunshine in the valley now in December." Like Hemingway, Steinbeck uses physical and geographical details to suggest the *absence* of positive qualities in his fictional characters. There is no sunshine in the valley, and the chrysanthemum plants aren't flowering, but what is natural in the annual vegetation cycle is out of kilter in Elisa. She experiences the world as a state of frustration.

Steinbeck has written an understated Chekhovian story in which ostensibly nothing much happens. It is a slice of life as Elisa lives it, sheltered and comfortable, yet — in Henry David Thoreau's words — life lived in a state of "quiet desperation."

The two male characters feel none of Elisa's lack of fulfillment. They live in a male world and take their opportunities for granted. Her husband, Henry Allen, is having a fine day. He's sold his thirty head of steer for a good price, and he's celebrating this Saturday night by taking his wife out to dinner and the movies in town. The traveling man is a trifle down on his luck, but it's nothing serious. He's found no customers this day so he lacks the money for his supper, but he knows a mark when he sees one. He flatters Elisa by agreeing with her and handing her a line about bringing some of her chrysanthemums to a lady he knows "down the road a piece." Elisa springs into action, delighted to be needed. Her tender shoots need her too, but she is not sufficiently absorbed by her gardening. The men do the real work of the world in this story. Gardening is a hobby she's proud of, and her husband encourages her to take pride in it, but she needs to feel of use in a larger dimension. Elisa mistakes this need for the freedom she imagines the transient knows on the road. Steinbeck gives her a clue as to the man's real condition in the state of his horse and mule, which she as a good gardener shouldn't have missed: "The horse and donkey drooped like unwatered flowers."

Instead, Elisa is caught up in her romantic fantasy of his nomadic life. Her sexual tension reduces her to a "fawning dog" as she envisions his life, but finally she realizes the man doesn't have the money for his dinner. "She stood up then, very straight, and her face was ashamed." Ashamed for what reason? Her lack of sensitivity to his poverty? Her sexual excitement? Her sense of captivity in a masculine world, where apparently only motherhood would bring opportunities for real work? Elisa brings the man two battered pots to fix and resumes talking, unable to leave him or her fantasy about the freedom she thinks he enjoys. He tells her outright that "it ain't the right kind of a life for a woman." Again she misreads the situation, taking his comment as a challenge. Her response is understandable, since she's never had his opportunity to choose a life on the road. She defends her ability to be his rival at sharpening scissors and banging out dents in pots and pans.

When the man leaves, Elisa is suddenly aware of her loneliness. She scrubs her body as rigorously as she's swept her house, punishing her skin with a pumice stone instead of pampering it with bubble bath. Then she puts on "the dress which was the symbol of her prettiness." An odd choice of words. Without understanding her instinctive rebellion against male expectations, Elisa refuses to be a sex symbol. Again she loses, denying herself pleasure in soft fabrics and beautiful colors. When Henry returns, he is bewildered by her mood and unable to reach her. She sees the chrysanthemums dying on the road, but she still can't face the truth about her sense of the repression and futility of her life. Wine at dinner and the idea of going to see a prize fight briefly bring her closer to the flesh and the instinctive life she has shunned outside her contact with her flowers, but they don't lift her mood. She feels as fragile and undervalued as her chrysanthemums. She begins to cry weakly, "like an old woman," as Henry drives her down the road.

Like Lawrence's heroine in "Odour of Chrysanthemums," Elisa is frustrated, cut off from the fullness of life by her physical destiny as a woman in a man's world. Does Steinbeck understand the sexual bias that undermines Elisa's sense of herself? He makes Henry as considerate a husband as a woman could wish for — he takes Elisa to the movies instead of going off to the prize fight himself. Like Hemingway, Steinbeck was sensitive to women's frustration, depicting it often in his fiction, even if he didn't look too closely at its probable causes in the society of his time.

Questions for Discussion

1. Based on Steinbeck's description in the first three paragraphs, how would you characterize the initial tone of the story? What do you associate with Steinbeck's image of the valley as "a closed pot"? In what way does this initial description foreshadow the events of the story?
2. What kind of character is Elisa Allen? What are the physical boundaries of her world? What is Elisa's psychological state at the beginning of the story?
3. Characterize the two men who are part of Elisa's world. In what ways are they similar and different? How does their way of life compare and contrast with the life Elisa leads?
4. What is the role of the chrysanthemums in Elisa's life? What do they symbolize?
5. How does Elisa delude herself about the life of the tinker? What other fantasies does this lead her to indulge in?
6. In what way does the tinker manipulate Elisa to accomplish his goals?
7. When the tinker leaves, a change comes over Elisa. What has she suddenly realized, and what course of action does she adopt?
8. As Elisa, both realistically and symbolically, goes out into the world, has she achieved any resolution of her problem? Why does she end the story "crying weakly — like an old woman"?

Topics for Writing

1. Discuss Steinbeck's use of setting to establish theme in "The Chrysanthemums."

2. Consider the isolation of Elisa Allen.
3. Analyze Elisa's illusions about the tinker and his interest in her as contrasted with reality.
4. **RESPONDING CREATIVELY** Recall a time when you felt threatened and frustrated by events that isolated you. Write a narrative recounting this experience from a third-person point of view.
5. **CONNECTIONS** Compare male versus female societal and sexual roles in Lawrence's "Odour of Chrysanthemums" and Steinbeck's "The Chrysanthemums."
6. **CONNECTIONS** Discuss woman in a man's world: Steinbeck's Elisa and Silko's Yellow Woman.

Related Commentary

Jay Parini, Lawrence's and Steinbeck's "Chrysanthemums," p. 1560.

Related Story

D. H. Lawrence, Odour of Chrysanthemums, p. 875.

Suggested Readings

Marcus, Mordecai. "The Lost Dream of Sex and Children in 'The Chrysanthemums.'" *Modern Fiction Studies* 11 (1965): 54–58.
McMahan, Elizabeth. "'The Chrysanthemums': Study of a Woman's Sexuality." *Modern Fiction Studies* 14 (1968–69): 453–58.
Miller, William V. "Sexual and Spiritual Ambiguity in 'The Chrysanthemums.'" *Steinbeck Quarterly* 5 (1972): 68–75.
Renner, S. "The Real Woman behind the Fence in 'The Chrysanthemums.'" *Modern Fiction Studies* 31 (1985): 305–17.
Sweet, Charles A. "Ms. Elisa Allen and Steinbeck's 'The Chrysanthemums.'" *Modern Fiction Studies* 20 (1974): 210–14.

AMY TAN

Two Kinds (p. 1278)

"Two Kinds," which was first published in the February 1989 issue of *The Atlantic Monthly*, is an excerpt from Amy Tan's best-selling book *The Joy Luck Club*. It is a skillfully written story that will probably pose no difficulty for most students; plot, characters, setting, and theme are immediately clear. The narrator states what she's "learned" from her experience in her final paragraph: She has come to realize that "Pleading Child" and "Perfectly Contented" are "two halves of the same song."

Looking back to her childhood, the narrator appears to be "perfectly contented" with her memories. Her interpretation of her relationship with her mother is presented in a calm, even self-satisfied way. After her mother's death, she tunes the piano left to her in her parents' apartment. "I played a few bars [of the piano piece by Robert Schumann], surprised at how easily the notes came back to me." The painful memory of her fiasco as a piano student has dissipated. Now she is her own audience, and she is pleased with what she hears. There is no real emotional stress in "Two Kinds"; the girl has had a comfortable life. She has survived her mother and can dispose of her possessions as she likes. She is at peace with her past, fulfilling her mother's prophecy that "you can be best anything."

The mother earned her right to look on the bright side of life by surviving tremendous losses when she left China. Her desire to turn her daughter into a "Chinese Shirley Temple" is understandable but unfortunate, since it places a tremendous psychological burden on the child. A discussion about this story might center on parents' supporting children versus "pushing" them to succeed in tasks beyond their abilities or ambitions.

Still, the narrator doesn't appear to have suffered unduly from her mother's ambitions for her. By her own account she was more than a match for her mother in the contest of wills on the piano bench. After her wretched performance at the recital, the daughter refuses to practice anymore. Her mother shouts, "Only two kinds of daughters. . . . Those who are obedient and those who follow their own mind! Only one kind of daughter can live in this house. Obedient daughter!" The girl answers by saying the unspeakable: "I wish I'd never been born! I wish I were dead! Like [the mother's twin baby girls lost in China]." This ends the conflict, but the narrator goes on to tell us that she was unrelenting in victory: "In the years that followed, I failed her many times, each time asserting my will, my right to fall short of expectations. I didn't get straight As. I didn't become class president. I didn't get into Stanford. I dropped out of college." She tells us that only after her mother's death can she begin to see things in perspective, when she is free to create her version of the past.

Since most students in class will be of the age when they are also asserting their will against parents in a struggle to take control of their lives, they will probably sympathize with Tan's narrator and accept her judgments uncritically. Will any reader take the mother's side?

Questions for Discussion

1. Why is the setting of this story important? What do you learn from it about the experience of Asian immigrants in their first years in the United States?
2. What advantages are offered to the child? What disadvantages?
3. How typical is Tan's story of the mother-daughter conflict? Explain.
4. Explain the meaning of the last paragraph of the story.

Topics for Writing

1. **CONNECTIONS** Compare and contrast the theme of initiation in Ellison's "Battle Royal" and Tan's "Two Kinds."
2. **CONNECTIONS** Analyze the use of dialect in Wright's "The Man Who Was Almost a Man" and Tan's "Two Kinds."
3. **CONNECTIONS** Compare and contrast the mother in Tan's "Two Kinds" with Olga, the protagonist of Chekhov's "Angel."

Related Commentary

Amy Tan, In the Canon, for All the Wrong Reasons, p. 1583.

Suggested Readings

Tan, Amy. *The Joy Luck Club.* New York: Ballantine, 1989.
———. "The Language of Discretion." *The State of the Language.* Ed. Christopher Ricks. Berkeley: U of California P, 1990.

JAMES THURBER

The Secret Life of Walter Mitty (p. 1288)

Like a good joke, a successful comic story may be easy to enjoy but hard to explain. Thurber has rendered his hero so convincingly that "Walter Mitty" has long since entered the popular vocabulary as a shorthand term for a certain personality type. The triumph of the story does not come, however, at the expense of the henpecked and bullied daydreamer. Stephen A. Black rightly points out that Mitty's escapism risks a denial of the self in its retreat from reality, but it is important to note that Mitty's fantasy life, despite its dependence on pulp fiction clichés, is just as real on the page as his (equally stereotypical) impatient and condescending wife, the officious policeman, and the insolent parking-lot attendant. Thus the reader may respond with admiration to Mitty's imaginary competence, courage, and grace under pressure.

Throughout the story Thurber uses things from the real environment to trigger Mitty's fantasies, but he also shows that the fantasies can have an impact on his actual life. The phrase "You miserable cur" reminds Mitty of the forgotten puppy biscuit. Near the end, after the sergeant tells "Captain Mitty" that "It's forty kilometers through hell, sir," Mitty has his life in Connecticut in mind when he musingly replies, "After all, . . . what isn't?" In his fantasy, "the box barrage is closing in," but Mitty is just as courageous in standing up to the salvo of questions and criticism launched moments later by his wife, which elicits his vague remark, "Things close in." As he stands against the drugstore wall in the Waterbury rain to face the imaginary firing squad, the reader can agree that he *is* "Walter Mitty the Undefeated" — because his inner life remains, for his banal tormentors, "inscrutable to the last."

WILLIAM E. SHEIDLEY

Questions for Discussion

1. What is Walter Mitty actually doing in the first paragraph of the story?
2. Explain Mitty's attitude toward his wife. Why does she insist that he wear gloves and overshoes?
3. How familiar is Walter Mitty with medical terminology? What is the purpose for Mitty of his medical fantasy?

4. Do Mitty's fantasies help or hinder him in dealing with reality?
5. Explain Mitty's statement that "things close in."
6. Where do you think Walter Mitty gets his ideas of heroism? Is there any sense in which his real life can be called heroic?

Topics for Writing

1. Describe Walter Mitty's final wish.
2. Discuss the romantic and the banal: the basis of Thurber's humor in "The Secret Life of Walter Mitty."
3. Find as many connections as possible between Mitty's actual experiences and his fantasies. How are they related? What do you think will be the consequence, if any, of Mitty's imaginary execution?

Suggested Readings

Black, Stephen A. *James Thurber — His Masquerades: A Critical Study*. The Hague: Mouton, 1970. 15, 18–19, 32, 42–43, 49–50, 54, 56, 119.
Morseburger, Robert E. *James Thurber*. Twayne's United States Authors Series 62. New York: Twayne, 1964. 18–19, 44–48, 123, 151–52.

Leo Tolstoy

The Death of Ivan Ilych (p. 1293)

No one who comes to "The Death of Ivan Ilych" from a direction other than that of *War and Peace* and *Anna Karenina* is likely to share the opinion of some Tolstoy scholars that it is parable-thin in its evocation of life, providing only a transparent surface of detail through which Tolstoy's allegorical intentions are exposed. The story is studded with brilliantly realistic representations of experiences that the reader encounters with a twinge of sometimes embarrassed recognition — Peter Ivanovich's struggle with the pouffe, for example. But it is nonetheless a product of the period following Tolstoy's religious crisis and a story written by one whose explicit theory of art rested on a utilitarian moral didacticism.

The story's effectiveness depends on Tolstoy's avoiding, until the last possible moment, preaching the sermon that, as the headnote suggests, he eventually means to preach. The opening section places us in the shoes of Peter Ivanovich, causing us to sympathize with the desire to look away from death, at the same time that it subjects that desire to a devastating satiric attack. Then, by returning to a long chronological survey of Ivan Ilych's life, Tolstoy forces us to do exactly the opposite of what Peter Ivanovich does: to confront death and its meaning in an extended and excruciatingly matter-of-fact account. What we see is not a life, but a death — or a life viewed as death. For Ivan Ilych's life, as he eventually comes to realize, is a slow but accelerating process of dying. The narration, however, decelerates, so that the reader may expect it to be nearly over around section VI, whereas in fact there are six more (albeit shorter) sections to come, containing a series of painful revelations that burst through the screen Ivan Ilych has built up to hide himself from reality.

Tolstoy tortures the reader just as Ivan Ilych is tortured, so that the precept finally advanced by the story arrives as the answer to the reader's fervent need. Ivan Ilych is not a particularly bad man; and — bad or good — all men, as Gerasim remarks, come to the same spot. Tolstoy makes this recognition virtually intolerable by his vivid rendering of Ivan Ilych's suffering. Then he offers a way out by proposing that one simple motion of the soul toward charity can release the sufferer from his mortal anguish. Tolstoy prepares us for this revelation by stressing the relief Ivan Ilych finds in the kindness of Gerasim, whose health, strength, and repose are bound up with his simple acceptance of sickness and death as necessary parts of life. Some critics have claimed that Tolstoy's art fails to encompass the illumination Ivan Ilych receives at the end, which rests on doctrines extrinsic to the text; but at least it can be said that he avoids sentimental piety by providing for an ironic interpretation when he caps Ivan Ilych's triumphant assertion "Death is finished. . . . It is no more!" with the paradoxical conclusion "He drew in a breath, stopped in the midst of a sigh, stretched out, and died."

The preoccupations and activities of Ivan Ilych and his peers during Ilych's lifetime in the society portrayed by Tolstoy contrast sharply with those of the unselfish peasant Gerasim. They are directed to no constructive end, serving only to gratify the ego with a sense of power and to hide the fear of death under a surface awareness of pleasure and propriety. Ivan Ilych is never more content than when manipulating the inert objects which are so plentiful in the story — as when decorating his new house — and he does his best to relate to people as he relates to things, insulating himself from true human contact. After he has received his death blow from the quite inert knob of a window frame, however, Ivan Ilych experiences a similar dehumanizing treatment by the doctors, his wife, and his friends, none of whom can bear to face the implications of his evident mortality. As his sickness steadily reduces him to a state of infantile dependency, Ilych comes to recognize first his own powerlessness and then the error in his strategy of living. Finally, as the coffin-womb he has built for himself falls away and he is reborn into the light of spiritual understanding, he sees the fundamental truth he has worked so hard to deny: The feelings of others are as real as his own. At this moment, moved by pity for his wife and son, he at last finds something worthwhile to do; and, in doing it, he attains the sense of ease and "rightness" that has previously eluded him. That the single positive act of Ivan Ilych's life is to die may be seen as either a grim irony or an exciting revelation, depending on the perspective from which the reader views it. But either way the conclusion of the story embodies the kernel of Tolstoy's social theme. As Edward Wasiolek puts it, "Death for Tolstoy now, as the supremely shared experience, is the model of all solidarity, and only the profound consciousness of its significance can bring one to the communion of true brotherhood."

WILLIAM E. SHEIDLEY

Questions for Discussion

1. How does the authorial voice qualify our view of Ivan Ilych's survivors' reactions to his death in section I?
2. Evaluate Peter Ivanovich's view of Ivan Ilych's son when he meets him near the end of section I.

3. Comment on the implications of Ivan Ilych's hanging a medallion bearing the motto *respice finem* (consider your end) on his watch chain.
4. What is wrong with Ivan Ilych's marriage? with his work? with his ambitions?
5. By examining the authorial comments in sections III and IV, define the attitude toward Ivan Ilych that Tolstoy asks the reader to share. Does this attitude change?
6. Consider the opening sentence of section VI. Is this section a low point in the story? If so, what kind of rise ensues?
7. Why does Ivan Ilych find relief in having his legs supported by Gerasim?
8. What is the effect of the shift to the present tense about one-third of the way through section VIII?
9. In section IX, Ivan Ilych complains to God in language similar to that of Job. Compare and contrast their plights.
10. What is the meaning of Ivan Ilych's reversion to childhood shortly before his death?
11. How might Ivan Ilych's dream of the black sack be interpreted?

Topics for Writing

1. Stop after reading section I and write a paragraph or two on the theme and tone of the story as you understand them so far. After reading the rest of the story, write a paragraph evaluating your original response. Write an essay examining the opening section as a story in itself, but one fully understood only after reading sections II–XII.
2. Consider bridge as an epitome of the life Ivan Ilych and his friends try to live.
3. Discuss Tolstoy's use of symbolic, descriptive details in "The Death of Ivan Ilych."
4. Using "The Death of Ivan Ilych" as the basis of your knowledge of society, write a manifesto calling for revolution or reform.
5. **RESPONDING CREATIVELY**   Write a sermon, using the demise of Ivan Ilych Golovin as your occasion.

Related Commentaries

Peter Rudy, Tolstoy's Revisions in "The Death of Ivan Ilych," p. 1567.
Leo Tolstoy, Chekhov's Intent in "The Darling" ["Angel"], p. 1642.

Suggested Readings

Christian, R. F. *Tolstoy: A Critical Introduction.* Cambridge: Cambridge UP, 1969. 236–38.
Greenwood, E. B. *Tolstoy: The Comprehensive Vision.* New York: St. Martin's, 1975. 118–23.
Simmons, Ernest J. *Introduction to Tolstoy's Writings.* Chicago: U of Chicago P, 1968. Esp. 148–50.
Wasiolek, Edward. *Tolstoy's Major Fiction.* Chicago: U of Chicago P, 1978. Esp. 165–79.

JEAN TOOMER

Blood-Burning Moon (p. 1335)

One of the questions the reader brings to the writing of many American authors is the crucial issue of identity. In a nation of many different nationalities whose American experience has been forged by many different economic and social pressures, the first question the reader usually has to ask of the writer is "Who are you?" The question of identity, however, has not been emphasized in the case of African American writers. The African American designation in itself has been such a strong mark of identification that it is usually the point where all discussion of their writing begins. Jean Toomer is the remarkable exception to this generalization. It is his identity as a creative artist that is the most ambiguous aspect of his writing, just as his ambivalence toward his racial identity was the most complex issue of his guarded life.

There is almost nothing in Toomer's early education or background that would prepare the reader for his one major work, the experimental collection *Cane*, published in 1923. Many of the pieces, both poetry and prose, such as "Blood-Burning Moon," that made up the book, were published in "little magazines" edited and presented for the white audience for modernist writing. At some point after the publication of this groundbreaking collection Toomer chose to cross the racial boundary and pass as white, and he no longer identified himself with the African American community. It was almost as though the brief years when his stories and poems were conceived were part of an adventure into blackness, in which he achieved a spiritual empathy that is as unexpected as it is impressive.

The romanticism and the idealizations of Toomer's response to rural black life seem to have been the result, as he wrote himself, of three brief months he spent in Georgia in 1922, when he was already twenty-seven years old. "This was the first time I'd ever heard the folk-songs and spirituals. They were very rich and sad and joyous and beautiful." As one reviewer of *Cane* wrote in 1923, "Toomer has not interviewed the Negro, has not asked opinions about him, has not drawn conclusions about him from his reactions to outside stimuli, but has made the much more searching, and much more self-forgetting effort of seeing life with him, through him." The reviewer was responding to Toomer's empathy. The book itself is such an amalgam of styles and attitudes, responding to the challenge of an eclectic range of current experimental writing, that it has always been difficult to find any single term of it that would describe all its facets. The book as a whole is more closely related to the fashionable literary modernism of Toomer's era than it is a close description of southern black life.

If *Cane* itself is only in part a portrait of the South, "Blood-Burning Moon" can be considered the archetype of many stories that followed it, with its painful love triangle, its conflict between the races, and the orgy of violence that is the story's inevitable ending. The classic figures who appear in many later stories and novels make their early appearance here: the light-skinned African American woman flattered by white attention but confused in her response, the white lover, sympathetic, but only to a point, and imperturbably racist beyond that point, and the strong, possessive, inarticulate black man unable to control his rage. Richard Wright's Bigger Thomas, the unforgettable black protagonist in his novel of the 1930s, *Native Son* (1940), clearly has Tom Burwell as a predecessor. The setting and the tone of Toomer's story also prefigure the scene and the tension of William Faulkner's well-known story "That Evening Sun." Perhaps a reason for Toomer's withdrawal from the literary scene was that he understood he had already achieved a great deal — and there was little for him in repeating what he had accomplished in a few months of breathless creativity.

Questions for Discussion

1. As Louisa is walking up the road she feels confident that the white man, Bob Stone, loves her. What impression do readers get from Stone's thoughts later in the story? What does Toomer intend us to feel about Louisa's assurance?
2. What is Toomer suggesting in the sentence, "His black balanced, and pulled against, the white of Stone"?
3. Skin color is always a crucial element in any story of racial conflict. How does Toomer describe Louisa's skin color? How would we interpret that description?
4. Does Tom Burwell have a premonition that the night will somehow lead to violence, even before he speaks to Louisa? What are the signs?
5. When Tom Burwell first approaches Louisa he thinks he won't be able to talk to her, but then he delivers a long and impassioned proposal. Does this contradict what the author has already told us about his character? Do we believe him when he says, "Seems like th love I feel fo yo done stolen tongue"? Or does this remind us of other local-color stories of southern life?
6. Is the reader surprised by Bob Stone's virulent racism?
7. The ending of the story is preordained by the triangle the author has presented. What statements by the characters make it clear that Burwell will be lynched at the story's end?

Topics for Writing

1. Many blues songs include the line, "I got a gal, works in the white folk's yard." Using this line, describe Louisa's situation and discuss the tensions that this kind of domestic employment caused in the African American community.
2. The syntax of the story shifts from the modernism of the opening sentences to the dialect of the African American characters. Analyze the linguistic shifts and relate them to the plot and to the characters.
3. When Bob Stone is hurrying to find Louisa with Burwell he stumbles over a dog, and the entire countryside suddenly fills with sounds "heralding the blood-shot eyes of southern awakening." Analyze this last statement for its multiple levels of meaning.
4. As the silent lynch mob comes for Burwell, Toomer writes, "The moving body of their silence preceded them over the crest of the hill into factory town. It flattened the Negroes beneath it." Discuss the historical background of these sentences, and comment on their application to the climax of the story.
5. Using library materials, compare the character of Tom Burwell to the figure of Bigger Thomas in Richard Wright's novel *Native Son*.

Suggested Readings

O'Daniel, Therman B., ed. *Jean Toomer: A Critical Evaluation.* Washington, DC: Howard UP, 1988.
Pabre, Genevieve, and Michel Feith, eds. *Jean Toomer and the Harlem Renaissance.* New Brunswick, NJ: Rutgers UP, 2001.
Rusch, Frederik L., ed. *A Jean Toomer Reader: Selected Unpublished Writings.* New York: Oxford UP, 1993.
Toomer, Jean. *Cane: An Authoritative Text, Backgrounds, and Criticism.* Ed. Darwin T. Turner. New York: Norton, 1988.
———. *Selected Essays and Literary Criticism.* Ed. Robert B. Jones. Knoxville: U of Tennessee P, 1996.
———. *The Wayward and the Seeking: A Collection of Writings.* Ed. with an intro. by Darwin T. Turner. Washington, DC: Howard UP, 1980.

JOHN UPDIKE

A & P (p. 1343)

Although Updike was a precociously successful writer who spent his apprenticeship living in New York City and writing for *The New Yorker* magazine, much of the strength of his writing stems from his ability to take the reader back to the atmosphere of the small town where he grew up. "A & P" showcases this ability. This story about a nineteen-year-old at a checkout counter in an A & P supermarket skillfully sustains the point of view of a teenage boy from a small-town working-class family.

The incident the story describes is slight. What gives "A & P" its substance is the voice of the narrator. He is obviously what the author thinks of as an ordinary teenager, impatient with old people, not interested in his job, and deeply aroused by girls. The longest descriptive passage — almost a third of the story itself — dwells on the body of one of the girls; as the story's slight action unfolds, the bodies of that girl and one of her friends are mentioned several times again. The narrator's adolescent desire and adoration are amusingly played off his clumsy bravado and the idiom of sexist stereotypes he is trying to master. "You never know for sure how girls' minds work (do you really think it's a mind in there or just a little buzz like a bee in a glass jar?)." His view of adult women is no less callow: "We're right in the middle of town, and the women generally put on a shirt or shorts or something before they get out of the car into the street. And anyway these are usually women with six children and varicose veins mapping their legs and nobody, including them, could care less."

It is probably true that when the story was written, in the late 1950s, its attitudes were not considered unusual. Today we have to ask ourselves whether the deplorable sexism is redeemed by the artfulness of the story, the technique Updike brings to constructing his narrator's voice.

Questions for Discussion

1.   What does the language of the story tell us about the narrator's social background?
2.   Are there any details in the story that place it in a specific part of the United States, or could it be happening anywhere within a few miles of a beach? Explain.
3.   Is the boy's discomfort with older people limited to women, or is he also uncomfortable with men? Is there anyone in the store he *is* comfortable with? Explain.
4.   Do you think Updike shares the narrator's attitudes?

Topics for Writing

1.   Analyze the strengths and the limitations of the first-person narrative in "A & P."
2.   **CONNECTIONS**   Consider "acting like a man": the bag boy in Updike's "A & P" and Dave in Wright's "The Man Who Was Almost a Man."
3.   **CONNECTIONS**   Compare and contrast adolescent narrators in Updike's "A & P" and Joyce's "Araby."

Related Commentary

John Updike, Kafka and "The Metamorphosis," p. 1588.

Suggested Readings

Cantor, Jay. "On Giving Birth to One's Own Mother." *TriQuarterly* 75 (Spring–Summer 1989): 78–91.
Detweiler, Robert. *John Updike.* Rev. ed. Boston: G. K. Hall, 1987.
Fleischauer, John F. "John Updike's Prose Style: Definition at the Periphery of Meaning." *Critique: Studies in Contemporary Fiction* 30.4 (Summer 1989): 277–90.
Greiner, Donald J. *The Other Updike: Poems, Short Stories, Prose, Play.* Columbus: Ohio UP, 1981.
Luscher, Robert M. "John Updike's Olinger Stories: New Light among the Shadows." *Journal of the Short Story in English* 11 (Autumn 1988): 99–117.
Lyons, E. "John Updike: The Beginning and the End." *Critique* 14.2 (1972): 44–59.
Newman, Judie. *John Updike.* New York: St. Martin's, 1988.
Samuels, C. T. "Art of Fiction: John Updike." *Paris Review* 12 (1968): 84–117.
Seib, P. "Lovely Way through Life: An Interview with John Updike." *Southwest Review* 66 (1981): 341–50.
Taylor, Charles C. *John Updike: A Bibliography.* Ann Arbor, MI: Books Demand UMI, 1989.
Thorburn, David, and Howard Eiland. *John Updike: A Collection of Critical Essays.* New York: Prentice-Hall, 1979.
Updike, John. *Hugging the Shore.* New York: Random House, 1983.
———. *Picked-Up Pieces.* New York: Knopf, 1976.
———. *Too Far to Go.* New York: Ballantine, 1979.

Wilhelm, Albert E. "Rebecca Cune: Updike's Wedge Between the Maples." *Notes on Modern American Literature* 7.2 (Fall 1983): Item 9.

———. "The Trail-of-Bread-Crumbs Motif in Updike's Maples Stories." *Studies in Short Fiction* 25.1 (Winter 1988): 71–73.

HELENA MARÍA VIRAMONTES

The Moths (p. 1349)

Although Viramontes has written in many styles, this story shows the influence of one of her teachers, Nobel Prize–winner Gabriel García Márquez. It has close affinities to the subject matter and the characters of a typical García Márquez story, and the literary style reflects García Márquez's commitment to magic realism. Viramontes's magic realism, however, is more rooted in the everyday than that of many other writers using this idiom, and her story about a girl's difficult relationship with her mother and her sisters reflects Viramontes's American upbringing. Students will likely have a strong response to the story's imagery and to the unyielding tale the girl tells of her grandmother's death. The image of small gray moths that come from her grandmother's soul and flutter out of her mouth at the moment of her death is unforgettable, and like so much of the metaphor and symbolism that is at the root of magic realist technique, it is never adequately explained. It is up to Viramontes's readers to make what they can of it.

Students will find it helpful in studying the story to follow one image through various points in the narrative. An image we can follow is the girl's hands. For Viramontes, the girl's hands become a symbol of her emotional difficulties with her family. Already in the second paragraph we are told that one reason the girl didn't fit in with her sisters was that her hands "were too big to handle the fineries of crocheting or embroidery." Her sisters have given her the cruel nickname "bull hands." The girl tells us casually that because she had doubted her grandmother's cure for her fever, her hands "grow like a liar's nose." Her grandmother cures her swollen hands with "a balm [made] out of dried moth wings and Vicks." When the girl tries to talk to her mother about the seriousness of her grandmother's illness, she feels her hands "hanging helplessly" by her side. She falls asleep and is awakened when her hands fall from her lap. As she crushes the chili peppers for her grandmother's tripe stew, she describes herself as doing it with her "bull hand."

Viramontes is not afraid to take chances, and her language is as startling as her imagery. The girl speaks of her grandmother's "pasty gray eye" beaming at her and "burning holes" in her suspicions about the old woman's folk medicines. She talks of a sunset as a moment when "the sun is finally defeated, finally sinks into the realization that it cannot with all its power to heal or burn, exist forever." Beneath the verbal fireworks, however, Viramontes has a simple story to tell. The girl is hardened by the verbal abuse and the whippings she has received at the hands of her family. Only her grandmother has let her escape from them into something like an ordinary life. When the grandmother dies the girl is alone, and she carefully cleans the old woman's body, taking her grandmother into the bathtub with her, holding her in her arms. Sitting in the water with the body, she is finally able to cry. Students will respond to the story's literary qualities — to its language and poetic imagery — but they will first be moved by the immediacy and the poignancy of the girl's experience.

Questions for Discussion

1. Discuss the image of the girl's hands and how the obsession with her hands follows her through the story.
2. One of the girl's difficulties with her family is her refusal to attend church. What does she experience the one time in the story she does visit a chapel?
3. Much of the girl's protest against her family sounds like a typical American teenager's complaints. What is different, or not different, about her complaints about her Latino family?
4. The story jumps from one time frame to another as the girl remembers her life with her *abuelita*. At what moment is the story occurring? How do we know it from the text?
5. How does the author relate the moment of the old woman's death to the eternal rhythms of life and our experience?
6. What is the contrast the author intends when she describes the water running into the bath as filled with "vitality and steam"?
7. Discuss what the author is telling us when she says that the girl, after her grandmother's death, "wanted to go to where the moths were"?
8. Discuss the symbolism of the moths.

Topics for Writing

1. In the same sentence in which Viramontes tells us that the protagonist's sisters have nicknamed her "bull hands," Viramontes describes her sisters' "waterlike voices," using a strong simile. Find other strong similes and metaphors in the text and discuss their importance to the story.
2. When the girl challenges her family's belief in the grandmother's folk medicine, she is challenging their adherence to old-fashioned traditions the way that many young people do. Analyze how this challenge is developed and resolved in the narrative.

Suggested Reading

Viramontes, Helena María, and Maria Herrera-Sobek, eds. *Chicana Creativity and Criticism: New Frontiers in American Literature.* Albuquerque: U of New Mexico P, 1996.

KURT VONNEGUT JR.

Harrison Bergeron (p. 1354)

This humorous fantasy story deserves to become a classic in American literature, like James Thurber's "The Secret Life of Walter Mitty." Vonnegut has stretched the basic premise of American democracy — that all men (and women) are created equal — to its literal limit. In his opening paragraph he explains how this admirable social ideal was realized in the year 2081, and then he shows the consequences of the idea as experienced in the family life of George and Hazel Bergeron and their fourteen-year-old son Harrison.

As a storyteller, Vonnegut makes good use of the traditional elements of fiction in structuring a conventional plot, but you could point out to students that the most dramatic events of the plot (ironically enough) occur in a television program that George and Hazel are watching together in their living room, parodying the "normal" activities of the average twenty-first-century family. On the screen, they see their son shot and killed by the U.S. Handicapper General in a television studio after he has defied the law of the land by freeing himself, a beautiful ballerina, and several musicians of their handicaps.

The most memorable aspect of Vonnegut's story is his description of the effect of the handicap on George Bergeron — the various noises of buzzers, ball peen hammers, and riveting guns transmitted by his "ear radio" are guaranteed to keep him from thinking about anything for too long. Their effect is terribly painful, as it is meant to be. By destroying individual human thought, the government has created a nation of sheep, content in their passivity to accept whatever they see on television, including the murder of their only son.

Questions for Discussion

1. How does the "ear radio" worn by everyone possessing above-normal intelligence in Vonnegut's story anticipate the earphones worn now by people listening to tapes and CDs?
2. How do the noises transmitted by George Bergeron's earphones suggest the effect of the frequent television advertisements infiltrating programs broadcast by the media today?
3. In what way does "Harrison Bergeron" contradict the idea of human equality at the basis of democracy in the United States? How can you defend the idea, despite what happens in the story?
4. Why doesn't Hazel wear a handicap? How does George deal with his handicap?
5. Why isn't Harrison content with the status quo? Does his age alone (fourteen) adequately explain his rebellion against the laws of his society?

Topic for Writing

1. Analyze Vonnegut's use of simile and metaphor in "Harrison Bergeron" to suggest the emotional effect of the handicap radio on George Bergeron.

Suggested Reading

Vonnegut, Kurt, Jr. *Welcome to the Monkey House.* New York: Dell, 1968.

ALICE WALKER

Everyday Use (p. 1360)

In this very accessible but powerful story, Alice Walker deals with issues that college readers should find thought-provoking and relevant to their lives. It is a story about family, heritage, and personal pride, and the way that one young woman's search for identity causes her to devalue the very aspects of her past that are most important. While searching for objects and symbols to enshrine as reflections of her zealous racial pride, Dee overlooks the human beings whose strength and courage she should really be interested in preserving and emulating.

Dee has always been seen, by herself and others, as different from her family and the people around her. She is smart, ambitious, wanting more out of life than her family seems to have. Of course, there is nothing wrong in any of this, and as many young people do, Dee moves away to find herself and a better life. The irony arises after she finds this new life. Then, her need to feel a connection to a past, a people, and a history asserts itself, and Dee searches for her identity in a socially trendy fashion, reaching back to African tradition in hairstyle, clothing, and name, "Wangero." The problem is that in "reaching back" to Africa, she reaches right past her own relatives, whose lives she considers common, ignorant, and unimportant.

This is illustrated most powerfully by her rejection of her birth name, which, she tells her mother contemptuously, is a name "after the people who oppress me." Her mother, puzzled, reminds her that she was named after her aunt, who was named after *her* mother, who was named after *her* mother . . . and reflects that the name could probably be traced back beyond the Civil War to slave days. You would think that a young woman who is so interested in preserving her "heritage" would show some interest in these women whose name she bears and whose lives of struggle and oppression she truly springs from, but Dee doesn't care at all. Dee is only interested in pieces of history that are aesthetically appealing and will enhance her life by making her (or her surroundings) look good. The stories of dead women, who lived (in Dee's view) in ignorance, poverty, and passive acceptance of oppression have no value for her.

Dee's shallowness and her superficial vision of family history are again displayed as we watch her select objects from her mother's house to take away as mementos. She takes the churn top and dasher, which her mother obviously still puts to practical use, without even asking permission, because she needs a centerpiece for a table. She places no value on the function of these objects or on another person's need for them, only on her own appreciation of their "artistic" qualities. Her mother allows her to have her way, but finally stands up to her and says no when she tries to take the handmade quilts. These quilts have been promised to Maggie, the rather pathetic younger sister who has always lived in Dee's shadow. Here, Mrs. Johnson's protective instincts are aroused, as she sees that Maggie will give in to Dee as she has always done unless her mother prevents it. She knows that Maggie is the one who will really value the quilts, putting them to "everyday use," as they were intended.

It is Maggie who is really in touch with her heritage, who has a "memory like an elephant" and who knows the family history because she knew and loved the people who created it. Maggie and her mother still live the same kind of life that their ancestors lived, in the same place, with the same kind of house, furniture, and food (which "Wangero" is so condescendingly "delighted" with). Dee, who is frenetically searching for objects that will make her feel connected to her roots, is smugly convinced that only she "understands her heritage." But, in reality, she doesn't understand anything about her family and in fact, has always looked down upon them all. Maggie is the one who deserves the family heirlooms, as she and her mother are the ones who really understand their meaning and value their creators.

Questions for Discussion

1. Describe the mother in this story. What kind of person is she? How does she seem to feel about Dee? about Maggie?
2. How did Dee relate to her family before she left home? What role did she assume for herself? Does this change after she leaves home?
3. How do you feel about Dee? Do you sympathize with her desire to "improve" herself and her family? Where do you think she goes wrong?
4. Discuss the relationship between Maggie and Dee.
5. Why has Dee assumed African dress, hairstyle, and name? How would you characterize the attitudes of her and her new husband/boyfriend toward their race? positive or negative? honest or simply "politically correct"?
6. Discuss Dee's mother's and sister's reactions to her new persona, "Wangero." Do you sympathize with them?
7. How would you describe the way that Dee reacts to the food and objects in her mother's house?
8. Why does Mrs. Johnson decide to stand up to Dee and not allow her to take the quilts at the end of the story?
9. Why do you think Maggie is so content at the end?

Topics for Writing

1. Discuss Dee's final comment to her mother that she (the mother) "doesn't understand" her heritage.
2. **RESPONDING CREATIVELY** Argue with Mrs. Johnson, and try to convince her that Dee/Wangero deserves the quilts.
3. Discuss the positive and negative aspects of Wangero's and Hakim-a-barber's search for identity.

Related Commentary

Alice Walker, "Zora Neale Hurston: A Cautionary Tale and a Partisan View," p. 1661.

Suggested Readings

Banks, Erma Davis, and Keith Byerman. *Alice Walker: An Annotated Bibliography 1968–1986.* New York: Garland, 1989.

Bell, Roseann P., Bettye J. Parker, and Beverly Guy-Sheftall, eds. *Sturdy Black Bridges: Visions of Black Women in Literature.* New York: Anchor, 1979.

Bloom, Harold. *Alice Walker.* New York: Chelsea House, 1990.

Byerman, Keith, and Erma Banks. "Alice Walker: A Selected Bibliography, 1968–1988." *Callaloo: An Afro-American and African Journal of Arts and Letters* 12.2 (Spring 1989): 343–45.

Byrne, Mary Ellen. "Welty's 'A Worn Path' and Walker's 'Everyday Use': Companion Pieces." *Teaching English in a Two-Year College* 16(2) (May 1989): 129–33.

Cooke, Michael. *Afro-American Literature in the Twentieth Century: The Achievement of Intimacy.* New Haven: Yale UP, 1984.

Davis, T. M. "Alice Walker's Celebration of Self in Southern Generations." In *Women Writers of the Contemporary South.* Ed. Peggy Whitman Prenshaw. Jackson: UP of Mississippi, 1984. 83–94.

Erickson, P. "Cast Out Alone/To Heal/and Re-create/Ourselves: Family Based Identity in the Work of Alice Walker." *College Language Association Journal* 23 (1979): 71–94.

Evans, Mari, ed. *Black Women Writers (1950–1980): A Critical Evaluation.* New York: Anchor, 1984. 453–95.

Mariani, Philomena, ed. *Critical Fictions: The Politics of Imaginative Writing.* Seattle: Bay Press, 1991.

Petry, Alice Hall. "Alice Walker: The Achievement of the Short Fiction." *Modern Language Studies* 19.1 (Winter 1989): 12–27.

Stade, G. "Womanist Fiction and Male Characters." *Partisan Review* 52 (1985): 265–70.

Winchell, Donna Haisty. *Alice Walker.* Boston: Twayne, 1990.

EUDORA WELTY

Why I Live at the P.O. (p. 1368)

This story may be troublesome to some readers, especially if they have been sensitized to racial issues in short fiction through a discussion of Achebe's criticism of Conrad's "Heart of Darkness." The word "nigger" used as a racial slur occurs three times in Welty's story. The narrator who uses the word is clearly an uneducated bigot, but her contempt for people of color living in her community is underscored by her assumption that they are fit only for the lowest kind of work. Here are the passages concerned:

> So I merely slammed the door behind me and went down and made some green-tomato pickle. Somebody had to do it. Of course Mama had turned both the niggers loose; she always said no earthly power could hold one anyway on the Fourth of July, so she wouldn't even try. It turned out that Jaypan fell in the lake and came within a very narrow limit of drowning.

> There was a nigger girl going along on a little wagon right in front. "Nigger girl," I says, "come help me haul these things down the hill, I'm going to live in the post office." Took her nine trips in her express wagon. Uncle Rondo came out on the porch and threw her a nickel.

In both cases, African Americans are assumed to be stupid workhorses, barely tolerated as human beings and undeserving of respect. In the first instance the two house servants are "turned loose" (like animals?) on the Fourth of July, but they are so immature and irresponsible that they go wild on their chance to celebrate Independence Day (irony?); they get drunk, and one of them, Jaypan, nearly drowns. In the second case, African Americans are presumed to be so stupid that a black child won't mind stopping her play with a wagon to help move a white woman; the child will also be satisfied being paid a pittance for working so hard. Welty is writing a humorous story, of course, told from the point of view of a Mississippi cracker, but humor doesn't negate the racism, any more than Marlowe's naiveté condones his judgments about Africans in "Heart of Darkness." Racist jokes aren't any more tolerable because they are meant to be "funny."

Insensitive literary critics discussing "Why I Live at the P.O." usually comment on "the exasperation and frustration, loneliness and near-madness" of the narrator, trapped in a provincial Mississippi town. Or they view her as "a solid and practical person struggling to keep her self-possession and balance in the midst of a childish, neurotic, and bizarre family." In Welty's commentary on the story, she stresses the normalcy of characters like Sister (the narrator) and her family in the South. Thrown against one another with limited social resources, they bicker and feud but usually reconcile their differences, because family solidarity is important to them. At the end of the story we learn that Sister's outburst has been provoked after five days of living by herself in the post office; Welty has said that once the character's anger has cooled, she'd move back home. She writes, "I was trying to show how, in these tiny little places such as where they come from, the only entertainment people have is dramatizing the family situation, which they do fully knowing what they are doing. They're having a good time. They're not caught up; it's not pathological. It's a Southern kind of exaggeration."

Questions for Discussion

1. Can we equate Sister's voice with Welty's opinions? Explain.
2. Does the humor in the story soften or increase the tension between the members of the family? Why or why not?
3. Why do the two sisters fight so much?

Topics for Writing

1. **RESPONDING CREATIVELY**   Retell the story through the eyes of the house servant Jaypan or the little girl with the express wagon.
2. **CONNECTIONS**   Compare Mississippi small towns as backgrounds for Welty's "Why I Live at the P.O." and Faulkner's "A Rose for Emily."

Suggested Readings

See page 263.

Eudora Welty

A Worn Path (p. 1377)

Try not to force the Christian or mythological schemes of allegory the story supports until you encourage students to savor the beauty of the literal narration. Phoenix Jackson is an embodiment of love, faith, sacrifice, charity, self-renunciation, and triumph over death in herself, quite apart from the typological implications of her name or the allusions to the stations of the cross in her journey. Phoenix transcends her merely archetypal significance just as she transcends the stereotype of old black mammies on which she is built. Welty accomplishes this act of creation by entering fully into the consciousness of her character. There she discovers the little child that still lives within the old woman and causes her to dream of chocolate cake, dance with a scarecrow, and delight in a Christmas toy. Phoenix is right when she says, "I wasn't as old as I thought," but she does not merit the condescension of the hunter's exclamation, "I know you old colored people! Wouldn't miss going to town to see Santa Claus!" Even in her greatest discomfort, lying in the weeds, losing her memory, getting her shoes tied, "stealing" a nickel, or taking one as a handout, Phoenix retains her invincible dignity, an essential component of the single glimpse we receive of her triumphant homeward march, bearing aloft the bright symbol of life she has retrieved through her exertions.

In her comments on the story (included in Part Two, p. 1592), Welty implies that the meaning of Phoenix's journey is that of any human exertion carried out in good faith despite the uncertainty of the outcome: "The path is the thing that matters." In keeping with this theme, Welty repeatedly shows Phoenix asserting life in the face of death. Her name itself, taken from the mythical bird that periodically immolates itself and rises reborn from its ashes, embodies the idea. (She even makes a noise like "a solitary little bird" in the first paragraph.) Phoenix makes her journey at the time of the death and rebirth of the year; her own skin color is like the sun bursting through darkness; she overcomes discouragement as she tops the hill; she extricates herself from a thorn bush (of which much may be made in a Christian allegorical interpretation); she passes "big dead trees" and a buzzard; she traverses a field of dead corn; she sees a "ghost" that turns out to be a dancing scarecrow; she is overcome by a "black dog" but rescued by a death-dealing hunter whose gun she faces down and whom she beats out of a shiny nickel; and she emerges from a deathlike trance in the doctor's office to return with the medicine her grandson needs to stay alive. Phoenix's strength lies in the purpose of her journey, and her spirit is contagious. The hunter, the woman who ties her shoes, and the doctor's attendant all perform acts of charity toward her, and lest the reader overlook the one word that lies at the heart of Welty's vision, the nurse says "Charity" while "making a check mark in a book."

Questions for Discussion

1. Notice Phoenix's identification with "a solitary little bird." What other birds does she encounter on her journey? Explain their implications.
2. What techniques does Welty use to suggest the laboriousness of Phoenix's trip?

3. Before she crosses the creek, Phoenix says, "Now comes the trial." Does she pass it? How? To what extent is this event a microcosm of the whole story? Are there other microcosmic episodes?

4. What effect do Phoenix's sequential reactions to the scarecrow, the abandoned cabins, and the spring have on the reader's view of her?

5. What is your opinion of the hunter? What conclusion might be drawn from the fact that even though he kills birds and patronizes Phoenix, he helps her in a way he does not know?

6. Interpret the passage that begins with Phoenix bending for the nickel and ends with her parting from the hunter.

7. Describe Natchez as Phoenix perceives it. Is it a worthy culmination for her journey?

8. In her comments reprinted in Part Two (p. 1591), Welty remarks that Phoenix's victory comes when she sees the doctor's diploma "nailed up on the wall." In what sense is this moment the climax of the story? What is different about the ensuing action from the action that leads up to this moment? Are there any similarities?

9. How does Phoenix describe her grandson? What is Welty's reason for using these terms?

10. Explain the irony in the way the nurse records Phoenix's visit.

Topics for Writing

1. Explain why many readers think that Phoenix Jackson's grandson is dead.

2. Discuss the symbolism of birds in "A Worn Path."

3. After your first reading of "A Worn Path," write a paragraph giving your opinion of Phoenix Jackson. Then study some symbolic interpretations of the story (such as those by Ardelino, Isaacs, and Keys, cited in Suggested Readings). Reread the story and write another assessment of the central character. Does she bear up under the freight of symbolic meaning the critics ask her to carry? Does her relation to these archetypes help to account for your original response?

4. **RESPONDING CREATIVELY** Read Welty's account of how she came to write "A Worn Path" in Part Two. Following her example, write an account of what you imagine to be the day's experience of someone you catch a glimpse of who strikes your fancy. Use the intimate interior third-person limited-omniscient point of view that Welty employs for Phoenix Jackson.

Related Commentaries

Eudora Welty, Is Phoenix Jackson's Grandson Really Dead?, p. 1591.
Eudora Welty, Plot and Character in Chekhov's "The Darling" ["Angel"], p. 1645.

Suggested Readings

Ardelino, Frank. "Life out of Death: Ancient Myth and Ritual in Welty's 'A Worn Path.' " *Notes on Mississippi Writers* 9 (1976): 1–9.
Bloom, Harold. *Eudora Welty.* New York: Chelsea House, 1986.

Desmond, John F. *A Still Moment: Essay on the Art of Eudora Welty.* Metuchen, NJ: Scarecrow, 1978.

Isaacs, Neil D. "Life for Phoenix." *Sewanee Review* 71 (1963): 75–81.

Keys, Marilynn. " 'A Worn Path': The Way of Dispossession." *Studies in Short Fiction* 16 (1979): 354–56.

Kieft, Ruth M. *Eudora Welty.* Rev. ed. Boston: G. K. Hall, 1987.

MacNeil, Robert. *Eudora Welty: Seeing Black and White.* Westport, CT: Greenwood, 1990.

Phillips, Robert L., Jr. "A Structural Approach to Myth in the Fiction of Eudora Welty." *Eudora Welty: Critical Essays.* Ed. Peggy Whitman Prenshaw. Jackson: UP of Mississippi, 1979. 56–67, esp. 60.

Preenshaw, Peggy W., ed. *Eudora Welty: Thirteen Essays.* Jackson: UP of Mississippi, 1983.

Schmidt, Peter. *The Heart of the Story: Eudora Welty's Short Fiction.* Jackson: UP of Mississippi, 1991.

Turner, W. Craig, and Lee Harding, eds. *Critical Essays on Eudora Welty.* Boston: G. K. Hall, 1989.

Welty, Eudora. *The Eye of the Story.* New York: Vintage, 1990.

———. *One Writer's Beginnings.* New York: Warner, 1984.

EDITH WHARTON

Roman Fever (p. 1385)

Nearly every detail of this seemingly meandering narration that leads up to the final sequence of three dramatic revelations has a function in preparing for the climax. Wharton knits better than Grace Ansley, and her story does not fully unravel until the last words are spoken. When the secret is finally out, the reader experiences a flash of ironic insight that Wharton has been preparing from the beginning through her masterful delineation of the characters and their situation.

Face to face with "the great accumulated wreckage of passion and splendor" that spreads before them, and deserted in their advancing age by the pair of daughters who are now their sole concerns, the two widows may evoke the reader's condescending pity. They seem as small and pale as the images of one another each sees, in Wharton's metaphor, "through the wrong end of her little telescope." But as the two characters become differentiated, Alida Slade takes on depth and coloration. As the story of her flashy but parasitic life and of the jealousy and guilty resentment she has harbored toward her friend gradually emerges, the reader can no longer pity her but can hardly admire her either. Her revelation that it was she, not Delphin Slade, who wrote the letter inviting Grace to a tryst in the Colosseum may be unexpected, but it follows perfectly from her character as Wharton has established it. Its blow to Mrs. Ansley is severe, and it seems the more cruel to the reader, who has no reason as yet to revise the original estimate of her as merely pitiable. Mrs. Ansley staggers, but to the reader's surprise and gratification she gradually recovers herself. Impelled by the shock for once to assert herself, she caps Mrs. Slade's revelation with an even more dramatic one of her own.

Grace Ansley's reticence, and the quietness of her life in contrast to Alida Slade's, expresses neither emotional pallor nor weakness of character. She had the spunk to take what she wanted from Delphin Slade twenty-five years before, and she has been content with her memory ever since, not needing, as Alida Slade would have (and indeed *has*) needed, to get reassurance by parading her conquest in public. Thus, it is Mrs. Ansley who manifests greater independence and vitality. Mrs. Slade, by contrast, has been conventional and dependent. Widowhood is such an uncomfortable lot for her because she can no longer shine with the reflected brilliance of her husband. Barbara may be unlike Horace Ansley because Delphin Slade was really her father, but her differences from Jenny derive from the fact that Grace Ansley, not Alida Slade, is her mother.

Wharton has constructed her plot with a precision O. Henry would have admired, but she has based it less on contrivances of circumstance than on an understanding of her characters. By placing them in a setting that spans millennia — from ancient Rome to the airplane — she implies the universality of the passions, triumphs, and defeats that make up the lives of even these New York society ladies, whose wealth and status do not protect them from the human condition after all.

WILLIAM E. SHEIDLEY

Questions for Discussion

1. What do Barbara and Jenny think of their mothers? How accurate is their estimate?
2. Why does Grace Ansley place an "undefinable stress" on "me" and "I" in replying to Alida Slade's questions about her reaction to their view of the Roman ruins?
3. Why does Alida Slade consider Grace and Horace Ansley "two nullities"?
4. Compare and contrast the two ladies' responses to widowhood and advancing age. Who takes them harder? Why?
5. Alida Slade remembers that "Mrs. Horace Ansley, twenty-five years ago, had been exquisitely lovely." Explain the importance of this fact to Mrs. Slade, to Mrs. Ansley, and to the structure of the plot.
6. What is Roman fever — literally and figuratively?
7. Why has Alida Slade "always gone on hating" Grace Ansley?
8. What reaction does Alida Slade seem to have expected from Grace Ansley in response to her confession that she forged the letter? Why?
9. Alida Slade remarks, "Well, girls are ferocious sometimes." What about ladies?
10. Near the end of the story, why does Grace Ansley pity Alida Slade? Why does Mrs. Slade at first reject that pity?
11. Comment on the meaning of the way the ladies walk offstage.

Topics for Writing

1. Analyze the importance of setting in "Roman Fever."
2. Show how Wharton manipulates point of view in "Roman Fever."
3. Explain how "Roman Fever" conforms to Wharton's principles of the short story as stated in the excerpt from her book *The Writing of Fiction* (included in Part Two, p. 1594).

4. On your first reading of the story, mark passages whose significance is not entirely clear — such as Grace Ansley's peculiar intonations when acknowledging her memory of a former visit to Rome. After reading the story to the end, return to the marked passages and write explanations of them.

5. Which of the two ladies is more guilty of reprehensible behavior? Consider arguments on both sides, or organize a debate.

6. **RESPONDING CREATIVELY** Write a story of your own about a secret that comes out or a misunderstanding that is resolved. Try to make both the perpetuation of the error or deception and the emergence of the truth dependent on character rather than circumstance.

Related Commentary

Edith Wharton, Every Subject Must Contain within Itself Its Own Dimensions, p. 1594.

Suggested Readings

Flynn, Dale Bachman. "Salamanders in the Fire: The Short Stories of Edith Wharton." *Dissertation Abstracts International* 45.12 (June 1985): 3638A.

Hollbrook, David. *Edith Wharton.* New York: St. Martin's, 1991.

Howe, Irving, ed. *Edith Wharton: A Collection of Critical Essays.* New York: Prentice-Hall, 1962.

Lewis, R. W. B. *Edith Wharton: A Biography.* New York: Harper, 1985.

McDowell, Margaret B. *Edith Wharton.* Boston: Twayne, 1991.

Petry, Alice Hall. "A Twist of Crimson Silk: Edith Wharton's 'Roman Fever.'" *Studies in Short Fiction* 24.2 (Spring 1987): 163–66.

Vita-Finzi, Penelope. *Edith Wharton and the Art of Fiction.* New York: St. Martin's, 1990.

Wharton, Edith. *The Collected Letters of Edith Wharton.* New York: Macmillan, 1987.

White, Barbara A. "Neglected Areas: Wharton's Short Stories and Incest, Part II." *Edith Wharton Review* 8.2 (Fall 1991): 3–10, 32.

JOHN EDGAR WIDEMAN

newborn thrown in trash and dies (p. 1396)

Students will already have noticed that several stories in this collection are told from a child's point of view. This angry, turbulent story is unique in that it is told from the point of view of a newborn child who will not live out even a single day. It is also unique in that the author has made no effort to present the story in the voice of a newborn child, and he has not placed any limitations on the knowledge or the perceptions of this barely conscious being. What we hear in the newborn's voice is, instead, the voice of the author, and it is a voice that is so filled with rage that often the details of the simple narrative become blurred in the swirl of his angry feelings. It is as though the story of the death of the newborn girl has aroused so many emotions in Wideman that he struggles furiously to express all of them at once.

In the tumult of the prose we learn that the baby was dropped down a trash chute from the tenth floor of a building on New York City's Westside on August 12, 1991. It was, in fact, a newspaper story that spurred Wideman to write this darkly imagined account of the newborn's few hours of life. Out of the welter of the baby's imagined emotions, the author has her tell us, "I know things I have no business knowing." He first begins to tell us something about her by having her describe the floors of the building that she passed in her descent, but already on the ninth floor he becomes distracted by the knowledge that there is gambling in the building, and he devotes half a page to evoking the fixations, the speech, and the habits of the gamblers. With that digression the account of the floors of the building is abandoned for a page-long paragraph headed *The Floor of Facts*. Here he lets the girl tell her story. Her nineteen-year-old mother walked forty-five feet from the door of the apartment where she was staying to the trash chute where she dropped her child. Close to the end of the paragraph, as she plunges down the chute, the child wonders, in a moment that is almost too painful for the reader, "am I doing it right. I didn't know any better."

For the rest of the story the author takes up again his recounting of the building's floors, but now each of them is named symbolically. The girl falls past *A Floor of Opinions, Floor of Wishes, Floor of Power, Floor of Regrets, Floor of Love,* and *The Floor That Stands for All the Other Floors Missed or Still to Come.* Each of the floors is another glimpse into the life of the black ghetto, and the view we are given is desolate and unforgiving. On *A Floor of Opinions* the girl states flatly that "my death will serve no purpose" and that even the choices she makes about what to notice on the floors has no real purpose. She says without rancor, "I believe all floors are not equally interesting. Less reason to notice some than others. . . . Though we may slight some and rattle on about others, that does not change the fact that each floor exists and the life on it is real, whether we pause to notice or not."

Wideman does not state explicitly what he means by the concept of the floors, but we can infer that it is the unfolding of the life she might have experienced. It is often a raw presentiment. For *Wishes* the girl is sorry she will miss Christmas and wishes she could have seen Christmas morning instead of this August afternoon. With *Regrets* it is a glimpse of the floors above the one where she was dropped, which she regrets not seeing. As harsh as these and the metaphoric glimpse of white domination in the floor titled *Power* have been, Wideman's furious indictment of the ghetto experience rises to a crescendo in the last of his floors, *Love,* and the floor *that stands for all the floors.* In the floor called *Love* the girl is raped by her father when she is still a young girl, and in the final paragraph her stepbrother is killed in a meaningless schoolyard shooting. Although the voice of the story is the child's, the bitter knowledge and the angry emotions are the author's.

Questions for Discussion

1. The story makes no pretense of limiting itself to the voice or point of view of the newborn child who is supposed to be speaking. Why did Wideman choose this method of telling his story?
2. Is the baby's experience presented as unique? Could the story be interpreted as an indictment of the ghetto community?

3.   In *A Floor of Opinions* Wideman writes, "I believe facts sometimes speak for themselves but never speak for us." What is he saying?
4.   The girl's death occurs in August. Why does she long for winter and Christmas?
5.   The description of El Presidente seems to be a metaphor for the power of the white community. What suggests or doesn't suggest that this is the interpretation the author intends?
6.   How can we interpret the sentences describing El Presidente: "El Presidente often performs on TV. We can watch him jog, golf, fish, travel, lie, preen, mutilate the language"?
7.   In his casual recounting of the stepbrother's death does Wideman leave the reader with any hope for the black community?
8.   Are the floors he describes of the building real or symbolic?

Topics for Writing

1.   Discuss the baby's statement: "In my opinion my death will have no purpose." Suggest ways in which the death could be said to have some purpose.
2.   Discuss the figure of El Presidente, with special emphasis on the statement "his job is keeping things in the building as they are."
3.   **CONNECTIONS**   Compare this story to others in the anthology that are told from a child's point of view and discuss how the authors have made use of this literary device to present their own ideas.
4   Comment on what you understand about the author's view of the black community after reading the story.

Suggested Readings

Wideman, John Edgar. *All Stories Are True.* New York: Random House, 1992.
———. *The Collected Stories of John Edgar Wideman.* New York: Pantheon, 1992.

WILLIAM CARLOS WILLIAMS

The Use of Force (p. 1403)

Although William Carlos Williams is best known as a poet, he also wrote a number of short stories, a successful play, and three novels chronicling the life of his wife's Norwegian immigrant family in the United States. Most of his short stories were written in the 1930s, during the Depression, and many of them were published in small magazines that were committed to the struggle for equality and social justice that dominated American intellectual life in those years. In the 1920s, when Williams was still thinking of himself as an experimental poet, he had written avant-garde prose, but the new stories, because of their political commitment, were written in a more direct style, and their subject matter was the ordinary life of the people who came to him as patients. The term for writing like this in the 1930s was "hard-hitting." Certainly Williams's new spare, unsentimental style was influenced by the stories of Ernest Hemingway, published several years earlier, but the setting in the poor neighborhoods of Rutherford, New Jersey, and the depressed, anxious people of the stories are his own.

The stubbornness of the girl in "The Use of Force" will remind some readers of the refusal of Melville's Bartleby to give in to authority in "Bartleby, the Scrivener," but Williams takes his story a step further. He reveals to the reader that the girl has a reason for her refusal to be examined. She is sick, and she is afraid of treatment. He also has the honesty to admit that he became so angry in the struggle with the girl that he felt pleasure in forcing her to give in.

The story certainly may suggest submerged sexual overtones to some readers in the fact that the patient is a girl and the doctor is trying to force a wooden instrument into her mouth, but there is nothing in the text to suggest that Williams intends to describe anything more than a professional visit to help a sick girl and her worried parents. Today we are more casual about infections like the one the girl is suffering from, but in Williams's time there were no antibiotics. He takes it for granted that his readers understand the necessity for him to get the girl's mouth open. To leave her as she is would probably be to leave her to die. As Williams writes, "I have seen at least two children lying dead in bed of neglect in such cases." He has to try to save her.

Questions for Discussion

1. Today, would a doctor try to examine a child's throat during a house call, or would the patient come to a medical office to have the preliminary examination performed by a nurse?
2. Williams tells us almost nothing about the kitchen where the girl is waiting or about the appearance of her parents. Why? (Students might suggest several possible answers.)
3. When Williams writes that the girl's parents "weren't telling me more than they had to," what is he saying about the relationship between a doctor and his patients?
4. The spare language of the story gives it some of the feeling of a medical report. Do students feel this is helpful or unhelpful in creating the mood of the story?
5. Is it stubbornness or terror that is driving the girl to act the way she is?
6. Why does the girl feel defeated when Williams finally is able to examine her throat? Does she comprehend that she is dangerously ill?

Topic for Writing

1. There have been many changes in the relationship between doctors and patients in the United States since Williams wrote the story. Discuss whether or not you feel that Williams would have been happy with the changes, using examples from the story.

Suggested Reading

Coles, Robert, ed. *William Carlos Williams: The Doctor Stories.* New York: New Directions, 1984.

Tobias Wolff

The Rich Brother (p. 1407)

Although Wolff has chosen to title his sorrowing tale "The Rich Brother," the subject that dominates the story is not a portrayal of the richer of two brothers. The story's subject is something more conclusive: a depiction of the helplessly intertwined relationship between two brothers who can neither leave each other nor accept each other. The title could as easily have been "The Poor Brother." If the story had been written at the beginning of the development of the short story two hundred years ago it would probably have been titled something like "The Sorrowful Tale of Two Brothers," and there would have been a subtitle that read, "In Which It Is Shown That Wealth Brings Not Happiness, Nor Poverty Joy." Wolff has chosen to weight his story by making the poor brother a crashing example of almost total emotional and practical ineptitude, but it is still only the relationship between the brothers that is the subject of the story. We aren't asked to make any decisions between prosperity and poverty, except to observe that prosperity has its advantages.

Structurally the story will present few problems to students. Its entire time span covers only a few hours in an automobile, although there is considerable preparation for the moment of crisis in the ride in the lengthy descriptions of the events in their lives that have brought the two men to where they are. The carefully weighted antagonism between the brothers is thrown into disequilibrium by the sudden intrusion of the third figure, a shabby con man posing as someone needing a lift. Wolff has carefully allowed each of them the opportunity to present their values, with an attempt at a kind of hip cynicism on the part of Pete, the successful brother, who clearly is solidly representative of his community's ideal of success, even to his mid-life fling with skydiving. Wolff contrasts this with the earnest moralizing of the younger brother, Donald, who attempts to put his brother on the defensive by relating incidents from their childhood in which his older brother was abusive. They have clearly been over this same emotional ground so many times before that there will be no decision possible this time, any more than they have managed to force each other into some kind of surrender the other times they have had these arguments.

With Donald's gullible response to the story told by the man wanting a lift — a story so transparently untrue that the older brother decides the man wasn't even trying particularly hard to deceive them — even the reader becomes impatient with the younger brother's vague moralizing. The story's moral weight is tipped toward the successful brother, if only by default. His younger sibling is clearly so helpless that his self-justifications become an embarrassment. It is with some relief that the reader watches Pete stop the car and drop Donald beside the road in the darkness, and it is with a sad understanding that we see Pete slow the car a few moment later so he can turn and go to pick his brother up again.

The story is presented as a face-off between two lifestyles, with the moral defenses that bolster each of the paths that the brothers have taken. The reality that it is a description of the brothers' emotional dependence on one another, manifested in ways that they can barely understand and accept only with difficulty.

Questions for Discussion

1. What is a Century 21 franchise? What is the advantage to having a franchise in California? How does this detail add to Wolff's characterization of the older brother?
2. In describing Donald the author mentions "Perfect Masters." What is he referring to?
3. Why does Pete try to justify himself to his brother in his description of his skydiving adventures?
4. Explain Pete's gesture in giving Donald $100. Is there a hidden aggression in the gesture?
5. Is Pete finding some pleasure in hearing of his brother's mishaps? Is this a natural human response when others relate their failures? How does Wolff express this idea?
6. Donald says to his brother, "You don't know when to quit. You just keep hitting away." What is he saying?
7. Was Pete consciously trying to kill his brother when they were children?
8. Why does Pete allow his brother to pick up the passenger? Is he being honest?
9. What does Pete mean by his judgment of the passenger's story: "He hadn't even tried"?

Topics for Writing

1. Discuss the concept of dependency, and relate it to the two men in the story.
2. Although neither brother is described as contented with his life, there seems to be more sympathy toward the older brother on the part of the writer. Discuss whether or not this seems to be so, and comment on his possible reasons.
3. **RESPONDING CREATIVELY** Discuss the dreams that the two brothers have of each other, and put their dreams into the context of the present situation.
4. Comment on the role the passenger plays in the story, and relate it to the long tradition of the confidence trickster in our society.

Related Commentary

Tobias Wolff, On "The Rich Brother," p. 1595.

Suggested Readings

Wolff, Tobias. *Back in the World: Stories.* Boston: Houghton, 1985.
———. *The Barracks Thief and Other Stories.* New York: Bantam, 1984.
———. *In the Garden of the North American Martyrs: A Collection of Short Stories.* New York: Ecco, 1981.
Woodruff, Jay, ed. "In the Garden of the North American Martyrs." *A Piece of Work: Five Writers Discuss Their Revisions.* Iowa City: U of Iowa P, 1993.

VIRGINIA WOOLF

Kew Gardens (p. 1421)

This sketch might puzzle some students, since its point of view (clearly dictated by Woolf) seems so unusual. No particular person is having his or her story told. Rather, Woolf seems to be telling the story of a snail in a plot of flowers in Kew Gardens. "Cosmic" rather than "omniscient" might be the best word to describe Woolf's perspective, which blends blue sky and green earth so closely as to exclude the people strolling the garden paths between the two elements.

Woolf's story is experimental, and her concentration as she attempts to record "the essential life" of the creatures in the garden is almost palpable. According to the critic Susan Dick, in 1919 Woolf learned from studying Chekhov that "inconclusive stories are legitimate." Dick goes on to say that the narrator in a typical story by Woolf functions "as a perceptive observer of the external scene. . . . [or] the narrator dramatizes from within the minds of the characters . . . their perceptions of themselves and their world." In "Kew Gardens," Woolf moves seamlessly in and out of her characters' minds, recording their thoughts and feelings more substantially than the actual words they exchange.

The thoughts and words of the first couple, a married pair with two children, shape the reader's expectations for the rest of the story. Simon, the husband, thinks of Lily, an earlier love, to whom he'd proposed marriage in Kew Gardens when he was young. He remembers the shoe she wore, "with the square silver buckle at the toe," which symbolized her attractiveness and her lack of interest in his proposal. His wife, Eleanor, when he asks her if she ever thinks of the past, answers him bluntly, perhaps jealous that he is thinking of the beautiful Lily. Eleanor's memory of past love in Kew Gardens is the kiss given to her by "an old grey-haired woman with a wart on her nose, the mother of all my kisses all my life." We hear no more of this old woman (Eleanor's art teacher?), and we are not told why the kiss was so unsettling that Eleanor's "hand shook all the afternoon so that I couldn't paint." The married couple leave with their children, as much strangers to us as when they appeared.

The snail is the next character, and his conflict is a physical problem: How should he get around a dead leaf? This shift to the nonhuman prepares the reader for Woolf's shift to a cosmic view. The couples on the garden paths are reduced to colors as she lets the descriptive elements of the scene dissolve "like drops of water in the yellow and green atmosphere." The heat of the summer afternoon overcomes everything, reducing the "gross and heavy bodies" to a drowsy torpidity, but their voices continue as a manifestation of their spiritual essence, "as if they were flames lolling from the thick waxen bodies of candles." The silence is found to be composed of pure sound, the sound of buses, people, and the petals of flowers, whose colors seem to Woolf to be heard in the air.

Questions for Discussion

1. How does Woolf organize her sketch so that her description seems continuous and coherent?
2. Describe the people in the scene. What other living elements in the garden are treated as characters?

3. What is Woolf's tone? To which social class does she belong? Comment on her treatment of the two "elderly women of the lower middle class." How are they described? What can you tell about Woolf's attitude toward them from the words they exchange?
4. What is Woolf's attitude toward romantic love? old age? Do these two elements serve as the extremes of dramatic human conflicts in her sketch? Explain.

Topics for Writing

1. **RESPONDING CREATIVELY** Rewrite "Kew Gardens" as it might be the following afternoon, when it's raining.
2. Analyze Woolf's range of vocabulary in this sketch. How does she suggest a poetic atmosphere in her descriptions of the garden and its inhabitants and visitors?

Related Commentary

Katherine Mansfield, Review of Woolf's "Kew Gardens," p. 1529.

Suggested Readings

Baldwin, Dean. *Virginia Woolf: A Study of the Short Fiction.* Boston: Twayne, 1986.

Beja, Morris, ed. *Critical Essays on Virginia Woolf.* Boston: G. K. Hall, 1985.

Bishop, Edward L. "Pursuing 'It' Through 'Kew Gardens.'" *Studies in Short Fiction* 19.3 (Summer 1982): 269–75.

Homans, Margaret. *Virginia Woolf: A Collection of Critical Essays.* Englewood Cliffs, NJ: Prentice-Hall, 1993.

Marcus, Jane, ed. *New Feminist Essays on Virginia Woolf.* Lincoln: U of Nebraska P, 1981.

Oakland, John. "Virginia Woolf's *Kew Gardens.*" *English Studies: A Journal of English Language and Literature* 68.3 (June 1987): 264–73.

Woolf, Virginia. *The Complete Shorter Fiction of Virginia Woolf.* San Diego: Harcourt, 1985.

———. *The Essays of Virginia Woolf.* San Diego: Harcourt, 1988.

RICHARD WRIGHT

The Man Who Was Almost a Man (p. 1427)

Dave Saunders dislikes being laughed at, and his discomfort at becoming an object of amusement for accidentally shooting old Jenny, the mule, precipitates his final step into manhood. Although the anecdote around which Wright builds the story is comical enough, the reader probably should accede to Dave's wish to be taken seriously, for the fate that lies ahead of this young man as he rolls toward his unknown destination atop a boxcar with nothing in his pocket but an unloaded gun is likely to be grim.

At the same time, however, Dave's self-esteem and independence deserve respect. At the beginning of the story he dissociates himself from the field hands and fixes on his ambition to declare his manhood by owning a gun. Throughout the story the idea that *boys* do not have guns recurs, and Dave not only wants a gun but also chafes at being called "boy" by his parents and at being treated as a child. Just before he goes out to master the gun and hop a freight, Dave grumbles, "They treat me like a mule, n then they beat me." His resolution to escape his inferior status will involve not only leaving home but taking potshots at the facade of white society just as he wants to shoot at "Jim Hawkins' big white house" in order "to let him know Dave Saunders is a man." The question Wright leaves hanging for the reader as his story trails off into ellipses is whether Dave has killed the mule in himself or whether he himself, like Jenny, may become the victim of his own wild shots.

William E. Sheidley

Questions for Discussion

1. Explain the pun in the last sentence of the first paragraph.
2. Define our first impression of Dave. What reasons do we have to admire him? to laugh at him? to pity him?
3. What does it take to be a man in the world of the story? Is a gun enough? How does one get a gun?
4. What is ironic about the way Dave gets the money to buy his gun?
5. How is Dave treated by his father? Why does Ma say of the gun, "It be fer Pa"?
6. With the gun under his pillow, Dave feels "a sense of power. Could kill a man with a gun like this. Kill anybody, black or white." What does Dave still have to learn before he can be called a man? How does the story bring it home to him?
7. Explain what happens the first time Dave fires the gun. What does he do differently the next time?
8. Why does Wright describe the death of the mule in such detail?
9. Explain why being laughed at is so painful for Dave. What might enable him to join in and laugh at himself?
10. Comment on the possible implications of Dave's remark "They treat me like a mule, n then they beat me," both within the story and in a broader social and historical context. Does Dave's killing the mule have a symbolic significance?
11. Where might Dave be headed as he hops on the Illinois Central? What might he find at the end of his journey?
12. Why is the title not "The Boy Who Was Almost a Man"?

Topics for Writing

1. Examine the tone of Wright's story.
2. Discuss the treatment of Wright's social themes in "The Man Who Was Almost a Man." (See the story's headnote.)
3. **RESPONDING CREATIVELY** Write a sequel to Wright's story, another episode in the life of Dave Saunders — something that happens on the train ride or when he arrives in New Orleans or Chicago or wherever. Try to

sustain and develop as many themes and motives already present in Wright's story as you can, but make the material your own by imagining what you think happens, not necessarily what you guess Wright would have written. Decide whether to adopt Wright's style and point of view or employ a different mode of narration. Remember that the story is set during the Great Depression.

Related Commentaries

Leslie Lee, Scene from the Screenplay of *Almos' a Man*, p. 1521.
Richard Wright, Reading Fiction, p. 1597.

Suggested Readings

Felgar, Robert. *Richard Wright*. Boston: Twayne, 1980.
Hakutani, Yoshinobu, ed. *Critical Essays on Richard Wright*. Boston: G. K. Hall, 1982.
Margolies, Edward. *The Art of Richard Wright*. Carbondale: Southern Illinois UP, 1969.
McCall, Dan. *The Example of Richard Wright*. New York: Harcourt, 1969.
Reilly, John M. *Richard Wright: The Critical Reception*. New York: Burt Franklin, 1978.
Wright, Richard. *Uncle Tom's Children*. New York: Harper, 1989.

Hiyase Yamamoto

Wilshire Bus (p. 1437)

In this small sketch of a painful moment of racial insensitivity the reader is placed on a bus in Los Angeles, but it is a story that in its simplest applications could have been set in almost any American city. What gives Yamamoto's story its individual character, however, is that in Los Angeles it could be possible for three Oriental nations to be represented on the same bus ride. Students will be most interested by this complex response of the Chinese couple and the Japanese woman (with her memory of an elderly Korean whom she observed from a bus) to the drunken Anglo passenger's racist remarks. Although situations like this one are often used to illustrate the pervasiveness of racist attitudes, the reader is left with the conclusion that the response of someone hearing the remarks is defined almost as precisely by his or her own place in the emotional equation.

It probably will be easier for students to understand the subtleties of the story if they understand that to many Asian Americans it is an accepted idea that it is virtually impossible to tell someone of Chinese descent from someone of Japanese or Korean descent. In a number of studies conducted during World War II, it was found that Chinese Americans felt little discomfort walking the streets of American cities, while Japanese Americans experienced strong anxieties. The same studies also found that Anglo Americans could not distinguish between the two groups. The emotions of the two groups of Asian Americans were entirely condi-

tioned by their own expectations. For Koreans there is the same personal evaluation of any obvious white response.

We find some of the same complex responses in the incident on the bus. The
woman who is the central character is Japanese, and as the man rails at the couple
who have aroused his ire by turning to look at him, the woman "was startled to
realize that what she was actually doing was gloating over the fact that the drunken
man had specified the Chinese as the unwanted." Then her memory of seeing the
elderly man's I AM KOREAN button emphasizes for her the complicated levels
of her response to the situation.

Perhaps the simplest reaction of everyone involved in the incident is the
short speech by the American of European descent who apologizes for what the
drunken passenger has said. He himself was not the subject of the man's remarks,
and he has no emotional wounds from the exchange. With his gesture of friend-
ship he tries to apologize for the other man's boorishness, and although there is
little he can do to soften the effect, his effort assures the reader of the author's
consciousness of the complexities of the racial equation.

Although the author tells us early in the story that the Japanese woman is
upset with herself for "a grave sin of omission," the only specific gesture she
seems to make is to smile at the Chinese woman in a friendly manner. The antagonism felt by many Chinese toward the Japanese, dating from the brutalities of the
Japanese invasion of China in the 1930s, is still so intense that she shouldn't have
been surprised if the woman perhaps intuited that she was of Japanese descent.
We are never told what she failed to do, although she might be wishing that she
had said something at the time of the incident. When she bursts into tears with
her husband it is for her feeling of helplessness at what she witnessed. Her strongest insight is that perhaps people are wrong when they excuse someone for a
drunken act. "People say, do not regard what he says, now he is in liquor." Her
angry decision is that "[p]erhaps it is the only time he ought to be regarded." It is
probably not meant ironically that she puts the entire incident behind her by allowing her husband to feel that, yes, women are silly.

Questions for Discussion

1. What is meant by *somatotonic*? Why does the author use such a little-known
   medical term?
2. Why does the author carefully contrast the clothing of the drunk and the
   Chinese couple?
3. Does the Chinese woman do something to cause the outburst? Would it
   have been enough to upset the man if he had been sober?
4. Is the reference to Trinidad surprising? What does it suggest about the man?
6. Would a button reading I AM JAPANESE have deflected the man's rage?
7. Is there some mixing of idioms in his phrase "slant eyed pickaninnies"?
8. There doesn't seem to be any specific act of omission. What does the reader
   intuit of the woman's feeling that she should have done something?
9. Why does her husband look around smugly at his roommates when she
   begins to cry?

Topics for Writing

1. Discuss Yamamoto's conclusion that "People say, do not regard what he says, now he is in liquor. Perhaps it is the only time he ought to be regarded." Comment on the statement's serious moral implications.
2. Discuss the distinctions that Asian Americans make about one another's roles in American society, and compare them to the same complex attitudes on the part of the various European American groups in the society, for example, Polish Americans and Italian Americans.
3. Comment on the society's tolerance for alcohol abuse and compare this to what the reaction of the reader would be if the man were described as being under the influence of other drugs.

THEMATIC INDEX

Story Pairs

1. Nachtigal, *Peter Klaus the Goatherd*, and Irving, *Rip Van Winkle* [German folktale and American revision as a short story]
2. Flaubert, *A Simple Heart*, and Maupassant, *Clochette* [Stories about a devoted house servant in rural France]
3. Allen, *Whirlwind Man Steals Yellow Woman*, and Silko, *Yellow Woman* [Native American folktale and contemporary retelling as a short story]
4. Crane, *The Open Boat*, and *The Sinking of the* Commodore [A short story masterpiece and the newspaper narrative on which it is based]
5. Lawrence, *Odour of Chrysanthemums*, and Steinbeck, *The Chrysanthemums* [Stories about the role of women as reflected in the institution of marriage]
6. Carver, *The Bath*, and *A Small, Good Thing* [two versions of the same plot written in two different literary styles]
7. Hemingway, *Hills Like White Elephants*, and Banks, *Black Man and White Woman in Dark Green Rowboat* [A short story masterpiece retold as if it took place today]

On Writing

Amis, *The Immortals*
Atwood, *Happy Endings*
Barth, *Lost in the Funhouse*
Cortázar, *A Continuity of Parks*
García Márquez, *A Very Old Man with Enormous Wings*
Lavin, *The Widow's Son*
Moore, *How to Become a Writer*
Paley, *A Conversation with My Father*
Sontag, *The Way We Live Now*
Stein, *Miss Furr and Miss Skeene*

Fantasy and the Supernatural

Allen, *The Kugelmass Episode*
Amis, *The Immortals*
Carter, *The Company of Wolves*
Cheever, *The Swimmer*
Clemens, *The Celebrated Jumping Frog of Calaveras County*
García Márquez, *A Very Old Man with Enormous Wings*
Gilman, *The Yellow Wallpaper*
Gogol, *The Overcoat*
Hawthorne, *The Birthmark*
Hawthorne, *Young Goodman Brown*
Hurston, *Spunk*
Idris, *The Chair Carrier*
Irving, *Rip Van Winkle*
Jackson, *The Lottery*
Johnson, *Menagerie, A Child's Fable*
Kafka, *A Hunger Artist*
Kafka, *The Metamorphosis*
Lawrence, *The Rocking-Horse Winner*
Le Guin, *The Ones Who Walk Away from Omelas*
Murakami, *The Seventh Man*
Paz, *My Life with the Wave*
Poe, *The Fall of the House of Usher*
Proulx, *The Blood Bay*
Silko, *Yellow Woman*
Thurber, *The Secret Life of Walter Mitty*
Vonnegut, *Harrison Bergeron*
Wideman, *newborn thrown in trash and dies*

Hawthorne, *The Birthmark*
Hawthorne, *Young Goodman Brown*
Hemingway, *Hills Like White Elephants*
Hurston, *The Gilded Six-Bits*
Hurston, *Sweat*
Jin, *The Bridegroom*
Joyce, *The Dead*
Klíma, *The White House*
Lahiri, *The Interpreter of Maladies*
Lawrence, *Odour of Chrysanthemums*

Mansfield, *Bliss*
Mason, *Shiloh*
Maupassant, *The Necklace*
Maupassant, *Clochette*
Mishima, *Patriotism*
Munro, *Family Furnishings*
Silko, *Yellow Woman*
Steinbeck, *The Chrysanthemums*
Thurber, *The Secret Life of Walter Mitty*
Wharton, *Roman Fever*

Parents and Children

Beattie, *Find and Replace*
Carver, *The Bath*
Carver, *A Small, Good Thing*
Cather, *Paul's Case*
Danticat, *Night Women*
Faulkner, *That Evening Sun*
Fitzgerald, *Babylon Revisited*
Gaitskill, *Tiny, Smiling Daddy*
Jen, *Who's Irish*
Kafka, *The Metamorphosis*
Kincaid, *Girl*
Lavin, *The Widow's Son*
Lawrence, *The Rocking-Horse Winner*
Mansfield, *The Garden-Party*
Moody, *Boys*

Flannery O'Connor, *Everything That Rises Must Converge*
Flannery O'Connor, *Good Country People*
Olsen, *I Stand Here Ironing*
Paley, *A Conversation with My Father*
Roth, *The Conversion of the Jews*
Tan, *Two Kinds*
Viramontes, *The Moths*
Walker, *Everyday Use*
Welty, *Why I Live at the P.O.*
Welty, *A Worn Path*
Wideman, *newborn thrown in trash and dies*
Wright, *The Man Who Was Almost a Man*

War and Revolution

Achebe, *Civil Peace*
Babel, *My First Goose*
Bierce, *An Occurrence at Owl Creek Bridge*
Borowski, *This Way for the Gas, Ladies and Gentlemen*
Camus, *The Guest*
Conrad, *Heart of Darkness*
Gordimer, *The Ultimate Safari*

Mukherjee, *The Management of Grief*
O'Brien, *The Things They Carried*
Frank O'Connor, *Guests of the Nation*
Ozick, *The Shawl*
Thurber, *The Secret Life of Walter Mitty*
Toomer, *Blood-Burning Moon*
Vonnegut, *Harrison Bergeron*

Looking at the Wall

Alexie, *The Lone Ranger and Tonto Fistfight in Heaven*
Allison, *River of Names*
Atwood, *Rape Fantasies*
Anderson, *Death in the Woods*
Baldwin, *Sonny's Blues*
Banks, *Black Man and White Woman in Dark Green Rowboat*
Berriault, *Who Is It Can Tell Me Who I Am?*
Bierce, *An Occurrence at Owl Creek Bridge*

Borges, *The End of the Duel*
Borowski, *This Way for the Gas, Ladies and Gentlemen*
Boyle, *Friendly Skies*
Carver, *The Bath*
Carver, *A Small, Good Thing*
Carver, *What We Talk About When We Talk About Love*
Conrad, *Heart of Darkness*
Crane, *The Open Boat*

GUIDE TO COMMENTARIES

Writers on Writing

Writers on Other Writers

Biographical and Historical Contexts

Critics on Writers

Robert Coles
Tillie Olsen: The Iron and the Riddle,
 p. 1478

Joan Dayan
Amorous Bondage: Poe, Ladies, and
 Slaves, p. 1712

James W. Gargano
The Question of Poe's Narrators in "The
 Tell-Tale Heart" and "The Cask of
 Amontillado," p. 1701

Sandra M. Gilbert and Susan Gubar
A Feminist Reading of Gilman's "The
 Yellow Wallpaper," p. 1493

Janice H. Harris
Levels of Meaning in Lawrence's "The
 Rocking-Horse Winner," p. 1499

Carolyn G. Heilbrun
A Feminist Perspective on Katherine
 Anne Porter and "The Jilting of
 Granny Weatherall," p. 1501

J. Gerald Kennedy
On "The Fall of the House of Usher,"
 p. 1704

Dorothy Tuck McFarland
"On Good Country People," p. 1681

J. Hillis Miller
A Deconstructive Reading of Melville's
 "Bartleby, the Scrivener," p. 1537

Jay Parini
Lawrence's and Steinbeck's Chrysanthe-
 mums, p. 1560

David S. Reynolds
Poe's Art of Transformation in "The Cask
 of Amontillado," p. 1708

Edward Said
The Past and the Present: Joseph Conrad
 and the Fiction of Autobiography,
 p. 1572

Arthur M. Saltzman
A Reading of "What We Talk About
 When We Talk About Love," p. 1622

A. O. Scott
Looking for Raymond Carver, p. 1624

Kathleen Westfall Shute
On "The Bath" and "A Small, Good
 Thing," p. 1617

Lionell Trilling
The Greatness of Conrad's "Heart of
 Darkness," p. 1587

SHORT STORIES ON FILM AND VIDEO

Sherman Alexie
*The Lone Ranger and Tonto Fistfight in
    Heaven*
Movie Title: *Smoke Signals*
89 min., color, 1998
Cast: Adam Beach, Evan Adams
Directed by Chris Eyre
Distributed by Miramax Pictures Home
    Video

Ambrose Bierce
An Occurrence at Owl Creek Bridge
Movie Title: *An Occurrence at Owl Creek
    Bridge*
27 min., b&w, 1962
Cast: Roger Jacquet, Ann Cornaly,
    Anker Larsen, Stephanie Fey
Directed by Robert Enrico
Distributed by New York Film Annex

Angela Carter
The Company of Wolves
Movie Title: *The Company of Wolves*
95 min., color, 1985
Cast: Angela Lansbury, David Warner,
    Stephen Rea, Tusse Silberg, Sarah
    Patterson
Directed by Neil Jordan
Distributed by Live Entertainment and
    Vestron Video

Raymond Carver
*What We Talk About When We Talk
    About Love*
Movie Title: *Short Cuts*
189 min., color, 1993
Cast: Jennifer Jason Leigh, Tim Robbins,
    Madeleine   Stowe,   Frances
    McDormand, Peter Gallagher, Lily
    Tomlin, Andie McDowell, Jack
    Lemmon, Lyle Lovett, Huey Lewis,
    Matthew Modine, Lili Taylor, Chris-
    topher Penn, Robert Downey Jr.
Directed by Robert Altman
Distributed by Columbia Tristar Home
    Video

Willa Cather
Paul's Case
Movie Title: *Paul's Case*
52 min., color, 1980
Cast: Eric Roberts, Michael Higgins,
    Lindsay Crouse
Directed by Lamont Johnson
Distributed by Moneterey Home Video

John Cheever
The Swimmer
Movie Title: *The Swimmer*
94 min., color, 1968
Cast: Burt Lancaster, Janet Langard
Directed by Frank Perry
Distributed by Goodtimes Home Video

Anton Chekhov
The Lady with the Little Dog
Movie Title: *The Lady with the Dog*
86 min., b&w, 1960
In Russian with English subtitles
Videocassette Release of a 1959 motion
    picture
Cast: Iya Savvina, Alexei Batalov
Directed by Yosef Heifitz
Distributed by Tapeworm Video Dis-
    tributors

Kate Chopin
The Story of an Hour
Movie Title: *Kate Chopin's The Story of
    an Hour*
24 min., color, 1982
Originally released as a major motion
    picture in 1982
Cast: Gwendolyn Coleman, Laura
    Lanfranchi, Shannon Baker, Paul
    Zakrzewski
Directed by Marita Simpson
Distributed by ISHTAR Films

Movie Title: *The Joy that Kills*
56 min., color, 1999
Cast: Frances Conroy, Jeffrey De Munn,
    Rosalind Cash
Directed by Tina Rathborne
Distributed by Films for the Humani-
    ties

Movie Title: *Five Stories of an Hour*
25 min., color, 1991
Four dramatic renditions of Kate
    Chopin's "The Story of an Hour," in
    addition to her original story
Cast: Zoe Wanamaker, Julian Cartside,
    Jilly Blond
Directed by Paul Kafno, Greg Lanning,
    David Hodgson
Distributed by Films for the Humani-
    ties

Samuel Clemens
*The Celebrated Jumping Frog of
    Calaveras County*
Movie Title: *Mark Twain's The Notorious
    Jumping Frog of Calaveras County*
25 min., color, 1989
Directed by Dan Bessie
Distributed by Barr Films

Joseph Conrad
Heart of Darkness
Movie Title: *Heart of Darkness*
120 min., color, 1993
Made for television
Cast: Tim Roth, John Malkovich, James
    Fox
Directed by Nicholas Roeg
Distributed by Turner Home Entertain-
    ment Company

Movie Title: *Apocalypse Now*
153 min., color, 1979
Cast: Martin Sheen, Marlon Brando,
    Robert Duvall
Directed by Francis Ford Coppola
Distributed by Paramount Home Video

Stephen Crane
The Open Boat
Movie Title: *The Open Boat*
29 min., b&w, 1965
Part of the "American Story Classics"
    series
Distributed by Film Video Library

William Faulkner
A Rose for Emily
Movie Title: *A Rose for Emily*
27 min., color, 1983

Cast: Angelica Huston, John Carradine
Distributed by Pyramid Media

F. Scott Fitzgerald
Babylon Revisited
Movie Title: *The Last Time I Saw Paris*
116 min., color, 1954
Cast: Elizabeth Taylor, Van Johnson,
    Donna Reed, Eva Gabor
Directed by Richard Brooks
Distributed by MGM Home Entertain-
    ment

Mary Wilkins Freeman
The Revolt of "Mother"
Movie Title: *The Revolt of Mother*
60 min., color, 1988
Cast: Amy Madigan, Jay O'Saunders
Distributed by Monterey Home Video

Gabriel García Márquez
A Very Old Man with Enormous Wings
Movie Title: *A Very Old Man with Enor-
    mous Wings*
90 min., color, 1991
In Spanish with English subtitles
Cast: Daisy Granados, Asdrubal
    Melendez, Luis Alberto Ramirez,
    Fernando Birri
Distributed by Orion Home Video

Charlotte Perkins Gilman
The Yellow Wallpaper
Movie Title: *The Yellow Wallpaper*
14 min., color, 1977
Cast: Sigurd Wurschmidt, Tom
    Dalhgren, Susan Lynch
Distributed by Women Make Movies

Nikolai Gogol
The Overcoat
Movie Title: *The Overcoat*
93 min., b&w, 1959
In Russian with English subtitles
Cast: Rolan Bykov
Directed by Alexei Batalov
Distributed by Hen's Tooth Video

Nathaniel Hawthorne
The Birthmark
Movie Title: *The Birthmark*

15 min., color, 1978
Part of the Short Story Series
Distributed by Indiana University Audio Visual Center

Young Goodman Brown
Movie Title: *Young Goodman Brown*
44 min., color, 2000
Cast: John P. Ryan, Tom Shell, Judy Geeson, Dorothy Lyman
Directed by Peter George
Distributed by Films for the Humanities and Sciences

Movie Title: *Young Goodman Brown*
30 min., color, 1971
Distributed by Pyramid Media

Washington Irving
Rip Van Winkle
Movie Title: *Rip Van Winkle*
30 min., color, 1993
Animation
Narrated by Angelica Huston
Distributed by Baker & Taylor Video

Movie Title: *Rip Van Winkle*
60 min., color, 1985
Part of the "Faerie Tale Theatre" Series
Cast: Harry Dean Stanton, Talia Shire
Directed by Francis Ford Coppola
Distributed by CBS/Fox Video

Movie Title: *Rip Van Winkle*
18 min., color, 1994
Animation
Narrated by Joseph Sicati
Distributed by AIMS Media

Shirley Jackson
The Lottery
Movie Title: *The Lottery by Shirley Jackson*
19 min., color, 1980
Distributed by Encyclopedia Britannica Educational Corporation

Henry James
The Real Thing
Movie Title: *The Real Thing*
15 min., color, 1978
No. 8 of The Short Story Series

Cast: Stanley Anderson, Joyce Polk, John Muir
Directed by John Robbins
Distributed by Indiana University Audio Visual Center

Sarah Orne Jewett
A White Heron
Movie Title: *A White Heron*
26 min., color, 1978
Distributed by New Letters on the Air

James Joyce
The Dead
Movie Title: *The Dead*
82 min., color, 2000
Cast: Angelica Huston, Donal McCann, Helena Carroll, Cathleen Delany
Directed by John Huston
Distributed by Artisan Home Entertainment

Franz Kafka
A Hunger Artist
Movie Title: *A Hunger Artist*
23 min., b&w, 1983
Distributed by Film Ideas

Movie Title: *The Metamorphosis of Mr. Samsa*
10 min., color, 1991
Animation
Directed by Caroline Leaf
Distributed by National Film Board of Canada

D. H. Lawrence
Odour of Chrysanthemums
Movie Title: *Odour of Chrysanthemums*
24 min., color, 1995
Cast: Jack Shepherd, Philip Jackson
Written and Presented by Graham Martin
Distributed by Films for the Humanities & Sciences

The Rocking-Horse Winner
Movie Title: *The Rocking-Horse Winner*
91 min., b&w, 1949
Cast: John Mills, Valerie Hobson
Directed by Anthony Pelessier
Distributed by Home Vision Cinema

Jack London
To Build a Fire
Movie Title: *To Build a Fire*
56 min., color, 1969
Narrated by Orson Welles
Distributed by Educational Video Network

Movie Title: *To Build a Fire*
60 min., color, 1974
Cast: Ion Hogg
Distributed by WNET-TV Educational Television

Katherine Mansfield
Bliss
Movie Title: *Exit 10*
35 min., color, 1979
Directed by Stephen Gyllenhaal
Distributed by Phoenix

The Garden-Party
Movie Title: *The Garden-Party*
24 min., color, 1974
Distributed by AIMS Multimedia

Guy de Maupassant
The Necklace
Movie Title: *The Necklace by Guy de Maupassant*
20 min., color, 1980
Distributed by Encyclopedia Britannica Education Corporation

Movie Title: *The Necklace*
22 min., color, 1982
Directed by Bernard Wilets
Distributed by Barr Films

Herman Melville
Bartleby, the Scrivener
Movie Title: *Bartleby*
28 min., color, 1969
Distributed by Encyclopedia Britannica Education Corporation

Movie Title: *Bartleby, the Scrivener*
79 min., color, 1970
Cast: Paul Scofield, John McEnery
Directed by Anthony Friedman
Distributed by The Video Catalog

Movie Title: *Bartleby by Herman Melville*
38 min., color, 1990
Cast: Patrick Cambell, James Westerfield
Directed by Larry Yust
Distributed by Encyclopedia Britannica Education Corporation

Movie Title: *Bartleby, the Scrivener*
59 min., color, 1988
A teleplay by Israel Horovitz
Cast: Nicholas Kepros, Joel Colodner
Distributed by Films for the Humanities

Yukio Mishima
Patriotism
Movie Title: *Rite of Love and Death*
21 min., b&w, 1968
English version of the 1967 Japanese motion picture entitled *Yukoku*
Cast: Yukio Mishima, Miss Tsuruoka
Distributed by Grove Press, Film Division

Joyce Carol Oates
Where Are You Going, Where Have You Been?
Movie Title: *Smooth Talk*
92 min., color, 1985
Cast: Laura Dern, Treat Williams, Mary Kay Place, Levon Helm
Directed by Joyce Chopra
Distributed by Vestron Video

Flannery O'Connor
Good Country People
Movie Title: *Good Country People*
32 min., color, 1975
Cast: Johnnie Collins III, Shirley Slater, June Whitley Taylor
Directed by Jeffrey E. Jackson
Distributed by Valley Video

Frank O'Connor
Guests of the Nation
Movie Title: *Guests of the Nation*
58 min., color, 1981
Cast: Frank Coverse, Richard Cottrell, Charlie Stavola

Directed by John Desmond
Distributed by Broadway Theatre Archive

Octavio Paz
My Life with the Wave
Movie Title: *My Life with the Wave*
30 min., color, 1998
Partial Animation
Hosted by Levar Burton
Distributed by Great Plains National

Edgar Allan Poe
The Cask of Amontillado
Movie Title: *The Cask of Amontillado*
29 min., b&w, 1965
Part of the "American Story Classics" series
Distributed by Film Video Library

The Fall of the House of Usher
Movie Title: *House of Usher*
92 min., color, 1989
Cast: Oliver Reed, Donald Pleasence, Romy Windsor
Directed by Alan Birkinshaw
Distributed by Polygram Video

Movie Title: *The Fall of the House of Usher*
70 min., b&w, 1952
Videocassette Release of a 1952 motion picture
Cast: Gwendoline Watford, Kaye Tendeter, Irving Steen
Directed by Ivan Bennett
Distributed by Sinister Cinema

Movie Title: *The Fall of the House of Usher*
85 min., color, 1993
Cast: Vincent Price, Mark Damon, Myrna Fahey
Directed by Roger Corman
Distributed by GoodTimes Home Video

Movie Title: *Edgar Allen Poe's The Fall of the House of Usher*
92 min., color, 1990
Cast: Oliver Reed, Donald Pleasence, Romy Windsor
Directed by Alan Birkinshaw
Distrubuted by RCA/Columbia Pictures Home Video

The Tell-Tale Heart
Movie Title: *The Tell-Tale Heart*
30 min., b&w, 1980
Cast: Alex Cord, Sam Jaffe
Distributed by Churchill Films

Katherine Anne Porter
The Jilting of Granny Weatherall
Movie Title: *The American Short Story Collection: The Jilting of Granny Weatherall*
57 min., color, 1993
Cast: Geraldine Fitzgerald, Lois Smith
Part of The American Short Story Series
Hosted by Henry Fonda
Distributed by Monterey Video

William Sidney Porter
The Last Leaf
Movie Title: *The Last Leaf*
21 min., color, 1993
Cast: Wendy Bunts, Shannon Rossiter, Bob Penny, David Laird Scott
Directed by James Rogers
Distributed by Pyramid Film & Video

Movie Title: *O. Henry's The Last Leaf*
25 min., color, 2001
Release Date: December 11, 2001
Distributed by Monterey Video

John Steinbeck
The Chrysanthemums
Movie Title: *The Chrysanthemum: A Film Production of John Steinbeck's Short Story*
22 min., color, 1990
Directed: Steve Rosen
Distributed by Pyramid Media

Amy Tan
Two Kinds
Movie Title: *Joy Luck Club*
139 min., color, 2000
Cast: Tsai Chin, Kieu Chinh, Lisa Lu
Directed by Wayne Wong
Distributed by Hollywood Pictures Home Video

James Thurber
The Secret Life of Walter Mitty
Movie Title: *The Secret Life of Walter Mitty*
110 min., color, 1947
Cast: Danny Kaye, Virginia Mayo, Boris Karloff, Fay Bainter
Directed by Norman Z. McLeod
Distributed by MGM Home Entertainment

Leo Tolstoy
The Death of Ivan Ilych
Movie Title: *The Death of Ivan Ilych*
60 min., color, 1995
Part of The Living Literature: The Classics & You Series
Director: Tony Labriola
Distributed by Insight Media

John Updike
A & P
Movie Title: *A & P*
31 min., color, 1999
Cast: Sean Patrick Hayes, Randy Oglesby, Amy Smart
Directed by Bruce R. Schwartz
Distributed by Films for the Humanities and Sciences

Kurt Vonnegut, Jr.
Harrison Bergeron
Movie Title: *Harrison Bergeron*
99 min., color, 1995
Cast: Sean Astin, Miranda De Pencier, Christopher Plummer
Directed by Bruce Pittman
Distributed by Republic Entertainment

Eudora Welty
A Worn Path
Movie Title: *A Worn Path*
32 min., color, 1994
Cast: Cora Lee Day, Conchata Ferrell, Jodie Markell, Brad Dourif
Director: Bruce R. Schwartz
Distributed by Films for the Humanities and Sciences

Richard Wright
The Man Who Was Almost a Man
Movie Title: *Almos' a Man*
39 min., color, 1977
Cast: LeVar Burton
Directed by Stan Lathan
Distributed by Moneterey Home Video

Directory of Film and Video Distributors

AIMS Multimedia
9710 DeSoto Avenue
Chatsworth, CA 91311-4409
(800) 367-2467, (818) 773-4300

Artisan Home Entertainment
See local retailer
Baker & Taylor, Inc.
2709 Water Ridge Parkway
Charlotte, NC 28217
(800) 775-1800, (704) 329-9011

Barr Films
See local retailer

Broadway Theatre Archive
c/o Nederlander Digital Entertainment
1450 Broadway, 20th floor

New York, NY 10007
(212) 822-4246
CBS/FOX Video
See local retailer

Churchill Films
6677 North Northwest Highway
Chicago, IL 60631
(800) 334-7830

Columbia Tristar Home Video
See local retailer

Coronet/MTI Film & Video
2349 Chaffee Drive
St. Louis, MO 63146
(800) 221-1274, (314) 569-0211

Creative Arts Television Archive
P.O. Box 739
Kent, CT 06757
(860) 868-1771

Educational Video Network
1401 19th Street
Huntsville, TX 77340
(936)295-5767

**Encyclopaedia Britannica
Educational Corporation**
310 S. Michigan Avenue
Chicago, IL 60604
(312) 347-7900, (800) 621-3900

Film Ideas
308 North Wolf Road
Wheeling, IL 60090
(800) 475-3456

Film Video Library
University of Michigan
919 S. University Avenue
Room 2178 Shapiro
Ann Arbor, MI 48109-1185
(313) 764-5360

**Films for the Humanities
and Sciences**
P.O. Box 2053
Princeton, NJ 08543-2053
(800) 257-5126, (609) 275-1400

Goodtimes Home Video
16 East 40th Street
New York, NY 10016
(212) 951-3000

Great Plains National
Broadcast Sales & Acquisitions
P.O. Box 80669
Lincoln, NE 68501-0669
(800) 228-4630

Grove Press, Film Division
841 Broadway
New York, NY 10003
(212) 614-7850

Hen's Tooth Video
See local retailer

Hollywood Pictures Home Video
See local retailer

Home Vision Cinema
4423 North Ravenswood Avenue
Chicago, IL 60640-5802
(800) 826-3456, (312) 878-2600

**Indiana University Audio
Visual Center**
Franklin Hall, Room 0001
Bloomington, IN 47405-5901
(812) 855-2853

Insight Media
2162 Broadway
New York, NY 10024
(800) 223-9910, (212) 721-6316

International Film Bureau
332 S. Michigan Avenue, Suite 450
Chicago, IL 60604-4382
(312) 427-4545

Ishtar Films
15030 Ventura Boulevard, Suite 766
Sherman Oaks, CA 91403
(800) 428-7136

Library of Congress
Motion Picture, Broadcasting & Re-
  corded Sound Division
101 Independence Avenue SE
Washington, DC 20540-4690
(202) 707-5840

Live Entertainment
See local retailer

Media Concepts, Inc.
331 North Broad Street
Philadelphia, PA 19107
(215) 923-2545

MGM Home Entertainment
See local retailer

Monterey Home Video
566 St. Charles Dr.
Thousand Oaks, CA 91360
(800) 424-2593, (805) 494-7199

National Film Board of Canada
350 Fifth Avenue, Suite 4820
New York, NY 10118
(212) 629-8890

New Letters on the Air
University of Missouri at Kansas City
5101 Rockhill Road
Kansas City, MO 64110
(888) 548-2477, (816) 235-1159

New York Film Annex
1618 W. 4th Street
Brooklyn, NY 11223
(718) 382-8868

Orion Home Video
See local retailer

Paramount Home Video
See local retailer
PBS Video
1320 Braddock Place
Alexandria, VA 22314
(800) 424-7963, (703) 739-5380

Phoenix/BFA Films
2349 Chaffee Drive
St. Louis, MO 63146
(800) 221-1274, (314) 569-0211

Polygram Video
See local retailer

Pyramid Media
2801 Colorado Avenue
Santa Monica, CA, 90404
(800) 421-2304, (310) 828-7577

RCA/Columbia Pictures Home Video
See local retailer

Republic Entertainment
See local retailer

Sinister Cinema
See local retailer

Tapeworm Video Distributors
27833 Avenue Hopkins, Unit 6
Valencia, CA 01355
(800) 367-8437, (805) 257-4904

Time-Life Video and Television
2000 Duke Street
Alexandria, VA 22314
(703) 838-7000

Turner Home Entertainment Company
See local retailer

Universal Studios Home Video
See local retailer

University of California Extension Media Center
2000 Center Street, Suite 400
Berkeley, CA 94704
(510) 642-0460

Valley Video
See local retailer

Vestron Video, Inc.
See local retailer

Video Catalog
1000 Westgate Drive
Saint Paul, MN 55114
(612) 659-3700

Warner Home Video
See local retailer

WNET-TV Educational Television
356 W. 58th Street
New York, NY 10019
(212) 560-2000

Women Make Movies
462 Broadway, Suite 500
New York, NY 10013
(212) 925-0606